50% OFF Online NEX Prep Course!

Dear Customer,

We consider it an honor and a privilege that you chose our NEX Study Guide. As a way of showing our appreciation and to help us better serve you, we have partnered with Mometrix Test Preparation to offer you **50% off their online NEX Prep Course**. Many NEX courses are needlessly expensive and don't deliver enough value. With their course, you get access to the best NEX prep material, and **you only pay half price**.

Mometrix has structured their online course to perfectly complement your printed study guide. The NEX Prep Course contains **in-depth lessons** that cover all the most important topics, **250+ video reviews** that explain difficult concepts, over **450 practice questions** to ensure you feel prepared, and more than **670 digital flashcards**, so you can study while you're on the go.

Online NEX Prep Course

Topics Included:

- Verbal
  - Reading in Context
  - Finding the Meaning and Assessing the Text
  - Word Knowledge
- Mathematics
  - Numbers and Operations
  - Measurement
  - Algebra
  - Data Information
- Science
  - Science Cognitive Skills
  - Biology
  - Anatomy and Physiology
  - Chemistry
  - Health

Course Features:

- NEX Study Guide
  - Get content that complements our best-selling study guide.
- Full-Length Practice Tests
  - With over 450 practice questions, you can test yourself again and again.
- Mobile Friendly
  - If you need to study on the go, the course is easily accessible from your mobile device.
- NEX Flashcards
  - Our course includes a flashcard mode with over 670 content cards to help you study.

To receive this discount, visit them at mometrix.com/university/nex or simply scan this QR code with your smartphone. At the checkout page, enter the discount code: **NEX50TPB**

If you have any questions or concerns, please contact them at support@mometrix.com.

Sincerely,

 in partnership with

FREE Test Taking Tips Video/DVD Offer

To better serve you, we created videos covering test taking tips that we want to give you for FREE. **These videos cover world-class tips that will help you succeed on your test.**

We just ask that you send us feedback about this product. Please let us know what you thought about it—whether good, bad, or indifferent.

To get your **FREE videos**, you can use the QR code below or email freevideos@studyguideteam.com with "Free Videos" in the subject line and the following information in the body of the email:

   a. The title of your product

   b. Your product rating on a scale of 1-5, with 5 being the highest

   c. Your feedback about the product

If you have any questions or concerns, please don't hesitate to contact us at info@studyguideteam.com.

Thank you!

NEX Nursing Entrance Exam Study Guide

4 Practice Tests and NLN Prep
[Includes Detailed Answer Explanations]

Lydia Morrison

Written and edited by TPB Publishing.

TPB Publishing is not associated with or endorsed by any official testing organization. TPB Publishing is a publisher of unofficial educational products. All test and organization names are trademarks of their respective owners. Content in this book is included for utilitarian purposes only and does not constitute an endorsement by TPB Publishing of any particular point of view.

Interested in buying more than 10 copies of our product? Contact us about bulk discounts:
bulkorders@studyguideteam.com

ISBN 13: 9781637754146

Table of Contents

Welcome

Dear Reader,

Welcome to your new Test Prep Books study guide! We are pleased that you chose us to help you prepare for your exam. There are many study options to choose from, and we appreciate you choosing us. Studying can be a daunting task, but we have designed a smart, effective study guide to help prepare you for what lies ahead.

Whether you're a parent helping your child learn and grow, a high school student working hard to get into your dream college, or a nursing student studying for a complex exam, we want to help give you the tools you need to succeed. We hope this study guide gives you the skills and the confidence to thrive, and we can't thank you enough for allowing us to be part of your journey.

In an effort to continue to improve our products, we welcome feedback from our customers. We look forward to hearing from you. Suggestions, success stories, and criticisms can all be communicated by emailing us at info@studyguideteam.com.

Sincerely,
Test Prep Books Team

FREE Videos/DVD OFFER

Doing well on your exam requires both knowing the test content and understanding how to use that knowledge to do well on the test. We offer completely FREE test taking tip videos. **These videos cover world-class tips that you can use to succeed on your test.**

To get your **FREE videos**, you can use the QR code below or email freevideos@studyguideteam.com with "Free Videos" in the subject line and the following information in the body of the email:

    a. The title of your product
    b. Your product rating on a scale of 1-5, with 5 being the highest
    c. Your feedback about the product

If you have any questions or concerns, please don't hesitate to contact us at info@studyguideteam.com.

Quick Overview

Thankfully, you have this study guide to help you get ready. Use this guide to help keep your studying on track and refer to it often.

This study guide contains several key sections that will help you be successful on your exam. The guide contains tips for what you should do the night before and the day of the test. Also included are test-taking tips. Knowing the right information is not always enough. Many well-prepared test takers struggle with exams. These tips will help equip you to accurately read, assess, and answer test questions.

A large part of the guide is devoted to showing you what content to expect on the exam and to helping you better understand that content. In this guide are practice test questions so that you can see how well you have grasped the content. Then, answer explanations are provided so that you can understand why you missed certain questions.

Don't try to cram the night before you take your exam. This is not a wise strategy for a few reasons. First, your retention of the information will be low. Your time would be better used by reviewing information you already know rather than trying to learn a lot of new information. Second, you will likely become stressed as you try to gain a large amount of knowledge in a short amount of time. Third, you will be depriving yourself of sleep. So be sure to go to bed at a reasonable time the night before. Being well-rested helps you focus and remain calm.

Be sure to eat a substantial breakfast the morning of the exam. If you are taking the exam in the afternoon, be sure to have a good lunch as well. Being hungry is distracting and can make it difficult to focus. You have hopefully spent lots of time preparing for the exam. Don't let an empty stomach get in the way of success!

When travelling to the testing center, leave earlier than needed. That way, you have a buffer in case you experience any delays. This will help you remain calm and will keep you from missing your appointment time at the testing center.

Be sure to pace yourself during the exam. Don't try to rush through the exam. There is no need to risk performing poorly on the exam just so you can leave the testing center early. Allow yourself to use all of the allotted time if needed.

Remain positive while taking the exam even if you feel like you are performing poorly. Thinking about the content you should have mastered will not help you perform better on the exam.

Once the exam is complete, take some time to relax. Even if you feel that you need to take the exam again, you will be well served by some down time before you begin studying again. It's often easier to convince yourself to study if you know that it will come with a reward!

2

Test-Taking Strategies

1. Predicting the Answer

When you feel confident in your preparation for a multiple-choice test, try predicting the answer before reading the answer choices. This is especially useful on questions that test objective factual knowledge. By predicting the answer before reading the available choices, you eliminate the possibility that you will be distracted or led astray by an incorrect answer choice. You will feel more confident in your selection if you read the question, predict the answer, and then find your prediction among the answer choices. After using this strategy, be sure to still read all of the answer choices carefully and completely. If you feel unprepared, you should not attempt to predict the answers. This would be a waste of time and an opportunity for your mind to wander in the wrong direction.

2. Reading the Whole Question

Too often, test takers scan a multiple-choice question, recognize a few familiar words, and immediately jump to the answer choices. Test authors are aware of this common impatience, and they will sometimes prey upon it. For instance, a test author might subtly turn the question into a negative, or he or she might redirect the focus of the question right at the end. The only way to avoid falling into these traps is to read the entirety of the question carefully before reading the answer choices.

3. Looking for Wrong Answers

Long and complicated multiple-choice questions can be intimidating. One way to simplify a difficult multiple-choice question is to eliminate all of the answer choices that are clearly wrong. In most sets of answers, there will be at least one selection that can be dismissed right away. If the test is administered on paper, the test taker could draw a line through it to indicate that it may be ignored; otherwise, the test taker will have to perform this operation mentally or on scratch paper. In either case, once the obviously incorrect answers have been eliminated, the remaining choices may be considered. Sometimes identifying the clearly wrong answers will give the test taker some information about the correct answer. For instance, if one of the remaining answer choices is a direct opposite of one of the eliminated answer choices, it may well be the correct answer. The opposite of obviously wrong is obviously right! Of course, this is not always the case. Some answers are obviously incorrect simply because they are irrelevant to the question being asked. Still, identifying and eliminating some incorrect answer choices is a good way to simplify a multiple-choice question.

4. Don't Overanalyze

Anxious test takers often overanalyze questions. When you are nervous, your brain will often run wild, causing you to make associations and discover clues that don't actually exist. If you feel that this may be a problem for you, do whatever you can to slow down during the test. Try taking a deep breath or counting to ten. As you read and consider the question, restrict yourself to the particular words used by the author. Avoid thought tangents about what the author *really* meant, or what he or she was *trying* to say. The only things that matter on a multiple-choice test are the words that are actually in the question. You must avoid reading too much into a multiple-choice question, or supposing that the writer meant something other than what he or she wrote.

3

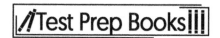
5. No Need for Panic

It is wise to learn as many strategies as possible before taking a multiple-choice test, but it is likely that you will come across a few questions for which you simply don't know the answer. In this situation, avoid panicking. Because most multiple-choice tests include dozens of questions, the relative value of a single wrong answer is small. As much as possible, you should compartmentalize each question on a multiple-choice test. In other words, you should not allow your feelings about one question to affect your success on the others. When you find a question that you either don't understand or don't know how to answer, just take a deep breath and do your best. Read the entire question slowly and carefully. Try rephrasing the question a couple of different ways. Then, read all of the answer choices carefully. After eliminating obviously wrong answers, make a selection and move on to the next question.

6. Confusing Answer Choices

When working on a difficult multiple-choice question, there may be a tendency to focus on the answer choices that are the easiest to understand. Many people, whether consciously or not, gravitate to the answer choices that require the least concentration, knowledge, and memory. This is a mistake. When you come across an answer choice that is confusing, you should give it extra attention. A question might be confusing because you do not know the subject matter to which it refers. If this is the case, don't eliminate the answer before you have affirmatively settled on another. When you come across an answer choice of this type, set it aside as you look at the remaining choices. If you can confidently assert that one of the other choices is correct, you can leave the confusing answer aside. Otherwise, you will need to take a moment to try to better understand the confusing answer choice. Rephrasing is one way to tease out the sense of a confusing answer choice.

7. Your First Instinct

Many people struggle with multiple-choice tests because they overthink the questions. If you have studied sufficiently for the test, you should be prepared to trust your first instinct once you have carefully and completely read the question and all of the answer choices. There is a great deal of research suggesting that the mind can come to the correct conclusion very quickly once it has obtained all of the relevant information. At times, it may seem to you as if your intuition is working faster even than your reasoning mind. This may in fact be true. The knowledge you obtain while studying may be retrieved from your subconscious before you have a chance to work out the associations that support it. Verify your instinct by working out the reasons that it should be trusted.

8. Key Words

Many test takers struggle with multiple-choice questions because they have poor reading comprehension skills. Quickly reading and understanding a multiple-choice question requires a mixture of skill and experience. To help with this, try jotting down a few key words and phrases on a piece of scrap paper. Doing this concentrates the process of reading and forces the mind to weigh the relative importance of the question's parts. In selecting words and phrases to write down, the test taker thinks about the question more deeply and

4

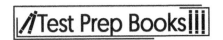

carefully. This is especially true for multiple-choice questions that are preceded by a long prompt.

9. Subtle Negatives

One of the oldest tricks in the multiple-choice test writer's book is to subtly reverse the meaning of a question with a word like *not* or *except*. If you are not paying attention to each word in the question, you can easily be led astray by this trick. For instance, a common question format is, "Which of the following is...?" Obviously, if the question instead is, "Which of the following is not...?," then the answer will be quite different. Even worse, the test makers are aware of the potential for this mistake and will include one answer choice that would be correct if the question were not negated or reversed. A test taker who misses the reversal will find what he or she believes to be a correct answer and will be so confident that he or she will fail to reread the question and discover the original error. The only way to avoid this is to practice a wide variety of multiple-choice questions and to pay close attention to each and every word.

10. Reading Every Answer Choice

It may seem obvious, but you should always read every one of the answer choices! Too many test takers fall into the habit of scanning the question and assuming that they understand the question because they recognize a few key words. From there, they pick the first answer choice that answers the question they believe they have read. Test takers who read all of the answer choices might discover that one of the latter answer choices is actually *more* correct. Moreover, reading all of the answer choices can remind you of facts related to the question that can help you arrive at the correct answer. Sometimes, a misstatement or incorrect detail in one of the latter answer choices will trigger your memory of the subject and will enable you to find the right answer. Failing to read all of the answer choices is like not reading all of the items on a restaurant menu: you might miss out on the perfect choice.

11. Spot the Hedges

One of the keys to success on multiple-choice tests is paying close attention to every word. This is never truer than with words like *almost*, *most*, *some*, and *sometimes*. These words are called "hedges" because they

indicate that a statement is not totally true or not true in every place and time. An absolute statement will contain no hedges, but in many subjects, the answers are not always straightforward or absolute. There are always exceptions to the rules in these subjects. For this reason, you should favor those multiple-choice questions that contain hedging language. The presence of qualifying words indicates that the author is taking special care with his or her words, which is certainly important when composing the right answer. After all, there are many ways to be wrong, but there is only one way to be right! For this reason, it is wise to avoid answers that are absolute when taking a multiple-choice test. An absolute answer is one that says things are either all one way or all another.

They often include words like *every*, *always*, *best*, and *never*. If you are taking a multiple-choice test in a subject that doesn't lend itself to absolute answers, be on your guard if you see any of these words.

12. Long Answers

In many subject areas, the answers are not simple. As already mentioned, the right answer often requires

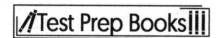

hedges. Another common feature of the answers to a complex or subjective question are qualifying clauses, which are groups of words that subtly modify the meaning of the sentence. If the question or answer choice describes a rule to which there are exceptions or the subject matter is complicated, ambiguous, or confusing, the correct answer will require many words in order to be expressed clearly and accurately. In essence, you should not be deterred by answer choices that seem excessively long. Oftentimes, the author of the text will not be able to write the correct answer without offering some qualifications and modifications. Your job is to read the answer choices thoroughly and completely and to select the one that most accurately and precisely answers the question.

13. Restating to Understand

Sometimes, a question on a multiple-choice test is difficult not because of what it asks but because of how it is written. If this is the case, restate the question or answer choice in different words. This process serves a couple of important purposes. First, it forces you to concentrate on the core of the question. In order to rephrase the question accurately, you have to understand it well. Rephrasing the question will concentrate your mind on the key words and ideas. Second, it will present the information to your mind in a fresh way. This process may trigger your memory and render some useful scrap of information picked up while studying.

14. True Statements

Sometimes an answer choice will be true in itself, but it does not answer the question. This is one of the main reasons why it is essential to read the question carefully and completely before proceeding to the answer choices. Too often, test takers skip ahead to the answer choices and look for true statements. Having found one of these, they are content to select it without reference to the question above. The savvy test taker will always read the entire question before turning to the answer choices. Then, having settled on a correct answer choice, he or she will refer to the original question and ensure that the selected answer is relevant. The mistake of choosing a correct-but-irrelevant answer choice is especially common on questions related to specific pieces of objective knowledge.

15. No Patterns

One of the more dangerous ideas that circulates about multiple-choice tests is that the correct answers tend to fall into patterns. These erroneous ideas range from a belief that B and C are the most common right answers, to the idea that an unprepared test-taker should answer "A-B-A-C-A-D-A-B-A." It cannot be emphasized enough that pattern-seeking of this type is exactly the WRONG way to approach a multiple-choice test. To begin with, it is highly unlikely that the test maker will plot the correct answers according to some predetermined pattern. The questions are scrambled and delivered in a random order. Furthermore, even if the test maker was following a pattern in the assignation of correct answers, there is no reason why the test taker would know which pattern he or she was using. Any attempt to discern a pattern in the answer choices is a waste of time and a distraction from the real work of taking the test. A test taker would be much better served by extra preparation before the test than by reliance on a pattern in the answers.

Bonus Content

We host multiple bonus items online, including all four practice tests in digital format. Scan the QR code or go to this link to access this content:

testprepbooks.com/bonus/nex

The first time you access the page, you will need to register as a "new user" and verify your email address.

If you have any issues, please email support@testprepbooks.com.

Introduction to the NEX

Function of the Test

The National League for Nursing (NLN) Nursing Entrance Examination (NEX) is designed for students seeking acceptance into nursing programs in the United States. Although there were previously two versions of the Pre-Admission Examination (PAX) (the RN and the PN), the NLN has streamlined the exam offerings and combined these versions into the sole NEX exam. To be eligible for the exam, candidates must have obtained a high school diploma or GED. Each nursing program can set their own minimum passing score required for prospective candidates.

There are three main content domains on the NLN NEX: Verbal, Math, and Science. As such, the exam is designed to assess the background knowledge and skills in these academic areas, as well as the general reasoning ability of prospective nursing students.

Test Administration

The NLN NEX consists of three tests with 163 questions administered via computer. Candidates can register online through the NLN testing services website and test at proctored locations (usually nursing schools) across the country, or remotely with a live virtual proctor. Alternatively, some nursing programs offer registration and dates of administration directly on their websites. Test takers should review the websites or admissions information of the programs for which they seek entry.

Special accommodations are available for students with documented disabilities. Official requests must be made on the NLN testing services website. Candidates with disabilities should contact the nursing school where they will be taking the test to make the necessary arrangements.

Test Format

The NLN NEX has three sections: Verbal, Math, and Science. The questions in the verbal section assesses word knowledge and reading comprehension. In the mathematics section, questions address basic computations and quantitative reasoning skills, graphs, algebra, and word problems. The science section includes questions about general biology, chemistry, and human health, anatomy, and physiology. There are 163 questions on the exam. The breakdown is as follows:

Section	Number of Scored Questions	Number of Unscored Questions	Time Allotted
Verbal	50	8	60 minutes
Math	40	5	60 minutes
Science	55	5	60 minutes
Total	145	18	3 hours

Note that there are additional, unscored items in each section. As these are unscored, they do not affect the percentage of questions answered correctly in the section nor the overall score. Some nursing programs allow the use of calculators, while others do not. Candidates will need to confirm the policy at the school administering their exam.

Scoring

Score reports are available immediately after completing the exam. There is no set "passing score;" instead, each nursing program sets their own standards. These percentiles are usually published in the information about

8

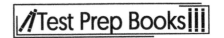

admissions on their website. If a candidate "fails" one section, the entire test must be retaken. A score (from 1-300) and percentile rank for each of the three sections is reported as well as an overall composite percentile rank.

Study Prep Plan for the NEX Test

1   **Schedule -** Use one of our study schedules below or come up with one of your own.

2   **Relax -** Test anxiety can hurt even the best students. There are many ways to reduce stress. Find the one that works best for you.

3   **Execute -** Once you have a good plan in place, be sure to stick to it.

One Week Study Schedule

Day 1	Verbal
Day 2	Math
Day 3	Measurement
Day 4	Science
Day 5	Chemistry
Day 6	NEX Practice Test #1
Day 7	Take Your Exam!

Two Week Study Schedule

Day 1	Verbal	Day 8	Human Anatomy and Physiology
Day 2	Comparing Different Ways of Presenting Ideas	Day 9	Anatomy and Physiology of the Neuromuscular System
Day 3	Math	Day 10	Chemistry
Day 4	Algebra	Day 11	Health
Day 5	Measurement	Day 12	NEX Practice Test #1
Day 6	Data & Information	Day 13	NEX Practice Test #2
Day 7	Science	Day 14	Take Your Exam!

One Month Study Schedule						
Day 1	Verbal	Day 11	Mean, Median, Mode, and Range	Day 21	Health Promotion/ Disease Prevention
Day 2	Reading Comprehension	Day 12	Science	Day 22	NEX Practice Test #1
Day 3	Comparing Different Ways of Presenting Ideas	Day 13	Anaerobic Respiration	Day 23	Answer Explanations #1
Day 4	Math	Day 14	Human Anatomy and Physiology	Day 24	NEX Practice Test #2
Day 5	Rational Numbers and Their Operations	Day 15	Anatomy and Physiology of the Respiratory System	Day 25	Answer Explanations #2
Day 6	Algebra	Day 16	Anatomy and Physiology of the Neuromuscular System	Day 26	NEX Practice Test #3
Day 7	Writing an Expression from a Written Description	Day 17	Anatomy and Physiology of the Endocrine System	Day 27	Answer Explanations #3
Day 8	Measurement	Day 18	Chemistry	Day 28	NEX Practice Test #4
Day 9	Geometric Quantities	Day 19	Chemical Equations	Day 29	Answer Explanations #4
Day 10	Data & Information	Day 20	Health	Day 30	Take Your Exam!

Build your own prep plan by visiting:
testprepbooks.com/prep

11

As you study for your test, we'd like to take the opportunity to remind you that you are capable of great things! With the right tools and dedication, you truly can do anything you set your mind to. The fact that you are holding this book right now shows how committed you are. In case no one has told you lately, you've got this! Our intention behind including this coloring page is to give you the chance to take some time to engage your creative side when you need a little brain-break from studying. As a company, we want to encourage people like you to achieve their dreams by providing good quality study materials for the tests and certifications that improve careers and change lives. As individuals, many of us have taken such tests in our careers, and we know how challenging this process can be. While we can't come alongside you and cheer you on personally, we can offer you the space to recall your purpose, reconnect with your passion, and refresh your brain through an artistic practice. We wish you every success, and happy studying!

Verbal

Word Knowledge

Synonyms

Synonyms are words that mean the same or nearly the same if given a list of words in the same language. When presented with several words and asked to choose the synonym, more than one word may be similar to the original. However, one word is generally the strongest match. Synonyms should always share the same part of speech. For instance, *shy* and *timid* are both adjectives and hold similar meanings. The words *shy* and *loner* are similar, but shy is an adjective, while loner is a noun. Another way to test for the best synonym is to reread the question with each possible word and determine which one makes the most sense. Consider the words: adore, sweet, kind, and nice.

Now consider the following sentence: *He will love you forever.*

> He will adore you forever.

> He will sweet you forever.

> He will kind you forever.

> He will nice you forever.

In the first sentence, the word *love* is used as a verb. The best synonym from the list that shares the same part of speech is *adore*. Adore is a verb, and when substituted in the sentence, it is the only substitution that makes grammatical and semantic sense.

Synonyms can be found for nouns, adjectives, verbs, adverbs, and prepositions. Here are some examples of synonyms from different parts of speech:

- Nouns: clothes, wardrobe, attire, apparel
- Verbs: run, spring, dash
- Adjectives: fast, quick, rapid, swift
- Adverbs: slowly, nonchalantly, leisurely
- Prepositions: near, proximal, neighboring, close

Here are several more examples of synonyms in the English language:

Word	Synonym	Meaning
smart	intelligent	having or showing a high level of intelligence
exact	specific	clearly identified
almost	nearly	not quite but very close
to annoy	to bother	to irritate
to answer	to reply	to form a written or verbal response
building	edifice	a structure that stands on its own with a roof and four walls
business	commerce	the act of purchasing, negotiating, trading, and selling
defective	faulty	when a device is not working or not working well

Vocabulary

In order to understand synonyms, one must have a good foundation of vocabulary. *Vocabulary* is the words a person uses on a daily basis. Having a good vocabulary is important. It's important in writing and in conversation. Many of the questions on the test may have words that you don't know. Therefore, it's important to learn ways to find out a word's meaning.

It's hard to use vocabulary correctly. Imagine being thrust into a foreign country. If you didn't know right words to use to ask for the things you need, you could run into trouble! Asking for help from people who don't share the same vocabulary is hard. Language helps us understand each other. The more vocabulary words a person knows, the easier they can ask for things they need. This section of the study guide focuses on getting to know vocabulary through basic grammar.

Prefixes and Suffixes

In this section, we will look at the *meaning* of various prefixes and suffixes when added to a root word. A *prefix* is a combination of letters found at the beginning of a word. A *suffix* is a combination of letters found at the end. A *root word* is the word that comes after the prefix, before the suffix, or between them both. Sometimes a root word can stand on its own without either a prefix or a suffix. More simply put:

Prefix + Root Word = Word

Root Word + Suffix = Word

Prefix + Root Word + Suffix = Word

Root Word = Word

Knowing the definitions of common prefixes and suffixes is helpful. It's helpful when you are trying to find out the meaning of a word you don't know. Also, knowing prefixes can help you find out the number of things, the negative of something, or the time and space of an object! Understanding suffixes can help when trying to find out the meaning of an adjective, noun, or verb.

The following charts look at some of the most common prefixes, what they mean, and how they're used to find out a word's meaning:

Number and Quantity Prefixes

Prefix	Definition	Example
bi-	two	bicycle, bilateral
mono-	one, single	monopoly, monotone
poly-	many	polygamy, polygon
semi-	half, partly	semiannual, semicircle
uni-	one	unicycle, universal

Here's an example of a number prefix:

The girl rode on a *bicycle* to school.

Look at the word *bicycle*. The root word (*cycle*)comes from the Greek and means *wheel*. The prefix *bi-* means *two*. The word *bicycle* means two wheels! When you look at any bicycles, they all have two wheels. If you had a unicycle, your bike would only have one wheel, because *uni-* means *one*.

16

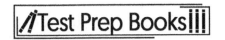

Negative Prefixes

Prefix	Definition	Example
a-	without, lack of	amoral, atypical
in-	not, opposing	inability, inverted
non-	not	nonexistent, nonstop
un-	not, reverse	unable, unspoken

Here's an example of a negative prefix:

The girl was *insensitive* to the boy who broke his leg.

Look at the word *insensitive*. In the chart above, the prefix *in-* means *not* or *opposing*. Replace the prefix with *not*. Now place *not* in front of the word *sensitive*. Now we see that the girl was "not sensitive" to the boy who broke his leg. In simpler terms, she showed that she did not care. These are easy ways to use prefixes and suffixes in order to find out what a word means.

Time and Space Prefixes

Prefix	Definition	Example
a-	in, on, of, up, to	aloof, associate
ab-	from, away, off	abstract, absent
ad-	to, towards	adept, adjacent
ante-	before, previous	antebellum, antenna
anti-	against, opposing	anticipate, antisocial
cata-	down, away, thoroughly	catacomb, catalogue
circum-	around	circumstance, circumvent
com-	with, together, very	combine, compel
contra-	against, opposing	contraband, contrast
de-	from	decrease, descend
dia-	through, across, apart	diagram, dialect
dis-	away, off, down, not	disregard, disrespect
epi-	upon	epidemic, epiphany
ex-	out	example, exit
hypo-	under, beneath	hypoallergenic, hypothermia
inter-	among, between	intermediate, international
intra-	within	intrapersonal, intravenous
ob-	against, opposing	obtain, obscure
per-	through	permanent, persist
peri-	around	periodontal, periphery
post-	after, following	postdate, postoperative
pre-	before, previous	precede, premeditate
pro-	forward, in place of	program, propel
retro-	back, backward	retroactive, retrofit
sub-	under, beneath	submarine, substantial
super-	above, extra	superior, supersede
trans-	across, beyond, or over	transform, transmit
ultra-	beyond, excessively	ultraclean, ultralight

17

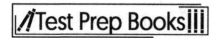

Here's an example of a space prefix:

> The teacher's motivational speech helped *propel* her students toward greater academic achievement.

Look at the word *propel*. The prefix *pro-* means *forward*. *Forward* means something related to time and space. *Propel* means to drive or move in a forward direction. Therefore, knowing the prefix *pro-* helps interpret that the students are moving forward *toward greater academic achievement*.

Miscellaneous Prefixes

Prefix	Definition	Example
belli-	war, warlike	bellied, belligerent
bene-	well, good	benediction, beneficial
equi-	equal	equidistant, equinox
for-	away, off, from	forbidden, forsaken
fore-	previous	forecast, forebode
homo-	same, equal	homogeneous, homonym
hyper-	excessive, over	hyperextend, hyperactive
in-	in, into	insignificant, invasive
magn-	large	magnetic, magnificent
mal-	bad, poorly, not	maladapted, malnourished
mis-	bad, poorly, not	misplace, misguide
mor-	death	mortal, morgue
neo-	new	neoclassical, neonatal
omni-	all, everywhere	omnipotent, omnipresent
ortho-	right, straight	orthodontist, orthopedic
over-	above	overload, overstock,
pan-	all, entire	panacea, pander
para-	beside, beyond	paradigm, parameter
phil-	love, like	philanthropy, philosophic
prim-	first, early	primal, primer
re-	backward, again	reload, regress
sym-	with, together	symmetry, symbolize
vis-	to see	visual, visibility

Here's another prefix example:

> The computer was *primitive*; it still had a floppy disk drive!

The word *primitive* has the prefix *prim-*. The prefix *prim-* indicates being *first* or *early*. *Primitive* refers to the historical development of something. Therefore, the sentence is saying that the computer is an older model, because it still has a floppy disk drive.

The charts that follow review some of the most common suffixes. They also include examples of how the suffixes that are used to determine the meaning of a word. Remember, suffixes are added to the *end* of a root word:

18

Adjective Suffixes

Suffix	Definition	Example
-able (-ible)	capable of being	teachable, accessible
-esque	in the style of, like	humoresque, statuesque
-ful	filled with, marked by	helpful, deceitful
-ic	having, containing	manic, elastic
-ish	suggesting, like	malnourish, tarnish
-less	lacking, without	worthless, fearless
-ous	marked by, given to	generous, previous

Here's an example of an adjective suffix:

The live model looked so *statuesque* in the window display; she didn't even move!

Look at the word *statuesque*. The suffix *-esque* means *in the style of* or *like*. If something is *statuesque*, it's *like a statue*. In this sentence, the model looks like a statue.

Noun Suffixes

Suffix	Definition	Example
-acy	state, condition	literacy, legacy
-ance	act, condition, fact	distance, importance
-ard	one that does	leotard, billiard
-ation	action, state, result	legislation, condemnation
-dom	state, rank, condition	freedom, kingdom
-er (-or)	office, action	commuter, spectator
-ess	feminine	caress, princess
-hood	state, condition	childhood, livelihood
-ion	action, result, state	communion, position
-ism	act, manner, doctrine	capitalism, patriotism
-ist	worker, follower	stylist, activist
-ity (-ty)	state, quality, condition	community, dirty
-ment	result, action	empowerment, segment
-ness	quality, state	fitness, rudeness
-ship	position	censorship, leadership
-sion (-tion)	state, result	tension, transition
-th	act, state, quality	twentieth, wealth
-tude	quality, state, result	attitude, latitude

Look at the following example of a noun suffix:

The *spectator* cheered when his favorite soccer team scored a goal.

Look at the word *spectator*. The suffix *-or* means *action*. In this sentence, the *action* is to *spectate* (watch something). Therefore, a *spectator* is someone involved in watching something.

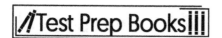

Verb Suffixes

Suffix	Definition	Example
-ate	having, showing	facilitate, integrate
-en	cause to be, become	frozen, written
-fy	make, cause to have	modify, rectify
-ize	cause to be, treat with	realize, sanitize

Here's an example of a verb suffix:

The preschool had to *sanitize* the toys every Tuesday and Thursday.

In the word *sanitize*, the suffix *-ize* means *cause to be* or *treat with*. By adding the suffix *-ize* to the root word *sanitary*, the meaning of the word becomes active: *cause to be sanitary*.

Context Clues

It's common to find words that aren't familiar in writing. When you don't know a word, there are some "tricks" that can be used to find out its meaning. *Context clues* are words or phrases in a sentence or paragraph that provide hints about a word and what it means. For example, if an unknown word is attached to a noun with other surrounding words as clues, these can help you figure out the word's meaning. Consider the following example:

After the treatment, Grandma's natural rosy cheeks looked *wan* and ghostlike.

The word we don't know is *wan*. The first clue to its meaning is in the phrase *After the treatment,* which tells us that something happened after a procedure (possibly medical). A second clue is the word *rosy*, which describes Grandma's natural cheek color that changed after the treatment. Finally, the word *ghostlike* infers that Grandma's cheeks now look white. By using the context clues in the sentence, we can figure out that the meaning of the word *wan* means *pale*.

Below are more ways to use context clues to find out the meaning of a word we don't know:

Contrasts

Look for context clues that *contrast* the unknown word. When reading a sentence with a word we don't know, look for an opposite word or idea. Here's an example:

Since Mary didn't cite her research sources, she lost significant points for *plagiarizing* the content of her report.

In this sentence, *plagiarizing* is the word we don't know. Notice that when Mary *didn't cite her research sources,* it resulted in her losing points for *plagiarizing the content of her report*. These contrasting ideas tell us that Mary did something wrong with the content. This makes sense because the definition of *plagiarizing* is "taking the work of someone else and passing it off as your own."

Contrasts often use words like *but, however, although,* or phrases like *on the other hand.* For example:

The *gargantuan* television won't fit in my car, but it will cover the entire wall in the den.

The word we don't know is *gargantuan*. Notice that the television is too big to fit in a car, *but it will cover the entire wall in the den*. This tells us that the television is extremely large. The word *gargantuan* means *enormous*.

20

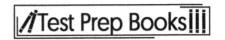

Synonyms

Another way to find out a word you don't know is to think of synonyms for that word. *Synonyms* are words with the same meaning. To do this, replace synonyms one at a time. Then read the sentence after each synonym to see if the meaning is clear. By replacing a word we don't know with a word we do know, it's easier to uncover its meaning. For example:

Gary's clothes were *saturated* after he fell into the swimming pool.

In this sentence, we don't know the word *saturated*. To brainstorm synonyms for *saturated*, think about what happens to Gary's clothes after falling into the swimming pool. They'd be *soaked* or *wet*. These both turn out to be good synonyms to try. The actual meaning of *saturated* is "thoroughly soaked."

Antonyms

Sometimes sentences contain words or phrases that oppose each other. Opposite words are known as *antonyms*. An example of an antonym is *hot* and *cold*. For example:

Although Mark seemed *tranquil*, you could tell he was actually nervous as he paced up and down the hall.

The word we don't know is *tranquil*. The sentence says that Mark was in fact not *tranquil*. He was *actually nervous*. The opposite of the word *nervous* is *calm*. *Calm* is the meaning of the word *tranquil*.

Explanations or Descriptions

Explanations or descriptions of other things in the sentence can also provide clues to an unfamiliar word. Take the following example:

Golden Retrievers, Great Danes, and Pugs are the top three *breeds* competing in the dog show.

We don't know the word *breeds*. Look at the sentence for a clue. The subjects (*Golden Retrievers, Great Danes,* and *Pugs*) describe different types of dogs. This description helps uncover the meaning of the word *breeds*. The word *breeds* means "a particular type of animal."

Inferences

Inferences are clues to an unknown word that tell us its meaning. These inferences can be found within the sentence where the word appears. Or, they can be found in a sentence before the word or after the word. Look at the following example:

The *wretched* old lady was kicked out of the restaurant. She was so mean and nasty to the waiter!

Here, we don't know the word *wretched*. The first sentence says that the *old lady was kicked out of the restaurant*, but it doesn't say why. The sentence after tells us why: *She was so mean and nasty to the waiter!* This infers that the old lady was *kicked out* because she was *so mean and nasty* or, in other words, *wretched*.

When you prepare for a vocabulary test, try reading harder materials to learn new words. If you don't know a word on the test, look for prefixes and suffixes to find out what the word means and get rid of wrong answers. If two answers both seem right, see if there are any differences between them. Then select the word that best fits. Context clues in the sentence or paragraph can also help you find the meaning of a word you don't know. By learning new words, a person can expand their knowledge. They can also improve the quality of their writing.

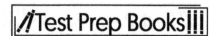

Words Frequently Confused

The English language is interesting because many of its words sound so similar or identical that they confuse readers and writers alike. Errors involving these words are hard to spot because they *sound* right even when they're wrong. Also, because these mistakes are so pervasive, many people think they're correct.

They're vs. Their vs. There

This set of words is probably the all-time winner of misuse. The word *they're* is a contraction of "they are." Remember that contractions combine two words, using an apostrophe to replace any eliminated letters. If a question asks whether the writer is using the word *they're* correctly, change the word to "they are" and reread the sentence. Look at the following example:

Legislators can be proud of they're work on this issue.

This sentence *sounds* correct, but replace the contraction *they're* with "they are" to see what happens:

Legislators can be proud of they are work on this issue.

The result doesn't make sense, which shows that it's an incorrect use of the word *they're*. Did the writer mean to use the word *their* instead? The word *their* indicates possession because it shows that something *belongs* to something else. Now put the word *their* into the sentence:

Legislators can be proud of their work on this issue.

To check the answer, find the word that comes right after the word *their* (which in this case is *work*). Pose this question: whose *work* is it? If the question can be answered in the sentence, then the word signifies possession. In the sentence above, it's the legislators' work. Therefore, the writer is using the word *their* correctly.

If the words *they're* and *their* don't make sense in the sentence, then the correct word is almost always *there*. The word *there* can be used in many different ways, so it's easy to remember to use it when *they're* and *their* don't work. Now test these methods with the following sentences:

Their going to have a hard time passing these laws.

Enforcement officials will have there hands full.

They're are many issues to consider when discussing car safety.

In the first sentence, asking the question "Whose going is it?" doesn't make sense. Thus the word *their* is incorrect. However, when replaced with the conjunction *they're* (or *they are*), the sentence works. Thus, the correct word for the first sentence should be *they're*.

In the second sentence, ask this question: "Whose hands are full?" The answer (*enforcement officials*) is correct in the sentence. Therefore, the word *their* should replace *there* in this sentence.

In the third sentence, changing the word *they're* to "they are" ("They are are many issues") doesn't make sense. Ask this question: "Whose are is it?" This makes even less sense, since neither of the words *they're* or *their* makes sense. Therefore, the correct word must be *there*.

Who's vs. Whose

Who's is a contraction of "who is" while the word *whose* indicates possession. Look at the following sentence:

> Who's job is it to protect America's drivers?

The easiest way to check for correct usage is to replace the word *who's* with "who is" and see if the sentence makes sense:

> Who is job is it to protect America's drivers?

By changing the contraction to "Who is" the sentence no longer makes sense. Therefore, the correct word must be *whose*.

Your vs. You're

The word *your* indicates possession, while *you're* is a contraction for "you are." Look at the following example:

> Your going to have to write your congressman if you want to see action.

Again, the easiest way to check correct usage is to replace the word *Your* with "You are" and see if the sentence still makes sense.

> You are going to have to write your congressman if you want to see action.

By replacing Your with "You are," the sentence still makes sense. Thus, in this case, the writer should have used "You're."

Its vs. It's

Its is a word that indicates possession, while the word *it's* is a contraction of "it is." Once again, the easiest way to check for correct usage is to replace the word with "it is" and see if the sentence makes sense. Look at the following sentence:

> It's going to take a lot of work to pass this law.

Replacing *it's* with "it is" results in this: "It is going to take a lot of work to pass this law." This makes sense, so the contraction (*it's*) is correct. Now look at another example:

> The car company will have to redesign it's vehicles.

Replacing *it's* with "it is" results in this: "The car company will have to redesign it is vehicles." This sentence doesn't make sense, so the contraction (*it's*) is incorrect.

Than vs. Then

Than is used in sentences that involve comparisons, while *then* is used to indicate an order of events. Consider the following sentence:

> Japan has more traffic fatalities than the U.S.

The use of the word *than* is correct because it compares Japan to the U.S. Now look at another example:

> Laws must be passed, and then we'll see a change in behavior.

Here the use of the word *then* is correct because one thing happens after the other.

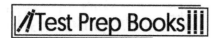
Affect vs. Effect

Affect is a verb that means to change something, while *effect* is a noun that indicates such a change. Look at the following sentence:

> There are thousands of people affected by the new law.

This sentence is correct because *affected* is a verb that tells what's happening. Now look at this sentence:

> The law will have a dramatic effect.

This sentence is also correct because *effect* is a noun and the thing that happens.

Note that a noun version of *affect* is occasionally used. It means "emotion" or "desire," usually in a psychological sense.

Two vs. Too vs. To

Two is the number (2). *Too* refers to an amount of something, or it can mean *also*. *To* is used for everything else. Look at the following sentence:

> Two senators still haven't signed the bill.

This is correct because there are *two* (2) senators. Here's another example:

> There are too many questions about this issue.

In this sentence, the word *too* refers to an amount ("too many questions"). Now here's another example:

> Senator Wilson is supporting this legislation, too.

In this sentence, the word *also* can be substituted for the word *too*, so it's also correct. Finally, one last example:

> I look forward to signing this bill into law.

In this sentence, the tests for *two* and *too* don't work. Thus, the word *to* fits the bill!

Other pairs of words cause mix-ups but are not necessarily homonyms. Here are a few of those:

That/Which

The pronouns *that* and *which* are both used to refer to nouns—but they are not interchangeable. The rule is to use the word *that* in essential clauses and phrases that help convey the meaning of the sentence. Use the word *which* in nonessential (less important) clauses. Typically, *which* clauses are enclosed in commas.

> The morning <u>that I fell asleep in class</u> caused me a lot of trouble.

> This morning's coffee, <u>which had too much creamer</u>, woke me up.

Who/Whom

We use the pronouns *who* and *whom* to refer to people. We always use *who* when it is the subject of the sentence or clause. We never use *whom* as the subject; it is always the object of a verb or preposition.

> <u>Who</u> hit the baseball for the home run? (subject)

> The baseball fell into the glove of <u>whom</u>? (object of the preposition of)

24

The umpire called <u>whom</u> "out"? (object of the verb called)

Disinterested/Uninterested
Disinterested is used to describe a neutral feeling towards something; *uninterested* means bored.

The jury remains <u>disinterested</u> during the trial.

I was <u>uninterested</u> during the lecture.

Fewer/Less
Fewer is used for things you can count; *less* is used for things you cannot count, as well as time.

He has <u>fewer</u> playing cards.

He has <u>less</u> talent.

You have <u>less</u> than a minute.

Farther/Further
Farther is used when discussing distance; *further* means "more"

His paper airplane flew <u>farther</u> than mine.

He needed <u>further</u> information.

Among/Between
Among is used when referring to more than two things; *between* is usually used when referring to just two things, or when naming specific distinct items, even if more than two.

Surfing is <u>among</u> my favorite hobbies.

She sat <u>between</u> Bill and Ronald.

Hear/Here
Hear is a verb that means to perceive sound by using one's ears, *here* is an adverb meaning at, on, or in this place.

I can <u>hear</u> the birds chirping.

The book was found <u>here</u>.

i.e./e.g.
i.e. is short for the Latin phrase *id est,* which means "in other words." *e.g.* is short for the Latin phrase *exempli gratia*, which means "for example."

Our new house is a money pit – <u>i.e.</u>, things are constantly breaking and we have spent tens of thousands of dollars on repairs.

The textbook also comes with online features (<u>e.g.</u>, interactive quizzes, instructional videos).

Lie/Lay

Lie is a verb meaning to recline in a flat position, and using it does not require a direct object; *lay* is a verb that means to place something in its resting position, and using it requires a direct object.

> I'm going to <u>lie</u> down after I call Terry.
> I usually <u>lay</u> my sweater on the back of the chair.

Note

Some people have problems with these:

> regardless/irregardless
> a lot/alot

Irregardless and *alot* are always incorrect. Don't use them.

Reading Comprehension

Events, Plots, Characters, Settings, and Ideas

Putting Events in Order

One of the most crucial skills for conquering the Reading Comprehension questions is the ability to recognize the sequences of events for each passage and place them in the correct order. Every passage has a plot, whether it is from a short story, a manual, a newspaper article or editorial, or a history text. And each plot has a logical order, which is also known as a sequence. Some of the most straightforward sequences can be found in technology directions, science experiments, instructional materials, and recipes. These forms of writing list actions that must occur in a proper sequence in order to get sufficient results. Other forms of writing, however, use style and ideas in ways that completely change the sequence of events. Poetry, for instance, may introduce repetitions that make the events seem cyclical. Postmodern writers are famous for experimenting with different concepts of place and time, creating "cut scenes" that distort straightforward sequences and abruptly transport the audience to different contexts or times. Even everyday newspaper articles, editorials, and historical sources may experiment with different sequential forms for stylistic effect.

Most questions that call for test takers to apply their sequential knowledge use key words such as **sequence**, **sequence of events**, or **sequential order** to cue the test taker in to the task at hand. In social studies or history passages, the test questions might employ key words such as **chronology** or **chronological order** to cue the test taker. In some cases, sequence can be found through comprehension techniques. These literal passages number the sequences, or they use key words such as *firstly, secondly, finally, next,* or *then*. The sequences of these stories can be found by rereading the passage and charting these numbers or key words. In most cases, however, readers have to correctly order events through inferential and evaluative reading techniques; they have to place events in a logical order without explicit cues.

Making Inferences

Predictions

Some texts use suspense and foreshadowing to captivate readers. For example, an intriguing aspect of murder mysteries is that the reader is never sure of the culprit until the author reveals the individual's identity. Authors often build suspense and add depth and meaning to a work by leaving clues to provide hints or predict future events in the story; this is called foreshadowing. While some instances of foreshadowing are subtle, others are quite obvious.

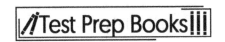

Inferences

Another way to read actively is to identify examples of inference within text. Making an inference requires the reader to read between the lines and look for what is implied rather than what is explicitly stated. That is, using information that is known from the text, the reader is able to make a logical assumption about information that is not explicitly stated but is probably true.

Authors employ literary devices such as tone, characterization, and theme to engage the audience by showing details of the story instead of merely telling them. For example, if an author said *Bob is selfish*, there's little left to infer. If the author said, *Bob cheated on his test, ignored his mom's calls, and parked illegally*, the reader can infer Bob is selfish. Authors also make implications through character dialogue, thoughts, effects on others, actions, and looks. Like in life, readers must assemble all the clues to form a complete picture.

Read the following passage:

"Hey, do you wanna meet my new puppy?" Jonathan asked.

"Oh, I'm sorry but please don't—" Jacinta began to protest, but before she could finish, Jonathan had already opened the passenger side door of his car and a perfect white ball of fur came bouncing towards Jacinta.

"Isn't he the cutest?" beamed Jonathan.

"Yes—achoo!—he's pretty—aaaachooo!!—adora—aaa—aaaachoo!" Jacinta managed to say in between sneezes. "But if you don't mind, I—I—achoo!—need to go inside."

Which of the following can be inferred from Jacinta's reaction to the puppy?
    a. She hates animals.
    b. She is allergic to dogs.
    c. She prefers cats to dogs.
    d. She is angry at Jonathan.

An inference requires the reader to consider the information presented and then form their own idea about what is probably true. Based on the details in the passage, what is the best answer to the question? Important details to pay attention to include the tone of Jacinta's dialogue, which is overall polite and apologetic, as well as her reaction itself, which is a long string of sneezes. Answer choices (a) and (d) both express strong emotions ("hates" and "angry") that are not evident in Jacinta's speech or actions. Answer choice (c) mentions cats, but there is nothing in the passage to indicate Jacinta's feelings about cats. Answer choice (b), "she is allergic to dogs," is the most logical choice. Based on the fact she began sneezing as soon as a fluffy dog approached her, it makes sense to guess that Jacinta might be allergic to dogs. Using the clues in the passage, it is reasonable to guess that this is true even though Jacinta never directly states, "Sorry, I'm allergic to dogs!"

Making inferences is crucial for readers of literature because literary texts often avoid presenting complete and direct information to readers about characters' thoughts or feelings, or they present this information in an unclear way, leaving it up to the reader to interpret clues given in the text. In order to make inferences while reading, readers should ask themselves:

- What details are being presented in the text?
- Is there any important information that seems to be missing?
- Based on the information that the author *does* include, what else is probably true?
- Is this inference reasonable based on what is already known?

27

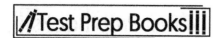

Conclusions

Active readers should also draw conclusions. When doing so, the reader should ask the following questions: What is this piece about? What does the author believe? Does this piece have merit? Do I believe the author? Would this piece support my argument? The reader should first determine the author's intent. Identify the author's viewpoint and connect relevant evidence to support it. Readers may then move to the most important step: deciding whether to agree and determining whether they are correct. Always read cautiously and critically. Interact with text, and record reactions in the margins. These active reading skills help determine not only what the author thinks, but what you think as the reader.

Analyzing Relationships within Passages

Inferences are useful in gaining a deeper understanding of how people, events, and ideas are connected in a passage. Readers can use the same strategies used with general inferences and analyzing texts—paying attention to details and using them to make reasonable guesses about the text—to read between the lines and get a more complete picture of how (and why) characters are thinking, feeling, and acting.

Read the following passage from O. Henry's story "The Gift of the Magi":

> One dollar and eighty-seven cents. That was all. And sixty cents of it was in pennies. Pennies saved one and two at a time by bulldozing the grocer and the vegetable man and the butcher until one's cheeks burned with the silent imputation of parsimony that such close dealing implied. Three times Della counted it. One dollar and eighty-seven cents. And the next day would be Christmas.
>
> There was clearly nothing to do but flop down on the shabby little couch and howl. So Della did it.

These paragraphs introduce the reader to the character Della. Even though the author doesn't include a direct description of Della, the reader can already form a general impression of her personality and emotions. One detail that should stick out to the reader is repetition: "one dollar and eighty-seven cents." This amount is repeated twice in the first paragraph, along with other descriptions of money: "sixty cents of it was in pennies," "pennies saved one and two at a time." The story's preoccupation with money parallels how Della herself is constantly thinking about her finances—"three times Della counted" her meager savings. Already the reader can guess that Della is having money problems. Next, think about her emotions.

The first paragraph describes haggling over groceries "until one's cheeks burned"—another way to describe blushing. People tend to blush when they are embarrassed or ashamed, so readers can infer that Della is ashamed by her financial situation. This inference is also supported by the second paragraph, when she flops down and howls on her "shabby little couch." Clearly, she's in distress. Without saying, "Della has no money and is embarrassed to be poor," O. Henry is able to communicate the same impression to readers through his careful inclusion of details.

A character's **motive** is their reason for acting a certain way. Usually, characters are motivated by something that they want. In the passage, above, why is Della upset about not having enough money? There's an important detail at the end of the first paragraph: "the next day would be Christmas." Why is money especially important around Christmas? Christmas is a holiday when people exchange gifts. If Della is struggling with money, she's probably also struggling to buy gifts. So a shrewd reader should be able to guess that Della's motivation is wanting to buy a gift for someone—but she's currently unable to afford it, leading to feelings of shame and frustration.

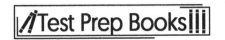

In order to understand characters in a text, readers should keep the following questions in mind:

- What words does the author use to describe the character? Are these words related to any specific emotions or personality traits (for example, characteristics like rude, friendly, unapproachable, or innocent)?

- What does the character say? Does their dialogue seem to be straightforward, or are they hiding some thoughts or emotions?

- What actions can be observed from this character? How do their actions reflect their feelings?

- What does the character want? What do they do to get it?

Understanding Main Ideas and Details

Determining the Relationship Between Ideas

It is very important to know the difference between the topic and the main idea of the text. Even though these two are similar because they both present the central point of a text, they have distinctive differences. A **topic** is the subject of the text; This can usually be described in a concise one- to two-word phrase. On the other hand, the **main idea** is more detailed and provides the author's central point of the text. It can be expressed through a complete sentence and is often found in the beginning, the middle, or at the end of a paragraph. In most nonfiction books, the first sentence of the passage usually (but not always) states the main idea.

Review the passage below to explore the topic versus the main idea:

Cheetahs are one of the fastest mammals on the land, reaching up to 70 miles an hour over short distances. Even though cheetahs can run as fast as 70 miles an hour, they usually only have to run half that speed to catch up with their choice of prey. Cheetahs cannot maintain a fast pace over long periods of time because their bodies will overheat. After a chase, cheetahs need to rest for approximately 30 minutes prior to eating or returning to any other activity.

In the example above, the topic of the passage is "Cheetahs" simply because that is the subject of the text. The main idea of the text is "Cheetahs are one of the fastest mammals on the land but can only maintain a fast pace for shorter distances." While it covers the topic, it is more detailed and refers to the text in its entirety. The text continues to provide additional details called **supporting details**, which will be discussed in the next section.

How Details Develop the Main Idea

Supporting details help readers better develop and understand the main idea. Supporting details answer questions like *who, what, where, when, why,* and *how.* Different types of supporting details include examples, facts and statistics, anecdotes, and sensory details.

Persuasive and informative texts often use supporting details. In persuasive texts, authors attempt to make readers agree with their points of view, and supporting details are often used as "selling points." If authors make a statement, they need to support the statement with evidence in order to adequately persuade readers. Informative texts use supporting details such as examples and facts to inform readers. Review the previous "Cheetahs" passage to find examples of supporting details.

Cheetahs are one of the fastest mammals on the land, reaching up to 70 miles an hour over short distances. Even though cheetahs can run as fast as 70 miles an hour, they usually only have to run half that speed to catch up with their choice of prey. Cheetahs cannot maintain a fast pace over long periods of time because their bodies will overheat. After a chase, cheetahs need to rest for approximately 30 minutes prior to eating or returning to any other activity.

29

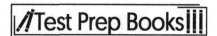
In the example, supporting details include:

- Cheetahs reach up to 70 miles per hour over short distances.
- They usually only have to run half that speed to catch up with their prey.
- Cheetahs will overheat if they exert a high speed over longer distances.
- Cheetahs need to rest for 30 minutes after a chase.

Look at the diagram below (applying the cheetah example) to help determine the hierarchy of topic, main idea, and supporting details.

Point of View and Purpose

Author's Point of View and Purpose

When it comes to an author's writing, readers should always identify a **position** or **stance**. No matter how objective a text may seem, readers should assume the author has preconceived beliefs. One can reduce the likelihood of accepting an invalid argument by looking for multiple articles on the topic, including those with varying opinions. If several opinions point in the same direction and are backed by reputable peer-reviewed sources, it's more likely that the author has a valid argument. Positions that run contrary to widely held beliefs and existing data should invite scrutiny. There are exceptions to the rule, so readers should be careful consumers of information.

While themes, symbols, and motifs are buried deep within the text and can sometimes be difficult to infer, an author's **purpose** is usually obvious from the beginning. There are four purposes of writing: to inform, to persuade, to describe, and to entertain. **Informative** writing presents facts in an accessible way. **Persuasive** writing appeals to emotions and logic to inspire the reader to adopt a specific stance. Readers should be wary of this type of writing, as it can mask a lack of objectivity with powerful emotion. **Descriptive** writing is designed to paint a picture in the reader's mind, while texts that **entertain** are often narratives designed to engage and delight the reader.

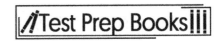

The various writing styles are usually blended, with one purpose dominating the rest. A persuasive text, for example, might begin with a humorous tale to make readers more receptive to the persuasive message, or a recipe in a cookbook designed to inform might be preceded by an entertaining anecdote that makes the recipes more appealing.

Author's Position and Response to Different Viewpoints

If an author presents a differing opinion or a counterargument in order to refute it, the reader should consider how and why the information is being presented. It is meant to strengthen the original argument and shouldn't be confused with the author's intended conclusion, but it should also be considered in the reader's final evaluation.

Authors can also use bias if they ignore the opposing viewpoint or present their side in an unbalanced way. A strong argument considers the opposition and finds a way to refute it. Critical readers should look for an unfair or one-sided presentation of the argument and be skeptical, as a bias may be present. Even if this bias is unintentional, if it exists in the writing, the reader should be wary of the validity of the argument. Readers should also look for the use of stereotypes, which refer to specific groups. Stereotypes are often negative connotations about a person or place and should always be avoided. When a critical reader finds stereotypes in a piece of writing, they should be critical of the argument, and consider the validity of anything the author presents. Stereotypes reveal a flaw in the writer's thinking and may suggest a lack of knowledge or understanding about the subject.

Inferring the Author's Purpose in the Passage

In nonfiction writing, authors employ argumentative techniques to present their opinion to readers in the most convincing way. Persuasive writing usually includes at least one type of appeal: an appeal to logic (**logos**), emotion (**pathos**), or credibility and trustworthiness (**ethos**). When a writer appeals to logic, they are asking readers to agree with them based on research, evidence, and an established line of reasoning. An author's argument might also appeal to readers' emotions, perhaps by including personal stories and anecdotes (a short narrative of a specific event). A final type of appeal—appeal to authority—asks the reader to agree with the author's argument on the basis of their expertise or credentials. Consider three different approaches to arguing the same opinion:

Logic (Logos)

Below is an example of an appeal to logic. The author uses evidence to disprove the logic of the school's rule (the rule was supposed to reduce discipline problems, but the number of problems has not been reduced; therefore, the rule is not working) and he or she calls for its repeal.

> Our school should abolish its current ban on campus cell phone use. The ban was adopted last year as an attempt to reduce class disruptions and help students focus more on their lessons. However, since the rule was enacted, there has been no change in the number of disciplinary problems in class. Therefore, the rule is ineffective and should be done away with.

Emotion (Pathos)

An author's argument might also appeal to readers' emotions, perhaps by including personal stories and anecdotes. The next example presents an appeal to emotion. By sharing the personal anecdote of one student and speaking about emotional topics like family relationships, the author invokes the reader's empathy in asking them to reconsider the school rule.

> Our school should abolish its current ban on campus cell phone use. If students aren't able to use their phones during the school day, many of them feel isolated from their loved ones. For example, last semester, one student's grandmother had a heart attack in the morning. However, because he couldn't use his cell phone, the student didn't know about his grandmother's condition until the end of the day—when

she had already passed away, and it was too late to say goodbye. By preventing students from contacting their friends and family, our school is placing undue stress and anxiety on students.

Credibility (Ethos)

Finally, an appeal to authority includes a statement from a relevant expert. In this case, the author uses a doctor in the field of education to support the argument. All three examples begin from the same opinion—the school's phone ban needs to change—but rely on different argumentative styles to persuade the reader.

> Our school should abolish its current ban on campus cell phone use. According to Dr. Bartholomew Everett, a leading educational expert, "Research studies show that cell phone usage has no real impact on student attentiveness. Rather, phones provide a valuable technological resource for learning. Schools need to learn how to integrate this new technology into their curriculum." Rather than banning phones altogether, our school should follow the advice of experts and allow students to use phones as part of their learning.

Rhetorical Questions

Another commonly used argumentative technique is asking **rhetorical questions**, questions that do not actually require an answer but that push the reader to consider the topic further.

> I wholly disagree with the proposal to ban restaurants from serving foods with high sugar and sodium contents. Do we really want to live in a world where the government can control what we eat? I prefer to make my own food choices.

Here, the author's rhetorical question prompts readers to put themselves in a hypothetical situation and imagine how they would feel about it.

Tone and Figurative Language

How Words Affect Tone

Tone refers to the writer's attitude toward the subject matter. For example, the tone conveys how the writer feels about the topic he or she is writing about. A lot of nonfiction writing has a neutral tone, which is an important tone for the writer to take. A neutral tone demonstrates that the writer is presenting a topic impartially and letting the information speak for itself.

On the other hand, nonfiction writing can be just as effective and appropriate if the tone isn't neutral. For instance, consider this example:

> Seat belts save more lives than any other automobile safety feature. Many studies show that airbags save lives as well; however, not all cars have airbags. For instance, some older cars don't. Furthermore, air bags aren't entirely reliable. For example, studies show that in 15% of accidents, airbags don't deploy as designed; but, on the other hand, seat belt malfunctions are extremely rare. The number of highway fatalities has plummeted since laws requiring seat belt usage were enacted.

In this passage, the writer mostly chooses to retain a neutral tone when presenting information. If the writer would instead include their own personal experience of losing a friend or family member in a car accident, the tone would change dramatically. The tone would no longer be neutral and would show that the writer has a personal stake in the content, allowing them to interpret the information in a different way. When analyzing tone, consider what the writer is trying to achieve in the text and how they *create* the tone using style.

Verbal

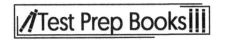

An author's choice of words—also referred to as **diction**—helps to convey their meaning in a particular way. Through diction, an author can convey a particular tone—e.g., a humorous tone, a serious tone—in order to support the thesis in a meaningful way to the reader.

Connotation and Denotation

Connotation is when an author chooses words or phrases that invoke ideas or feelings other than their literal meaning. An example of the use of connotation is the word *cheap*, which suggests something is poor in value or negatively describes a person as reluctant to spend money. When something or someone is described this way, the reader is more inclined to have a particular image or feeling about it or him/her. Thus, connotation can be a very effective language tool in creating emotion and swaying opinion. However, connotations are sometimes hard to pin down because varying emotions can be associated with a word. Generally, though, connotative meanings tend to be fairly consistent within a specific cultural group.

Denotation refers to words or phrases that mean exactly what they say. It is helpful when a writer wants to present hard facts or vocabulary terms with which readers may be unfamiliar. Some examples of denotation are the words *inexpensive* and *frugal*. *Inexpensive* refers to the cost of something, not its value, and *frugal* indicates that a person is conscientiously watching their spending. These terms do not elicit the same emotions that *cheap* does.

Authors sometimes choose to use both, but what they choose and when they use it is what critical readers need to differentiate. One method isn't inherently better than the other; however, one may create a better effect, depending upon an author's intent. If, for example, an author's purpose is to inform, to instruct, and to familiarize readers with a difficult subject, their use of connotation may be helpful. However, it may also undermine credibility and confuse readers. An author who wants to create a credible, scholarly effect in their text would most likely use denotation, which emphasizes literal, factual meaning and examples.

How Figurative Language Affects the Meaning of Words

It's important to be able to recognize and interpret **figurative,** or non-literal, language. Literal statements rely directly on the denotations of words and express exactly what's happening in reality. Figurative language uses non-literal expressions to present information in a creative way. Consider the following sentences:

a. His pillow was very soft, and he fell asleep quickly.

b. His pillow was a fluffy cloud, and he floated away on it to the dream world.

Sentence *A* is literal, employing only the real meanings of each word. Sentence *B* is figurative. It employs a metaphor by stating that his pillow was a cloud. Of course, he isn't actually sleeping on a cloud, but the reader can draw on images of clouds as light, soft, fluffy, and relaxing to get a sense of how the character felt as he fell asleep. Also, in sentence *B*, the pillow becomes a vehicle that transports him to a magical dream world. The character isn't literally floating through the air—he's simply falling asleep! But by utilizing figurative language, the author creates a scene of peace, comfort, and relaxation that conveys stronger emotions and more creative imagery than the purely literal sentence. While there are countless types of figurative language, there are a few common ones that any reader should recognize.

Simile and **metaphor** are comparisons between two things, but their formats differ slightly. A simile says that two things are *similar* and makes a comparison using "like" or "as"—*A* is like *B*, or *A* is as [some characteristic] as *B*—whereas a metaphor states that two things are exactly the same—*A* is *B*. In both cases, simile and metaphor invite the reader to think more deeply about the characteristics of the two subjects and consider where they overlap. An

This material is provided for exam preparation purposes only and does not indicate an endorsement of any specific scientific, political, or religious point of view. © TPB Publishing. You have been licensed one copy of this document for personal use only. Any other reproduction or redistribution is strictly prohibited. All rights reserved.

Verbal

example of metaphor can be found in the above sentence about the sleeper ("His pillow was a fluffy cloud"). For an example of simile, look at the first line of Robert Burns' famous poem:

My love is like a red, red rose

This is comparison using "like," and the two things being compared are love and a rose. Some characteristics of a rose are that it's fragrant, beautiful, blossoming, colorful, vibrant—by comparing his love to a rose, Burns asks the reader to apply these qualities to his love. In this way, he implies that his love is also fresh, blossoming, and brilliant.

Similes can also compare things that appear dissimilar. Here's a song lyric from Florence and the Machine:

Happiness hit her like a bullet in the back

"Happiness" has a very positive connotation, but getting "a bullet in the back" seems violent and aggressive, not at all related to happiness. By using an unexpected comparison, the writer forces readers to think more deeply about the comparison and ask themselves how could getting shot be similar to feeling happy. "A bullet in the back" is something that she doesn't see coming; it's sudden and forceful; and presumably, it has a strong impact on her life. So, in this way, the author seems to be saying that unexpected happiness made a sudden and powerful change in her life.

Another common form of figurative language is **personification,** when a non-human object is given human characteristics. William Blake uses personification here:

... the stars threw down their spears,

And watered heaven with their tears

He imagines the stars as combatants in a heavenly battle, giving them both action (throwing down their spears) and emotion (the sadness and disappointment of their tears). Personification helps to add emotion or develop relationships between characters and non-human objects. In fact, most people use personification in their everyday lives:

My alarm clock betrayed me! It didn't go off this morning!

The last piece of chocolate cake was staring at me from the refrigerator.

Next is **hyperbole,** a type of figurative language that uses extreme exaggeration. Sentences like, "I love you to the moon and back," or "I will love you for a million years," are examples of hyperbole. They aren't literally true—unfortunately, people cannot jump to outer space or live for a million years—but they're creative expressions that communicate the depth of feeling of the author.

Another way that writers add deeper meaning to their work is through **allusions.** An allusion is a reference to something from history, literature, or another cultural source. When the text is from a different culture or a time period, readers may not be familiar with every allusion. However, allusions tend to be well-known because the author wants the reader to make a connection between what's happening in the text and what's being referenced.

I can't believe my best friend told our professor that I was skipping class to finish my final project! What a Judas!

This sentence contains a Biblical allusion to Judas, a friend and follower of Jesus who betrayed Jesus to the Romans. In this case, the allusion to Judas is used to give a deeper impression of betrayal and disloyalty from a trusted friend. Commonly used allusions in Western texts may come from the Bible, Greek or Roman mythology, or well-known

34

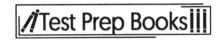
literature such as Shakespeare. By familiarizing themselves with these touchstones of history and culture, readers can be more prepared to recognize allusions.

How Figurative Language Influences the Author's Purpose

A **rhetorical strategy**—also referred to as a **rhetorical mode**—is the structural way an author chooses to present their argument. Though the terms noted below are similar to the organizational structures noted earlier, these strategies do not imply that the entire text follows the approach. For example, a cause and effect organizational structure is solely that, nothing more. A persuasive text may use cause and effect as a strategy to convey a singular point. Thus, an argument may include several of the strategies as the author strives to convince their audience to take action or accept a different point of view. It's important that readers are able to identify an author's thesis and position on the topic in order to be able to identify the careful construction through which the author speaks to the reader.

The following are some of the more common rhetorical strategies:

- **Cause and effect**—establishing a logical correlation or causation between two ideas
- **Classification/division**—the grouping of similar items together or division of something into parts
- **Comparison/contrast**—the distinguishing of similarities/differences to expand on an idea
- **Definition**—used to clarify abstract ideas, unfamiliar concepts, or to distinguish one idea from another
- **Description**—use of vivid imagery, active verbs, and clear adjectives to explain ideas
- **Exemplification**—the use of examples to explain an idea
- **Narration**—anecdotes or personal experience to present or expand on a concept
- **Problem/Solution**—presentation of a problem or problems, followed by proposed solution(s)

How Rhetorical Language Conveys Meaning, Emotion, or Persuades Readers

A **rhetorical device** is the phrasing and presentation of an idea that reinforces and emphasizes a point in an argument. A rhetorical device is often quite memorable. One of the more famous uses of a rhetorical device is in John F. Kennedy's 1961 inaugural address: "Ask not what your country can do for you, ask what you can do for your country." The contrast of ideas presented in the phrasing is an example of the rhetorical device of antimetabole. Some other common examples are provided in the following chart, but test takers should be aware that this is not a complete list.

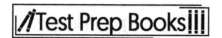

Observe this chart:

Device	Definition	Example
Allusion	A reference to a famous person, event, or significant literary text as a form of significant comparison	"We are apt to shut our eyes against a painful truth, and listen to the song of that siren till she transforms us into beasts." Patrick Henry
Anaphora	The repetition of the same words at the beginning of successive words, phrases, or clauses, designed to emphasize an idea	"We shall not flag or fail. We shall go on to the end. We shall fight in France, we shall fight on the seas and oceans, we shall fight with growing confidence ... we shall fight in the fields and in the streets, we shall fight in the hills. We shall never surrender." Winston Churchill
Understatement	A statement meant to portray a situation as less important than it actually is to create an ironic effect	"The war in the Pacific has not necessarily developed in Japan's favor." Emperor Hirohito, surrendering Japan in World War II
Parallelism	A syntactical similarity in a structure or series of structures used for impact of an idea, making it memorable	"A penny saved is a penny earned." Ben Franklin
Rhetorical question	A question posed that is not answered by the writer though there is a desired response, most often designed to emphasize a point	"Can anyone look at our reduced standing in the world today and say, 'Let's have four more years of this?'" Ronald Reagan

Organizing Ideas

How a Section Fits into a Passage and Helps Develop the Ideas

Being able to determine what is most important while reading is critical to synthesis. It is the difference between being able to tell what is necessary to full comprehension and that which is interesting but not necessary.

When determining the importance of an author's ideas, consider the following:

- Ask how critical an author's particular idea, assertion, or concept is to the overall message.

- Ask "is this an interesting fact or is this information essential to understanding the author's main idea?"

- Make a simple chart. On one side, list all of the important, essential points an author makes and on the other, list all of the interesting yet non-critical ideas.

- Highlight, circle, or underline any dates or data in non-fiction passages. Pay attention to headings, captions, and any graphs or diagrams.

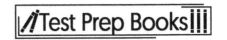

- When reading a fictional passage, delineate important information such as theme, character, setting, conflict (what the problem is), and resolution (how the problem is fixed). Most often, these are the most important aspects contained in fictional text.

- If a non-fiction passage is instructional in nature, take physical note of any steps in the order of their importance as presented by the author. Look for words such as *first*, *next*, *then*, and *last*.

Determining the importance of an author's ideas is critical to synthesis in that it requires the test taker to parse out any unnecessary information and demonstrate they have the ability to make sound determination on what is important to the author, and what is merely a supporting or less critical detail.

Analyzing How a Text is Organized

Depending on what the author is attempting to accomplish, certain formats or text structures work better than others. For example, a sequence structure might work for narration but not for identifying similarities and differences between concepts. Similarly, a comparison-contrast structure is not useful for narration. It's the author's job to put the right information in the correct format.

Readers should be familiar with the five main literary structures:

Sequence Structure

Sequence structure (sometimes referred to as the order structure) is when the order of events proceeds in a predictable order. In many cases, this means the text goes through the plot elements: exposition, rising action, climax, falling action, and resolution. Readers are introduced to characters, setting, and conflict in the **exposition**. In the **rising action**, there's an increase in tension and suspense. The **climax** is the height of tension and the point of no return. **Tension** decreases during the falling action. In the **resolution**, any conflicts presented in the exposition are resolved, and the story concludes. An informative text that is structured sequentially will often go in order from one step to the next.

Problem-Solution

In the **problem-solution structure**, authors identify a potential problem and suggest a solution. This form of writing is usually divided into two parts (the problem and the solution) and can be found in informational texts. For example, cell phone, cable, and satellite providers use this structure in manuals to help customers troubleshoot or identify problems with services or products.

Comparison-Contrast

When authors want to discuss similarities and differences between separate concepts, they arrange thoughts in a **comparison-contrast paragraph structure**. **Venn diagrams** are an effective graphic organizer for comparison-contrast structures because they feature two overlapping circles that can be used to organize similarities and differences. A comparison-contrast essay organizes one paragraph based on similarities and another based on differences. A comparison-contrast essay can also be arranged with the similarities and differences of individual traits addressed within individual paragraphs. Words such as *however*, *but*, and *nevertheless* help signal a contrast in ideas.

Descriptive

Descriptive writing is designed to appeal to your senses. Much like an artist who constructs a painting, good descriptive writing builds an image in the reader's mind by appealing to the five senses: *sight, hearing, taste, touch,* and *smell.* However, overly descriptive writing can become tedious; likewise, sparse descriptions can make settings and characters seem flat. Good authors strike a balance by applying descriptions only to facts that are integral to the passage.

Cause and Effect

Passages that use the **cause and effect structure** are simply asking *why* by demonstrating some type of connection between ideas. Words such as *if, since, because, then,* or *consequently* indicate a relationship. By switching the order of a complex sentence, the writer can rearrange the emphasis on different clauses. Saying, *If Sheryl is late, we'll miss the dance,* is different from saying *We'll miss the dance if Sheryl is late.* One emphasizes Sheryl's tardiness while the other emphasizes missing the dance. Paragraphs can also be arranged in a cause and effect format. Cause-and-effect writing discusses the impact of decisions that have been made or could be made. Researchers often apply this paragraph structure to the scientific method.

Understanding the Meaning and Purpose of Transition Words

The writer should act as a guide, showing the reader how all the sentences fit together. Consider this example:

> Seat belts save more lives than any other automobile safety feature. Many studies show that airbags save lives as well. Not all cars have airbags. Many older cars don't. Air bags aren't entirely reliable. Studies show that in 15% of accidents, airbags don't deploy as designed. Seat belt malfunctions are extremely rare.

There's nothing wrong with any of these sentences individually, but together they're disjointed and difficult to follow. The best way for the writer to communicate information is through the use of transition words. Here are examples of transition words and phrases that tie sentences together, enabling a more natural flow:

- To show causality: *as a result, therefore,* and *consequently*
- To compare and contrast: *however, but,* and *on the other hand*
- To introduce examples: *for instance, namely,* and *including*
- To show order of importance: *foremost, primarily, secondly,* and *lastly*

Note: This is not a complete list of transitions. There are many more that can be used; however, most fit into these or similar categories. The point is that the words should clearly show the relationship between sentences, supporting information, and the main idea.

Here is an update to the previous example using transition words. These changes make it easier to read and bring clarity to the writer's points:

> Seat belts save more lives than any other automobile safety feature. Many studies show that airbags save lives as well; however, not all cars have airbags. For instance, some older cars don't. Furthermore, air bags aren't entirely reliable. For example, studies show that in 15% of accidents, airbags don't deploy as designed; but, on the other hand, seat belt malfunctions are extremely rare.

Also, be prepared to analyze whether the writer is using the best transition word or phrase for the situation. Take this sentence for example: "As a result, seat belt malfunctions are extremely rare." This sentence doesn't make sense in the context above because the writer is trying to show the contrast between seat belts and airbags, not the causality.

How the Passage Organization Supports the Author's Ideas

Even if the writer includes plenty of information to support their point, the writing is only coherent when the information is in a logical order. **Logical sequencing** is really just common sense, but it's also an important writing technique. First, the writer should introduce the main idea, whether for a paragraph, a section, or the entire piece. Second, they should present evidence to support the main idea by using transitional language. This shows the reader how the information relates to the main idea and the sentences around it. The writer should then take time to interpret the information, making sure necessary connections are obvious to the reader. Finally, the writer can summarize the information in a closing section.

38

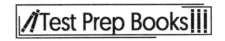

Note: Though most writing follows this pattern, it isn't a set rule. Sometimes writers change the order for effect. For example, the writer can begin with a surprising piece of supporting information to grab the reader's attention, and then transition to the main idea. Thus, if a passage doesn't follow the logical order, don't immediately assume it's wrong. However, most writing usually settles into a logical sequence after a nontraditional beginning.

Introductions and Conclusions

Examining the writer's strategies for introductions and conclusions puts the reader in the right mindset to interpret the rest of the text. Look for methods the writer might use for **introductions** such as:

- Stating the main point immediately, followed by outlining how the rest of the piece supports this claim.

- Establishing important, smaller pieces of the main idea first, and then grouping these points into a case for the main idea.

- Opening with a quotation, anecdote, question, seeming paradox, or other piece of interesting information, and then using it to lead to the main point.

- Whatever method the writer chooses, the introduction should make their intention clear, establish their voice as a credible one, and encourage a person to continue reading.

Conclusions tend to follow a similar pattern. In them, the writer restates their main idea a final time, often after summarizing the smaller pieces of that idea. If the introduction uses a quote or anecdote to grab the reader's attention, the conclusion often makes reference to it again. Whatever way the writer chooses to arrange the conclusion, the final restatement of the main idea should be clear and simple for the reader to interpret. Finally, conclusions shouldn't introduce any new information.

Comparing Different Ways of Presenting Ideas

Evaluating Two Different Texts

Every passage has its own unique scope, purpose, and emphasis, or what it covers, why it is written, and what its specific focus is centered upon. Additionally, each passage is written with a particular audience in mind, and each passage affects its audience differently. The scope, purpose, and emphasis of each passage can be found by comparing the parts of the piece with the whole framework of the piece. Word choices, grammatical choices, and syntactical choices can help the reader figure out the scope, purpose, and emphasis. These choices are embedded in the words and sentences of the passage (the parts). They help show the intentions and goals of the author (the "whole").

For example, if an author uses strong language like *enrage, ignite, infuriate,* and *antagonize*, then they may be cueing the reader in to their own rage, or they may be trying to incite anger in others. Likewise, if an author continually uses short, simple sentences, he or she might be trying to incite excitement or nervousness. These different choices and styles affect the overall message, or purpose. Sometimes the subject matter or audience is discussed explicitly, but often, test takers have to break a passage down, also known as decoding the passage. In this way, test takers can find the passage's target audience and intentions. Meanwhile, the impact of the article can be personal or historical, depending upon the passage—it can either speak to the test taker personally or capture a historical era.

When two passages are analyzed in juxtaposition—or side-by-side—it can help the audience have a clearer picture of the scope, purpose, emphasis, audience, and impact. Evaluating and comparing passages side-by-side helps shed light on similarities and differences that are helpful for test takers. The key is to figure out both the parts and the "wholes" of each passage. Compare the word choices, grammatical choices, and syntactical choices of each passage, and then compare the big picture of each passage. As a result, test takers will have a stronger basis for understanding the intricate details and broader frameworks of all passages they encounter.

39

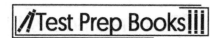

Evaluating Two Different Passages

Every passage offered has its own view, tone, style, organization, purpose, or impact. It is extremely important to compare the parts to the "wholes" of each passage. Additionally, these parts and "wholes" are better understood through **intertextual analysis** (for example, comparing the texts as if they were side by side). The viewpoint of the text can be found through a close analysis of the author's biases, or personal opinions or perceptions. All biases are embedded in the word choices, grammatical choices, and syntactical choices of each passage. For example, if an author continually uses negative words like *dislike*, *hate*, *despise*, *detrimental*, or *loathe*, they are trying to illustrate their own hatred of something or convey a character's hatred of something. These negative terms inevitably affect the view and tone of a passage. Comparing terminologies and biases can help a test taker better understand the similarities and differences of two or more passages. Similarly, the purposes of each can be better highlighted with a closer examination of word choices, grammatical choices, and syntactical choices.

Organization, on the other hand, is more easily understood by studying the passage on its own. Organizational differences on the page are likely to jump out at the test taker. A poetry passage, for instance, is traditionally organized differently than a prose passage. Test takers can see the differences in structures: one uses paragraphs, while the other uses stanzas. If organizational differences cannot be deduced through visual analysis, test takers should try to take a closer look at the sequence of events or the content of each paragraph. Organization, nevertheless, is not something that is separate from view, tone, purpose, style, and impact. It can skew or connect a viewpoint, shift or solidify tone, reinforce or undermine purpose, express or conceal a particular style, or establish or disestablish the impact of passage. Organization is the backbone of every form of written expression—it unifies all the parts and sets the parameters for the wholes. Thus, organization should be analyzed strategically when comparing passages.

The Relationship Between Evidence and Main Ideas and Details

Summarizing Information from a Passage

Summarizing is an effective way to draw a conclusion from a passage. A summary is a shortened version of the original text, written by the reader in their own words. Focusing on the main points of the original text and including only the relevant details can help readers reach a conclusion. It's important to retain the original meaning of the passage.

Like summarizing, **paraphrasing** can also help a reader fully understand different parts of a text. Paraphrasing calls for the reader to take a small part of the passage and list or describe its main points. Paraphrasing is more than rewording the original passage, though. It should be written in the reader's own words, while still retaining the meaning of the original source. This will indicate an understanding of the original source, yet still help the reader expand on their interpretation.

Readers should pay attention to the **sequence**, or the order in which details are laid out in the text, as this can be important to understanding its meaning as a whole. Writers will often use transitional words to help the reader understand the order of events and to stay on track. Words like *next, then, after*, and *finally* show that the order of events is important to the author. In some cases, the author omits these transitional words, and the sequence is implied. Authors may even purposely present the information out of order to make an impact or have an effect on the reader. An example might be when a narrative writer uses **flashback** to reveal information.

Relationship Between the Main Idea and Details of a Passage

In order to understand any text, readers first must determine the **topic**, or what the text is about. In non-fiction writing, the topic can generally be expressed in a few words. For example, a passage might be about college education, moving to a new neighborhood, or dog breeds. Slightly more specific information is found in the **main idea**, or what the writer wants readers to know about the topic. An article might be about the history of popular dog

40

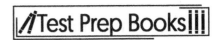

breeds; another article might tell how certain dog breeds are unfairly stereotyped. In both cases, the topic is the same—dog breeds—but the main ideas are quite different.

Each writer has a distinct purpose for writing and a different set of details for what they want us to know about dog breeds. When a writer expresses their main idea in one sentence, this is known as a **thesis statement**. If a writer uses a thesis statement, it can generally be found at the beginning of the passage. Finally, the most specific information in a text is in the **supporting details**. An article about dog breed stereotyping might discuss a case study of pit bulls and provide statistics about how many dog attacks are caused by pit bulls versus other breeds.

Main Idea of a Passage

Topics and main ideas are critical parts of writing. The **topic** is the subject matter of the piece. An example of a topic would be *the use of cell phones in a classroom.*

The **main idea** is what the writer wants to say about that topic. A writer may make the point that the use of cell phones in a classroom is a serious problem that must be addressed in order for students to learn better. Therefore, the topic is cell phone usage in a classroom, and the main idea is that it's *a serious problem needing to be addressed.* The topic can be expressed in a word or two, but the main idea should be a complete thought.

An author will likely identify the topic immediately within the title or the first sentence of the passage. The main idea is usually presented in the introduction. In a single passage, the main idea may be identified in the first or last sentence, but it will most likely be directly stated and easily recognized by the reader. Because it is not always stated immediately in a passage, it's important that readers carefully read the entire passage to identify the main idea.

The main idea should not be confused with the thesis statement. A **thesis statement** is a clear statement of the writer's specific stance and can often be found in the introduction of a nonfiction piece. The thesis is a specific sentence (or two) that offers the direction and focus of the discussion.

In order to illustrate the main idea, a writer will use **supporting details**, which provide evidence or examples to help make a point. Supporting details are typically found in nonfiction pieces that seek to inform or persuade the reader.

Determining Which Details Support a Main Idea

An important skill is the ability to determine which details in a passage support the main idea. In the example of cell phone usage in the classroom, where the author's main idea is to show the seriousness of this problem and the need to "unplug", supporting details would be critical for effectively making that point. Supporting details used here might include statistics on a decline in student focus and studies showing the impact of digital technology usage on students' attention spans. The author could also include testimonies from teachers surveyed on the topic.

It's important that readers evaluate the author's supporting details to be sure that they are credible, provide evidence of the author's point, and directly support the main idea. Although shocking statistics grab readers' attention, their use may provide ineffective information in the piece. Details like this are crucial to understanding the passage and evaluating how well the author presents their argument and evidence.

Though there are several types of conflicts and several potential themes within them, the following are the most common:

- Individual against the self—relevant to themes of self-awareness, internal struggles, pride, coming of age, facing reality, fate, free will, vanity, loss of innocence, loneliness, isolation, fulfillment, failure, and disillusionment

- Individual against nature— relevant to themes of knowledge vs. ignorance, nature as beauty, quest for discovery, self-preservation, chaos and order, circle of life, death, and destruction of beauty

- Individual against society— relevant to themes of power, beauty, good, evil, war, class struggle, totalitarianism, role of men/women, wealth, corruption, change vs. tradition, capitalism, destruction, heroism, injustice, and racism

- Individual against another individual— relevant to themes of hope, loss of love or hope, sacrifice, power, revenge, betrayal, and honor

For example, in Hawthorne's *The Scarlet Letter*, one possible narrative conflict could be the individual against the self, with a relevant theme of internal struggles. This theme is alluded to through characterization—Dimmesdale's moral struggle with his love for Hester and Hester's internal struggles with the truth and her daughter, Pearl. It's also alluded to through plot—Dimmesdale's suicide and Hester helping the very townspeople who initially condemned her.

Sometimes, a text can convey a **message** or **universal lesson**—a truth or insight that the reader infers from the text, based on analysis of the literary and/or poetic elements. This message is often presented as a statement. For example, a potential message in Shakespeare's *Hamlet* could be "Revenge is what ultimately drives the human soul." This message can be immediately determined through plot and characterization in numerous ways, but it can also be determined through the setting of Norway, which is bordering on war.

How Authors Develop Theme

Authors employ a variety of techniques to present a theme. They may compare or contrast characters, events, places, ideas, or historical or invented settings to speak thematically. They may use analogies, metaphors, similes, allusions, or other literary devices to convey the theme. An author's use of diction, syntax, and tone can also help convey the theme. Authors will often develop themes through the development of characters, use of the setting, repetition of ideas, use of symbols, and through contrasting value systems. Authors of both fiction and nonfiction genres will use a variety of these techniques to develop one or more themes.

Regardless of the literary genre, there are commonalities in how authors, playwrights, and poets develop themes or central ideas.

Authors often do research, the results of which contribute to theme. In prose fiction and drama, this research may include real historical information about the setting the author has chosen or include elements that make fictional characters, settings, and plots seem realistic to the reader. In nonfiction, research is critical since information contained within this literature must be accurate.

In fiction, authors present a narrative conflict that will contribute to the overall theme. This conflict may involve the storyline the storyline itself and some trouble within characters that needs resolution. In nonfiction, this conflict may be an explanation or commentary on factual people and events.

Authors will sometimes use character motivation to convey theme, such as in the example from *Hamlet* regarding revenge. In fiction, the characters an author creates will think, speak, and act in ways that effectively convey the

42

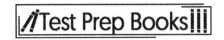

theme to readers. In nonfiction, the characters are factual, as in a biography, but authors pay particular attention to presenting those motivations to make them clear to readers.

Authors also use literary devices as a means of conveying theme. For example, the use of Moon symbolism in Mary Shelley's *Frankenstein* is significant, as its phases can be compared to the phases that the Creature undergoes as he struggles with his identity.

The selected point of view can also contribute to a work's theme. The use of first-person point of view in a fiction or non-fiction work engages the reader's response differently than third person point of view. The central idea or theme from a first-person narrative may differ from a third-person limited text.

In literary nonfiction, authors usually identify the purpose of their writing, which differs from fiction, where the general purpose is to entertain. The purpose of nonfiction is usually to inform, persuade, or entertain the audience. The stated purpose of a non-fiction text will drive how the central message or theme, if applicable, is presented.

Authors identify an audience for their writing, which is critical in shaping the theme of the work. For example, the audience for J.K. Rowling's *Harry Potter* series would be different than the audience for a biography of George Washington. The audience an author chooses to address is closely tied to the purpose of the work. The choice of an audience also drives the choice of language and level of diction an author uses. Ultimately, the intended audience determines the level to which that subject matter is presented and the complexity of the theme.

Drawing Conclusions, Making Inferences, and Evaluating Evidence

Making Generalizations Based on Evidence

One way to make generalizations is to look for main topics. When doing so, pay particular attention to any titles, headlines, or opening statements made by the author. Topic sentences or repetitive ideas can be clues in gleaning inferred ideas. For example, if a passage contains the phrase *While some consider DNA testing to be infallible, it is an inherently flawed technique,* the test taker can infer the rest of the passage will contain information that points to problems with DNA testing.

The test taker may be asked to make a generalization based on prior knowledge but may also be asked to make predictions based on new ideas. For example, the test taker may have no prior knowledge of DNA other than its genetic property to replicate. However, if the reader is given passages on the flaws of DNA testing with enough factual evidence, the test taker may arrive at the inferred conclusion or generalization that the author does not support the infallibility of DNA testing in all identification cases.

When making generalizations, it is important to remember that the critical thinking process involved must be fluid and open to change. While a reader may infer an idea from a main topic, general statement, or other clues, they must be open to receiving new information within a particular passage. New ideas presented by an author may require the test taker to alter a generalization. Similarly, when asked questions that require making an inference, it's important to read the entire test passage and all of the answer options. Often, a test taker will need to refine a generalization based on new ideas that may be presented within the text itself.

Using Main Ideas to Draw Conclusions

Determining conclusions requires being an active reader, as a reader must make a prediction and analyze facts to identify a conclusion. There are a few ways to determine a logical conclusion, but careful reading is the most important. It's helpful to read a passage a few times, noting details that seem important to the text. A reader should also identify key words in a passage to determine the logical conclusion or determination that flows from the information presented.

43

Textual evidence helps readers draw a conclusion about a passage. **Textual evidence** refers to information—facts and examples that support the main point; it will likely come from outside sources and can be in the form of quoted or paraphrased material. In order to draw a conclusion from evidence, it's important to examine the credibility and validity of that evidence as well as how (and if) it relates to the main idea.

If an author presents a differing opinion or a **counterargument** in order to refute it, the reader should consider how and why the information is being presented. It is meant to strengthen the original argument and shouldn't be confused with the author's intended conclusion, but it should also be considered in the reader's final evaluation.

Sometimes, authors explicitly state the conclusion they want readers to understand. Alternatively, a conclusion may not be directly stated. In that case, readers must rely on the implications to form a logical conclusion:

> On the way to the bus stop, Michael realized his homework wasn't in his backpack. He ran back to the house to get it and made it back to the bus just in time.

In this example, though it's never explicitly stated, it can be inferred that Michael is a student on his way to school in the morning. When forming a conclusion from implied information, it's important to read the text carefully to find several pieces of evidence to support the conclusion.

Describing the Steps of an Argument

Strong arguments tend to follow a fairly defined format. In the introduction, background information regarding the problem is shared, , the implications of the issue are stated, and the author's thesis or claims are given. Supporting evidence is then presented in the body paragraphs, along with the counterargument, which then gets refuted with specific evidence. Lastly, in the conclusion, the author summarizes the points and claims again.

Evidence Used to Support a Claim or Conclusion

Premises are the why, and **conclusions** are the what. Stated differently, premises are the evidence or facts supporting why the conclusion is logical and valid. Reading Comprehension questions do not require evaluation of the factual accuracy of the arguments; instead, the questions evaluate the test taker's ability to assess an argument's logical strength. For example, John eats all red food. Apples are red. Therefore, John eats apples. This argument is logically sound, despite having no factual basis in reality. Below is an example of a practice argument.

> Julie is an American track athlete. She's the star of the number one collegiate team in the country. Her times are consistently at the top of national rankings. Julie is extremely likely to represent the United States at the upcoming Olympics.

In this example, the conclusion, or the *what*, is that she will likely be on the American Olympic team. The author supports this conclusion with two premises. First, Julie is the star of an elite track team. Second, she runs some of the best times of the country. This is the *why* behind the conclusion. The following builds off this basic argument:

> Julie is an American track athlete. She's the star of the number one collegiate team in the country. Her times are consistently at the top of national rankings. Julie is extremely likely to represent the United States at the upcoming Olympics. Julie will continue to develop after the Olympic trials. She will be a frontrunner for the gold. Julie is likely to become a world-famous track star.

These additions to the argument make the conclusion different. Now, the conclusion is that Julie is likely to become a world-famous track star. The previous conclusion, Julie will likely be on the Olympic team, functions as a **sub-conclusion** in this argument. Like conclusions, premises must adequately support sub-conclusions. However, sub-conclusions function like premises, since sub-conclusions also support the overall conclusion.

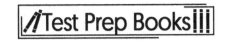

Determining Whether Evidence is Relevant and Sufficient

A **hasty generalization** involves an argument relying on insufficient statistical data or inaccurately generalizing. One common generalization occurs when a group of individuals under observation have some quality or attribute that is asserted to be universal or true for a much larger number of people than actually documented. Here's an example of a hasty generalization:

> A man smokes a lot of cigarettes, but so did his grandfather. The grandfather smoked nearly two packs per day since his World War II service until he died at ninety years of age. Continuing to smoke cigarettes will clearly not impact the grandson's long-term health.

This argument is a hasty generalization because it assumes that one person's addiction and lack of consequences will naturally be reflected in a different individual. There is no reasonable justification for such extrapolation. It is common knowledge that any smoking is detrimental to everyone's health. The fact that the man's grandfather smoked two packs per day and lived a long life has no logical connection with the grandson engaging in similar behavior. The hasty generalization doesn't take into account other reasons behind the grandfather's longevity. Nor does the author offer evidence that might support the idea that the man would share a similar lifetime if he smokes. It might be different if the author stated that the man's family shares some genetic trait rendering them immune to the effects of tar and chemicals on the lungs. If this were in the argument, we would assume it as truth and find the generalization to be valid rather than hasty. Of course, this is not the case in our example.

Determining Whether a Statement Is or Is Not Supported

The basic tenet of reading comprehension is the ability to read and understand a text. One way to understand a text is to look for information that supports the author's main idea, topic, or position statement. This information may be factual, or it may be based on the author's opinion. This section will focus on the test taker's ability to identify factual information, as opposed to opinionated bias. The test will ask test takers to read passages containing factual information, and then logically relate those passages by drawing conclusions based on evidence.

In order to identify factual information within one or more text passages, begin by looking for statements of fact. Factual statements can be either true or false. Identifying factual statements as opposed to opinion statements is important in demonstrating full command of evidence in reading. For example, the statement *The temperature outside was unbearably hot* may seem like a fact; however, it's not. While anyone can point to a temperature gauge as factual evidence, the statement itself reflects only an opinion. Some people may find the temperature unbearably hot. Others may find it comfortably warm. Thus, the sentence, *The temperature outside was unbearably hot,* reflects the opinion of the author who found it unbearable. If the text passage followed up the sentence with atmospheric conditions indicating heat indices above 140 degrees Fahrenheit, then the reader knows there is factual information that supports the author's assertion of *unbearably hot.*

In looking for information that can be proven or disproven, it's helpful to scan for dates, numbers, timelines, equations, statistics, and other similar data within any given text passage. These types of indicators will point to proven particulars. For example, the statement, *The temperature outside was unbearably hot on that summer day, July 10, 1913,* most likely indicates factual information, even if the reader is unaware that this is the hottest day on record in the United States. Be careful when reading biased words from an author. Biased words indicate opinion, as opposed to fact.

The following list contains a sampling of common biased words:

- Good/bad
- Great/greatest
- Better/best/worst
- Amazing

45

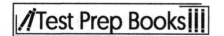

- Terrible/bad/awful
- Beautiful/handsome/ugly
- More/most
- Exciting/dull/boring
- Favorite
- Very
- Probably/should/seem/possibly

Remember, most of what is written is actually opinion or carefully worded information that seems like fact when it isn't. To say, *duplicating DNA results is not cost-effective* sounds like it could be a scientific fact, but it isn't. Factual information can be verified through independent sources.

The simplest type of test question may provide a text passage, then ask the test taker to distinguish the correct factual supporting statement that best answers the corresponding question on the test. However, be aware that most questions may ask the test taker to read more than one text passage and identify which answer best supports an author's topic. While the ability to identify factual information is critical, these types of questions require the test taker to identify chunks of details, and then relate them to one another.

Assessing Whether an Argument is Valid

Although different from conditions and If/Then Statements, **reasonableness** is another important foundational concept. Evaluating an argument for reasonableness and validity entails evaluating the evidence presented by the author to justify their conclusions. Everything contained in the argument should be considered, but remember to ignore outside biases, judgments, and knowledge. For the purposes of this test, the test taker is a one-person jury at a criminal trial using a standard of reasonableness under the circumstances presented by the argument.

These arguments are encountered on a daily basis through social media, entertainment, and cable news. An example is:

> Although many believe it to be a natural occurrence, some believe that the red tide that occurs in Florida each year may actually be a result of human sewage and agricultural runoff. However, it is arguable that both natural and human factors contribute to this annual phenomenon. On one hand, the red tide has been occurring every year since the time of explorers like Cabeza de Vaca in the 1500's. On the other hand, the red tide seems to be getting worse each year, and scientists from the Florida Fish & Wildlife Conservation say the bacteria found inside the tide feed off of nutrients found in fertilizer runoff.

The author's conclusion is that both natural phenomena and human activity contribute to the red tide that happens annually in Florida. The author backs this information up by historical data to prove the natural occurrence of the red tide, and then again with scientific data to back up the human contribution to the red tide. Both of these statements are examples of the premises in the argument. Evaluating the strength of the logical connection between the premises and conclusion is how reasonableness is determined. Another example is:

> The local railroad is a disaster. Tickets are exorbitantly priced, bathrooms leak, and the floor is sticky.

The author is clearly unhappy with the railroad service. They cite three examples of why they believe the railroad to be a disaster. An argument more familiar to everyday life is:

> Alexandra said the movie she just saw was amazing. We should go see it tonight.

Although not immediately apparent, this is an argument. The author is making the argument that they should go see the movie. This conclusion is based on the premise that Alexandra said the movie was amazing. There's an inferred

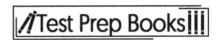

note that Alexandra is knowledgeable on the subject, and she's credible enough to prompt her friends to go see the movie. This seems like a reasonable argument. A less reasonable argument is:

> Alexandra is a film student, and she's written the perfect romantic comedy script. We should put our life savings toward its production as an investment in our future.

The author's conclusion is that they should invest their life savings into the production of a movie, and it is justified by referencing Alexandra's credibility and current work. However, the premises are entirely too weak to support the conclusion. Alexandra is only a film *student*, and the script is seemingly her first work. This is not enough evidence to justify investing one's life savings in the film's success.

Assumptions in an Argument

Think of assumptions as unwritten premises. Although they never explicitly appear in the argument, the author is relying on it to defend the argument, just like a premise. Assumptions are the most important part of an argument that will never appear in an argument.

An argument in the abstract is: The author concludes Z based on W and X premises. But the W and X premises actually depend on the unmentioned assumption of Y. Therefore, the author is really saying that X, W, and Y make Z correct, but Y is assumed.

People assume all of the time. Assumptions and inferences allow the human mind to process the constant flow of information. Many assumptions underlie even the most basic arguments. However, in the world of Legal Reasoning arguments, assumptions must be avoided. An argument must be fully presented to be valid; relying on an assumption is considered weak. The test requires that test takers identify these underlying assumptions. One example is:

> Peyton Manning is the most over-rated quarterback of all time. He lost more big games than anyone else. Plus, he allegedly assaulted his female trainer in college. Peyton clearly shouldn't make the Hall of Fame.

The author certainly relies on a lot of assumptions. A few assumptions are:

- Peyton Manning plays quarterback.
- He is considered to be a great quarterback by at least some people.
- He played in many big games.
- Allegations and past settlements without any admission of guilt from over a decade ago can be relied upon as evidence against Hall of Fame acceptance.
- The Hall of Fame voters factor in off-the-field incidents, even if true.
- The best players should make the Hall of Fame.
- Losing big games negates, at least in part, the achievement of making it to those big games
- Peyton Manning is retired, and people will vote on whether he makes the Hall of Fame at some point in the future.

The author is relying on all of these assumptions. Some are clearly more important to his argument than others. In fact, disproving a necessary assumption can destroy a premise and possibly an entire conclusion. For example, what if the Hall of Fame did not factor in any of the off-the-field incidents? Then the alleged assault no longer factors into the argument. Even worse, what if making the big games actually was more important than losing those games in

47

the eyes of the Hall of Fame voters? Then the whole conclusion falls apart and is no longer justified if that premise is disproven.

Assumption questions test this exact point by asking the test taker to identify which assumption the argument relies upon. If the author is making numerous assumptions, then the most important assumption must be chosen.

If the author truly relies on an assumption, then the argument will completely fall apart if the assumption isn't true. **Negating** a necessary assumption will *always* make the argument fall apart. This is a universal rule of logic and should be the first thing done in testing answer choices.

Here are some ways that underlying assumptions will appear as questions:

- Which of the following is a hidden assumption that the author makes to advance his argument?
- Which assumption, if true, would support the argument's conclusion (make it more logical)?
- The strength of the argument depends on which of the following?
- Upon which of the following assumptions does the author rely?
- Which assumption does the argument presuppose?

An example is:

> Frank Underwood is a terrible president. The man is a typical spend, spend, spend liberal. His employment program would exponentially increase the annual deficit and pile on the national debt. Not to mention, Underwood is also on the verge of starting a war with Russia.

Upon which of the following assumptions does the author's argument most rely?
a. Frank Underwood is a terrible president.
b. The United States cannot afford Frank Underwood's policy plans without spending more than the country raises in revenue.
c. No spend, spend, spend liberal has ever succeeded as president.
d. Starting a war with Russia is beneficial to the United States.

Use the negation rule to find the correct answer in the choices below.

Choice *A* is not an assumption—it is the author's conclusion. This type of restatement will never be the correct answer, but test it anyway. After negating the choice, what remains is: *Frank Underwood is a fantastic president.* Does this make the argument fall apart? No, it just becomes the new conclusion. The argument is certainly worse since it does not seem reasonable for someone to praise a president for being a spend, spend, spend liberal or raising the national debt; however, the argument still makes *logical* sense. Eliminate this choice.

Choice *B* is certainly an assumption. It underlies the premises that the country cannot afford Underwood's economic plans. When reversed to: *The United States can afford Frank Underwood's policy plans without spending more than the country raises in revenue,* this destroys the argument. If the United States can afford his plans, then the annual deficit and national debt won't increase; therefore, Underwood being a terrible president would only be based on the final premise. The argument is much weaker without the two sentences involving the financials. Keep it as a benchmark while working through the remaining choices.

Choice *C* is irrelevant. The author is not necessarily claiming that all loose-pocket liberals make for bad presidents. His argument specifically pertains to Underwood. Negate it— *Some spend, spend, spend liberals have succeeded as president.* This does not destroy the argument. Some other candidate could have succeeded as president. However, the author is pointing out that those policies would be disastrous considering the rising budget and debt. The author

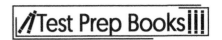

Verbal

is not making an appeal to historical precedent. Although not a terrible choice, it is certainly weaker than Choice *B*. Eliminate this choice.

Choice *D* is definitely not an assumption made by the author. The author is assuming that a war with Russia is disastrous. Negate it anyway—*Starting a war with Russia is not beneficial for the United States.* This does not destroy the argument; it makes it stronger. Eliminate this choice.

Analyzing Two Arguments and Evaluating the Types of Evidence Used to Support Each Claim

Arguments use evidence and reasoning to support a position or prove a point. Claims are typically controversial and may be faced with some degree of contention. Thus, authors support claims with evidence. Two arguments might present different types of evidence that readers will need to evaluate for merit, worthiness, accuracy, relevance, and impact. Evidence can take on many forms such as numbers (statistics, measurements, numerical data, etc.), expert opinions or quotes, testimonies, anecdotal evidence or stories from individuals, and textual evidence, such as that obtained from documents like diaries, newspapers, and laws.

49

This material is provided for exam preparation purposes only and does not indicate an endorsement of any specific scientific, political, or religious point of view. © TPB Publishing. You have been licensed one copy of this document for personal use only. Any other reproduction or redistribution is strictly prohibited. All rights reserved.

Practice Quiz

Word Knowledge

Select the word that most correctly completes the sentence.

1. When the baseball game was over, the first thing Jackson did was run towards the dugout to grab his water bottle to relieve his arid throat. Arid means:
    a. humid
    b. scorched
    c. parched
    d. dusty

2. Driving across the United States, the two friends became inseparable each time they arrived in a new state. They shared many good memories on that trip they would remember for the rest of their lives. Inseparable means:
    a. closer
    b. distant
    c. suffering
    d. irritable

Reading Comprehension

Questions 3–5 are based on the following passage:

> As long ago as 1860 it was the proper thing to be born at home. At present, so I am told, the high gods of medicine have decreed that the first cries of the young shall be uttered upon the anesthetic air of a hospital, preferably a fashionable one. So young Mr. and Mrs. Roger Button were fifty years ahead of style when they decided, one day in the summer of 1860, that their first baby should be born in a hospital. Whether this anachronism had any bearing upon the astonishing history I am about to set down will never be known.
>
> I shall tell you what occurred, and let you judge for yourself.
>
> The Roger Buttons held an enviable position, both social and financial, in ante-bellum Baltimore. They were related to the This Family and the That Family, which, as every Southerner knew, entitled them to membership in that enormous peerage which largely populated the Confederacy. This was their first experience with the charming old custom of having babies—Mr. Button was naturally nervous. He hoped it would be a boy so that he could be sent to Yale College in Connecticut, at which institution Mr. Button himself had been known for four years by the somewhat obvious nickname of "Cuff."
>
> On the September morning consecrated to the enormous event he arose nervously at six o'clock, dressed himself, adjusted an impeccable stock, and hurried forth through the streets of Baltimore to the hospital, to determine whether the darkness of the night had borne in new life upon its bosom.
>
> When he was approximately a hundred yards from the Maryland Private Hospital for Ladies and Gentlemen he saw Doctor Keene, the family physician, descending the front steps, rubbing his hands together with a washing movement—as all doctors are required to do by the unwritten ethics of their profession.

50

Mr. Roger Button, the president of Roger Button & Co., Wholesale Hardware, began to run toward Doctor Keene with much less dignity than was expected from a Southern gentleman of that picturesque period. "Doctor Keene!" he called. "Oh, Doctor Keene!"

The doctor heard him, faced around, and stood waiting, a curious expression settling on his harsh, medicinal face as Mr. Button drew near.

"What happened?" demanded Mr. Button, as he came up in a gasping rush. "What was it? How is she? A boy? Who is it? What—"

"Talk sense!" said Doctor Keene sharply. He appeared somewhat irritated.

"Is the child born?" begged Mr. Button.

Doctor Keene frowned. "Why, yes, I suppose so—after a fashion." Again he threw a curious glance at Mr. Button.

The Curious Case of Benjamin Button, F. S. Fitzgerald, 1922

3. What kind of tone does the above passage have?
   a. Nervous and excited
   b. Sad and angry
   c. Shameful and confused
   d. Grateful and joyous

4. What does the author mean to do by adding the following description?

   ...rubbing his hands together with a washing movement—as all doctors are required to do by the unwritten ethics of their profession.

   a. Suggest that Mr. Button is tired of the doctor
   b. Try to explain the details of the doctor's profession
   c. Hint to readers that the doctor is an unethical man
   d. Give readers a visual picture of what the doctor is doing

5. Which of the following best describes the development of this passage?
   a. It starts in the middle of a narrative in order to transition smoothly to a conclusion.
   b. It is a chronological narrative from beginning to end.
   c. The sequence of events is backwards—we go from future events to past events.
   d. To introduce the setting of the story and its characters

See answers on the next page.

Answer Explanations

Word Knowledge

1. C: Jackson wanted to relieve his *parched* throat. *Parched* is the correct answer because it means *thirsty*, or *arid*. Choice *A*, humid, means moist, and usually refers to the weather. Choice *B*, scorched, means blackened or baked, and doesn't fit in this context. Choice *D* is incorrect; although *dusty* can cause dryness, it is not the same as the word *thirsty* or *arid*.

2. A: The two friends became inseparable, or *closer*. For this question, it's important to look at the context of the sentence. The second sentence says the friends shared good memories on the trip, which would not make the friends distant or irritable, Choices *B* and *D*. Choice *C*, suffering, carries a negative connotation, and *closer* or *inseparable* are positive words. Therefore, Choice *A* is correct.

Reading Comprehension

3. A: We are told in the fourth paragraph that Mr. Button "arose nervously." We also see him running without caution to the doctor to find out about his wife and baby—this indicates his excitement. We also see him stuttering in a nervous yet excited fashion as he asks the doctor if it's a boy or girl. Though the doctor may seem a bit abrupt at the end, indicating a bit of anger or shame, neither of these choices is the overwhelming tone of the entire passage. Despite the circumstances, joy and gratitude are not the main tone in the passage.

4. D: The author describes a visual image—the doctor rubbing his hands together—first and foremost. The author may be trying to make a comment about the profession; however, the author does not "explain the details of the doctor's profession" as Choice *B* suggests.

5. D: We know we are being introduced to the setting because we are given the year in the very first paragraph, along with the season: "one day in the summer of 1860." This is a classic structure for an introduction of the setting. In the third paragraph we also get a long explanation of Mr. Button, who is related to him, and what his life is like.

Math

Numbers and Operations

Base-10 Numerals, Number Names, and Expanded Form

Numbers used in everyday life are constituted in a **base-10 system**. Each digit in a number, depending on its location, represents some multiple of 10, or quotient of 10 when dealing with decimals. Each digit to the left of the decimal point represents a higher multiple of 10. Each digit to the right of the decimal point represents a quotient of a higher multiple of 10 for the divisor. For example, consider the number 7,631.42. The digit one represents simply the number one. The digit 3 represents 3×10. The digit 6 represents:

$$6 \times 10 \times 10 \text{ (or } 6 \times 100)$$

The digit 7 represents $7 \times 10 \times 10 \times 10$ (or $7 \times 1{,}000$). The digit 4 represents $4 \div 10$. The digit 2 represents ($2 \div 10$) $\div 10$, or $2 \div (10 \times 10)$ or $2 \div 100$.

A number is written in **expanded form** by expressing it as the sum of the value of each of its digits. The expanded form in the example above, which is written with the highest value first down to the lowest value, is expressed as:
$$7{,}000 + 600 + 30 + 1 + .4 + .02$$

When verbally expressing a number, the integer part of the number (the numbers to the left of the decimal point) resembles the expanded form without the addition between values. In the above example, the numbers read "seven thousand six hundred thirty-one." When verbally expressing the decimal portion of a number, the number is read as a whole number, followed by the place value of the furthest digit (non-zero) to the right. In the above example, 0.42 is read "forty-two hundredths." Reading the number 7,631.42 in its entirety is expressed as "seven thousand six hundred thirty-one and forty-two hundredths." The word *and* is used between the integer and decimal parts of the number.

Composing and Decomposing Multi-Digit Numbers

Composing and decomposing numbers aids in conceptualizing what each digit of a multi-digit number represents. The standard, or typical, form in which numbers are written consists of a series of digits representing a given value based on their place value. Consider the number 592.7. This number is composed of 5 hundreds, 9 tens, 2 ones, and 7 tenths.

Composing a number requires adding the given numbers for each place value and writing the numbers in standard form. For example, composing 4 thousands, 5 hundreds, 2 tens, and 8 ones consists of adding as follows: $4{,}000 + 500 + 20 + 8$, to produce 4,528 (standard form).

Decomposing a number requires taking a number written in standard form and breaking it apart into the sum of each place value. For example, the number 83.17 is decomposed by breaking it into the sum of 4 values (for each of the 4 digits): 8 tens, 3 ones, 1 tenth, and 7 hundredths. The decomposed or "expanded" form of 83.17 is:
$$80 + 3 + 0.1 + 0.07$$

Place Value of a Given Digit

The number system that is used consists of only ten different digits or characters. However, this system is used to represent an infinite number of values. The **place value system** makes this infinite number of values possible. The position in which a digit is written corresponds to a given value. Starting from the decimal point (which is implied, if

53

not physically present), each subsequent place value to the left represents a value greater than the one before it. Conversely, starting from the decimal point, each subsequent place value to the right represents a value less than the one before it.

The names for the place values to the left of the decimal point are as follows:

...	Billions	Hundred-Millions	Ten-Millions	Millions	Hundred-Thousands	Ten-Thousands	Thousands	Hundreds	Tens	Ones

*Note that this table can be extended infinitely further to the left.

The names for the place values to the right of the decimal point are as follows:

Decimal Point (.)	Tenths	Hundredths	Thousandths	Ten-Thousandths	...

*Note that this table can be extended infinitely further to the right.

When given a multi-digit number, the value of each digit depends on its place value. Consider the number 682,174.953. Referring to the chart above, it can be determined that the digit 8 is in the ten-thousands place. It is in the fifth place to the left of the decimal point. Its value is 8 ten-thousands or 80,000. The digit 5 is two places to the right of the decimal point. Therefore, the digit 5 is in the hundredths place. Its value is 5 hundredths or $\frac{5}{100}$ (equivalent to .05).

Base-10 System

Value of Digits

In accordance with the **base-10 system**, the value of a digit increases by a factor of ten each place it moves to the left. For example, consider the number 7. Moving the digit one place to the left (70), increases its value by a factor of 10 ($7 \times 10 = 70$). Moving the digit two places to the left (700) increases its value by a factor of 10 twice ($7 \times 10 \times 10 = 700$). Moving the digit three places to the left (7,000) increases its value by a factor of 10 three times ($7 \times 10 \times 10 \times 10 = 7,000$), and so on.

Conversely, the value of a digit decreases by a factor of ten each place it moves to the right. (Note that multiplying by $\frac{1}{10}$ is equivalent to dividing by 10). For example, consider the number 40. Moving the digit one place to the right (4) decreases its value by a factor of 10 ($40 \div 10 = 4$). Moving the digit two places to the right (0.4), decreases its value by a factor of 10 twice ($40 \div 10 \div 10 = 0.4$) or:

$$40 \times \frac{1}{10} \times \frac{1}{10} = 0.4$$

Moving the digit three places to the right (0.04) decreases its value by a factor of 10 three times ($40 \div 10 \div 10 \div 10 = 0.04$) or ($40 \times \frac{1}{10} \times \frac{1}{10} \times \frac{1}{10} = 0.04$), and so on.

Exponents to Denote Powers of 10

The value of a given digit of a number in the base-10 system can be expressed utilizing powers of 10. A power of 10 refers to 10 raised to a given exponent such as 10^0, 10^1, 10^2, 10^3, etc. For the number 10^3, 10 is the base and 3 is the exponent. A base raised by an exponent represents how many times the base is multiplied by itself. Therefore, $10^1 = 10$, $10^2 = 10 \times 10 = 100$, $10^3 = 10 \times 10 \times 10 = 1,000$, $10^4 = 10 \times 10 \times 10 \times 10 = 10,000$, etc. Any base with a zero exponent equals one.

Powers of 10 are utilized to decompose a multi-digit number without writing all the zeroes. Consider the number 872,349. This number is decomposed to:

$$800,000 + 70,000 + 2,000 + 300 + 40 + 9$$

When utilizing powers of 10, the number 872,349 is decomposed to:

$$(8 \times 10^5) + (7 \times 10^4) + (2 \times 10^3) + (3 \times 10^2) + (4 \times 10^1) + (9 \times 10^0)$$

The power of 10 by which the digit is multiplied corresponds to the number of zeroes following the digit when expressing its value in standard form. For example, 7×10^4 is equivalent to 70,000 or 7 followed by four zeros.

Rounding Multi-Digit Numbers

Rounding numbers changes the given number to a simpler and less accurate number than the exact given number. Rounding allows for easier calculations which estimate the results of using the exact given number. The accuracy of the estimate and ease of use depends on the place value to which the number is rounded. Rounding numbers consists of:

- Determining what place value the number is being rounded to
- Examining the digit to the right of the desired place value to decide whether to round up or keep the digit
- Replacing all digits to the right of the desired place value with zeros

To round 746,311 to the nearest ten thousands, the digit in the ten thousands place should be located first. In this case, this digit is 4 (7<u>4</u>6,311). Then, the digit to its right is examined. If this digit is 5 or greater, the number will be rounded up by increasing the digit in the desired place by one. If the digit to the right of the place value being rounded is 4 or less, the number will be kept the same. For the given example, the digit being examined is a 6, which means that the number will be rounded up by increasing the digit to the left by one.

Therefore, the digit 4 is changed to a 5. Finally, to write the rounded number, any digits to the left of the place value being rounded remain the same and any to its right are replaced with zeros. For the given example, rounding 746,311 to the nearest ten thousand will produce 750,000. To round 746,311 to the nearest hundred, the digit to the right of the three in the hundreds place is examined to determine whether to round up or keep the same number. In this case, that digit is a one, so the number will be kept the same and any digits to its right will be replaced with zeros. The resulting rounded number is 746,300.

Rounding place values to the right of the decimal follows the same procedure, but digits being replaced by zeros can simply be dropped. To round 3.752891 to the nearest thousandth, the desired place value is located (3.75<u>2</u>891) and the digit to the right is examined. In this case, the digit 8 indicates that the number will be rounded up, and the 2 in the thousandths place will increase to a 3. Rounding up and replacing the digits to the right of the thousandths place produces 3.753000 which is equivalent to 3.753. Therefore, the zeros are not necessary, and the rounded number should be written as 3.753.

When rounding up, if the digit to be increased is a 9, the digit to its left is increased by 1 and the digit in the desired place value is changed to a zero. For example, the number 1,598 rounded to the nearest ten is 1,600. Another example shows the number 43.72961 rounded to the nearest thousandth is 43.730 or 43.73.

Solving Multistep Mathematical and Real-World Problems

Problem Situations for Operations

Addition and subtraction are **inverse operations**. Adding a number and then subtracting the same number will cancel each other out, resulting in the original number, and vice versa. For example,

$$8 + 7 - 7 = 8$$

and

$$137 - 100 + 100 = 137$$

Similarly, multiplication and division are inverse operations. Therefore, multiplying by a number and then dividing by the same number results in the original number, and vice versa. For example,

$$8 \times 2 \div 2 = 8$$

and

$$12 \div 4 \times 4 = 12$$

Inverse operations are used to work backwards to solve problems. In the case that 7 and a number add to 18, the inverse operation of subtraction is used to find the unknown value:

$$18 - 7 = 11$$

If a school's entire 4th grade was divided evenly into 3 classes each with 22 students, the inverse operation of multiplication is used to determine the total students in the grade:

$$22 \times 3 = 66$$

Additional scenarios involving inverse operations are included in the tables below.

There are a variety of real-world situations in which one or more of the operators is used to solve a problem. The tables below display the most common scenarios.

Addition & Subtraction

	Unknown Result	Unknown Change	Unknown Start
Adding to	5 students were in class. 4 more students arrived. How many students are in class? $5 + 4 =?$	8 students were in class. More students arrived late. There are now 18 students in class. How many students arrived late? $8+? = 18$ Solved by inverse operations $18- 8 =?$	Some students were in class early. 11 more students arrived. There are now 17 students in class. How many students were in class early? $?+11 = 17$ Solved by inverse operations $17- 11 =?$
Taking from	15 students were in class. 5 students left class. How many students are in class now? $15- 5 =?$	12 students were in class. Some students left class. There are now 8 students in class. How many students left class? $12-? = 8$ Solved by inverse operations $8+? = 12 \rightarrow 12- 8 =?$	Some students were in class. 3 students left class. Then there were 13 students in class. How many students were in class before? $?- 3 = 13$ Solved by inverse operations $13 + 3 =?$

	Unknown Total	Unknown Addends (Both)	Unknown Addends (One)
Putting together/ taking apart	The homework assignment is 10 addition problems and 8 subtraction problems. How many problems are in the homework assignment? $10 + 8 =?$	Bobby has $9. How much can Bobby spend on candy and how much can Bobby spend on toys? $9 =? +?$	Bobby has 12 pairs of pants. 5 pairs of pants are shorts, and the rest are long. How many pairs of long pants does he have? $12 = 5+?$ Solved by inverse operations $12- 5 =?$

	Unknown Difference	Unknown Larger Value	Unknown Smaller Value
Comparing	Bobby has 5 toys. Tommy has 8 toys. How many more toys does Tommy have than Bobby? $5+? = 8$ Solved by inverse operations $8- 5 =?$ Bobby has $6. Tommy has $10. How many fewer dollars does Bobby have than Tommy? $10- 6 =?$	Tommy has 2 more toys than Bobby. Bobby has 4 toys. How many toys does Tommy have? $2 + 4 =?$ Bobby has 3 fewer dollars than Tommy. Bobby has $8. How many dollars does Tommy have? $?- 3 = 8$ Solved by inverse operations $8 + 3 =?$	Tommy has 6 more toys than Bobby. Tommy has 10 toys. How many toys does Bobby have? $?+6 = 10$ Solved by inverse operations $10- 6 =?$ Bobby has $5 less than Tommy. Tommy has $9. How many dollars does Bobby have? $9 - 5 =?$

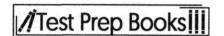

Multiplication and Division

	Unknown Product	Unknown Group Size	Unknown Number of Groups
Equal groups	There are 5 students, and each student has 4 pieces of candy. How many pieces of candy are there in all? $5 \times 4 =?$	14 pieces of candy are shared equally by 7 students. How many pieces of candy does each student have? $7 \times? = 14$ Solved by inverse operations $14 \div 7 =?$	If 18 pieces of candy are to be given out 3 to each student, how many students will get candy? $? \times 3 = 18$ Solved by inverse operations $18 \div 3 =?$
	Unknown Product	**Unknown Factor**	**Unknown Factor**
Arrays	There are 5 rows of students with 3 students in each row. How many students are there? $5 \times 3 =?$	If 16 students are arranged into 4 equal rows, how many students will be in each row? $4 \times? = 16$ Solved by inverse operations $16 \div 4 =?$	If 24 students are arranged into an array with 6 columns, how many rows are there? $? \times 6 = 24$ Solved by inverse operations $24 \div 6 =?$
	Larger Unknown	**Smaller Unknown**	**Multiplier Unknown**
Comparing	A small popcorn costs $1.50. A large popcorn costs 3 times as much as a small popcorn. How much does a large popcorn cost? $1.50 \times 3 =?$	A large soda costs $6 and that is 2 times as much as a small soda costs. How much does a small soda cost? $2 \times? = 6$ Solved by inverse operations $6 \div 2 =?$	A large pretzel costs $3 and a small pretzel costs $2. How many times as much does the large pretzel cost as the small pretzel? $? \times 2 = 3$ Solved by inverse operations $3 \div 2 =?$

Remainders in Division Problems

If a given total cannot be divided evenly into a given number of groups, the amount left over is the **remainder**. Consider the following scenario: 32 textbooks must be packed into boxes for storage. Each box holds 6 textbooks. How many boxes are needed? To determine the answer, 32 is divided by 6, resulting in 5 with a remainder of 2. A remainder may be interpreted three ways:

- Add 1 to the quotient
  How many boxes will be needed? Six boxes will be needed because five will not be enough.

- Use only the quotient
  How many boxes will be full? Five boxes will be full.

- Use only the remainder
  If you only have 5 boxes, how many books will not fit? Two books will not fit.

Strategies and Algorithms to Perform Operations on Rational Numbers

A *rational number* is any number that can be written in the form of a ratio or fraction. Integers can be written as fractions with a denominator of 1:

$$5 = \frac{5}{1}$$

$$-342 = \frac{-342}{1}$$

Decimals that terminate and/or repeat can also be written as fractions:

$$47 = \frac{47}{100}$$

$$.\overline{33} = \frac{1}{3}$$

For more on converting decimals to fractions, see the section *Converting Between Fractions, Decimals, and Percent.*

When adding or subtracting fractions, the numbers must have the same denominators. In these cases, numerators are added or subtracted, and denominators are kept the same. For example, $\frac{2}{7} + \frac{3}{7} = \frac{5}{7}$ and

$$\frac{4}{5} - \frac{3}{5} = \frac{1}{5}$$

If the fractions to be added or subtracted do not have the same denominator, a common denominator must be found. This is accomplished by changing one or both fractions to a different but equivalent fraction. Consider the example $\frac{1}{6} + \frac{4}{9}$. First, a common denominator must be found. One method is to find the **least common multiple (LCM)** of the denominators 6 and 9. This is the lowest number that both 6 and 9 will divide into evenly. In this case the LCM is 18. Both fractions should be changed to equivalent fractions with a denominator of 18. To obtain the numerator of the new fraction, the old numerator is multiplied by the same number by which the old denominator is multiplied. For the fraction $\frac{1}{6}$, 6 multiplied by 3 will produce a denominator of 18.

Therefore, the numerator is multiplied by 3 to produce the new numerator:

$$\left(\frac{1 \times 3}{6 \times 3} = \frac{3}{18}\right)$$

For the fraction $\frac{4}{9}$, multiplying both the numerator and denominator by 2 produces $\frac{8}{18}$. Since the two new fractions have common denominators, they can be added:

$$\left(\frac{3}{18} + \frac{8}{18} = \frac{11}{18}\right)$$

When multiplying or dividing rational numbers, these numbers may be converted to fractions and multiplied or divided accordingly. When multiplying fractions, all numerators are multiplied by each other and all denominators are multiplied by each other. For example:

$$\frac{1}{3} \times \frac{6}{5}$$

$$\frac{1 \times 6}{3 \times 5}$$

$$\frac{6}{15}$$

and

$$\frac{-1}{2} \times \frac{3}{1} \times \frac{11}{100}$$

$$\frac{-1 \times 3 \times 11}{2 \times 1 \times 100}$$

$$\frac{-33}{200}$$

When dividing fractions, the problem is converted by multiplying by the reciprocal of the divisor. This is done by changing division to multiplication and "flipping" the second fraction, or divisor. For example:

$$\frac{1}{2} \div \frac{3}{5} \rightarrow \frac{1}{2} \times \frac{5}{3}$$

and

$$\frac{5}{1} \div \frac{1}{3} \rightarrow \frac{5}{1} \times \frac{3}{1}$$

To complete the problem, the rules for multiplying fractions should be followed.

Note that when adding, subtracting, multiplying, and dividing mixed numbers (ex. $4\frac{1}{2}$), it is easiest to convert these to improper fractions (larger numerator than denominator). To do so, the denominator is kept the same. To obtain the numerator, the whole number is multiplied by the denominator and added to the numerator. For example, $4\frac{1}{2} = \frac{9}{2}$ and $7\frac{2}{3} = \frac{23}{3}$. Also, note that answers involving fractions should be converted to the simplest form.

Rational Numbers and Their Operations

Irregular Products and Quotients
The following shows examples where multiplication does not result in a product greater than both factors, and where division does not result in a quotient smaller than the dividend.

If multiplying numbers where one or more has a value less than one, the product will not be greater than both factors. For example, $6 \times \frac{1}{2} = 3$ and:

$$0.75 \times 0.2 = 0.15$$

60

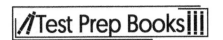

When dividing by a number less than one, the resulting quotient will be greater than the dividend. For example, $8 \div \frac{1}{2} = 16$, because division turns into a multiplication problem:

$$8 \div \frac{1}{2}$$

$$8 \times \frac{2}{1}$$

Another example is $0.5 \div 0.2$, which results in 2.5. The problem can be stated by asking how many times 0.2 will go into 0.5. The number being divided is larger than the number that goes into it, so the result will be a number larger than both factors.

Composing and Decomposing Fractions

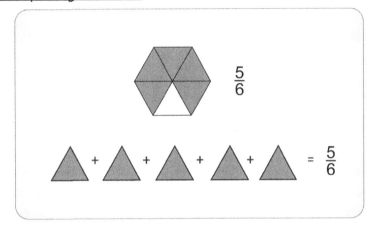

Fractions can be broken apart into sums of fractions with the same denominator. For example, the fraction $\frac{5}{6}$ can be **decomposed** into sums of fractions with all denominators equal to 6 and the numerators adding to 5.

The fraction $\frac{5}{6}$ is decomposed as:

$$\frac{3}{6} + \frac{2}{6}$$

$$\frac{2}{6} + \frac{2}{6} + \frac{1}{6}$$

$$\frac{3}{6} + \frac{1}{6} + \frac{1}{6}$$

$$\frac{1}{6} + \frac{1}{6} + \frac{1}{6} + \frac{2}{6}$$

$$\frac{1}{6} + \frac{1}{6} + \frac{1}{6} + \frac{1}{6} + \frac{1}{6}$$

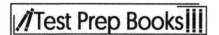

Math

A unit fraction is a fraction in which the numerator is 1. If decomposing a fraction into unit fractions, the sum will consist of a unit fraction added the number of times equal to the numerator. For example:

$$\frac{3}{4} = \frac{1}{4} + \frac{1}{4} + \frac{1}{4} \text{ (unit fractions } \frac{1}{4} \text{ added 3 times)}$$

Composing fractions is simply the opposite of decomposing. It is the process of adding fractions with the same denominators to produce a single fraction. For example:

$$\frac{3}{7} + \frac{2}{7} = \frac{5}{7}$$

and

$$\frac{1}{5} + \frac{1}{5} + \frac{1}{5} = \frac{3}{5}$$

Decrease in Value of a Unit Fraction

A **unit fraction** is one in which the numerator is 1 ($\frac{1}{2}, \frac{1}{3}, \frac{1}{8}, \frac{1}{20}$, etc.). The denominator indicates the number of equal pieces that the whole is divided into. The greater the number of pieces, the smaller each piece will be. Therefore, the greater the denominator of a unit fraction, the smaller it is in value. Unit fractions can also be compared by converting them to decimals. For example, $\frac{1}{2} = 0.5, \frac{1}{3} = 0.\overline{3}, \frac{1}{8} = 0.125, \frac{1}{20} = 0.05$, etc.

Use of the Same Whole when Comparing Fractions

Fractions all represent parts of the same whole. Fractions may have different denominators, but they represent parts of the same one whole, like a pizza. For example, the fractions $\frac{5}{7}$ and $\frac{2}{3}$ can be difficult to compare because they have different denominators. The first fraction may represent a whole divided into seven parts, where five parts are used. The second fraction represents the same whole divided into three parts, where two are used. It may be helpful to convert one or more of the fractions so that they have common denominators for converting to equivalent fractions by finding the LCM of the denominator. Comparing is much easier if fractions are converted to the equivalent fractions of $\frac{15}{21}$ and $\frac{14}{21}$. These fractions show a whole divided into 21 parts, where the numerators can be compared because the denominators are the same.

Order of Operations

When reviewing calculations consisting of more than one operation, the order in which the operations are performed affects the resulting answer. Consider the expression:

$$5 \times 2 + 7$$

Performing multiplication then addition results in an answer of 17 ($5 \times 2 = 10$; $10 + 7 = 17$). However, if the problem is written $5 \times (2 + 7)$, the order of operations dictates that the operation inside the parentheses must be performed first. The resulting answer is 45:

$$2 + 7 = 9, \text{then } 5 \times 9 = 45$$

The *order* in which operations should be performed is remembered using the acronym PEMDAS. **PEMDAS** stands for parentheses, exponents, multiplication/division, and addition/subtraction. Multiplication and division are performed in the same step, working from left to right with whichever comes first. Addition and subtraction are performed in the same step, working from left to right with whichever comes first.

Consider the following example:

$$8 \div 4 + 8(7 - 7)$$

Performing the operation inside the parentheses produces $8 \div 4 + 8(0)$ or:

$$8 \div 4 + 8 \times 0$$

There are no exponents, so multiplication and division are performed next from left to right resulting in: $2 + 8 \times 0$, then $2 + 0$. Finally, addition and subtraction are performed to obtain an answer of 2. Now consider the following example:

$$6 \times 3 + 3^2 - 6$$

Parentheses are not applicable. Exponents are evaluated first,

$$6 \times 3 + 9 - 6$$

Then multiplication/division forms $18 + 9 - 6$. At last, addition/subtraction leads to the final answer of 21.

Properties of Operations

Properties of operations exist that make calculations easier and solve problems for missing values. The following table summarizes commonly used properties of real numbers.

Property	Addition	Multiplication
Commutative	$a + b = b + a$	$a \times b = b \times a$
Associative	$(a + b) + c = a + (b + c)$	$(a \times b) \times c = a \times (b \times c)$
Identity	$a + 0 = a; \ 0 + a = a$	$a \times 1 = a; \ 1 \times a = a$
Inverse	$a + (-a) = 0$	$a \times \dfrac{1}{a} = 1; \ a \neq 0$
Distributive	$a(b + c) = ab + ac$	

The commutative property of addition states that the order in which numbers are added does not change the sum. Similarly, the commutative property of multiplication states that the order in which numbers are multiplied does not change the product. The associative property of addition and multiplication state that the grouping of numbers being added or multiplied does not change the sum or product, respectively. The commutative and associative properties are useful for performing calculations. For example, $(47 + 25) + 3$ is equivalent to $(47 + 3) + 25$, which is easier to calculate.

The identity property of addition states that adding zero to any number does not change its value. The identity property of multiplication states that multiplying a number by one does not change its value. The inverse property of addition states that the sum of a number and its opposite equals zero. Opposites are numbers that are the same with different signs (ex. 5 and -5; $-\frac{1}{2}$ and $\frac{1}{2}$). The inverse property of multiplication states that the product of a number (other than zero) and its reciprocal equals one. Reciprocal numbers have numerators and denominators that are inverted (ex. $\frac{2}{5}$ and $\frac{5}{2}$). Inverse properties are useful for canceling quantities to find missing values (see algebra content). For example, $a + 7 = 12$ is solved by adding the inverse of 7 (which is -7) to both sides in order to isolate a.

The distributive property states that multiplying a sum (or difference) by a number produces the same result as multiplying each value in the sum (or difference) by the number and adding (or subtracting) the products. Consider

63

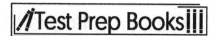

the following scenario: You are buying three tickets for a baseball game. Each ticket costs $18. You are also charged a fee of $2 per ticket for purchasing the tickets online. The cost is calculated:

$$3 \times 18 + 3 \times 2$$

Using the distributive property, the cost can also be calculated $3(18 + 2)$.

Representing Rational Numbers and Their Operations

Concrete Models

Concrete objects are used to develop a tangible understanding of operations of rational numbers. Tools such as tiles, blocks, beads, and hundred charts are used to model problems. For example, a hundred chart (10×10) and beads can be used to model multiplication. If multiplying 5 by 4, beads are placed across 5 rows and down 4 columns producing a product of 20. Similarly, tiles can be used to model division by splitting the total into equal groups. If dividing 12 by 4, 12 tiles are placed one at a time into 4 groups. The result is 4 groups of 3. This is also an effective method for visualizing the concept of remainders.

Representations of objects can be used to expand on the concrete models of operations. Pictures, dots, and tallies can help model these concepts. Utilizing concrete models and representations creates a foundation upon which to build an abstract understanding of the operations.

Rational Numbers on a Number Line

A **number line** typically consists of integers (…3,2,1,0,-1,-2,-3…), and is used to visually represent the value of a rational number. Each rational number has a distinct position on the line determined by comparing its value with the displayed values on the line. For example, if plotting -1.5 on the number line below, it is necessary to recognize that the value of -1.5 is .5 less than -1 and .5 greater than -2. Therefore, -1.5 is plotted halfway between -1 and -2.

Number lines can also be useful for visualizing sums and differences of rational numbers. Adding a value indicates moving to the right (values increase to the right), and subtracting a value indicates moving to the left (numbers decrease to the left). For example, $5 - 7$ is displayed by starting at 5 and moving to the left 7 spaces, if the number line is in increments of 1. This will result in an answer of -2.

Multiplication and Division Problems

Multiplication and division are **inverse operations** that can be represented by using rectangular arrays, area models, and equations. Rectangular arrays include an arrangement of rows and columns that correspond to the factors and display product totals.

Another method of multiplication can be done with the use of an **area model**. An area model is a rectangle that is divided into rows and columns that match up to the number of place values within each number. Take the example 29×65. These two numbers can be split into simpler numbers:

$$29 = 25 + 4 \text{ and } 65 = 60 + 5$$

The products of those 4 numbers are found within the rectangle and then summed up to get the answer. The entire process is:

$$(60 \times 25) + (5 \times 25) + (60 \times 4) + (5 \times 4) = 1,500 + 240 + 125 + 20 = 1,885$$

Here is the actual area model:

	25	**4**
60	60x25 1,500	60x4 240
5	5x25 125	5x4 20

```
        1 , 5 0 0
            2 4 0
            1 2 5
    +          2 0
        _____
        1 , 8 8 5
```

Multiplying decimals involves the same procedure as multiplying whole numbers, but including the decimal places in the end result. The problem involves multiplying the two numbers together, ignoring the decimal places, and then inserting the total number of decimal places in the original numbers into the result. For example, given the problem 87.5×0.45, the answer is found by multiplying 875×45 to obtain $39,375$ and then inputting a decimal point three places to the left because there are three total decimal places in the original problem. Therefore, the answer is 39.375.

Dividing a number by a single digit or two digits can be turned into repeated subtraction problems. An area model can be used throughout the problem that represents multiples of the divisor. For example, the answer to $8,580 \div 55$ can be found by subtracting 55 from 8,580 one at a time and counting the total number of subtractions necessary.

However, a simpler process involves using larger multiples of 55. First, $100 \times 55 = 5,500$ is subtracted from 8,580, and 3,080 is leftover. Next, $50 \times 55 = 2,750$ is subtracted from 3,080 to obtain380. $5 \times 55 = 275$ is subtracted from 330 to obtain 55, and finally, $1 \times 55 = 55$ is subtracted from 55 to obtain zero. Therefore, there is no remainder, and the answer is:

$$100 + 50 + 5 + 1 = 156$$

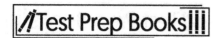

Here is a picture of the area model and the repeated subtraction process:

$$8580 \div 55$$

	55
100	5500
50	2750
5	275
1	55

$$
\begin{array}{r}
55\overline{\smash{\big)}\,8580} \\
-5500 \quad \text{(100 x 55)} \\
\hline
3080 \\
-2750 \quad \text{(50 x 55)} \\
\hline
330 \\
-275 \quad \text{(5 x 55)} \\
\hline
55 \\
-55 \quad \text{(1 x 55)} \\
\hline
0
\end{array}
$$

Checking the answer to a division problem involves multiplying the answer—the quotient—times the divisor to see if the dividend is obtained. If there is a remainder, the same process is computed, but the remainder is added on at the end to try to match the dividend. In the previous example, $156 \times 55 = 8,580$ would be the checking procedure. Dividing decimals involves the same repeated subtraction process. The only difference would be that the subtractions would involve numbers that include values in the decimal places. Lining up decimal places is crucial in this type of problem.

Comparing, Classifying, and Ordering Rational Numbers

A **rational number** is any number that can be written as a fraction or ratio. Within the set of rational numbers, several subsets exist that are referenced throughout the mathematics topics. Counting numbers are the first numbers learned as a child. Counting numbers consist of 1,2,3,4, and so on. Whole numbers include all counting numbers and zero (0,1,2,3,4,...). Integers include counting numbers, their opposites, and zero (...,-3,-2,-1,0,1,2,3,...). Rational numbers are inclusive of integers, fractions, and decimals that terminate, or end (1.7, 0.04213) or repeat $(0.136\overline{5})$.

When comparing or ordering numbers, the numbers should be written in the same format (decimal or fraction), if possible. For example, $\sqrt{49}$, 7.3, and $\frac{15}{2}$ are easier to order if each one is converted to a decimal, such as 7, 7.3, and 7.5 (converting fractions and decimals is covered in the following section). A number line is used to order and compare the numbers. Any number that is to the right of another number is greater than that number. Conversely, a number positioned to the left of a given number is less than that number.

Converting Between Fractions, Decimals, and Percent

To convert a fraction to a decimal, the numerator is divided by the denominator. For example, $\frac{3}{8}$ can be converted to a decimal by dividing 3 by 8 $(\frac{3}{8} = 0.375)$. To convert a decimal to a fraction, the decimal point is dropped, and the value is written as the numerator. The denominator is the place value farthest to the right with a digit other than zero. For example, to convert .48 to a fraction, the numerator is 48, and the denominator is 100 (the digit 8 is in the hundredths place). Therefore, $0.48 = \frac{48}{100}$. Fractions should be written in the simplest form, or reduced. To reduce a fraction, the numerator and denominator are divided by the largest common factor. In the previous example, 48 and 100 are both divisible by 4. Dividing the numerator and denominator by 4 results in a reduced fraction of $\frac{12}{25}$.

66

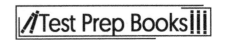

To convert a decimal to a percent, the number is multiplied by 100. To convert .13 to a percent, 0.13 is multiplied by 100 to get 13 percent. To convert a fraction to a percent, the fraction is converted to a decimal and then multiplied by 100. For example, $\frac{1}{5} = 0.20$ and 0.20 multiplied by 100 produces 20 percent.

To convert a percent to a decimal, the value is divided by 100. For example, 125 percent is equal to 1.25 ($\frac{125}{100}$). To convert a percent to a fraction, the percent sign is dropped, and the value is written as the numerator with a denominator of 100. For example, $80\% = \frac{80}{100}$. This fraction can be reduced ($\frac{80}{100} = \frac{4}{5}$).

Understanding Proportional Relationships and Percent

Applying Ratios and Unit Rates

A **ratio** is a comparison of two quantities that represent separate groups. For example, if a recipe calls for 2 eggs for every 3 cups of milk, this is expressed as a ratio. Ratios can be written three ways:

- With the word "to"
- Using a colon
- As a fraction.

In the previous example, the ratio of eggs to cups of milk is written as 2 to 3, 2:3, or $\frac{2}{3}$. When writing ratios, the order is very important. The ratio of eggs to cups of milk is not the same as the ratio of cups of milk to eggs, 3:2.

In simplest form, both quantities of a ratio should be written as integers. These should also be reduced just as a fraction is reduced. For example, 5:10 is reduced to 1:2. Given a ratio where one or both quantities are expressed as a decimal or fraction, multiply both by the same number to produce integers. To write the ratio $\frac{1}{3}$ to 2 in simplest form, both quantities are multiplied by 3. The resulting ratio is 1 to 6.

A problem involving ratios may give a comparison between two groups. The problem may then provide a total and ask for a part, or provide a part and ask for a total. Consider the following: The ratio of boys to girls in the 11th grade class is 5:4. If there are a total of 270 11th grade students, how many are girls? The total number of **ratio pieces** should be determined first. The total number of 11th grade students is divided into 9 pieces. The ratio of boys to total students is 5:9, and the ratio of girls to total students is 4:9. Knowing the total number of students, the number of girls is determined by setting up a proportion:

$$\frac{4}{9} = \frac{x}{270}$$

A rate is a ratio comparing two quantities expressed in different units. A unit rate is a ratio in which the second quantity is one unit. Rates often include the word *per*. Examples include miles per hour, beats per minute, and price per pound. The word per is represented with a / symbol or abbreviated with the letter *p* and units abbreviated. For example, miles per hour is written as mi/h. When given a rate that is not in its simplest form (the second quantity is not one unit), both quantities are divided by the value of the second quantity. If 99 heartbeats were recorded in $1\frac{1}{2}$ minutes, both quantities are divided by $1\frac{1}{2}$ to determine the heart rate of 66 beats per minute.

Percent

The word **percent** means per hundred. Similar to a unit rate in which the second quantity is always one unit, a percent is a rate where the second quantity is always 100 units. If the results of a poll state that 47 percent of people support a given policy, this indicates that 47 out of every 100 individuals polled were in support. In other words, 47 per 100 support the policy. If an upgraded model of a car costs 110 percent of the cost of the base model, for every $100 that is spent for the base model, $110 must be spent to purchase the upgraded model. In other words, the upgraded model costs $110 per $100 for the cost of the base model.

When dealing with percentages, the numbers can be evaluated as a value in hundredths. For example, 15 percent is expressed as fifteen hundredths and is written as $\frac{15}{100}$ or 0.15.

Unit-Rate Problems

A rate is a ratio in which two terms are in different units. When rates are expressed as a quantity of one, they are considered **unit rates**. To determine a unit rate, the first quantity is divided by the second. Knowing a unit rate makes calculations easier than simply having a rate. For example, suppose a 3-pound bag of onions costs $1.77. To calculate the price of 5 pounds of onions, a proportion could show:

$$\frac{3}{1.77} = \frac{5}{x}$$

However, by knowing the unit rate, the value of pounds of onions is multiplied by the unit price. The unit price is calculated:

$$\frac{\$1.77}{3 \text{ lb}} = \$0.59/\text{lb}$$

Multiplying the weight of the onions by the unit price yields:

$$5 \text{ lb} \times \frac{\$0.59}{\text{lb}} = \$2.95$$

The lb units cancel out.

Similar to unit-rate problems, **unit conversions** appear in real-world scenarios including cooking, measurement, construction, and currency. Given the conversion rate, unit conversions are written as a fraction (ratio) and multiplied by a quantity in one unit to convert it to the corresponding unit. To determine how many minutes are in $3\frac{1}{2}$ hours, the conversion rate of 60 minutes to 1 hour is written as $\frac{60 \text{ min}}{1 \text{ h}}$.

Multiplying the quantity by the conversion rate results in:

$$3\frac{1}{2}\text{h} \times \frac{60 \text{ min}}{1 \text{ h}} = 210 \text{ min}$$

The h unit is canceled. To convert a quantity in minutes to hours, the fraction for the conversion rate is flipped to cancel the min unit. To convert 195 minutes to hours, $195 \text{ min} \times \frac{1 \text{ h}}{60 \text{ min}}$ is multiplied. The result is $\frac{195 \text{ h}}{60}$ which reduces to:

$$3\frac{1}{4}\text{h}$$

Converting units may require more than one multiplication. The key is to set up conversion rates so that units cancel each other out and the desired unit is left. To convert 3.25 yards to inches, given that 1 yd = 3 ft and 12 in = 1 ft, the calculation is performed by multiplying:

$$3.25 \text{ yd} \times \frac{3 \text{ ft}}{1 \text{ yd}} \times \frac{12 \text{ in}}{1 \text{ ft}}$$

68

The yd and ft units will cancel, resulting in 117in.

Using Proportional Relationships

A proportion is a statement consisting of two equal ratios. Proportions will typically give three of four quantities and require solving for the missing value. The key to solving proportions is to set them up properly. Consider the following: 7 gallons of gas costs $14.70. How many gallons can you get for $20? The information is written as equal ratios with a variable representing the missing quantity:

$$\left(\frac{gallons}{cost} = \frac{gallons}{cost}\right) : \frac{7}{14.70} = \frac{x}{20}$$

To solve for x, the proportion is cross-multiplied. This means the numerator of the first ratio is multiplied by the denominator of the second, and vice versa. The resulting products are shown equal to each other. Cross-multiplying results in:

$$(7)(20) = (14.7)(x)$$

By solving the equation for x (see the algebra content), the answer is that 9.5 gallons of gas may be purchased for $20.

Percent problems can also be solved by setting up proportions. Examples of common percent problems are:

a. What is 15% of 25?
b. What percent of 45 is 3?
c. 5 is $\frac{1}{2}$% of what number?

Setting up the proper proportion is made easier by following the format:

$$\frac{is}{of} = \frac{percent}{100}$$

A variable is used to represent the missing value. The proportions for each of the three examples are set up as follows:

a. $\frac{x}{25} = \frac{15}{100}$
b. $\frac{3}{45} = \frac{x}{100}$
c. $\frac{5}{x} = \frac{\frac{1}{2}}{100}$

By cross-multiplying and solving the resulting equation for the variable, the missing values are determined to be:

a. 3.75
b. 6.$\overline{6}$%
c. 1,000

Basic Concepts of Number Theory

Prime and Composite Numbers

Whole numbers are classified as either prime or composite. A **prime number** can only be divided evenly by itself and one. For example, the number 11 can only be divided evenly by 11 and one; therefore, 11 is a prime number. A helpful way to visualize a prime number is to use concrete objects and try to divide them into equal piles. If dividing

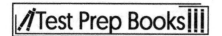

11 coins, the only way to divide them into equal piles is to create 1 pile of 11 coins or to create 11 piles of 1 coin each. Other examples of prime numbers include 2, 3, 5, 7, 13, 17, and 19.

A **composite number** is any whole number that is not a prime number. A composite number is a number that can be divided evenly by one or more numbers other than itself and one. For example, the number 6 can be divided evenly by 2 and 3. Therefore, 6 is a composite number. If dividing 6 coins into equal piles, the possibilities are 1 pile of 6 coins, 2 piles of 3 coins, 3 piles of 2 coins, or 6 piles of 1 coin. Other examples of composite numbers include 4, 8, 9, 10, 12, 14, 15, 16, 18, and 20.

To determine if a number is a prime or composite number, the number is divided by every whole number greater than one and less than its own value. If it divides evenly by any of these numbers, then the number is composite. If it does not divide evenly by any of these numbers, then the number is prime. For example, when attempting to divide the number 5 by 2, 3, and 4, none of these numbers divide evenly. Therefore, 5 must be a prime number.

Factors and Multiples of Numbers

The **factors** of a number are all integers that can be multiplied by another integer to produce the given number. For example, 2 is multiplied by 3 to produce 6. Therefore, 2 and 3 are both factors of 6. Similarly, $1 \times 6 = 6$ and $2 \times 3 = 6$, so 1, 2, 3, and 6 are all factors of 6. Another way to explain a factor is to say that a given number divides evenly by each of its factors to produce an integer. For example, 6 does not divide evenly by 5. Therefore, 5 is not a factor of 6.

Multiples of a given number are found by taking that number and multiplying it by any other whole number. For example, 3 is a factor of 6, 9, and 12. Therefore, 6, 9, and 12 are multiples of 3. The multiples of any number are an infinite list. For example, the multiples of 5 are 5, 10, 15, 20, and so on. This list continues without end. A list of multiples is used in finding the least common multiple, or LCM, for fractions when a common denominator is needed. The denominators are written down and their multiples listed until a common number is found in both lists. This common number is the LCM.

Prime factorization breaks down each factor of a whole number until only prime numbers remain. All composite numbers can be factored into prime numbers. For example, the prime factors of 12 are 2, 2, and 3:

$$2 \times 2 \times 3 = 12$$

To produce the prime factors of a number, the number is factored, and any composite numbers are continuously factored until the result is the product of prime factors only. A factor tree, such as the one below, is helpful when exploring this concept.

Here is an example of a factorization tree:

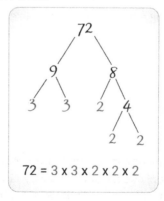

$$72 = 3 \times 3 \times 2 \times 2 \times 2$$

70

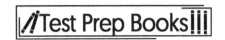

Determining the Reasonableness of Results

When solving math word problems, the solution obtained should make sense within the given scenario. The step of checking the solution will reduce the possibility of a calculation error or a solution that may be mathematically correct but not applicable in the real world. Consider the following scenarios:

A problem states that Lisa got 24 out of 32 questions correct on a test and asks to find the percentage of correct answers. To solve the problem, a student divided 32 by 24 to get 1.33, and then multiplied by 100 to get 133 percent. By examining the solution within the context of the problem, the student should recognize that getting all 32 questions correct will produce a perfect score of 100 percent. Therefore, a score of 133 percent with 8 incorrect answers does not make sense, and the calculations should be checked.

A problem states that the maximum weight on a bridge cannot exceed 22,000 pounds. The problem asks to find the maximum number of cars that can be on the bridge at one time if each car weighs 4,000 pounds. To solve this problem, a student divided 22,000 by 4,000 to get an answer of 5.5. By examining the solution within the context of the problem, the student should recognize that although the calculations are mathematically correct, the solution does not make sense. Half of a car on a bridge is not possible, so the student should determine that a maximum of 5 cars can be on the bridge at the same time.

Mental Math Estimation

Once a result is determined to be logical within the context of a given problem, the result should be evaluated by its nearness to the expected answer. This is performed by approximating given values to perform mental math. Numbers should be rounded to the nearest value possible to check the initial results.

Consider the following example: A problem states that a customer is buying a new sound system for their home. The customer purchases a stereo for $435, 2 speakers for $67 each, and the necessary cables for $12. The customer chooses an option that allows him to spread the costs over equal payments for 4 months. How much will the monthly payments be?

After making calculations for the problem, a student determines that the monthly payment will be $145.25. To check the accuracy of the results, the student rounds each cost to the nearest ten $(440 + 70 + 70 + 10)$ and determines that the total is approximately $590. Dividing by 4 months gives an approximate monthly payment of $147.50. Therefore, the student can conclude that the solution of $145.25 is very close to what should be expected.

When rounding, the place-value that is used in rounding can make a difference. Suppose the student had rounded to the nearest hundred for the estimation. The result $(400 + 100 + 100 + 0 = 600; \ 600 \div 4 = 150)$ will show that the answer is reasonable but not as close to the actual value as rounding to the nearest ten.

Algebra

Adding, Subtracting, Multiplying, and Factoring Linear Expressions

Algebraic expressions look similar to equations, but they do not include the equal sign. Algebraic expressions are comprised of numbers, variables, and mathematical operations. Some examples of algebraic expressions are $8x + 7y - 12z$, $3a^2$, and $5x^3 - 4y^4$.

Algebraic expressions consist of variables, numbers, and operations. A term of an expression is any combination of numbers and/or variables, and terms are separated by addition and subtraction. For example, the expression $5x^2 - 3xy + 4 - 2$ consists of 4 terms: $5x^2$, $-3xy$, $4y$, and -2. Note that each term includes its given sign (+ or −). The variable part of a term is a letter that represents an unknown quantity. The coefficient of a term is the number by

71

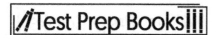

which the variable is multiplied. For the term $4y$, the variable is y, and the coefficient is 4. Terms are identified by the power (or exponent) of its variable.

A number without a variable is referred to as a constant. If the variable is to the first power (x^1 or simply x), it is referred to as a linear term. A term with a variable to the second power (x^2) is quadratic, and a term to the third power (x^3) is cubic. Consider the expression:

$$x^3 + 3x - 1$$

The constant is -1. The linear term is $3x$. There is no quadratic term. The cubic term is x^3.

An algebraic expression can also be classified by how many terms exist in the expression. Any like terms should be combined before classifying. A monomial is an expression consisting of only one term. Examples of monomials are: 17, $2x$, and $-5ab^2$. A binomial is an expression consisting of two terms separated by addition or subtraction. Examples include $2x - 4$ and $-3y^2 + 2y$. A trinomial consists of 3 terms. For example, $5x^2 - 2x + 1$ is a trinomial.

Algebraic expressions and equations can be used to represent real-life situations and model the behavior of different variables. For example, $2x + 5$ could represent the cost to play games at an arcade. In this case, 5 represents the price of admission to the arcade, and 2 represents the cost of each game played. To calculate the total cost, use the number of games played for x, multiply it by 2, and add 5.

Adding and Subtracting Linear Algebraic Expressions

An algebraic expression is simplified by combining like terms. A term is a number, variable, or product of a number and variables separated by addition and subtraction. For the algebraic expression $3x^2 - 4x + 5 - 5x^2 + x - 3$, the terms are $3x^2$, $-4x$, 5, $-5x^2$, x, and -3. Like terms have the same variables raised to the same powers (exponents). The like terms for the previous example are $3x^2$ and $-5x^2$, $-4x$ and x, 5 and -3. To combine like terms, the coefficients (numerical factor of the term including sign) are added, and the variables and their powers are kept the same. Note that if a coefficient is not written, it is an implied coefficient of 1 ($x = 1x$). The previous example will simplify to:

$$-2x^2 - 3x + 2$$

When adding or subtracting algebraic expressions, each expression is written in parentheses. The negative sign is distributed when necessary, and like terms are combined. Consider the following:

add $2a + 5b - 2$ to $a - 2b + 8c - 4$

The sum is set as follows:

$$(a - 2b + 8c - 4) + (2a + 5b - 2)$$

In front of each set of parentheses is an implied positive one, which, when distributed, does not change any of the terms. Therefore, the parentheses are dropped and like terms are combined:

$$a - 2b + 8c - 4 + 2a + 5b - 2$$

$$3a + 3b + 8c - 6$$

Consider the following problem:

Subtract $2a + 5b - 2$ from $a - 2b + 8c - 4$

72

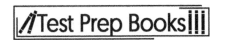

The difference is set as follows:

$$(a - 2b + 8c - 4) - (2a + 5b - 2)$$

The implied one in front of the first set of parentheses will not change those four terms. However, distributing the implied -1 in front of the second set of parentheses will change the sign of each of those three terms:

$$a - 2b + 8c - 4 - 2a - 5b + 2$$

Combining like terms yields the simplified expression:

$$-a - 7b + 8c - 2$$

Distributive Property

The **distributive property** states that multiplying a sum (or difference) by a number produces the same result as multiplying each value in the sum (or difference) by the number and adding (or subtracting) the products. Using mathematical symbols, the distributive property states:

$$a(b + c) = ab + ac$$

The expression $4(3 + 2)$ is simplified using the order of operations. Simplifying inside the parentheses first produces 4×5, which equals 20.

The expression $4(3 + 2)$ can also be simplified using the distributive property:

$$4(3 + 2)$$

$$4 \times 3 + 4 \times 2$$

$$12 + 8$$

$$20$$

Consider the following example: $4(3x - 2)$. The expression cannot be simplified inside the parentheses because $3x$ and -2 are not like terms and therefore cannot be combined. However, the expression can be simplified by using the distributive property and multiplying each term inside of the parentheses by the term outside of the parentheses: $12x - 8$. The resulting equivalent expression contains no like terms, so it cannot be further simplified.

Consider the expression:

$$(3x + 2y + 1) - (5x - 3) + 2(3y + 4)$$

Again, there are no like terms, but the distributive property is used to simplify the expression. Note there is an implied one in front of the first set of parentheses and an implied -1 in front of the second set of parentheses. Distributing the 1, -1, and 2 produces:

$$1(3x) + 1(2y) + 1(1) - 1(5x) - 1(-3) + 2(3y) + 2(4)$$

$$3x + 2y + 1 - 5x + 3 + 6y + 8$$

This expression contains like terms that are combined to produce the simplified expression:

$$-2x + 8y + 12$$

73

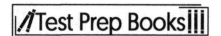

Algebraic expressions are tested to be equivalent by choosing values for the variables and evaluating both expressions. For example, $4(3x - 2)$ and $12x - 8$ are tested by substituting 3 for the variable x and calculating to determine if equivalent values result.

Evaluating Algebraic Expressions

To evaluate the expression, the given values for the variables are substituted (or replaced), and the expression is simplified using the order of operations. Parenthesis should be used when substituting. Consider the following: Evaluate $a - 2b + ab$ for $a = 3$ and $b = -1$.

To evaluate, any variable a is replaced with 3 and any variable b with -1, producing:

$$(3) - 2(-1) + (3)(-1)$$

Next, the order of operations is used to calculate the value of the expression, which is 2.

Here's another example:

$$\text{Evaluate } a - 2b + ab \text{ for } a = 3 \text{ and } b = -1$$

To evaluate an expression, the given values should be substituted for the variables and simplified using the order of operations. In this case:

$$(3) - 2(-1) + (3)(-1)$$

Parentheses are used when substituting.

Given an algebraic expression, students may be asked to simplify the expression. For example:

$$\text{Simplify } 5x^2 - 10x + 2 - 8x^2 + x - 1.$$

Simplifying algebraic expressions requires combining like terms. A term is a number, variable, or product of a number and variables separated by addition and subtraction. The terms in the above expression are: $5x^2, -10x, 2, -8x^2, x,$ and -1. Like terms have the same variables raised to the same powers (exponents). To combine like terms, the coefficients (numerical factor of the term including sign) are added, while the variables and their powers are kept the same. The example above simplifies to:

$$-3x^2 - 9x + 1$$

Let's try two more.

Evaluate $\frac{1}{2}x^2 - 3, x = 4$.

The first step is to substitute in 4 for x in the expression:

$$\frac{1}{2}(4)^2 - 3$$

Then, the order of operations is used to simplify.

The exponent comes first, $\frac{1}{2}(16) - 3$, then the multiplication $8 - 3$, and then, after subtraction, the solution is 5.

Evaluate $4|5 - x| + 2y, x = 4, y = -3$.

74

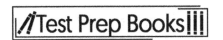

The first step is to substitute 4 in for *x* and -3 in for *y* in the expression:

$$4|5 - 4| + 2(-3)$$

Then, the absolute value expression is simplified, which is:

$$|5 - 4| = |1| = 1$$

The expression is $4(1) + 2(-3)$ which can be simplified using the order of operations.

First is the multiplication, $4 + (-6)$; then addition yields an answer of -2.

Creating Algebraic Expressions

A linear expression is a statement about an unknown quantity expressed in mathematical symbols. The statement "five times a number added to forty" can be expressed as $5x + 40$. A linear equation is a statement in which two expressions (at least one containing a variable) are equal to each other. The statement "five times a number added to forty is equal to ten" can be expressed as:

$$5x + 40 = 10$$

Real world scenarios can also be expressed mathematically. Suppose a job pays its employees $300 per week and $40 for each sale made. The weekly pay is represented by the expression $40x + 300$ where *x* is the number of sales made during the week.

Consider the following scenario: Bob had $20 and Tom had $4. After selling 4 ice cream cones to Bob, Tom has as much money as Bob. The cost of an ice cream cone is an unknown quantity and can be represented by a variable (*x*). The amount of money Bob has after his purchase is four times the cost of an ice cream cone subtracted from his original:

$$\$20 \rightarrow 20 - 4x$$

The amount of money Tom has after his sale is four times the cost of an ice cream cone added to his original:
$$\$4 \rightarrow 4x + 4$$

After the sale, the amount of money that Bob and Tom have is equal:

$$\rightarrow 20 - 4x = 4x + 4$$

When expressing a verbal or written statement mathematically, it is key to understand words or phrases that can be represented with symbols. The following are examples:

Symbol	Phrase
+	added to, increased by, sum of, more than
−	decreased by, difference between, less than, take away
x	multiplied by, 3 (4, 5...) times as large, product of
÷	divided by, quotient of, half (third, etc.) of
=	is, the same as, results in, as much as
$x, t, n, etc.$	a number, unknown quantity, value of

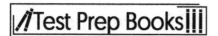

Adding, Subtracting, Multiplying, Dividing, and Factoring Polynomials

An expression of the form ax^n, where n is a non-negative integer, is called a **monomial** because it contains one term. A sum of monomials is called a **polynomial**. For example, $-4x^3 + x$ is a polynomial, while $5x^7$ is a monomial. A function equal to a polynomial is called a **polynomial function**.

The monomials in a polynomial are also called the **terms of the polynomial**.

The constants that precede the variables are called **coefficients**.

The highest value of the exponent of x in a polynomial is called the **degree** of the polynomial. So, $-4x^3 + x$ has a degree of 3, while $-2x^5 + x^3 + 4x + 1$ has a degree of 5. When multiplying polynomials, the degree of the result will be the sum of the degrees of the two polynomials being multiplied.

Addition and subtraction operations can be performed on polynomials with like terms. **Like terms** refers to terms that have the same variable and exponent. The two following polynomials can be added together by collecting like terms:

$$(x^2 + 3x - 4) + (4x^2 - 7x + 8)$$

The x^2 terms can be added as:

$$x^2 + 4x^2 = 5x^2$$

The x terms can be added as $3x + -7x = -4x$, and the constants can be added as:

$$-4 + 8 = 4$$

The following expression is the result of the addition:

$$5x^2 - 4x + 4$$

Let's try another:

$$(-2x^5 + x^3 + 4x + 1) + (-4x^3 + x)$$

$$-2x^5 + (1 - 4)x^3 + (4 + 1)x + 1$$

$$-2x^5 - 3x^3 + 5x + 1$$

Likewise, subtraction of polynomials is performed by subtracting coefficients of like powers of x. So,

$$(-2x^5 + x^3 + 4x + 1) - (-4x^3 + x)$$

$$-2x^5 + (1 + 4)x^3 + (4 - 1)x + 1$$

$$-2x^5 + 5x^3 + 3x + 1$$

To multiply two polynomials, multiply each term of the first polynomial by each term of the second polynomial and add the results. For example:

$$(4x^2 + x)(-x^3 + x)$$

$$4x^2(-x^3) + 4x^2(x) + x(-x^3) + x(x)$$

$$-4x^5 + 4x^3 - x^4 + x^2$$

In the case where each polynomial has two terms, like in this example, some students find it helpful to remember this as multiplying the First terms, then the Outer terms, then the Inner terms, and finally the Last terms, with the mnemonic FOIL. For longer polynomials, the multiplication process is the same, but there will be, of course, more terms, and there is no common mnemonic to remember each combination.

Factors for polynomials are similar to factors for integers—they are numbers, variables, or polynomials that, when multiplied together, give a product equal to the polynomial in question. One polynomial is a factor of a second polynomial if the second polynomial can be obtained from the first by multiplying by a third polynomial.

$6x^6 + 13x^4 + 6x^2$ can be obtained by multiplying together:

$$(3x^4 + 2x^2)(2x^2 + 3)$$

This means $2x^2 + 3$ and $3x^4 + 2x^2$ are factors of:

$$6x^6 + 13x^4 + 6x^2$$

In general, finding the factors of a polynomial can be tricky. However, there are a few types of polynomials that can be factored in a straightforward way.

If a certain monomial is in each term of a polynomial, it can be factored out. There are several common forms polynomials take, which if you recognize, you can solve. The first example is a perfect square trinomial. To factor this polynomial, first expand the middle term of the expression:

$$x^2 + 2xy + y^2$$

$$x^2 + xy + xy + y^2$$

Factor out a common term in each half of the expression (in this case x from the left and y from the right):
$$x(x + y) + y(x + y)$$

Then the same can be done again, treating $(x + y)$ as the common factor:

$$(x + y)(x + y) = (x + y)^2$$

Therefore, the formula for this polynomial is:

$$x^2 + 2xy + y^2 = (x + y)^2$$

Next is another example of a perfect square trinomial. The process is the similar, but notice the difference in sign:
$$x^2 - 2xy + y^2$$

$$x^2 - xy - xy + y^2$$

77

Factor out the common term on each side:

$$x(x - y) - y(x - y)$$

Factoring out the common term again:

$$(x - y)(x - y) = (x - y)^2$$

Thus,

$$x^2 - 2xy + y^2 = (x - y)^2$$

The next is known as a difference of squares. This process is effectively the reverse of binomial multiplication:

$$x^2 - y^2$$

$$x^2 - xy + xy - y^2$$

$$x(x - y) + y(x - y)$$

$$(x + y)(x - y)$$

Therefore,

$$x^2 - y^2 = (x + y)(x - y)$$

The following two polynomials are known as the sum or difference of cubes. These are special polynomials that take the form of $x^3 + y^3$ or $x^3 - y^3$. The following formula factors the sum of cubes:

$$x^3 + y^3 = (x + y)(x^2 - xy + y^2)$$

Next is the difference of cubes, but note the change in sign. The formulas for both are similar, but the order of signs for factoring the sum or difference of cubes can be remembered by using the acronym SOAP, which stands for "same, opposite, always positive." The first sign is the same as the sign in the first expression, the second is opposite, and the third is always positive. The next formula factors the difference of cubes:

$$x^3 - y^3 = (x - y)(x^2 + xy + y^2)$$

The following two examples are expansions of cubed binomials. Similarly, these polynomials always follow a pattern:

$$x^3 + 3x^2y + 3xy^2 + y^3 = (x + y)^3$$

$$x^3 - 3x^2y + 3xy^2 - y^3 = (x - y)^3$$

These rules can be used in many combinations with one another. For example, the expression $3x^3 - 24$ has a common factor of 3, which becomes:

$$3(x^3 - 8)$$

A difference of cubes still remains which can then be factored out:

$$3(x - 2)(x^2 + 2x + 4)$$

There are no other terms to be pulled out, so this expression is completely factored.

When factoring polynomials, a good strategy is to multiply the factors to check the result. Let's try another example:

$$4x^3 + 16x^2$$

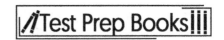

Both sides of the expression can be divided by 4, and both contain x^2, because $4x^3$ can be thought of as $4x^2(x)$, so the common term can simply be factored out:

$$4x^2(x + 4)$$

It sometimes can be necessary to rewrite the polynomial in some clever way before applying the above rules. Consider the problem of factoring $x^4 - 1$. This does not immediately look like any of the previous polynomials. However, it's possible to think of this polynomial as $x^4 - 1 = (x^2)^2 - (1^2)^2$, and now it can be treated as a difference of squares to simplify this:

$$(x^2)^2 - (1^2)^2$$

$$(x^2)^2 - x^2 1^2 + x^2 1^2 - (1^2)^2$$

$$x^2(x^2 - 1^2) + 1^2(x^2 - 1^2)$$

$$(x^2 + 1^2)(x^2 - 1^2)$$

$$(x^2 + 1)(x^2 - 1)$$

Creating Polynomials from Written Descriptions

Polynomials that represent mathematical or real-world problems can also be created from written descriptions, much like algebraic expressions. For example, polynomials might be created when working with formulas. Formulas are mathematical expressions that define the value of one quantity, given the value of one or more different quantities. Formulas look like equations because they contain variables, numbers, operators, and an equal sign. All formulas are equations, but not all equations are formulas. A formula must have more than one variable. For example, $2x + 7 = y$ is an equation and a formula (it relates the unknown quantities x and y). However, $2x + 7 = 3$ is an equation but not a formula (it only expresses the value of the unknown quantity x).

Formulas are typically written with one variable alone (or isolated) on one side of the equal sign. This variable can be thought of as the **subject** in that the formula is stating the value of the subject in terms of the relationship between the other variables. Consider the distance formula: $distance = rate \times time$ or $d = rt$. The value of the subject variable d (distance) is the product of the variable r and t (rate and time). Given the rate and time, the distance traveled can easily be determined by substituting the values into the formula and evaluating.

The formula $P = 2l + 2w$ expresses how to calculate the perimeter of a rectangle (P) given its length (l) and width (w). To find the perimeter of a rectangle with a length of 3 ft and a width of 2 ft, these values are substituted into the formula for l and w:

$$P = 2(3 \text{ ft}) + 2(2 \text{ ft})$$

Following the order of operations, the perimeter is determined to be 10ft. When working with formulas such as these, including units is an important step.

Given a formula expressed in terms of one variable, the formula can be manipulated to express the relationship in terms of any other variable. In other words, the formula can be rearranged to change which variable is the **subject**. To solve for a variable of interest by manipulating a formula, the equation may be solved as if all other variables were numbers. The same steps for solving are followed, leaving operations in terms of the variables instead of calculating numerical values. For the formula $P = 2l + 2w$, the perimeter is the subject expressed in terms of the length and width. To write a formula to calculate the width of a rectangle, given its length and perimeter, the previous formula relating the three variables is solved for the variable w. If P and l were numerical values, this is a

79

two-step linear equation solved by subtraction and division. To solve the equation $P = 2l + 2w$ for w, $2l$ is first subtracted from both sides:

$$P - 2l = 2w$$

Then both sides are divided by 2:

$$\frac{P - 2l}{2} = w$$

Test questions may involve creating a polynomial based on a formula. For example, using the perimeter of a rectangle formula, a problem may ask for the perimeter of a rectangle with a length of $2x + 12$ and a width of $x + 1$. Using the formula $P = 2l + 2w$, the perimeter would then be:

$$P = 2(2x + 12) + 2(x + 1)$$

This equals:

$$4x + 24 + 2x + 2 = 6x + 26$$

The area of the same rectangle, which uses the formula $A = l \times w$, would be:

$$A = (2x + 12)(x + 1)$$

$$2x^2 + 2x + 12x + 12$$

$$2x^2 + 14x + 12$$

Adding, Subtracting, Multiplying, Dividing Rational Expressions

A fraction, or ratio, wherein each part is a polynomial, defines **rational expressions**. Some examples include $\frac{2x+6}{x}$, $\frac{1}{x^2-4x+8}$, and $\frac{z^2}{x+5}$. Exponents on the variables are restricted to whole numbers, which means roots and negative exponents are not included in rational expressions.

Rational expressions can be transformed by factoring. For example, the expression $\frac{x^2-5x+6}{(x-3)}$ can be rewritten by factoring the numerator to obtain:

$$\frac{(x - 3)(x - 2)}{(x - 3)}$$

Therefore, the common binomial $(x - 3)$ can cancel so that the simplified expression is:

$$\frac{(x - 2)}{1} = (x - 2)$$

Additionally, other rational expressions can be rewritten to take on different forms. Some may be factorable in themselves, while others can be transformed through arithmetic operations. Rational expressions are closed under addition, subtraction, multiplication, and division by a nonzero expression. **Closed** means that if any one of these operations is performed on a rational expression, the result will still be a rational expression. The set of all real numbers is another example of a set closed under all four operations.

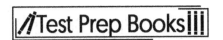
Adding and subtracting rational expressions is based on the same concepts as adding and subtracting simple fractions. For both concepts, the denominators must be the same for the operation to take place. For example, here are two rational expressions:

$$\frac{x^3 - 4}{(x - 3)} + \frac{x + 8}{(x - 3)}$$

Since the denominators are both $(x - 3)$, the numerators can be combined by collecting like terms to form:

$$\frac{x^3 + x + 4}{(x - 3)}$$

If the denominators are different, they need to be made common (the same) by using the **Least Common Denominator (LCD)**. Each denominator needs to be factored, and the LCD contains each factor that appears in any one denominator the greatest number of times it appears in any denominator. The original expressions need to be multiplied by a form of 1 such as $\frac{5}{5}$ or $\frac{x-2}{x-2}$, which will turn each denominator into the LCD. This process is like adding fractions with unlike denominators. It is also important when working with rational expressions to define what value of the variable makes the denominator zero. For this particular value, the expression is undefined.

Multiplication of rational expressions is performed like multiplication of fractions. The numerators are multiplied; then, the denominators are multiplied. The final fraction is then simplified. The expressions are simplified by factoring and cancelling out common terms. In the following example, the numerator of the second expression can be factored first to simplify the expression before multiplying:

$$\frac{x^2}{(x - 4)} \times \frac{x^2 - x - 12}{2}$$

$$\frac{x^2}{(x - 4)} \times \frac{(x - 4)(x + 3)}{2}$$

The $(x - 4)$ on the top and bottom cancel out:

$$\frac{x^2}{1} \times \frac{(x + 3)}{2}$$

Then multiplication is performed, resulting in:

$$\frac{x^3 + 3x^2}{2}$$

Dividing rational expressions is similar to the division of fractions, where division turns into multiplying by a reciprocal. Thus, the following expression can be rewritten as a multiplication problem:

$$\frac{x^2 - 3x + 7}{x - 4} \div \frac{x^2 - 5x + 3}{x - 4}$$

$$\frac{x^2 - 3x + 7}{x - 4} \times \frac{x - 4}{x^2 - 5x + 3}$$

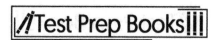

The $x - 4$ cancels out, leaving:

$$\frac{x^2 - 3x + 7}{x^2 - 5x + 3}$$

The final answers should always be completely simplified. If a function is composed of a rational expression, the zeros of the graph can be found from setting the polynomial in the numerator as equal to zero and solving. The values that make the denominator equal to zero will either exist on the graph as a **hole** or a **vertical asymptote**.

A **complex fraction** is a fraction in which the numerator and denominator are themselves fractions, of the form:

$$\frac{\left(\frac{a}{b}\right)}{\left(\frac{c}{d}\right)}$$

These can be simplified by following the usual rules for the order of operations, or by remembering that dividing one fraction by another is the same as multiplying by the reciprocal of the divisor. This means that any complex fraction can be rewritten using the following form:

$$\frac{\left(\frac{a}{b}\right)}{\left(\frac{c}{d}\right)} = \frac{a}{b} \times \frac{d}{c}$$

The following problem is an example of solving a complex fraction:

$$\frac{\left(\frac{5}{4}\right)}{\left(\frac{3}{8}\right)} = \frac{5}{4} \times \frac{8}{3} = \frac{40}{12} = \frac{10}{3}$$

Writing an Expression from a Written Description

When expressing a verbal or written statement mathematically, it is vital to understand words or phrases that can be represented with symbols. The following are examples:

Symbol	Phrase
+	Added to; increased by; sum of; more than
−	Decreased by; difference between; less than; take away
×	Multiplied by; 3(4,5...) times as large; product of
÷	Divided by; quotient of; half (third, etc.) of
=	Is; the same as; results in; as much as; equal to
x,t,n, etc.	A number; unknown quantity; value of; variable

Addition and subtraction are **inverse operations**. Adding a number and then subtracting the same number will cancel each other out, resulting in the original number, and vice versa. For example, $8 + 7 - 7 = 8$ and:

$$137 - 100 + 100 = 137$$

Similarly, multiplication and division are inverse operations. Therefore, multiplying by a number and then dividing by the same number results in the original number, and vice versa. For example, $8 \times 2 \div 2 = 8$ and $12 \div 4 \times 4 = 12$. Inverse operations are used to work backwards to solve problems. In the case that 7 and a number add to 18, the inverse operation of subtraction is used to find the unknown value ($18 - 7 = 11$). If a school's entire 4th grade was divided evenly into 3 classes each with 22 students, the inverse operation of multiplication is used to determine

82

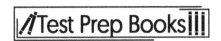

the total students in the grade ($22 \times 3 = 66$). Additional scenarios involving inverse operations are included in the tables below.

Recall that a rational expression is a fraction where the numerator and denominator are both polynomials. Some examples of rational expressions include the following: $\frac{4x^3y^5}{3z^4}$, $\frac{4x^3+3x}{x^2}$, and $\frac{x^2+7x+10}{x+2}$. Since these refer to expressions and not equations, they can be simplified but not solved. Using the rules in the previous Exponents and Roots sections, some rational expressions with monomials can be simplified. Other rational expressions such as the last example, $\frac{x^2+7x+10}{x+2}$, take more steps to be simplified. First, the polynomial on top can be factored from $x^2 + 7x + 10$ into $(x + 5)(x + 2)$. Then the common factors can be canceled, and the expression can be simplified to $(x + 5)$.

Consider this problem as an example of using rational expressions. Reggie wants to lay sod in his rectangular backyard. The length of the yard is given by the expression $4x + 2$, and the width is unknown. The area of the yard is $20x + 10$. Reggie needs to find the width of the yard. Knowing that the area of a rectangle is length multiplied by width, an expression can be written to find the width: $\frac{20x+10}{4x+2}$, area divided by length. Simplifying this expression by factoring out 10 on the top and 2 on the bottom leads to this expression:

$$\frac{10(2x + 1)}{2(2x + 1)}$$

By cancelling out the $2x + 1$, that results in $\frac{10}{2} = 5$. The width of the yard is found to be 5 by simplifying a rational expression.

Using Linear Equations to Solve Real-World Problems

Linear relationships describe the way two quantities change with respect to each other. The relationship is defined as linear because a line is produced if all the sets of corresponding values are graphed on a coordinate grid. When expressing the linear relationship as an equation, the equation is often written in the form $y = mx + b$ (slope-intercept form) where m and b are numerical values and x and y are variables (for example, $y = 5x + 10$). Given a linear equation and the value of either variable (x or y), the value of the other variable can be determined.

Imagine the following problem: The sum of a number and 5 is equal to -8 times the number.

To find this unknown number, a simple equation can be written to represent the problem. Key words such as difference, equal, and times are used to form the following equation with one variable: $n + 5 = -8n$. When solving for n, opposite operations are used. First, n is subtracted from $-8n$ across the equals sign, resulting in $5 = -9n$. Then, -9 is divided on both sides, leaving $n = -\frac{5}{9}$. This solution can be graphed on the number line with a dot as shown below:

Suppose a teacher is grading a test containing 20 questions with 5 points given for each correct answer, adding a curve of 10 points to each test. This linear relationship can be expressed as the equation $y = 5x + 10$ where x represents the number of correct answers, and y represents the test score. To determine the score of a test with a given number of correct answers, the number of correct answers is substituted into the equation for x and evaluated. For example, for 10 correct answers, 10 is substituted for x:

$$y = 5(10) + 10 \rightarrow y = 60$$

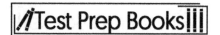

Math

Therefore, 10 correct answers will result in a score of 60. The number of correct answers needed to obtain a certain score can also be determined. To determine the number of correct answers needed to score a 90, 90 is substituted for y in the equation (y represents the test score) and solved:

$$90 = 5x + 10 \rightarrow 80 = 5x \rightarrow 16 = x$$

Therefore, 16 correct answers are needed to score a 90.

Linear relationships may be represented by a table of 2 corresponding values. Certain tables may determine the relationship between the values and predict other corresponding sets. Consider the table below, which displays the money in a checking account that charges a monthly fee:

Month	0	1	2	3	4
Balance	$210	$195	$180	$165	$150

An examination of the values reveals that the account loses $15 every month (the month increases by one and the balance decreases by 15). This information can be used to predict future values. To determine what the value will be in month 6, the pattern can be continued, and it can be concluded that the balance will be $120. To determine which month the balance will be $0, $210 is divided by $15 (since the balance decreases $15 every month), resulting in month 14.

Solving a System of Two Linear Equations

A **system of equations** is a group of equations that have the same variables or unknowns. These equations can be linear, but they are not always so. Finding a solution to a system of equations means finding the values of the variables that satisfy each equation. For a linear system of two equations and two variables, there could be a single solution, no solution, or infinitely many solutions.

A single solution occurs when there is one value for x and y that satisfies the system. This would be shown on the graph where the lines cross at exactly one point. When there is no solution, the lines are parallel and do not ever cross. With infinitely many solutions, the equations may look different, but they are the same line. One equation will be a multiple of the other, and on the graph, they lie on top of each other.

The process of elimination can be used to solve a system of equations. For example, the following equations make up a system:

$$x + 3y = 10 \text{ and } 2x - 5y = 9$$

Immediately adding these equations does not eliminate a variable, but it is possible to change the first equation by multiplying the whole equation by -2. This changes the first equation to:

$$-2x - 6y = -20$$

The equations can be then added to obtain $-11y = -11$. Solving for y yields $y = 1$. To find the rest of the solution, 1 can be substituted in for y in either original equation to find the value of $x = 7$. The solution to the system is $(7, 1)$ because it makes both equations true, and it is the point in which the lines intersect. If the system is **dependent**—having infinitely many solutions—then both variables will cancel out when the elimination method is used, resulting in an equation that is true for many values of x and y. Since the system is dependent, both equations can be simplified to the same equation or line.

84

A system can also be solved using **substitution.** This involves solving one equation for a variable and then plugging that solved equation into the other equation in the system. For example, $x - y = -2$ and $3x + 2y = 9$ can be solved using substitution. The first equation can be solved for x, where:

$$x = -2 + y$$

Then it can be plugged into the other equation:

$$3(-2 + y) + 2y = 9$$

Solving for y yields:

$$-6 + 3y + 2y = 9$$

That shows that $y = 3$. If $y = 3$, then $x = 1$.

This solution can be checked by plugging in these values for the variables in each equation to see if it makes a true statement.

Finally, a solution to a system of equations can be found graphically. The solution to a linear system is the point or points where the lines cross. The values of x and y represent the coordinates (x, y) where the lines intersect. Using the same system of equations as above, they can be solved for y to put them in slope-intercept form:

$$y = mx + b$$

These equations become $y = x + 2$ and:

$$y = -\frac{3}{2}x + 4.5$$

The slope is the coefficient of x, and the y-intercept is the constant value.

This system with the solution is shown below:

If the lines intersect, the point of intersection is the solution to the system. Every point on a line represents an ordered pair that makes its equation true. The ordered pair represented by this point of intersection lies on both lines and therefore makes both equations true. This ordered pair should be checked by substituting its values into both of the original equations of the system. Note that given a system of equations and an ordered pair, the ordered pair can be determined to be a solution or not by checking it in both equations.

If, when graphed, the lines representing the equations of a system do not intersect, then the two lines are parallel to each other or they are the same exact line. Parallel lines extend in the same direction without ever meeting. A system consisting of parallel lines has no solution. If the equations for a system represent the same exact line, then every point on the line is a solution to the system. In this case, there would be an infinite number of solutions. A system consisting of intersecting lines is referred to as independent; a system consisting of parallel lines is referred to as inconsistent; and a system consisting of coinciding lines is referred to as dependent.

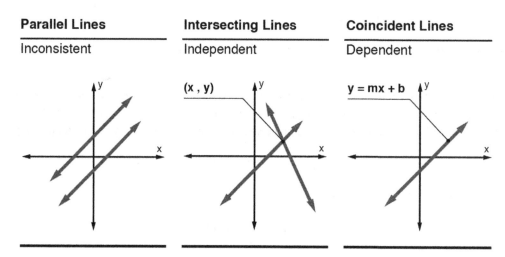

Matrices can also be used to solve systems of linear equations. Specifically, for systems, the coefficients of the linear equations in standard form are the entries in the matrix. Using the same system of linear equations as above, $x - y = -2$ and $3x + 2y = 9$, the matrix to represent the system is:

$$\begin{bmatrix} 1 & -1 \\ 3 & 2 \end{bmatrix} \begin{bmatrix} x \\ y \end{bmatrix} = \begin{bmatrix} -2 \\ 9 \end{bmatrix}$$

To solve this system using matrices, the inverse matrix must be found. For a general 2×2 matrix:

$$\begin{bmatrix} a & b \\ c & d \end{bmatrix}$$

The inverse matrix is found by the expression:

$$\frac{1}{ad - bc} \begin{bmatrix} d & -b \\ -c & a \end{bmatrix}$$

The inverse matrix for the system given above is:

$$\frac{1}{2 - -3} \begin{bmatrix} 2 & 1 \\ -3 & 1 \end{bmatrix} = \frac{1}{5} \begin{bmatrix} 2 & 1 \\ -3 & 1 \end{bmatrix}$$

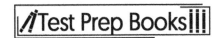

The next step in solving is to multiply this identity matrix by the system matrix above. This is given by the following equation:

$$\frac{1}{5}\begin{bmatrix} 2 & 1 \\ -3 & 1 \end{bmatrix}\begin{bmatrix} 1 & -1 \\ 3 & 2 \end{bmatrix}\begin{bmatrix} x \\ y \end{bmatrix} = \begin{bmatrix} 2 & 1 \\ -3 & 1 \end{bmatrix}\begin{bmatrix} -2 \\ 9 \end{bmatrix}\frac{1}{5}$$

which simplifies to

$$\frac{1}{5}\begin{bmatrix} 5 & 0 \\ 0 & 5 \end{bmatrix}\begin{bmatrix} x \\ y \end{bmatrix} = \frac{1}{5}\begin{bmatrix} 5 \\ 15 \end{bmatrix}$$

Solving for the solution matrix, the answer is:

$$\begin{bmatrix} 1 & 0 \\ 0 & 1 \end{bmatrix}\begin{bmatrix} x \\ y \end{bmatrix} = \begin{bmatrix} 1 \\ 3 \end{bmatrix}$$

Since the first matrix is the identity matrix, the solution is $x = 1$ and $y = 3$.

Finding solutions to systems of equations is essentially finding what values of the variables make both equations true. It is finding the input value that yields the same output value in both equations. For functions $g(x)$ and $f(x)$, the equation $g(x) = f(x)$ means the output values are being set equal to each other. Solving for the value of x means finding the x-coordinate that gives the same output in both functions. For example, $f(x) = x + 2$ and $g(x) = -3x + 10$ is a system of equations. Setting $f(x) = g(x)$ yields the equation:
$$x + 2 = -3x + 10$$

Solving for x, gives the x-coordinate $x = 2$ where the two lines cross. This value can also be found by using a table or a graph. On a table, both equations can be given the same inputs, and the outputs can be recorded to find the point(s) where the lines cross. Any method of solving finds the same solution, but some methods are more appropriate for some systems of equations than others.

Solving Inequalities and Graphing the Answer on a Number Line

Linear inequalities and linear equations are both comparisons of two algebraic expressions. However, unlike equations in which the expressions are equal to each other, linear inequalities compare expressions that are unequal. Linear equations typically have one value for the variable that makes the statement true. Linear inequalities generally have an infinite number of values that make the statement true.

Linear inequalities are a concise mathematical way to express the relationship between unequal values. More specifically, they describe in what way the values are unequal. A value could be greater than (>); less than (<); greater than or equal to (≥); or less than or equal to (≤) another value. The statement "five times a number added to forty is more than sixty-five" can be expressed as:

$$5x + 40 > 65$$

Common words and phrases that express inequalities are:

Symbol	Phrase
<	is under, is below, smaller than, beneath
>	is above, is over, bigger than, exceeds
≤	no more than, at most, maximum
≥	no less than, at least, minimum

If a problem were to say, "The sum of a number and 5 is greater than -8 times the number," then an inequality would be used instead of an equation. Using key words again, *greater than* is represented by the symbol >. The inequality $n + 5 > -8n$ can be solved using the same techniques, resulting in $n < -\frac{5}{9}$. The only time solving an inequality differs from solving an equation is when a negative number is either multiplied by or divided by each side of the inequality. The sign must be switched in this case. For this example, the graph of the solution changes to the following graph because the solution represents all real numbers less than $-\frac{5}{9}$. Not included in this solution is $-\frac{5}{9}$ because it is a *less than* symbol, not *equal to*.

When solving a linear inequality, the solution is the set of all numbers that makes the statement true. The inequality $x + 2 \geq 6$ has a solution set of 4 and every number greater than 4 (4.0001, 5, 12, 107, etc.). Adding 2 to 4 or any number greater than 4 would result in a value that is greater than or equal to 6. Therefore, $x \geq 4$ would be the solution set.

Solution sets for linear inequalities often will be displayed using a number line. If a value is included in the set ($\geq$ or $\leq$), there is a shaded dot placed on that value and an arrow extending in the direction of the solutions. For a variable > or $\geq$ a number, the arrow would point right on the number line (the direction where the numbers increase); and if a variable is < or $\leq$ a number, the arrow would point left (where the numbers decrease). If the value is not included in the set (> or <), an open circle on that value would be used with an arrow in the appropriate direction.

Observe this number line:

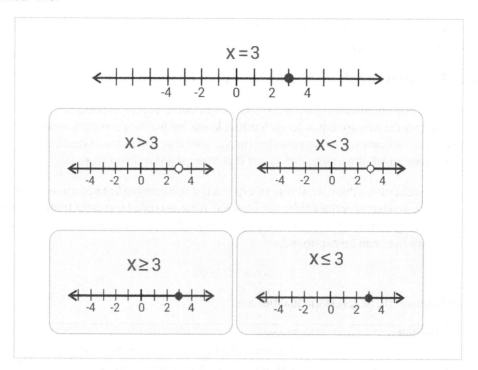

Students may be asked to write a linear inequality given a graph of its solution set. To do so, they should identify whether the value is included (shaded dot or open circle) and the direction in which the arrow is pointing.

In order to algebraically solve a linear inequality, the same steps should be followed as in solving a linear equation. The inequality symbol stays the same for all operations EXCEPT when multiplying or dividing by a negative number. If multiplying or dividing by a negative number while solving an inequality, the relationship reverses (the sign flips). Multiplying or dividing by a positive does not change the relationship, so the sign stays the same. In other words, $>$ switches to $<$ and vice versa. An example is shown below.

Solve $-2(x + 4) \leq 22$ for the value of x.

First, distribute -2 to the binomial by multiplying:

$$-2x - 8 \leq 22$$

Next, add 8 to both sides to isolate the variable:

$$-2x \leq 30$$

Divide both sides by -2 to solve for x:

$$x \geq -15$$

With a single equation in two variables, the solutions are limited only by the situation the equation represents. When two equations or inequalities are used, more constraints are added. For example, in a system of linear equations, there is often—although not always—only one answer. The point of intersection of two lines is the solution. For a system of inequalities, there are infinitely many answers.

The intersection of two solution sets gives the solution set of the system of inequalities. In the following graph, the darker shaded region is where two inequalities overlap. Any set of x and y found in that region satisfies both inequalities. The line with the positive slope is solid, meaning the values on that line are included in the solution.

The line with the negative slope is dotted, so the coordinates on that line are not included.

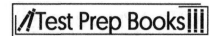

Quadratic Equations with One Variable

A **quadratic equation** can be written in the form:

$$y = ax^2 + bx + c$$

The u-shaped graph of a quadratic equation is called a **parabola**. The graph can either open up or open down (upside down u). The graph is symmetric about a vertical line, called the **axis of symmetry**. Corresponding points on the parabola are directly across from each other (same y-value) and are the same distance from the axis of symmetry (on either side). The axis of symmetry intersects the parabola at its **vertex**. The y-value of the vertex represents the minimum or maximum value of the function. If the graph opens up, the value of a in its equation is positive, and the vertex represents the minimum of the function. If the graph opens down, the value of a in its equation is negative, and the vertex represents the maximum of the function.

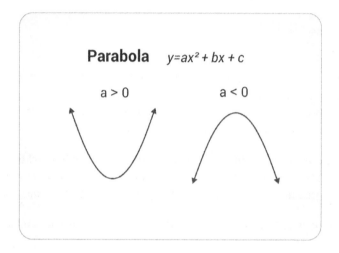

Parabola $y=ax^2 + bx + c$

A quadratic equation can be written in the standard form:

$$y = ax^2 + bx + c$$

It can be represented by a u-shaped graph called a **parabola**. For a quadratic equation where the value of a is positive, as the inputs increase, the outputs increase until a certain value (maximum of the function) is reached. As inputs increase past the value that corresponds with the maximum output, the relationship reverses, and the outputs decrease. For a quadratic equation where a is negative, as the inputs increase, the outputs (1) decrease, (2) reach a maximum, and (3) then increase.

Consider a ball thrown straight up into the air. As time passes, the height of the ball increases until it reaches its maximum height. After reaching the maximum height, as time increases, the height of the ball decreases (it is falling toward the ground). This relationship can be expressed as a quadratic equation where time is the input (x), and the height of the ball is the output (y).

Equations with one variable (linear equations) can be solved using the addition principle and multiplication principle. If $a = b$, then $a + c = b + c$, and $ac = bc$. Given the equation $2x - 3 = 5x + 7$, the first step is to combine the variable terms and the constant terms. Using the principles, expressions can be added and subtracted onto and off both sides of the equals sign, so the equation turns into $-10 = 3x$. Dividing by 3 on both sides through the multiplication principle with $c = \frac{1}{3}$ results in the final answer of $x = \frac{-10}{3}$.

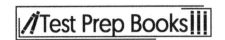

However, this same process cannot be used to solve nonlinear equations, including quadratic equations. Quadratic equations have a higher degree than linear ones (2 versus 1) and are not solved by simply using opposite operations. When an equation has a degree of 2, completing the square is an option. For example, the quadratic equation $x^2 - 6x + 2 = 0$ can be rewritten by completing the square. The goal of completing the square is to get the equation into the form:

$$(x - p)^2 = q$$

Using the example, the constant term 2 first needs to be moved over to the opposite side by subtracting. Then, the square can be completed by adding 9 to both sides, which is the square of half of the coefficient of the middle term $-6x$. The current equation is:

$$x^2 - 6x + 9 = 7$$

The left side can be factored into a square of a binomial, resulting in:

$$(x - 3)^2 = 7$$

To solve for x, the square root of both sides should be taken, resulting in $(x - 3) = \pm\sqrt{7}$, and:

$$x = 3 \pm \sqrt{7}$$

Other ways of solving quadratic equations include graphing, factoring, and using the quadratic formula. The equation $y = x^2 - 4x + 3$ can be graphed on the coordinate plane, and the solutions can be observed where it crosses the x-axis. The graph will be a parabola that opens up with two solutions at 1 and 3.

If quadratic equations take the form $ax^2 - b = 0$, then the equation can be solved by adding b to both sides and dividing by a to get:

$$x^2 = \frac{b}{a} \text{ or } x = \pm\sqrt{\frac{b}{a}}$$

Note that this is actually two separate solutions, unless b happens to be 0.

If a quadratic equation has no constant—so that it takes the form $ax^2 + bx = 0$—then the x can be factored out to get:

$$x(ax + b) = 0$$

Then, the solutions are $x = 0$, together with the solutions to $ax + b = 0$. Both factors x and $(ax + b)$ can be set equal to zero to solve for x because one of those values must be zero for their product to equal zero. For an equation $ab = 0$ to be true, either $a = 0$, or $b = 0$.

A given quadratic equation $x^2 + bx + c$ can be factored into $(x + A)(x + B)$, where $A + B = b$, and $AB = c$. Finding the values of A and B can take time, but such a pair of numbers can be found by guessing and checking. Looking at the positive and negative factors for c offers a good starting point.

For example, in $x^2 - 5x + 6$, the factors of 6 are 1, 2, and 3. Now,$(-2)(-3) = 6$, and $-2 - 3 = -5$. In general, however, this may not work, in which case another approach may need to be used.

A quadratic equation of the form $x^2 + 2xb + b^2 = 0$ can be factored into:

$$(x + b)^2 = 0$$

Similarly, $x^2 - 2xy + y^2 = 0$ factors into:

$$(x - y)^2 = 0$$

The first method of completing the square can be used in finding the second method, the quadratic formula. It can be used to solve any quadratic equation. This formula may be the longest method for solving quadratic equations and is commonly used as a last resort after other methods are ruled out.

It can be helpful in memorizing the formula to see where it comes from, so here are the steps involved.

The most general form for a quadratic equation is:

$$ax^2 + bx + c = 0$$

First, dividing both sides by a leaves us with:

$$x^2 + \frac{b}{a}x + \frac{c}{a} = 0$$

To complete the square on the left-hand side, $\frac{c}{a}$ can be subtracted on both sides to get:

$$x^2 + \frac{b}{a}x = -\frac{c}{a}$$

$(\frac{b}{2a})^2$ is then added to both sides.

This gives:

$$x^2 + \frac{b}{a}x + (\frac{b}{2a})^2 = (\frac{b}{2a})^2 - \frac{c}{a}$$

The left can now be factored and the right-hand side simplified to give:

$$(x + \frac{b}{2a})^2 = \frac{b^2 - 4ac}{4a}$$

Taking the square roots gives:

$$x + \frac{b}{2a} = \pm\frac{\sqrt{b^2 - 4ac}}{2a}$$

Solving for x yields the quadratic formula:

$$x = \frac{-b \pm \sqrt{b^2 - 4ac}}{2a}$$

It isn't necessary to remember how to get this formula but memorizing the formula itself is the goal.

If an equation involves taking a root, then the first step is to move the root to one side of the equation and everything else to the other side. That way, both sides can be raised to the index of the radical in order to remove it, and solving the equation can continue.

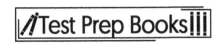

Measurement

Ratios and Proportions

Ratios

Ratios are used to show the relationship between two quantities. The ratio of oranges to apples in the grocery store may be 3 to 2. That means that for every 3 oranges, there are 2 apples. This comparison can be expanded to represent the actual number of oranges and apples, such as 36 oranges to 24 apples. Another example may be the number of boys to girls in a math class. If the ratio of boys to girls is given as 2 to 5, that means there are 2 boys to every 5 girls in the class; this can also be represented as 2: 5. Ratios can also be compared if the units in each ratio are the same. The ratio of boys to girls in the math class can be compared to the ratio of boys to girls in a science class by stating which ratio is higher and which is lower.

Rates are used to compare two quantities with different units. *Unit rates* are the simplest form of rate. With **unit rates**, the denominator in the comparison of two units is one. For example, if someone can type at a rate of 1,000 words in 5 minutes, then their unit rate for typing is $\frac{1,000}{5} = 200$ words in one minute or 200 words per minute. Any rate can be converted into a unit rate by dividing to make the denominator one. 1,000 words in 5 minutes has been converted into the unit rate of 200 words per minute.

Ratios and rates can be used together to convert rates into different units. For example, if someone is driving 50 kilometers per hour, that rate can be converted into miles per hour by using a ratio known as the **conversion factor**. Since the given value contains kilometers and the final answer needs to be in miles, the ratio relating miles to kilometers needs to be used. There are 0.62 miles in 1 kilometer. This, written as a ratio and in fraction form, is $\frac{0.62 \text{ miles}}{1 \text{ km}}$. To convert 50 km/hour into miles per hour, the following conversion needs to be set up:

$$\frac{50 \text{ km}}{\text{hour}} \times \frac{0.62 \text{ miles}}{1 \text{ km}} = 31 \text{ miles per hour}$$

The ratio between two similar geometric figures is called the **scale factor**. For example, a problem may depict two similar triangles, A and B. The scale factor from the smaller triangle A to the larger triangle B is given as 2 because the length of the corresponding side of the larger triangle, 16, is twice the corresponding side on the smaller triangle, 8. This scale factor can also be used to find the value of a missing side, x, in triangle A. Since the scale factor from the smaller triangle (A) to larger one (B) is 2, the larger corresponding side in triangle B (given as 25) can be divided by 2 to find the missing side in A ($x = 12.5$). The scale factor can also be represented in the equation $2A = B$ because two times the lengths of A gives the corresponding lengths of B. This is the idea behind similar triangles.

Unit Rate

Unit rate word problems will ask to calculate the rate or quantity of something in a different value. For example, a problem might say that a car drove a certain number of miles in a certain number of minutes and then ask how many miles per hour the car was traveling. These questions involve solving proportions. Consider the following examples:

1) Alexandra made $96 during the first 3 hours of her shift as a temporary worker at a law office. She will continue to earn money at this rate until she finishes in 5 more hours. How much does Alexandra make per hour? How much will Alexandra have made at the end of the day?

This problem can be solved in two ways. The first is to set up a proportion, as the rate of pay is constant. The second is to determine her hourly rate, multiply the 5 hours by that rate, and then add the $96.

To set up a proportion, put the money already earned over the hours already worked on one side of an equation. The other side has x over 8 hours (the total hours worked in the day). It looks like this:

$$\frac{96}{3} = \frac{x}{8}$$

Now, cross-multiply to get $768 = 3x$. To get x, divide by 3, which leaves $x = 256$. Alternatively, as x is the numerator of one of the proportions, multiplying by its denominator will reduce the solution by one step. Thus, Alexandra will make $256 at the end of the day. To calculate her hourly rate, divide the total by 8, giving $32 per hour.

Alternatively, it is possible to figure out the hourly rate by dividing $96 by 3 hours to get $32 per hour. Now her total pay can be figured by multiplying $32 per hour by 8 hours, which comes out to $256.

2) Jonathan is reading a novel. So far, he has read 215 of the 335 total pages. It takes Jonathan 25 minutes to read 10 pages, and the rate is constant. How long does it take Jonathan to read one page? How much longer will it take him to finish the novel? Express the answer in time.

To calculate how long it takes Jonathan to read one page, divide the 25 minutes by 10 pages to determine the page per minute rate. Thus, it takes 2.5 minutes to read one page.

Jonathan must read 120 more pages to complete the novel. (This is calculated by subtracting the pages already read from the total.) Now, multiply his rate per page by the number of pages. Thus,

$$120 \times 2.5 = 300$$

Expressed in time, 300 minutes is equal to 5 hours.

3) At a hotel, $\frac{4}{5}$ of the 120 rooms are booked for Saturday. On Sunday, $\frac{3}{4}$ of the rooms are booked. On which day are more of the rooms booked, and by how many more?

The first step is to calculate the number of rooms booked for each day. Do this by multiplying the fraction of the rooms booked by the total number of rooms.

Saturday: $\frac{4}{5} \times 120 = \frac{4}{5} \times \frac{120}{1} = \frac{480}{5} = 96$ rooms

Sunday: $\frac{3}{4} \times 120 = \frac{3}{4} \times \frac{120}{1} = \frac{360}{4} = 90$ rooms

Thus, more rooms were booked on Saturday by 6 rooms.

4) In a veterinary hospital, the veterinarian-to-pet ratio is 1:9. The ratio is always constant. If there are 45 pets in the hospital, how many veterinarians are currently in the veterinary hospital?

Set up a proportion to solve for the number of veterinarians:

$$\frac{1}{9} = \frac{x}{45}$$

Cross-multiplying results in $9x = 45$, which works out to 5 veterinarians.

Alternatively, as there are always 9 times as many pets as veterinarians, it is possible to divide the number of pets (45) by 9. This also arrives at the correct answer of 5 veterinarians.

5) At a general practice law firm, 30% of the lawyers work solely on tort cases. If 9 lawyers work solely on tort cases, how many lawyers work at the firm?

First, solve for the total number of lawyers working at the firm, which will be represented here with x. The problem states that 9 lawyers work solely on torts cases, and they make up 30% of the total lawyers at the firm. Thus, 30% multiplied by the total, x, will equal 9. Written as equation, this is:

$$30\% \times x = 9$$

It's easier to deal with the equation after converting the percentage to a decimal, leaving $0.3x = 9$. Thus, $x = \frac{9}{0.3} = 30$ lawyers working at the firm.

6) Xavier was hospitalized with pneumonia. He was originally given 35 mg of antibiotics. Later, after his condition continued to worsen, Xavier's dosage was increased to 60 mg. What was the percent increase of the antibiotics? Round the percentage to the nearest tenth.

An increase or decrease in percentage can be calculated by dividing the difference in amounts by the original amount and multiplying by 100. Written as an equation, the formula is:

$$\frac{new\ quantity - old\ quantity}{old\ quantity} \times 100$$

Here, the question states that the dosage was increased from 35 mg to 60 mg, so these are plugged into the formula to find the percentage increase.

$$\frac{60 - 35}{35} \times 100 = \frac{25}{35} \times 100$$

$$0.7142 \times 100 = 71.4\%$$

Proportions

Much like a scale factor can be written using an equation like $2A = B$, a **relationship** is represented by the equation $Y = kX$. X and Y are proportional because as values of X increase, the values of Y also increase. A relationship that is inversely proportional can be represented by the equation $Y = \frac{k}{X}$, where the value of Y decreases as the value of X increases and vice versa.

Proportional reasoning can be used to solve problems involving ratios, percentages, and averages. Ratios can be used in setting up proportions and solving them to find unknowns. For example, if a student completes an average of 10 pages of math homework in 3 nights, how long would it take the student to complete 22 pages? Both ratios can be written as fractions. The second ratio would contain the unknown.

The following proportion represents this problem, where x is the unknown number of nights:

$$\frac{10\ pages}{3\ nights} = \frac{22\ pages}{x\ nights}$$

Solving this proportion entails cross-multiplying (multiplying both sets of numbers that are diagonally across and setting them equal to each other) and results in the following equation: $10x = 22 \times 3$. Simplifying and solving for x results in the exact solution: $x = 6.6$ nights. The result would be rounded up to 7 because the homework would actually be completed on the 7th night.

The following problem uses ratios involving percentages:

If 20% of the class is girls and 30 students are in the class, how many girls are in the class?

To set up this problem, it is helpful to use the common proportion: $\frac{\%}{100} = \frac{is}{of}$. Within the proportion, % is the percentage of girls, 100 is the total percentage of the class, *is* is the number of girls, and *of* is the total number of students in the class. Most percentage problems can be written using this language. To solve this problem, the proportion should be set up as $\frac{20}{100} = \frac{x}{30}$ and then solved for x. Cross-multiplying results in the equation $20 \times 30 = 100x$, which results in the solution $x = 6$. There are 6 girls in the class.

Ratios can be used to solve problems that concern length, volume, and other units. For example, A problem may ask for the volume of a cone that has a radius, $r = 7$ m and a height, $h = 16$ m. Referring to the formulas provided on the test, the volume of a cone is given as: $V = \pi r^2 \frac{h}{3}$, where r is the radius, and h is the height. Plugging $r = 7$ and $h = 16$ into the formula, the following is obtained:

$$V = \pi(7^2)\frac{16}{3}$$

Therefore, the volume of the cone is found to be approximately 821 m^3. Sometimes, answers in different units are sought. If this problem wanted the answer in liters, 821 m^3 would need to be converted.

Using the equivalence statement 1 m^3 = 1,000 L, the following ratio would be used to solve for liters:

$$821 \text{ m}^3 \times \frac{1,000 \text{ L}}{1 \text{ m}^3}$$

Cubic meters in the numerator and denominator cancel each other out, and the answer is converted to 821,000 liters, or 8.21×10^5 L.

Other conversions can also be made between different given and final units. If the temperature in a pool is 30°C, what is the temperature of the pool in degrees Fahrenheit? To convert these units, an equation is used relating Celsius to Fahrenheit. The following equation is used:

$$T_{°F} = 1.8T_{°C} + 32$$

Plugging in the given temperature and solving the equation for T yields the result:

$$T_{°F} = 1.8(30) + 32 = 86°F$$

Both units in the metric system and U.S. customary system are widely used.

Here are some more examples of how to solve for proportions:

1) $\frac{75\%}{90\%} = \frac{25\%}{x}$

To solve for x, the fractions must be cross multiplied: $(75\%x = 90\% \times 25\%)$. To make things easier, let's convert the percentages to decimals: $(0.9 \times 0.25 = 0.225 = 0.75x)$. To get rid of x's coefficient, each side must be divided by that same coefficient to get the answer $x = 0.3$. The question could ask for the answer as a percentage or fraction in lowest terms, which are 30% and $\frac{3}{10}$, respectively.

2) $\frac{x}{12} = \frac{30}{96}$

Cross-multiply: $96x = 30 \times 12$

Multiply: $96x = 360$

Divide: $x = 360 \div 96$

Answer: $x = 3.75$

3) $\frac{0.5}{3} = \frac{x}{6}$

Cross-multiply: $3x = 0.5 \times 6$

Multiply: $3x = 3$

Divide: $x = 3 \div 3$

Answer: $x = 1$

You may have noticed there's a faster way to arrive at the answer. If there is an obvious operation being performed on the proportion, the same operation can be used on the other side of the proportion to solve for x. For example, in the first practice problem, 75% became 25% when divided by 3, and upon doing the same to 90%, the correct answer of 30% would have been found with much less legwork. However, these questions aren't always so intuitive, so it's a good idea to work through the steps, even if the answer seems apparent from the outset.

Units

The United States customary system and the metric system each consist of distinct units to measure lengths and volume of liquids. The U.S. customary units for length, from smallest to largest, are: inch (in), foot (ft), yard (yd), and mile (mi). The metric units for length, from smallest to largest, are: millimeter (mm), centimeter (cm), decimeter (dm), meter (m), and kilometer (km). The relative size of each unit of length is shown below.

U.S. Customary	Metric	Conversion
12 in = 1 ft	10 mm = 1 cm	1 in = 2.54 cm
36 in = 3 ft = 1 yd	10 cm = 1 dm(decimeter)	1 m ≈ 3.28 ft ≈ 1.09 yd
5,280 ft = 1,760 yd = 1 mi	100 cm = 10 dm = 1 m	1 mi ≈ 1.6 km
	1,000 m = 1 km	

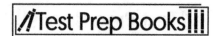

The U.S. customary units for volume of liquids, from smallest to largest, are: fluid ounces (fl oz), cup (c), pint (pt), quart (qt), and gallon (gal). The metric units for volume of liquids, from smallest to largest, are: milliliter (mL), centiliter (cL), deciliter (dL), liter (L), and kiloliter (kL). The relative size of each unit of liquid volume is shown below.

U.S. Customary	Metric	Conversion
8 fl oz = 1 c	10 mL = 1 cL	1 pt ≈ 0.473 L
2 c = 1 pt	10 cL = 1 dL	1 L ≈ 1.057 qt
4 c = 2 pt = 1 qt	1,000 mL = 100 cL = 10 dL = 1L	1 gal ≈ 3.785 L
4 qt = 1 gal	1,000 L = 1 kL	

The U.S. customary system measures weight (how strongly Earth is pulling on an object) in the following units, from least to greatest: ounce (oz), pound (lb), and ton. The metric system measures mass (the quantity of matter within an object) in the following units, from least to greatest: milligram (mg), centigram (cg), gram (g), kilogram (kg), and metric ton (MT).

The relative sizes of each unit of weight and mass are shown below.

U.S. Measures of Weight	Metric Measures of Mass
16 oz = 1 lb	10 mg = 1 cg
2,000 lb = 1 ton	100 cg = 1 g
	1,000 g = 1 kg
	1,000 kg = 1 MT

Metric System

Aside from the United States, most countries in the world have adopted the **metric system** embodied in the International System of Units (SI). The three main SI base units used in the metric system are the meter (m), the kilogram (kg), and the liter (L); meters measure length, kilograms measure mass, and liters measure volume.

These three units can use different prefixes, which indicate larger or smaller versions of the unit by powers of ten. This can be thought of as making a new unit, which is sized by multiplying the original unit in size by a factor.

These prefixes and associated factors are:

Metric Prefixes			
Prefix	Symbol	Multiplier	Exponential
kilo	k	1,000	10^3
hecto	h	100	10^2
deca	da	10	10^1
no prefix		1	10^0
deci	d	0.1	10^{-1}
centi	c	0.01	10^{-2}
milli	m	0.001	10^{-3}

The correct prefix is then attached to the base. Some examples:

1 milliliter equals .001 liters.

1 kilogram equals 1,000 grams.

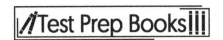

Some units of measure are represented as square or cubic units depending on the solution. For example, perimeter is measured in linear units, area is measured in square units, and volume is measured in cubic units.

Also, be sure to use the most appropriate unit for the thing being measured. A building's height might be measured in feet or meters while the length of a nail might be measured in inches or centimeters. Additionally, for SI units, the prefix should be chosen to provide the most succinct available value. For example, the mass of a bag of fruit would likely be measured in kilograms rather than grams or milligrams, and the length of a bacteria cell would likely be measured in micrometers rather than centimeters or kilometers.

Conversion Between Units
Converting measurements in different units between the two systems can be difficult because they follow different rules. The best method is to look up an English to Metric system conversion factor and then use a series of equivalent fractions to set up an equation to convert the units of one of the measurements into those of the other.

The table below lists some common conversion values that are useful for problems involving measurements with units in both systems:

English System	Metric System
1 inch	2.54 cm
1 foot	0.3048 m
1 yard	0.914 m
1 mile	1.609 km
1 ounce	28.35 g
1 pound	0.454 kg
1 fluid ounce	29.574 mL
1 quart	0.946 L
1 gallon	3.785 L

Consider the example where a scientist wants to convert 6.8 inches to centimeters. The table above is used to find that there are 2.54 centimeters in every inch, so the following equation should be set up and solved:

$$\frac{6.8 \text{ in}}{1} \times \frac{2.54 \text{ cm}}{1 \text{ in}} = 17.272 \text{ cm}$$

Notice how the inches in the numerator of the initial figure and the denominator of the conversion factor cancel out. (This equation could have been written simply as 6.8 in × 2.54 cm = 17.272 cm, but it was shown in detail to illustrate the steps). The goal in any conversion equation is to set up the fractions so that the units you are trying to convert from cancel out and the units you desire remain.

For a more complicated example, consider converting 2.15 kilograms into ounces. The first step is to convert kilograms into grams and then grams into ounces. Note that the measurement you begin with does not have to be put in a fraction.

So, in this case, 2.15 kg is by itself although it's technically the numerator of a fraction:

$$2.15 \text{ kg} \times \frac{1,000 \text{g}}{\text{kg}} = 2150 \text{ g}$$

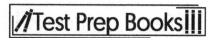

Then, use the conversion factor from the table to convert grams to ounces:

$$2{,}150 \text{ g} \times \frac{1 \text{ oz}}{28.35 \text{ g}} = 75.8$$

Geometric Quantities

Side Lengths of Shapes When Given the Area or Perimeter

The **perimeter** of a polygon is the distance around the outside of the two-dimensional figure or the sum of the lengths of all the sides. Perimeter is a one-dimensional measurement and is therefore expressed in linear units such as centimeters (cm), feet (ft), and miles (mi). The perimeter (P) of a figure can be calculated by adding together each of the sides.

Properties of certain polygons allow that the perimeter may be obtained by using formulas. A regular polygon is one in which all sides have equal length and all interior angles have equal measures, such as a square and an equilateral triangle. To find the perimeter of a regular polygon, the length of one side is multiplied by the number of sides.

A rectangle consists of two sides called the length (l), which have equal measures, and two sides called the width (w), which have equal measures. Therefore, the perimeter (P) of a rectangle can be expressed as:

$$P = l + l + w + w$$

This can be simplified to produce the following formula to find the perimeter of a rectangle:

$$P = 2l + 2w \text{ or } P = 2(l + w)$$

The perimeter of a square is measured by adding together all of the sides. Since a square has four equal sides, its perimeter can be calculated by multiplying the length of one side by 4. Thus, the formula is $P = 4 \times s$, where s equals one side. For example, the following square has side lengths of 5 meters:

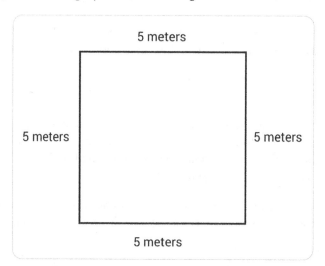

The perimeter is 20 meters because 4 times 5 is 20.

Like a square, a rectangle's perimeter is measured by adding together all of the sides. But as the sides are unequal, the formula is different. A rectangle has equal values for its lengths (long sides) and equal values for its widths (short sides), so the perimeter formula for a rectangle is:

$$P = l + l + w + w = 2l + 2w$$

100

l equals length
w equals width

Consider the following problem:

The total perimeter of a rectangular garden is 36m. If the length of each side is 12m, what is the width?

The formula for the perimeter of a rectangle is $P = 2L + 2W$, where P is the perimeter, L is the length, and W is the width. The first step is to substitute all of the data into the formula:

$$36 = 2(12) + 2W$$

Simplify by multiplying 2×12:

$$36 = 24 + 2W$$

Simplifying this further by subtracting 24 on each side gives:

$$36 - 24 = 24 - 24 + 2W$$

$$12 = 2W$$

Divide by 2:

$$6 = W$$

The width is 6 cm. Remember to test this answer by substituting this value into the original formula:

$$36 = 2(12) + 2(6)$$

A triangle's perimeter is measured by adding together the three sides, so the formula is $P = a + b + c$, where a, b, and c are the values of the three sides. The area is calculated by multiplying the length of the base times the height times ½, so the formula is:

$$A = \frac{1}{2} \times b \times h = \frac{bh}{2}$$

The base is the bottom of the triangle, and the height is the distance from the base to the peak. If a problem asks to calculate the area of a triangle, it will provide the base and height.

A circle's perimeter—also known as its circumference—is measured by multiplying the diameter (the straight line measured from one end to the direct opposite end of the circle) by π, so the formula is $\pi \times d$. This is sometimes expressed by the formula $C = 2 \times \pi \times r$, where r is the radius of the circle. These formulas are equivalent, as the radius equals half of the diameter.

Missing side lengths can be determined using subtraction. For example, if you are told that a triangle has a perimeter of 34 inches and that one side is 12 inches, another side is 16 inches, and the third side is unknown, you can calculate the length of that unknown side by setting up the following subtraction problem:

$$34 \text{ inches} = 12 \text{ inches} + 16 \text{ inches} + x$$

$$34 \text{ inches} = 28 \text{ inches} + x$$

$$6 \text{ inches} = x$$

101

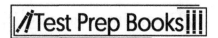

Therefore, the missing side length is 6 inches.

Area and Perimeter of Two-Dimensional Shapes

As mentioned, the **perimeter** of a polygon is the distance around the outside of the two-dimensional figure. Perimeter is a one-dimensional measurement and is therefore expressed in linear units such as centimeters (cm), feet (ft), and miles (mi). The perimeter (P) of a figure can be calculated by adding together each of the sides.

Properties of certain polygons allow that the perimeter may be obtained by using formulas. A rectangle consists of two sides called the length (l), which have equal measures, and two sides called the width (w), which have equal measures. Therefore, the perimeter (P) of a rectangle can be expressed as:

$$P = l + l + w + w$$

This can be simplified to produce the following formula to find the perimeter of a rectangle:

$$P = 2l + 2w \text{ or } P = 2(l + w)$$

A regular polygon is one in which all sides have equal length and all interior angles have equal measures, such as a square and an equilateral triangle. To find the perimeter of a regular polygon, the length of one side is multiplied by the number of sides. For example, to find the perimeter of an equilateral triangle with a side of length of 4 feet, 4 feet is multiplied by 3 (number of sides of a triangle). The perimeter of a regular octagon (8 sides) with a side of length of $\frac{1}{2}$ cm is:

$$\frac{1}{2} \text{cm} \times 8 = 4 \text{ cm}$$

The **area** of a polygon is the number of square units needed to cover the interior region of the figure. Area is a two-dimensional measurement. Therefore, area is expressed in square units, such as square centimeters (cm^2), square feet (ft^2), or square miles (mi^2). Regarding the area of a rectangle with sides of length x and y, the area is given by xy. For a triangle with a base of length b and a height of length h, the area is $\frac{1}{2}bh$. To find the area (A) of a parallelogram, the length of the base (b) is multiplied by the length of the height (h) $\rightarrow A = b \times h$. Similar to triangles, the height of the parallelogram is measured from one base to the other at a 90° angle (or perpendicular).

Area = bh

Perimeter = 2(a + b)

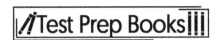

The area of a trapezoid can be calculated using the formula: $A = \frac{1}{2} \times h(b_1 + b_2)$, where h is the height and b_1 and b_2 are the parallel bases of the trapezoid.

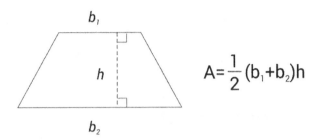

The area of a regular polygon can be determined by using its perimeter and the length of the **apothem**. The apothem is a line from the center of the regular polygon to any of its sides at a right angle. (Note that the perimeter of a regular polygon can be determined given the length of only one side.) The formula for the area (A) of a regular polygon is:

$$A = \frac{1}{2} \times a \times P$$

a is the length of the apothem, and P is the perimeter of the figure.

Consider the following regular pentagon:

To find the area, the perimeter (P) is calculated first: $8 \text{ cm} \times 5 \rightarrow P = 40 \text{ cm}$. Then the perimeter and the apothem are used to find the area (A):

$$A = \frac{1}{2} \times a \times P$$

$$A = \frac{1}{2} \times (6 \text{ cm}) \times (40 \text{ cm})$$

$$A = 120 \text{ cm}^2$$

Note that the unit is:

$$\text{cm}^2 \rightarrow \text{cm} \times \text{cm} = \text{cm}^2$$

103

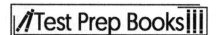
The area of irregular polygons is found by decomposing, or breaking apart, the figure into smaller shapes. When the area of the smaller shapes is determined, the area of the smaller shapes will produce the area of the original figure when added together. Consider the example below:

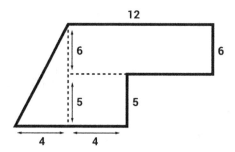

The irregular polygon is decomposed into two rectangles and a triangle. The area of the large rectangle ($A = l \times w \rightarrow A = 12 \times 6$) is 72 square units. The area of the small rectangle is 20 square units:

$$A = 4 \times 5$$

The area of the triangle:

$$A = \frac{1}{2} \times b \times h$$

$$A = \frac{1}{2} \times 4 \times 11$$

22 square units

The sum of the areas of these figures produces the total area of the original polygon:

$$A = 72 + 20 + 22$$

$$A = 114 \text{ square units}$$

The perimeter (P) of the figure below is calculated by:

$$P = 9\,\text{m} + 5\,\text{m} + 4\,\text{m} + 6\,\text{m} + 8\,\text{m} \rightarrow P = 32\,\text{m}$$

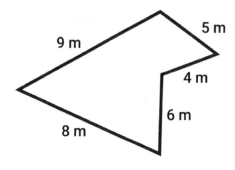

104

Area, Circumference, Radius, and Diameter of a Circle

A **circle** can be defined as the set of all points that are the same distance (known as the **radius**, r) from a single point (known as the **center** of the circle). The center has coordinates (h, k), and any point on the circle can be labelled with coordinates (x, y).

The **circumference** of a circle is the distance traveled by following the edge of the circle for one complete revolution, and the length of the circumference is given by $2\pi r$, where r is the radius of the circle. The formula for circumference is $C = 2\pi r$.

The area of a circle is calculated through the formula:

$$A = \pi \times r^2$$

The test will indicate either to leave the answer with π attached or to calculate to the nearest decimal place, which means multiplying by 3.14 for π.

Given two points on the circumference of a circle, the path along the circle between those points is called an **arc** of the circle. For example, the arc between B and C is denoted by a thinner line:

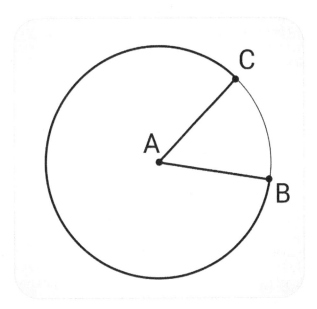

The length of the path along an arc is called the **arc length**. If the circle has radius r, then the arc length is given by multiplying the measure of the angle in radians by the radius of the circle.

Pythagorean Theorem

The Pythagorean theorem is an important concept in geometry. It states that for right triangles, the sum of the squares of the two shorter sides will be equal to the square of the longest side (also called the **hypotenuse**). The longest side will always be the side opposite to the 90° angle. If this side is called c, and the other two sides are a and b, then the Pythagorean theorem states that:

$$c^2 = a^2 + b^2$$

Since lengths are always positive, this also can be written as:

$$c = \sqrt{a^2 + b^2}$$

A diagram to show the parts of a triangle using the Pythagorean theorem is below.

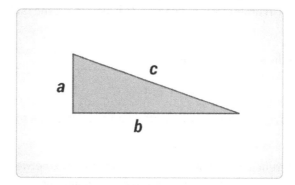

As an example of the theorem, suppose that Shirley has a rectangular field that is 5 feet wide and 12 feet long, and she wants to split it in half using a fence that goes from one corner to the opposite corner. How long will this fence need to be? To figure this out, note that this makes the field into two right triangles, whose hypotenuse will be the fence dividing it in half. Therefore, the fence length will be given by:

$$\sqrt{5^2 + 12^2} = \sqrt{169} = 13 \text{ feet long}$$

Volume and Surface Area of Three-Dimensional Shapes

Geometry in three dimensions is similar to geometry in two dimensions. The main new feature is that three points now define a unique **plane** that passes through each of them. Three-dimensional objects can be made by putting together two-dimensional figures in different surfaces. Below, some of the possible three-dimensional figures will be provided, along with formulas for their volumes and surface areas.

Volume is the measurement of how much space an object occupies, like how much space is in the cube. Volume questions will ask how much of something is needed to completely fill the object. The most common surface area and volume questions deal with spheres, cubes, and rectangular prisms.

Surface area of a three-dimensional figure refers to the number of square units needed to cover the entire surface of the figure. This concept is similar to using wrapping paper to completely cover the outside of a box. For example, if a triangular pyramid has a surface area of 17 square inches (written 17 in^2), it will take 17 squares, each with sides one inch in length, to cover the entire surface of the pyramid. Surface area is also measured in square units.

A **rectangular prism** is a box whose sides are all rectangles meeting at 90° angles. Such a box has three dimensions: length, width, and height. If the length is x, the width is y, and the height is z, then the volume is given by $V = xyz$.

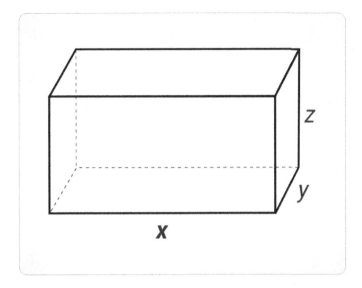

The **surface area** will be given by computing the surface area of each rectangle and adding them together. There is a total of six rectangles. Two of them have sides of length x and y, two have sides of length y and z, and two have sides of length x and z. Therefore, the total surface area will be given by:

$$SA = 2xy + 2yz + 2xz$$

A **cube** is a special type of rectangular solid in which its length, width, and height are the same. If this length is s, then the formula for the volume of a cube is $V = s \times s \times s$. The surface area of a cube is $SA = 6s^2$.

A **rectangular pyramid** is a figure with a rectangular base and four triangular sides that meet at a single vertex. If the rectangle has sides of length x and y, then the volume will be given by $V = \frac{1}{3}xyh$.

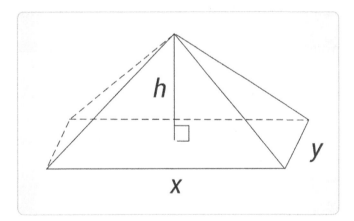

Many three-dimensional figures (solid figures) can be represented by nets consisting of rectangles and triangles. The surface area of such solids can be determined by adding the areas of each of its faces and bases. Finding the surface

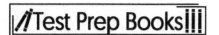
area using this method requires calculating the areas of rectangles and triangles. To find the area (A) of a rectangle, the length (l) is multiplied by the width:

$$(w) \rightarrow A = l \times w$$

The area of a rectangle with a length of 8 cm and a width of 4 cm is calculated:

$$A = (8 \text{ cm}) \times (4 \text{ cm}) \rightarrow A = 32 \text{ cm}^2$$

To calculate the area (A) of a triangle, the product of $\frac{1}{2}$, the base (b), and the height (h) is found:

$$A = \frac{1}{2} \times b \times h$$

Note that the height of a triangle is measured from the base to the vertex opposite of it forming a right angle with the base. The area of a triangle with a base of 11 cm and a height of 6 cm is calculated:

$$A = \frac{1}{2} \times (11 \text{ cm}) \times (6 \text{ cm})$$

$$A = 33 \text{ cm}^2$$

Consider the following triangular prism, which is represented by a net consisting of two triangles and three rectangles.

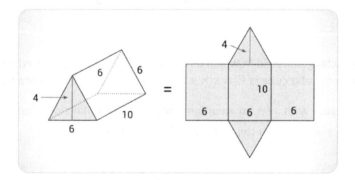

The surface area of the prism can be determined by adding the areas of each of its faces and bases.

$$Surface\ Area\ (SA) = area\ of\ triangle + area\ of\ triangle$$
$$+ area\ of\ rectangle + area\ of\ rectangle + area\ of\ rectangle$$

$$SA = \left(\frac{1}{2} \times b \times h\right) + \left(\frac{1}{2} \times b \times h\right) + (l \times w) + (l \times w) + (l \times w)$$

$$SA = \left(\frac{1}{2} \times 6 \times 4\right) + \left(\frac{1}{2} \times 6 \times 4\right) + (6 \times 10) + (6 \times 10) + (6 \times 10)$$

$$SA = (12) + (12) + (60) + (60) + (60)$$

$$SA = 204 \text{ square units}$$

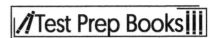

A **sphere** is a set of points all of which are equidistant from some central point. It is like a circle, but in three dimensions. The volume of a sphere of radius r is given by:

$$V = \frac{4}{3}\pi r^3$$

The surface area is given by $A = 4\pi r^2$.

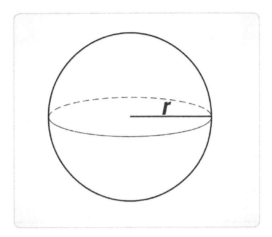

The volume of a **cylinder** is then found by adding a third dimension onto the circle. Volume of a cylinder is calculated by multiplying the area of the base (which is a circle) by the height of the cylinder. Doing so results in the equation:

$$V = \pi r^2 h$$

The volume of a **cone** is $\frac{1}{3}$ of the volume of a cylinder. Therefore, the formula for the volume of a **cone** is:

$$\frac{1}{3}\pi r^2 h$$

Solving Three-Dimensional Problems

Three-dimensional objects can be simplified into related two-dimensional shapes to solve problems. This simplification can make problem-solving a much easier experience. An isometric representation of a three-dimensional object can be completed so that important properties (e.g., shape, relationships of faces and surfaces) are noted. Edges and vertices can be translated into two-dimensional objects as well.

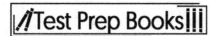

Consider this three-dimensional object that's been partitioned into two-dimensional representations of its faces:

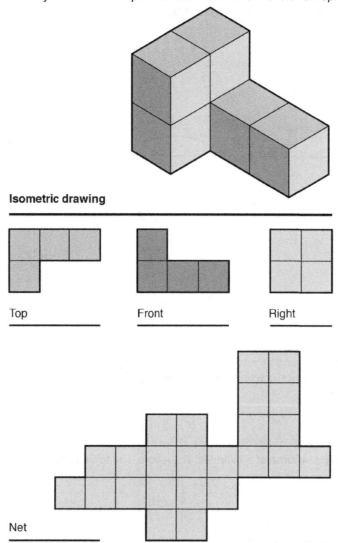

Isometric drawing

Top   Front   Right

Net

The net represents the sum of the three different faces. Depending on the problem, using a smaller portion of the given shape may be helpful, by simplifying the steps necessary to solve.

Many objects in the real world consist of three-dimensional shapes such as prisms, cylinders, and spheres. Surface area problems involve quantifying the outside area of such a three-dimensional object, and volume problems involve quantifying how much space the object takes up. Surface area of a prism is the sum of the areas, which is simplified into $SA = 2A + Bh$, where A is the area of the base, B is the perimeter of the base, and h is the height of the prism. The volume of the same prism is $V = Ah$.

The surface area of a cylinder is equal to the sum of the areas of each end and the side, which is:

$$SA = 2\pi rh + 2\pi r^2$$

Its volume is:

$$V = \pi r^2 h$$

110

Finally, the surface area of a sphere is $SA = 4\pi r^2$, and its volume is:

$$V = \frac{4}{3}\pi r^3$$

An example when one of these formulas should be used would be when calculating how much paint is needed for the outside of a house. In this scenario, surface area must be used. The sum of all individual areas of each side of the house must be found. Also, when calculating how much water a cylindrical tank can hold, a volume formula is used. Therefore, the amount of water that a cylindrical tank that is 8 feet tall with a radius of 3 feet is:

$$\pi \times 3^2 \times 8 = 226.1 \text{ cubic feet}$$

The formula used to calculate the volume of a cone is $\frac{1}{3}\pi r^2 h$. Essentially, the area of the base of the cone is multiplied by the cone's height. In a real-life example where the radius of a cone is 2 meters and the height of a cone is 5 meters, the volume of the cone is calculated by utilizing the formula:

$$\frac{1}{3}\pi 2^2 \times 5$$

After substituting 3.14 for π, the volume is 20.9 m^3.

Data & Information

Graphical Data Including Graphs, Tables, and More

A set of data can be visually displayed in various forms allowing for quick identification of characteristics of the set. **Histograms**, such as the one shown below, display the number of data points (vertical axis) that fall into given intervals (horizontal axis) across the range of the set. The histogram below displays the heights of black cherry trees in a certain city park. Each rectangle represents the number of trees with heights between a given five-point span. For example, the furthest bar to the right indicates that two trees are between 85 and 90 feet. Histograms can describe the center, spread, shape, and any unusual characteristics of a data set.

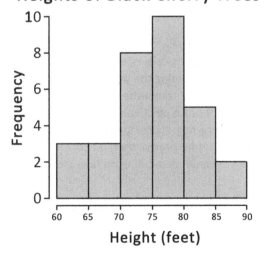

Heights of Black Cherry Trees

111

A **box plot**, also called a **box-and-whisker plot**, divides the data points into four groups and displays the five-number summary for the set as well as any outliers. The five-number summary consists of:

- The lower extreme: the lowest value that is not an outlier
- The higher extreme: the highest value that is not an outlier
- The median of the set: also referred to as the second quartile or Q_2
- The first quartile or Q_1: the median of values below Q_2
- The third quartile or Q_3: the median of values above Q_2

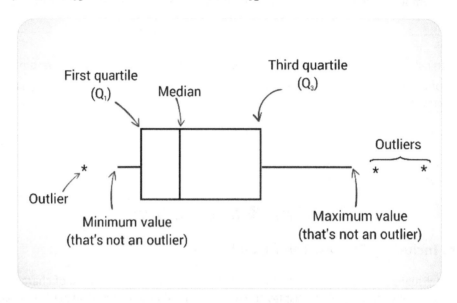

Suppose the box plot displays IQ scores for 12th grade students at a given school. The five-number summary of the data consists of: lower extreme (67); upper extreme (127); Q_2 or median (100); Q_1 (91); Q_3 (108); and outliers (135 and 140). Although all data points are not known from the plot, the points are divided into four quartiles each, including 25% of the data points. Therefore, 25% of students scored between 67 and 91, 25% scored between 91 and 100, 25% scored between 100 and 108, and 25% scored between 108 and 127. These percentages include the normal values for the set and exclude the outliers. This information is useful when comparing a given score with the rest of the scores in the set.

A **scatter plot** is a mathematical diagram that visually displays the relationship or connection between two variables. The independent variable is placed on the *x*-axis, or horizontal axis, and the dependent variable is placed on the *y*-axis, or vertical axis. When visually examining the points on the graph, if the points model a linear relationship, or if a line of best-fit can be drawn through the points with the points relatively close on either side, then a correlation exists. If the line of best-fit has a positive slope (rises from left to right), then the variables have a positive correlation. If the line of best-fit has a negative slope (falls from left to right), then the variables have a negative correlation. If a line of best-fit cannot be drawn, then no correlation exists. A positive or negative correlation can be categorized as strong or weak, depending on how closely the points are graphed around the line of best-fit.

Consider this display of correlations:

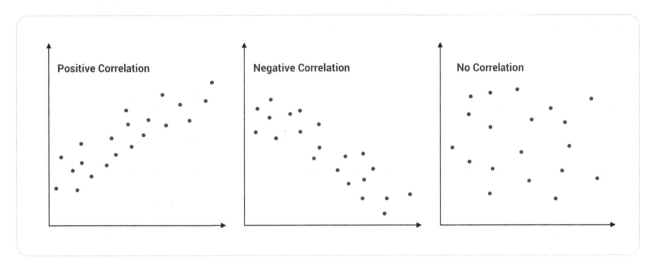

Like a scatter plot, a **line graph** compares variables that change continuously, typically over time. Paired data values (ordered pairs) are plotted on a coordinate grid with the x- and y-axis representing the variables. A line is drawn from each point to the next, going from left to right. The line graph below displays cell phone use for given years (two variables) for men, women, and both sexes (three data sets).

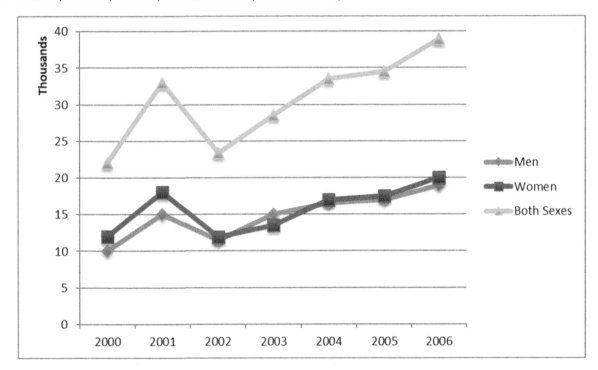

A **line plot**, also called **dot plot**, displays the frequency of data (numerical values) on a number line. To construct a line plot, a number line is used that includes all unique data values. It is marked with x's or dots above the value the number of times that the value occurs in the data set.

% Conformance to Goal

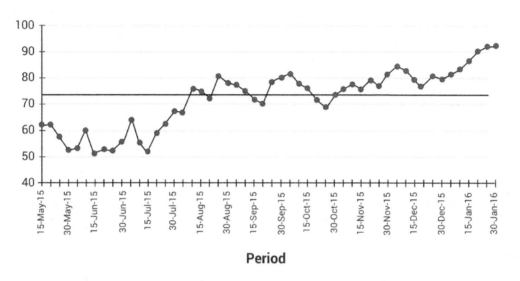

Period

A **bar graph** is a diagram in which the quantity of items within a specific classification is represented by the height of a rectangle. Each type of classification is represented by a rectangle of equal width. Here is an example of a bar graph:

Tablet Model Price Comparison

114

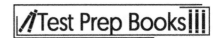

A **circle graph**, also called a **pie chart**, shows categorical data with each category representing a percentage of the whole data set. To make a circle graph, the percent of the data set for each category must be determined. To do so, the frequency of the category is divided by the total number of data points and converted to a percent. For example, if 80 people were asked what their favorite sport is and 20 responded basketball, basketball makes up 25% of the data:

$$\frac{20}{80} = 0.25 = 25\%$$

Each category in a data set is represented by a slice of the circle proportionate to its percentage of the whole.

A **stem-and-leaf plot** is a method of displaying sets of data by organizing numbers by their stems (usually the tens digit) and different leaf values (usually the ones digit).

For example, to organize a number of movie critic's ratings, as listed below, a stem-and-leaf plot could be utilized to display the information in a more condensed manner.

Movie critic scores: 47, 52, 56, 59, 61, 64, 66, 68, 68, 70, 73, 75, 79, 81, 83, 85, 86, 88, 88, 89, 90, 90, 91, 93, 94, 96, 96, 99.

	Movie Ratings
4	7
5	2 6 9
6	1 4 6 8 8
7	0 3 5 9
8	1 3 5 6 8 8 9
9	0 0 1 3 4 6 6 9
Key	6	1 represents 61

115

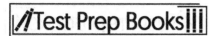

Looking at this stem and leaf plot, it is easy to ascertain key features of the data set. For example, what is the range of the data in the stem-and-leaf plot?

Using this method, it is easier to visualize the distribution of the scores and answer the question pertaining to the range of scores, which is:

$$99 - 47 = 52$$

A **tally chart** is a diagram in which tally marks are utilized to represent data. Tally marks are a means of showing a quantity of objects within a specific classification. Here is an example of a tally chart:

Number of days with rain	Number of weeks
0	‖
1	⊮ ‖
2	⊮ ‖‖
3	⊮ ⊮ ⊮
4	⊮
5	⊮ ‖
6	⊮
7	‖

Data is often recorded using fractions, such as half a mile, and understanding fractions is critical because of their popular use in real-world applications. Also, it is extremely important to label values with their units when using data. For example, regarding length, the number 2 is meaningless unless it is attached to a unit. Writing 2 cm shows that the number refers to the length of an object.

Graphing on the Coordinate Plane Using Mathematical Problems, Tables, and Patterns

Data can be recorded using a coordinate plane. Graphs are utilized frequently in real-world applications and can be seen in many facets of everyday life. A relationship can exist between the *x*- and *y*-coordinates that are plotted on a graph, and those values can represent a set of data that can be listed in a table. Going back and forth between the table and the graph is an important concept and defining the relationship between the variables is the key that links the data to a real-life application.

For example, temperature increases during a summer day. The *x*-coordinate can be used to represent hours in the day, and the *y*-coordinate can be used to represent the temperature in degrees. The graph would show the temperature at each hour of the day. Time is almost always plotted on the *x*-axis, and utilizing different units on each axis, if necessary, is important. Labeling the axes with units is also important.

Within the first quadrant of the coordinate plane, both the x and y values are positive. Most real-world problems can be plotted in this quadrant because most real-world quantities, such as time and distance, are positive. Consider the following table of values:

X	Y
1	2
2	4
3	6
4	8

Each row gives a coordinate pair. For example, the first row gives the coordinates (1,2). Each *x*-value tells you how far to move from the origin, the point (0,0), to the right, and each *y*-value tells you how far to move up from the origin.

Here is the graph of the points listed above in the table in addition to the origin:

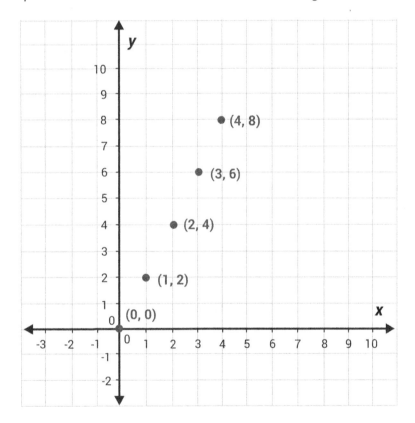

Notice that each *y*-value is found by doubling the *x*-value that forms the other portion of its coordinate pair.

Determining the Slope of a Line from a Graph, Equation, or Table

Rate of change for any line calculates the steepness of the line over a given interval. Rate of change is also known as the **slope** or rise/run. The slope of a linear function is given by the change in *y* divided by the change in *x*. So, the formula looks like this:

$$slope = \frac{y_2 - y_1}{x_2 - x_1}$$

117

In the graph below, two points are plotted. The first has the coordinates of (0, 1), and the second point is (2, 3). Remember that the x coordinate is always placed first in coordinate pairs. Work from left to right when identifying coordinates. Thus, the point on the left is point 1 (0, 1), and the point on the right is point 2 (2, 3).

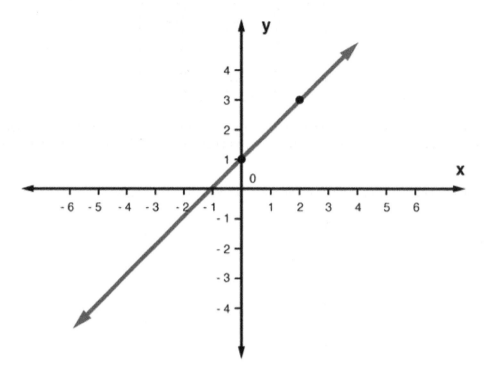

Now we just need to plug those numbers into the equation:

$$slope = \frac{3-1}{2-0}$$

$$slope = \frac{2}{2}$$

$$slope = 1$$

This means that for every increase of 1 for x, y also increased by 1. You can see this in the line. When x equaled 0, y equaled 1, and when x was increased to 1, y equaled 2.

Slope can be thought of as determining the rise over run:

$$slope = \frac{rise}{run}$$

The rise being the change vertically on the y axis and the run being the change horizontally on the x axis.

Proportional Relationships for Equations and Graphs

The rate of change for a linear function is constant and can be determined based on a few representations. One method is to place the equation in slope-intercept form: $y = mx + b$. Thus, m is the slope, and b is the y-intercept. In the graph below, the equation is $y = x + 1$, where the slope is 1 and the y-intercept is 1. For every vertical change of 1 unit, there is a horizontal change of 1 unit.

118

The x-intercept is -1, which is the point where the line crosses the x-axis:

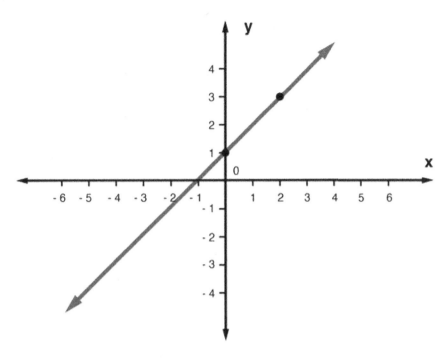

Let's look at an example of a proportional, or linear relationship, seen in the real world.

The graph above represents the relationship between distance traveled and time. To find the distance traveled in 80 minutes, the mark for 80 minutes is located at the bottom of the graph. By following this mark directly up on the graph, the corresponding point for 80 minutes is directly across from the 160 kilometer mark. This information indicates that the distance travelled in 80 minutes is 160 kilometers. To predict information not displayed on the graph, the way in which the variables change with respect to one another is determined. In this case, distance increases by 40 kilometers as time increases by 20 minutes. This information can be used to continue the data in the graph or convert the values to a table.

119

Let's try another example. Jim owns a car wash and charges $40 per car. The rent for the facility is $350 per month. An equation can be written to relate the number of cars Jim cleans to the money he makes per month. Let x represent the number of cars and y represent the profit Jim makes each month from the car wash. The equation $y = 40x - 350$ can be used to show Jim's profit or loss. Since this equation has two variables, the coordinate plane can be used to show the relationship and predict profit or loss for Jim. The following graph shows that Jim must wash at least nine cars to pay the rent, where $x = 9$. Anything nine cars and above yield a profit shown in the value on the y-axis.

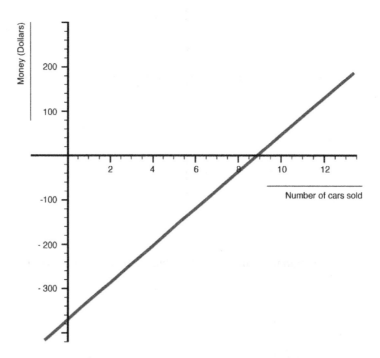

Features of Graphs and Tables for Linear and Nonlinear Relationships

As mentioned, linear relationships describe the way two quantities change with respect to each other. The relationship is defined as linear because a line is produced if all the sets of corresponding values are graphed on a coordinate grid. When expressing the linear relationship as an equation, the equation is often written in the form $y = mx + b$ (**slope-intercept form**) where m and b are numerical values and x and y are variables (for example, $y = 5x + 10$). The slope is the coefficient of x, and the y-intercept is the constant value. The slope of the line containing the same two points is:

$$m = \frac{y_2 - y_1}{x_2 - x_1}$$

and is also equal to rise/run. Given a linear equation and the value of either variable (x or y), the value of the other variable can be determined.

With polynomial functions such as quadratics, the x-intercepts represent zeros of the function. Finding the **zeros of polynomial functions** is the same process as finding the solutions of polynomial equations. These are the points at which the graph of the function crosses the x-axis. In the following quadratic equation, factoring the binomial leads to finding the zeros of the function:

$$x^2 - 5x + 6 = y$$

120

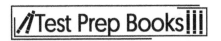

This equation factors into

$$(x - 3)(x - 2) = y$$

where 2 and 3 are found to be the zeros of the function when y is set equal to zero. The zeros of any function are the x-values where the graph of the function on the coordinate plane crosses the x-axis, which is the same as an x-intercept.

Determining the Graphical Properties and Sketch a Graph Given an Equation

Graphing a Linear Function

The process for graphing a line depends on the form in which its equation is written: slope-intercept form or standard form.

When an equation is written in slope-intercept form, $y = mx + b$, m represents the slope of the line and b represents the y-intercept. The y-intercept is the value of y when $x = 0$ and the point at which the graph of the line crosses the y-axis. The slope is the rate of change between the variables, expressed as a fraction. The fraction expresses the change in y compared to the change in x. If the slope is an integer, it should be written as a fraction with a denominator of 1. For example, 5 would be written as $\frac{5}{1}$.

To graph a line given an equation in slope-intercept form, the y-intercept should first be plotted. For example, to graph:

$$y = -\frac{2}{3}x + 7$$

the y-intercept of 7 would be plotted on the y-axis (vertical axis) at the point (0, 7). Next, the slope would be used to determine a second point for the line. Note that all that is necessary to graph a line is two points on that line. The slope will indicate how to get from one point on the line to another. The slope expresses vertical change (y) compared to horizontal change (x) and therefore is sometimes referred to as $\frac{rise}{run}$. The numerator indicates the change in the y value (move up for positive integers and move down for negative integers), and the denominator indicates the change in the x value. For the previous example, using the slope of $-\frac{2}{3}$, from the first point at the y-intercept, the second point should be found by counting down 2 and to the right 3. This point would be located at (3, 5).

When an equation is written in standard form, $Ax + By = C$, it is easy to identify the x- and y-intercepts for the graph of the line. Just as the y-intercept is the point at which the line intercepts the y-axis, the x-intercept is the point at which the line intercepts the x-axis. At the y-intercept, $x = 0$; and at the x-intercept, $y = 0$. Given an equation in standard form, $x = 0$ should be used to find the y-intercept. Likewise, $y = 0$ should be used to find the x-intercept. For example, to graph $3x + 2y = 6$, 0 for y results in $3x + 2(0) = 6$. Solving for y yields $x = 2$; therefore, an ordered pair for the line is (2, 0). Substituting 0 for x results in $3(0) + 2y = 6$. Solving for y yields $y =$

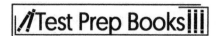

Math

3; therefore, an ordered pair for the line is (0, 3). The two ordered pairs (the *x*- and *y*-intercepts) can be plotted, and a straight line through them can be constructed.

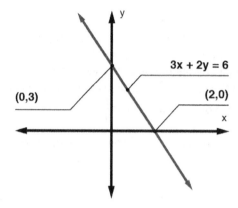

Graphing Linear and Nonlinear Relationships Between Two Quantities

A linear relationship between two quantities has a graph that is a straight line. The slope-intercept form of linear equation is $y = mx + b$, where m is the slope and b is the *y*-intercept. The slope of a line measures the steepness. If the slope is negative, the line decreases from left to right. If the slope is 0, the line is horizontal. If the slope is positive, the line increases from left to right. Here is an image that depicts the three cases:

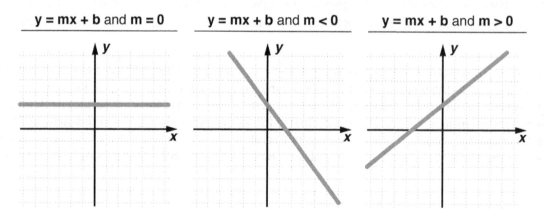

The point *b*, known as the *y*-intercept, is where the line crosses the *y*-axis. It is the point where the *x*-coordinate is 0. The x-intercept, which is where the line crosses the *x*-axis, can be found by letting the *y*-coordinate be equal to 0.

Consider the two lines $y = 5x + 2$ and $y = 10x + 4$. The first line has a slope of 5 and a y-intercept of 2. The second line has a slope of 10 and a y-intercept of 4. Therefore, we expect the second line to be steeper and to cross the y-axis at a higher point. Here are the graphs of each:

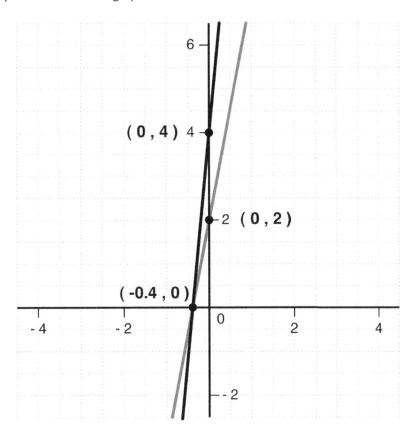

The gray line represents $y = 10x + 4$. Notices that it is steeper than the black line, which represents $y = 5x + 2$. Each line actually has the same y-intercept of (-0.4,0).

Linear relationships can also be represented using tables. In this case, there is a column for each variable. A corresponding x and y variable represents an ordered pair on a graph. Consider the same two lines as before. Here are two tables that show some ordered pairs on each line:

$y = 5x + 2$	
x	y
-1	-3
0	2
1	7
2	12
3	17

$y = 10x + 4$	
x	y
-1	-6
0	4
1	14
2	24
3	34

Because each table shows a point where $x = 0$, the y-intercept is shown here. Also, one can view the slope in the table as well. Because the x-values increase only by 1, one takes the difference of two corresponding y-values. This quantity shows the rate of change of each line.

123

Given the graph of a nonlinear relationship, one can look at intervals over which the function is increasing and decreasing, positive (above the x-axis) and negative (below the x-axis), and the end behavior. The end behavior refers to the trend of the graph at the ends of the x-axis (close to ∞ and −∞). Other characteristics involve relative maxima (maximum points), which are points in which the graph is higher than points on either side of this location. They are points where the graph changes from increasing to decreasing. Relative minima (minimum points) are points in which the graph is lower than the points on the other sides of this location. These are points where the graph changes from decreasing to increasing.

Consider the following graph of $y = x^3 + 2x^2 + 1$:

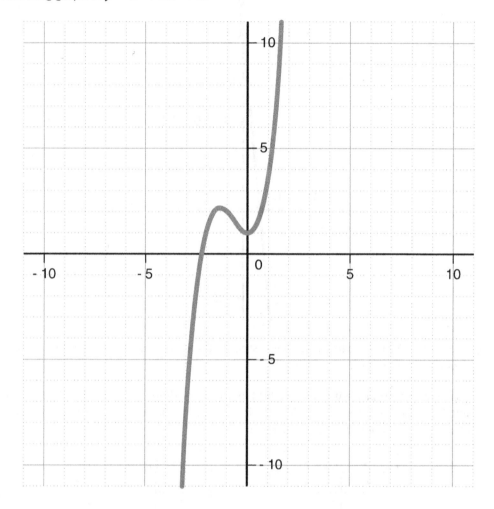

This graph has one local minimum and one local maximum. The graph is increasing until the point of the local maximum, and then it decreases to the local minimum. Then, the graph increases again. Note the end behavior: as $x \rightarrow \infty, y \rightarrow \infty$ and as $x \rightarrow -\infty, y \rightarrow -\infty$. This graph also has one x and one y-intercept.

A graph is symmetric with respect to the y-axis if one can fold the graph over the y-axis and the sides align. A graph is symmetric with respect to the x-axis if one can fold the graph over the x-axis and the sides align. Finally, a graph is periodic if it repeats itself over regular intervals.

Consider the graph of $y = \cos(x)$. It has a period of 2π and it is symmetric with respect to the y-axis.

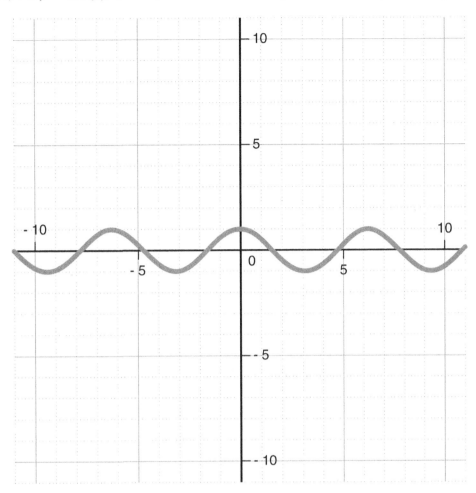

Mean, Median, Mode, and Range

Suppose that X is a set of data points $(x_1, x_2, x_3, \ldots x_n)$, and some description of the general properties of this data need to be found.

The first property that can be defined for this set of data is the **mean**. To find the mean, add up all the data points, then divide by the total number of data points. This can be expressed using **summation notation** as:

$$\bar{X} = \frac{x_1 + x_2 + x_3 + \cdots + x_n}{n} = \frac{1}{n}\sum_{i=1}^{n} x_i$$

For example, suppose that in a class of 10 students, the scores on a test were 50, 60, 65, 65, 75, 80, 85, 85, 90, 100. Therefore, the average test score will be:

$$\frac{1}{10}(50 + 60 + 65 + 65 + 75 + 80 + 85 + 85 + 90 + 100) = 75.5$$

The mean is a useful number if the distribution of data is normal (more on this later), which roughly means that the frequency of different outcomes has a single peak and is roughly equally distributed on both sides of that peak.

125

However, it is less useful in some cases where the data might be split or where there are some outliers. **Outliers** are data points that are far from the rest of the data. For example, suppose there are 90 employees and 10 executives at a company. The executives make $1,000 per hour, and the employees make $10 per hour. Therefore, the average pay rate will be:

$$\frac{1{,}000 \times 10 + 10 \times 90}{100} = \$109 \text{ per hour}$$

In this case, this average is not very descriptive.

Another useful measurement is the **median**. In a data set X consisting of data points $x_1, x_2, x_3, \dots x_n$, the median is the point in the middle. The middle refers to the point where half the data comes before it and half comes after, when the data is recorded in numerical order. If n is odd, then the median is:

$$x_{\frac{n+1}{2}}$$

If n is even, it is defined as:

$$\frac{1}{2}\left(x_{\frac{n}{2}} + x_{\frac{n}{2}+1}\right)$$

the mean of the two data points closest to the middle of the data points. In the previous example of test scores, the two middle points are 75 and 80. Since there is no single point, the average of these two scores needs to be found. The average is:

$$\frac{75 + 80}{2} = 77.5$$

The median is generally a good value to use if there are a few outliers in the data. It prevents those outliers from affecting the "middle" value as much as when using the mean.

Since an outlier is a data point that is far from most of the other data points in a data set, this means an outlier also is any point that is far from the median of the data set. The outliers can have a substantial effect on the mean of a data set, but they usually do not change the median or mode, or do not change them by a large quantity. For example, consider the data set (3, 5, 6, 6, 6, 8). This has a median of 6 and a mode of 6, with a mean of $\frac{34}{6} \approx 5.67$. Now, suppose a new data point of 1,000 is added so that the data set is now (3, 5, 6, 6, 6, 8, 1,000). The median and mode, which are both still 6, remain unchanged. However, the average is now $\frac{1{,}034}{7}$, which is approximately 147.7. In this case, the median and mode will be better descriptions for most of the data points.

Outliers in a given data set are sometimes the result of an error by the experimenter, but oftentimes, they are perfectly valid data points that must be taken into consideration.

One additional measure to define for X is the **mode**. This is the data point that appears more frequently. If two or more data points all tie for the most frequent appearance, then each of them is considered a mode. In the case of the test scores, where the numbers were 50, 60, 65, 65, 75, 80, 85, 85, 90, 100, there are two modes: 65 and 85.

The **first quartile** of a set of data X refers to the largest value from the first ¼ of the data points. In practice, there are sometimes slightly different definitions that can be used, such as the median of the first half of the data points (excluding the median itself if there are an odd number of data points). The term also has a slightly different use:

when it is said that a data point lies in the first quartile, it means it is less than or equal to the median of the first half of the data points. Conversely, if it lies *at* the first quartile, then it is equal to the first quartile.

When it is said that a data point lies in the **second quartile**, it means it is between the first quartile and the median.

The **third quartile** refers to data that lies between ½ and ¾ of the way through the data set. Again, there are various methods for defining this precisely, but the simplest way is to include all of the data that lie between the median and the median of the top half of the data.

Data that lies in the **fourth quartile** refers to all of the data above the third quartile.

Percentiles may be defined in a similar manner to quartiles. Generally, this is defined in the following manner:

If a data point lies in the **nth percentile**, this means it lies in the range of the first n% of the data.

If a data point lies at the **nth percentile**, then it means that n% of the data lies below this data point.

Given a data set X consisting of data points $(x_1, x_2, x_3, \dots x_n)$, the **variance of X** is defined to be:

$$\frac{\sum_{i=1}^{n}(x_i - \bar{X})^2}{n}$$

This means that the variance of X is the average of the squares of the differences between each data point and the mean of X. In the formula, $\bar{X}$ is the mean of the values in the data set, and x_i represents each individual value in the data set. The sigma notation indicates that the sum should be found with n being the number of values to add together. $i = 1$ means that the values should begin with the first value.

Given a data set X consisting of data points $(x_1, x_2, x_3, \dots x_n)$, the **standard deviation of X** is defined to be

$$s_x = \sqrt{\frac{\sum_{i=1}^{n}(x_i - \bar{X})^2}{n}}$$

In other words, the standard deviation is the square root of the variance.

Both the variance and the standard deviation are measures of how much the data tend to be spread out. When the standard deviation is low, the data points are mostly clustered around the mean. When the standard deviation is high, this generally indicates that the data are quite spread out, or else that there are a few substantial outliers.

As a simple example, compute the standard deviation for the data set (1, 3, 3, 5). First, compute the mean, which will be:

$$\frac{1+3+3+5}{4} = \frac{12}{4} = 3$$

Now, find the variance of X with the formula:

$$\sum_{i=1}^{4}(x_i - \bar{X})^2 = (1-3)^2 + (3-3)^2 + (3-3)^2 + (5-3)^2$$

$$-2^2 + 0^2 + 0^2 + 2^2 = 8$$

127

Therefore, the variance is $\frac{8}{4} = 2$. Taking the square root, the standard deviation will be $\sqrt{2}$.

Note that the standard deviation only depends upon the mean, not upon the median or mode(s). Generally, if there are multiple modes that are far apart from one another, the standard deviation will be high. A high standard deviation does not always mean there are multiple modes, however.

Describing a Set of Data

A set of data can be described in terms of its center, spread, shape and any unusual features. The center of a data set can be measured by its mean, median, or mode. The spread of a data set refers to how far the data points are from the center (mean or median). The spread can be measured by the range or by the quartiles and interquartile range. A data set with all its data points clustered around the center will have a small spread. A data set covering a wide range of values will have a large spread.

When a data set is displayed as a **histogram** or frequency distribution plot, the shape indicates if a sample is normally distributed, symmetrical, or has measures of skewness or kurtosis. When graphed, a data set with a **normal distribution** will resemble a bell curve.

If the data set is symmetrical, each half of the graph when divided at the center is a mirror image of the other. If the graph has fewer data points to the right, the data is **skewed right**. If it has fewer data points to the left, the data is **skewed left**.

Right-Skewed   Symmetric   Left-Skewed

Kurtosis is a measure of whether the data is heavy-tailed with a high number of outliers, or light-tailed with a low number of outliers.

128

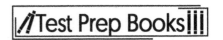

A description of a data set should include any unusual features such as gaps or outliers. A **gap** is a span within the range of the data set containing no data points. An **outlier** is a data point with a value either extremely large or extremely small when compared to the other values in the set.

Counting Techniques

The **addition rule** for probabilities states that the probability of A or B happening is:

$$P(A \cup B) = P(A) + P(B) - P(A \cap B)$$

Note that the subtraction of $P(A \cap B)$ must be performed, or else it would result in double counting any outcomes that lie in both A and in B. For example, suppose that a 20-sided die is being rolled. Fred bets that the outcome will be greater than 10, while Helen bets that it will be greater than 4 but less than 15. What is the probability that at least one of them is correct?

We apply the rule:

$$P(A \cup B) = P(A) + P(B) - P(A \cap B)$$

A is where outcome x is in the range $x > 10$, and B is where outcome x is in the range $4 < x < 15$.

$$P(A) = 10 \times \frac{1}{20} = \frac{1}{2}$$

$$P(B) = 10 \times \frac{1}{20} = \frac{1}{2}$$

$P(A \cap B)$ can be computed by noting that $A \cap B$ means the outcome x is in the range $10 < x < 15$, so

$$P(A \cap B) = 4 \times \frac{1}{20} = \frac{1}{5}$$

Therefore,

$$P(A \cup B) = P(A) + P(B) - P(A \cap B)$$

$$\frac{1}{2} + \frac{1}{2} - \frac{1}{5} = \frac{4}{5}$$

Note that in this particular example, we could also have directly reasoned about the set of possible outcomes $A \cup B$, by noting that this would mean that x must be in the range $5 \leq x$. However, this is not always the case, depending on the given information.

The **multiplication rule** for probabilities states the probability of A and B both happening is:

$$P(A \cap B) = P(A)P(B|A)$$

As an example, suppose that when Jamie wears black pants, there is a ½ probability that she wears a black shirt as well, and that she wears black pants ¾ of the time. What is the probability that she is wearing both a black shirt and black pants?

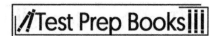

To figure this, use the above formula, where A will be "Jamie is wearing black pants," while B will be "Jamie is wearing a black shirt." It is known that $P(A)$ is ¾. It is also known that $P(B|A) = \frac{1}{2}$. Multiplying the two, the probability that she is wearing both black pants and a black shirt is:

$$P(A)P(B|A) = \frac{3}{4} \times \frac{1}{2} = \frac{3}{8}$$

Probability of an Event

Given a set of possible outcomes X, a **probability distribution** of X is a function that assigns a probability to each possible outcome. If the outcomes are $(x_1, x_2, x_3, \ldots x_n)$, and the probability distribution is p, then the following rules are applied.

- $0 \le p(x_i) \le 1$, for any i.
- $\sum_{i=1}^{n} p(x_i) = 1$.

In other words, the probability of a given outcome must be between zero and 1, while the total probability must be 1.

If $p(x_i)$ is constant, then this is called a **uniform probability distribution**, and $p(x_i) = \frac{1}{n}$. For example, on a six-sided die, the probability of each of the six outcomes will be $\frac{1}{6}$.

If seeking the probability of an outcome occurring in some specific range A of possible outcomes, written $P(A)$, add up the probabilities for each outcome in that range. For example, consider a six-sided die, and figure the probability of getting a 3 or lower when it is rolled. The possible rolls are 1, 2, 3, 4, 5, and 6. So, to get a 3 or lower, a roll of 1, 2, or 3 must be completed. The probabilities of each of these is $\frac{1}{6}$, so add these to get:

$$p(1) + p(2) + p(3) = \frac{1}{6} + \frac{1}{6} + \frac{1}{6} = \frac{1}{2}$$

An outcome occasionally lies within some range of possibilities B, and the probability that the outcomes also lie within some set of possibilities A needs to be figured. This is called a **conditional probability**. It is written as $P(A|B)$, which is read "the probability of A given B." The general formula for computing conditional probabilities is:

$$P(A|B) = \frac{P(A \cap B)}{P(B)}$$

However, when dealing with uniform probability distributions, simplify this a bit. Write $|A|$ to indicate the number of outcomes in A. Then, for uniform probability distributions, write:

$$P(A|B) = \frac{|A \cap B|}{|B|}$$

(recall that $A \cap B$ means "A intersect B," and consists of all of the outcomes that lie in both A and B)

This means that all possible outcomes do not need to be known. To see why this formula works, suppose that the set of outcomes X is $(x_1, x_2, x_3, \ldots x_n)$, so that $|X| = n$. Then, for a uniform probability distribution:

$$P(A) = \frac{|A|}{n}$$

130

However, this means:

$$(A|B) = \frac{P(A \cap B)}{P(B)} = \frac{\frac{|A \cap B|}{n}}{\frac{|B|}{n}} = \frac{|A \cap B|}{|B|}$$

The n's cancel out.

For example, suppose a die is rolled, and it is known that it will land between 1 and 4. However, how many sides the die has is unknown. Figure the probability that the die is rolled higher than 2. To figure this, $P(3)$ or $P(4)$ does not need to be determined, or any of the other probabilities, since it is known that a fair die has a uniform probability distribution. Therefore, apply the formula $\frac{|A \cap B|}{|B|}$. So, in this case B is (1, 2, 3, 4) and $A \cap B$ is (3, 4). Therefore,

$$\frac{|A \cap B|}{|B|} = \frac{2}{4} = \frac{1}{2}$$

Conditional probability is an important concept because, in many situations, the likelihood of one outcome can differ radically depending on how something else comes out. The probability of passing a test given that one has studied all of the material is generally much higher than the probability of passing a test given that one has not studied at all. The probability of a person having heart trouble is much lower if that person exercises regularly. The probability that a college student will graduate is higher when their SAT scores are higher, and so on. For this reason, there are many people who are interested in conditional probabilities.

Note that in some practical situations, changing the order of the conditional probabilities can make the outcome very different. For example, the probability that a person with heart trouble has exercised regularly is quite different than the probability that a person who exercises regularly will have heart trouble. The probability of a person receiving a military-only award, given that he or she is or was a soldier, is generally not very high, but the probability that a person being or having been a soldier, given that he or she received a military-only award, is 1.

However, in some cases, the outcomes do not influence one another this way. If the probability of A is the same regardless of whether B is given; that is, if $P(A|B) = P(A)$, then A and B are considered **independent**. In this case:

$$P(A|B) = \frac{P(A \cap B)}{P(B)} = P(A)$$

So, $P(A \cap B) = P(A)P(B)$. In fact, if $P(A \cap B) = P(A)P(B)$, it can be determined that $P(A|B) = P(A)$ and $P(A|B) = P(B)$ by working backward. Therefore, B is also independent of A.

An example of something being independent can be seen in rolling dice. In this case, consider a red die and a green die. It is expected that when the dice are rolled, the outcome of the green die should not depend in any way on the outcome of the red die. Or, to take another example, if the same die is rolled repeatedly, then the next number rolled should not depend on which numbers have been rolled previously. Similarly, if a coin is flipped, then the next flip's outcome does not depend on the outcomes of previous flips.

This can sometimes be counter-intuitive, since when rolling a die or flipping a coin, there can be a streak of surprising results. If, however, it is known that the die or coin is fair, then these results are just the result of the fact that over long periods of time, it is very likely that some unlikely streaks of outcomes will occur. Therefore, avoid making the mistake of thinking that when considering a series of independent outcomes, a particular outcome is "due to happen" simply because a surprising series of outcomes has already been seen.

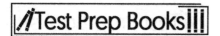

There is a second type of common mistake that people tend to make when reasoning about statistical outcomes: the idea that when something of low probability happens, this is surprising. It would be surprising that something with low probability happened after just one attempt. However, with so much happening all at once, it is easy to see at least something happen in a way that seems to have a very low probability. In fact, a lottery is a good example. The odds of winning a lottery are very small, but the odds that somebody wins the lottery each week are actually fairly high. Therefore, no one should be surprised when some low probability things happen.

A **simple event** consists of only one outcome. The most popular simple event is flipping a coin, which results in either heads or tails. A **compound event** results in more than one outcome and consists of more than one simple event. An example of a compound event is flipping a coin while tossing a die. The result is either heads or tails on the coin and a number from one to six on the die. The probability of a simple event is calculated by dividing the number of possible outcomes by the total number of outcomes. Therefore, the probability of obtaining heads on a coin is $\frac{1}{2}$, and the probability of rolling a 6 on a die is $\frac{1}{6}$. The probability of compound events is calculated using the basic idea of the probability of simple events. If the two events are independent, the probability of one outcome is equal to the product of the probabilities of each simple event. For example, the probability of obtaining heads on a coin and rolling a 6 is equal to:

$$\frac{1}{2} \times \frac{1}{6} = \frac{1}{12}$$

The probability of either A or B occurring is equal to the sum of the probabilities minus the probability that both A and B will occur. Therefore, the probability of obtaining either heads on a coin or rolling a 6 on a die is:

$$\frac{1}{2} + \frac{1}{6} - \frac{1}{12} = \frac{7}{12}$$

The two events aren't mutually exclusive because they can happen at the same time. If two events are mutually exclusive, and the probability of both events occurring at the same time is zero, the probability of event A or B occurring equals the sum of both probabilities. An example of calculating the probability of two mutually exclusive events is determining the probability of pulling a king or a queen from a deck of cards. The two events cannot occur at the same time.

Practice Quiz

1. Shawna buys $2\frac{1}{2}$ gallons of paint. If she uses $\frac{1}{3}$ of it on the first day, how much does she have left?

    a. $1\frac{5}{6}$ gallons

    b. $1\frac{1}{2}$ gallons

    c. $1\frac{2}{3}$ gallons

    d. 2 gallons

2. How will $\frac{4}{5}$ be written as a percent?

    a. 40%
    b. 125%
    c. 90%
    d. 80%

3. What are all the factors of 12?

    a. 12, 24, 36
    b. 1, 2, 4, 6, 12
    c. 12, 24, 36, 48
    d. 1, 2, 3, 4, 6, 12

4. At the beginning of the day, Xavier has 20 apples. At lunch, he meets his sister Emma and gives her half of his apples. After lunch, he stops by his neighbor Jim's house and gives him six of his apples. He then uses $\frac{3}{4}$ of his remaining apples to make an apple pie for dessert at dinner. At the end of the day, how many apples does Xavier have left?

    a. 4
    b. 6
    c. 2
    d. 1

5. How would the number 847.89632 be written if rounded to the nearest hundredth?

    a. 847.90
    b. 900
    c. 847.89
    d. 847.896

See answers on the next page.

Answer Explanations

1. C: If Shawna has used $\frac{1}{3}$ of the paint, she has $\frac{2}{3}$ remaining. The mixed fraction can be converted because $2\frac{1}{2}$ gallons is the same as $\frac{5}{2}$ gallons. The calculation is:

$$\frac{2}{3} \times \frac{5}{2} = \frac{10}{6} = \frac{5}{3} = 1\frac{2}{3} \text{ gallons}$$

2. D: To convert a fraction to a percent, the fraction is first converted to a decimal. To do so, the numerator is divided by the denominator:

$$4 \div 5 = 0.8$$

To convert a decimal to a percent, the number is multiplied by 100:

$$0.8 \times 100 = 80\%$$

3. D: A given number divides evenly by each of its factors to produce an integer (no decimals). To find the factors of 12, determine what whole numbers when multiplied equal 12. $1x12, 2x6$, and $3x4$ are all the ways to multiply to 12 using whole numbers, so the factors of 12 are: $1, 2, 3, 4, 6, 12$.

4. D: This problem can be solved using basic arithmetic. Xavier starts with 20 apples, then gives his sister half, so 20 is divided by 2.

$$\frac{20}{2} = 10$$

He then gives his neighbor six apples, so 6 is subtracted from 10.

$$10 - 6 = 4$$

Finally, he uses $\frac{3}{4}$ of his remaining apples to make a pie. Since $\frac{3}{4}$ of 4 is 3, he uses 3 apples, so 3 is subtracted from 4.

$$4 - 3 = 1$$

5. A: The hundredths place value is located two digits to the right of the decimal point (the digit 9 in the original number). To decide whether to round up or keep the digit, examine the digit to the right, and if it is 5 or greater, round up. In this case, the digit to the right is 6, so the hundredths place is rounded up. When rounding up, if the digit to be increased is a 9, the digit to its left is increased by one and the digit in the desired place value is made a zero. Therefore, the number is rounded to 847.90.

Science

Biology

Biology is the study of living organisms and the processes that are vital for life. Scientists who study biology study these organisms on a cellular level, individually or as populations, and look at the effects they have on their surrounding environment.

Water

Most cells are primarily composed of water and live in water-rich environments. Since water is such a familiar substance, it is easy to overlook its unique properties. Chemically, water is made up of two hydrogen atoms bonded to one oxygen atom by covalent bonds. The three atoms join to make a V-shaped molecule. Water is a polar molecule, meaning it has an unevenly distributed overall charge due to an unequal sharing of electrons. Due to oxygen's electronegativity and its more substantial positively charged nucleus, hydrogen's electrons are pulled closer to the oxygen. This causes the hydrogen atoms to have a slight positive charge and the oxygen atom to have a slight negative charge. In a glass of water, the molecules constantly interact and link for a fraction of a second due to intermolecular bonding between the slightly positive hydrogen atoms of one molecule and the slightly negative oxygen of a different molecule. These weak intermolecular bonds are called **hydrogen bonds**.

Water has several important qualities, including: cohesive and adhesive behaviors, temperature moderation ability, expansion upon freezing, and diverse use as a solvent.

Cohesion is the interaction of many of the same molecules. In water, cohesion occurs when there is hydrogen bonding between water molecules. Water molecules use this bonding ability to attach to each other and can work against gravity to transport dissolved nutrients to the top of a plant. A network of water-conducting cells can push water from the roots of a plant up to the leaves. Adhesion is the linking of two different substances. Water molecules can form a weak hydrogen bond with, or adhere to, plant cell walls to help fight gravity. The cohesive behavior of water also causes surface tension. If a glass of water is slightly overfull, water can still stand above the rim. This is because of the unique bonding of water molecules at the surface—they bond to each other and to the molecules below them, making it seem like it is covered with an impenetrable film. A raft spider could actually walk across a small body of water due to this surface tension.

Another important property of water is its ability to moderate temperature. Water can moderate the temperature of air by absorbing or releasing stored heat into the air. Water has the distinctive capability of being able to absorb or release large quantities of stored heat while undergoing only a small change in temperature. This is because of the relatively high **specific heat** of water, where specific heat is the amount of heat it takes for one gram of a material to change its temperature by 1 degree Celsius. The specific heat of water is one calorie per gram per degree Celsius, meaning that for each gram of water, it takes one calorie of heat to raise or lower the temperature of water by 1 degree Celsius.

When the temperature of water is reduced to freezing levels, water displays another interesting property: It expands instead of contracts. Most liquids become denser as they freeze because the molecules move around slower and stay closer together. Water molecules, however, form hydrogen bonds with each other as they move together. As the temperature lowers and they begin to move slower, these bonds become harder to break apart. When water freezes into ice, molecules are frozen with hydrogen bonds between them and they take up about 10 percent more volume than in their liquid state. The fact that ice is less dense than water is what makes ice float to the top of a glass of water.

Science

Lastly, the **polarity** of water molecules makes it a versatile solvent. **Ionic compounds**, such as salt, are made up of positively- and negatively-charged atoms, called **cations** and **anions**, respectively. Cations and anions are easily dissolved in water because of their individual attractions to the slight positive charge of the hydrogen atoms or the slight negative charge of the oxygen atoms in water molecules. Water molecules separate the individually charged atoms and shield them from each other so they don't bond to each other again, creating a homogenous solution of the cations and anions. Nonionic compounds, such as sugar, have polar regions, so are easily dissolved in water. For these compounds, the water molecules form hydrogen bonds with the polar regions (hydroxyl groups) to create a homogenous solution. Any substance that is attracted to water is termed **hydrophilic**. Substances that repel water are termed **hydrophobic**.

Biological Molecules

Basic units of organic compounds are often called **monomers**. Repeating units of linked monomers are called **polymers**. The most important large molecules, or polymers, found in all living things can be divided into four categories: carbohydrates, lipids, proteins, and nucleic acids. This may be surprising since there is so much diversity in the outward appearance and physical abilities of living things present on Earth. Carbon (C), hydrogen (H), oxygen (O), nitrogen (N), sulfur (S), and phosphorus (P) are the major elements of most biological molecules. Carbon is a common backbone of large molecules because of its ability to form four covalent bonds.

Carbohydrates

Carbohydrates consist of sugars and polymers of sugars. The simplest sugars are **monosaccharides**, which have the empirical formula of CH_2O. The formula for the monosaccharide glucose, for example, is $C_6H_{12}O_6$. Glucose is an important molecule for cellular respiration, the process of cells extracting energy by breaking bonds through a series of reactions. The individual atoms are then used to rebuild new small molecules. **Polysaccharides** are made up of a few hundred to a few thousand monosaccharides linked together. These larger molecules have two major functions. The first is that they can be stored as starches, such as **glycogen**, and then broken down later for energy. Secondly, they may be used to form strong materials, such as **cellulose**, which is the firm wall that encloses plant cells, and **chitin**, the carbohydrate insects use to build exoskeletons.

Use this chart to better understand the classification of carbs:

Classification of Carbs

Monosaccharides

Trioses	Tetroses	Pentoses	Hexoses or Heptoses

136

Lipids

Lipids are a class of biological molecules that are **hydrophobic**, meaning they don't mix well with water. They are mostly made up of large chains of carbon and hydrogen atoms, termed **hydrocarbon chains**. When lipids mix with water, the water molecules bond to each other and exclude the lipids because they are unable to form bonds with the long hydrocarbon chains. The three most important types of lipids are fats, phospholipids, and steroids.

Fats are made up of two types of smaller molecules: glycerol and fatty acids. **Glycerol** is a chain of three carbon atoms, with a **hydroxyl group** attached to each carbon atom. A hydroxyl group is made up of an oxygen and hydrogen atom bonded together. **Fatty acids** are long hydrocarbon chains that have a backbone of sixteen or eighteen carbon atoms. The carbon atom on one end of the fatty acid is part of a **carboxyl group.** A carboxyl group is a carbon atom that uses two of its four bonds to bond to one oxygen atom (double bond) and uses another one of its bonds to link to a hydroxyl group.

Fats are made by joining three fatty acid molecules and one glycerol molecule.

Glycerol   **Fatty Acid**

Phospholipids are made of two fatty acid molecules linked to one glycerol molecule. A **phosphate group** is attached to a third hydroxyl group of the glycerol molecule. A phosphate group consists of a phosphate atom connected to four oxygen atoms and has an overall negative charge.

Phospholipids have an interesting structure because their fatty acid tails are hydrophobic, but their phosphate group heads are hydrophilic. When phospholipids mix with water, they create double-layered structures, called **bilayers,** that shield their hydrophobic regions from water molecules. Cell membranes are made of phospholipid bilayers, which allow the cells to mix with aqueous solutions outside and inside, while forming a protective barrier and a semi-permeable membrane around the cell.

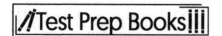

Steroids are lipids that consist of four fused carbon rings. The different chemical groups that attach to these rings are what make up the many types of steroids. **Cholesterol** is a common type of steroid found in animal cell membranes. Steroids are mixed in between the phospholipid bilayer and help maintain the structure of the membrane and aids in cell signaling.

Proteins

Proteins are essential for most all functions in living beings. The term *protein* is derived from the Greek word *proteios*, meaning *first* or *primary*. All proteins are made from a set of twenty amino acids that are linked in unbranched polymers. The combinations are numerous, which accounts for the diversity of proteins. Amino acids are linked by peptide bonds, while polymers of amino acids are called **polypeptides**. These polypeptides, either individually or in linked combination with each other, fold up to form coils of biologically-functional molecules, called proteins.

There are four levels of protein structure: primary, secondary, tertiary, and quaternary. The **primary structure** is the sequence of amino acids, similar to the letters in a long word. The **secondary structure** is beta sheets, or alpha helices, formed by hydrogen bonding between the polar regions of the polypeptide backbone. **Tertiary structure** is the overall shape of the molecule that results from the interactions between the side chains linked to the polypeptide backbone. **Quaternary structure** is the overall protein structure that occurs when a protein is made up of two or more polypeptide chains.

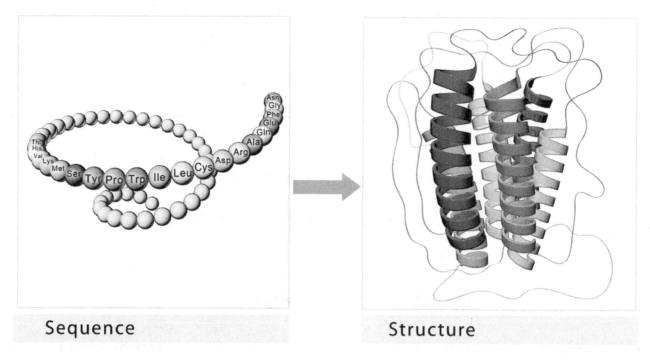

Sequence   Structure

Nucleic Acids

Nucleic acids can also be called **polynucleotides** because they are made up of chains of monomers called **nucleotides**. Nucleotides consist of a five-carbon sugar, a nitrogen-containing base, and a phosphate group. There are two types of nucleic acids: **deoxyribonucleic acid (DNA)** and **ribonucleic acid (RNA)**. Both DNA and RNA enable living organisms to pass on their genetic information and complex components to subsequent generations. While

138

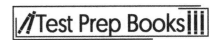

DNA is made up of two strands of nucleotides coiled together in a double-helix structure, RNA is made up of a single strand of nucleotides that folds onto itself.

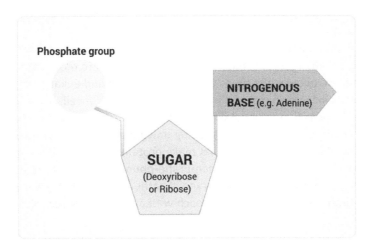

Metabolism

Metabolism is the set of chemical processes that occur within a cell for the maintenance of life. It includes both the synthesizing and breaking down of substances. A metabolic pathway begins with a molecule and ends with a specific product after going through a series of reactions, often involving an enzyme at each step. An **enzyme** is a protein that aids in the reaction. **Catabolic pathways** are metabolic pathways in which energy is released by complex molecules being broken down into simpler molecules. Contrast to catabolic pathways are **anabolic pathways**, which use energy to build complex molecules out of simple molecules. With cell metabolism, remember the **first law of thermodynamics**: Energy can be transformed, but it cannot be created or destroyed. Therefore, the energy released in a cell by a catabolic pathway is used up in anabolic pathways.

The reactions that occur within metabolic pathways are classified as either exergonic reactions or endergonic reactions. **Exergonic reactions** end in a release of free energy, while **endergonic reactions** absorb free energy from its surroundings. **Free energy** is the portion of energy in a system, such as a living cell, that can be used to perform work, such as a chemical reaction. It is denoted as the capital letter G and the change in free energy from a reaction or set of reactions is denoted as delta G (ΔG). When reactions do not require an input of energy, they are said to occur spontaneously. Exergonic reactions are considered spontaneous because they result in a negative delta G (– ΔG), where the products of the reaction have less free energy within them than the reactants. Endergonic reactions require an input of energy and result in a positive delta G (+ΔG), with the products of the reaction containing more free energy than the individual reactants. When a system no longer has free energy to do work, it has reached **equilibrium**. Since cells always work, they are no longer alive if they reach equilibrium.

Cells balance their energy resources by using the energy from exergonic reactions to drive endergonic reactions forward, a process called **energy coupling**. **Adenosine triphosphate**, or ATP, is a molecule that is an immediate source of energy for cellular work. When it is broken down, it releases energy used in endergonic reactions and anabolic pathways. ATP breaks down into adenosine diphosphate, or ADP, and a separate phosphate group, releasing energy in an exergonic reaction. As ATP is used up by reactions, it is also regenerated by having a new phosphate group added onto the ADP products within the cell in an endergonic reaction.

Enzymes are special proteins that help speed up metabolic reactions and pathways. They do not change the overall free energy release or consumption of reactions; they just make the reactions occur more quickly as it lowers the activation energy required. Enzymes are designed to act only on specific substrates. Their physical shape fits snugly

139

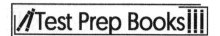

onto their matched substrates, so enzymes only speed up reactions that contain the substrates to which they are matched.

The Cell

Cells are the basic structural and functional unit of all organisms. They are the smallest unit of matter that is living. While there are many single-celled organisms, most biological organisms are more complex and made up of many different types of cells. There are two distinct types of cells: prokaryotic and eukaryotic. **Prokaryotic cells** include bacteria, while **eukaryotic cells** include animal and plant cells. Both types of cells are enclosed by a cell membrane, which is selectively permeable. Selective permeability essentially means that the membrane is a gatekeeper, allowing certain molecules and ions in and out, and keeping unwanted ones at bay, at least until they are ready for use. Both contain ribosomes, which are complexes that make protein inside the cell, and DNA. One major difference is that the DNA in eukaryotic cells are enclosed in a membrane-bound **nucleus**, where in prokaryotic cells, DNA is in the **nucleoid**, a region that is not enclosed by a membrane. Another major difference is that eukaryotic cells contain **organelles,** which are membrane-enclosed structures, each with a specific function, while prokaryotic cells do not have organelles.

Organelles Found in Eukaryotic Cells

The following cell organelles are found in both animal and plant cells unless otherwise noted:

Nucleus: The nucleus consists of three parts: nuclear envelope, nucleolus, and chromatin. The **nuclear envelope** is the double membrane that surrounds the nucleus and separates its contents from the rest of the cell. It is porous so substances can pass back and forth between the nucleus and the other parts of the cell. It is also continuous, with the endoplasmic reticulum that is present within the cytosol of the cell. The **nucleolus** is in charge of producing ribosomes. **Chromosomes** are comprised of tightly coiled proteins, RNA, and DNA and are collectively called chromatin.

Endoplasmic Reticulum (ER): The ER is a network of membranous sacs and tubes responsible for membrane synthesis and other metabolic and synthetic activities of the cell. There are two types of ER, rough and smooth. Rough ER is lined with ribosomes and is the location of protein synthesis. This provides a separate compartment for site-specific protein synthesis and is important for the intracellular transport of proteins. Smooth ER does not contain ribosomes and is the location of lipid synthesis.

Flagellum: The flagellum is found in protists and animal cells. It is a cluster of microtubules projected out of the plasma membrane and aids in cell motility.

Centrosome: The centrosome is the area of the cell where microtubules are created and organized for mitosis. Each centrosome contains two **centrioles.**

Cytoskeleton: The cytoskeleton in animal cells is made up of microfilaments, intermediate filaments, and microtubules. In plant cells, the cytoskeleton is made up of only microfilaments and microtubules. These structures reinforce the cell's shape and aid in cell movements.

Microvilli: Microvilli are found only in animal cells. They are protrusions in the cell membrane that increase the cell's surface area. They have a variety of functions, including absorption, secretion, and cellular adhesion.

Peroxisome: A peroxisome contains enzymes that are involved in many of the cell's metabolic functions, one of the most important being the breakdown of fatty acid chains. It produces hydrogen peroxide as a by-product of these processes and then converts the hydrogen peroxide to water.

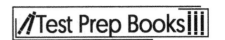

Mitochondrion: The mitochondrion, considered the cell's powerhouse, is one of the most important structures for maintaining regular cell function. It is where cellular respiration occurs and where most of the cell's ATP is generated.

Lysosome: Lysosomes are found exclusively in animal cells. They are responsible for digestion and can hydrolyze macromolecules.

Golgi Apparatus: The Golgi apparatus is responsible for synthesizing, modifying, sorting, transporting, and secreting cell products. Because of its large size, it was one of the first organelles studied in detail.

Ribosomes: Ribosomes are found either free in the cytosol, bound to the rough ER, or bound to the nuclear envelope. They are also found in prokaryotes. Ribosomes make up a complex that forms proteins within the cell.

Plasmodesmata: Found only in plant cells, plasmodesmata are cytoplasmic channels, or tunnels, that go through the cell wall and connect the cytoplasm of adjacent cells.

Chloroplast: Chloroplasts are found in protists, such as algae and plant cells. It is responsible for photosynthesis, which is the process of converting sunlight to chemical energy that is stored and used later to drive cellular activities.

Central Vacuole: A central vacuole is found only in plant cells, and is responsible for storage, breakdown of waste products, and hydrolysis of macromolecules.

Plasma Membrane: The plasma membrane is a phospholipid bilayer that encloses the cell. It is also found in prokaryotes.

Cell Wall: Cell walls are present in fungi, plant cells, and some protists. The cell wall is made up of strong fibrous substances, including cellulose (plants), chitin (fungi) and other polysaccharides, and protein. It is a layer outside of the plasma membrane that protects the cell from mechanical damage and helps maintain the cell's shape.

Cellular Respiration

Cellular respiration is a set of metabolic processes that converts energy from nutrients into ATP. Respiration can either occur aerobically, using oxygen, or anaerobically, without oxygen. While prokaryotic cells carry out respiration in the cytosol, most of the respiration in eukaryotic cells occurs in the mitochondria.

Aerobic Respiration

There are three main steps in aerobic cellular respiration: glycolysis, the citric acid cycle (also known as the Krebs cycle), and oxidative phosphorylation. **Glycolysis** is an essential metabolic pathway that converts glucose to pyruvate and allows for cellular respiration to occur. It does not require oxygen to be present. Glucose is a common molecule used for energy production in cells. During glycolysis, two three-carbon sugars are generated from the splitting of a glucose molecule. These smaller sugars are then converted into pyruvate molecules via oxidation and atom rearrangement. Glycolysis requires two ATP molecules to drive the process forward, but the end product of the process has four ATP molecules, for a net production of two ATP molecules. Also, two reduced nicotinamide adenine dinucleotide (NADH) molecules are created from when the electron carrier oxidized nicotinamide adenine dinucleotide (NAD+) peels off two electrons and a hydrogen atom.

In aerobically-respiring eukaryotic cells, the pyruvate molecules then enter the mitochondrion. Pyruvate is oxidized and converted into a compound called acetyl-CoA. This molecule enters the **citric acid cycle** to begin the process of aerobic respiration.

The citric acid cycle has eight steps. Remember that glycolysis produces two pyruvate molecules from each glucose molecule. Each pyruvate molecule oxidizes into a single acetyl-CoA molecule, which then enters the citric acid cycle. Therefore, two citric acid cycles can be completed and twice the number of ATP molecules are generated per glucose molecule.

Eight Steps of the Citric Acid Cycle

Step 1: Acetyl-CoA adds a two-carbon acetyl group to an oxaloacetate molecule and produces one citrate molecule.

Step 2: Citrate is converted to its isomer isocitrate by removing one water molecule and adding a new water molecule in a different configuration.

Step 3: Isocitrate is oxidized and converted to α-ketoglutarate. A carbon dioxide (CO_2) molecule is released and one NAD+ molecule is converted to NADH.

Step 4: α-Ketoglutarate is converted to succinyl-CoA. Another carbon dioxide molecule is released and another NAD+ molecule is converted to NADH.

Step 5: Succinyl-CoA becomes succinate by the addition of a phosphate group to the cycle. The oxygen molecule of the phosphate group attaches to the succinyl-CoA molecule and the CoA group is released. The rest of the phosphate group transfers to a guanosine diphosphate (GDP) molecule, converting it to guanosine triphosphate (GTP). GTP acts similarly to ATP and can actually be used to generate an ATP molecule at this step.

Step 6: Succinate is converted to fumarate by losing two hydrogen atoms. The hydrogen atoms join a flavin adenine dinucleotide (FAD) molecule, converting it to $FADH_2$, which is a hydroquinone form.

Step 7: A water molecule is added to the cycle and converts fumarate to malate.

Step 8: Malate is oxidized and converted to oxaloacetate. One lost hydrogen atom is added to an NAD molecule to create NADH. The oxaloacetate generated here then enters back into step one of the cycle.

At the end of glycolysis and the citric acid cycles, four ATP molecules have been generated. The NADH and FADH$_2$ molecules are used as energy to drive the next step of oxidative phosphorylation.

Oxidative Phosphorylation

Oxidative phosphorylation includes two steps: the electron transport chain and chemiosmosis. The inner mitochondrial membrane has four protein complexes, sequenced I to IV, used to transport protons and electrons through the inner mitochondrial matrix. Two electrons and a proton (H+) are passed from each NADH and FADH$_2$ to these channel proteins, pumping the hydrogen ions to the inner-membrane space using energy from the high-energy electrons to create a concentration gradient. NADH and FADH$_2$ also drop their high-energy electrons to the electron transport chain. NAD+ and FAD molecules in the mitochondrial matrix return to the Krebs cycle to pick up materials for the next delivery. From here, two processes happen simultaneously:

1. **Electron Transport Chain**: In addition to complexes I to IV, there are two mobile electron carriers present in the inner mitochondrial membrane, called **ubiquinone** and **cytochrome C**. At the end of this transport chain, electrons are accepted by an O_2 molecule in the matrix, and water is formed with the addition of two hydrogen atoms from chemiosmosis.

- 2. **Chemiosmosis**: This occurs in an ATP synthase complex that sits next to the four electron transporting complexes. ATP synthase uses **facilitated diffusion** (passive transport) to deliver protons across the concentration gradient from the inner mitochondrial membrane to the matrix. As the protons travel, the ATP synthase protein physically spins, and the kinetic energy generated is invested into phosphorylation of ADP molecules to generate ATP. Oxidative phosphorylation produces twenty-six to twenty-eight ATP molecules, bringing the total number of ATP generated through glycolysis and cellular respiration to thirty to thirty-two molecules.

Anaerobic Respiration

Some organisms do not live in oxygen-rich environments and must find alternate methods of respiration. Anaerobic respiration occurs in certain prokaryotic organisms. They utilize an electron transport chain similar to the aerobic respiration pathway; however, the terminal acceptor molecule is an electronegative substance that is not O_2. Some bacteria, for example, use the sulfate ion (SO_4^{2-}) as the final electron accepting molecule and the resulting byproduct is hydrogen sulfide (H_2S) instead of water.

Muscle cells that reach anaerobic threshold go through lactic acid respiration, while yeasts go through alcohol fermentation. Both processes only make two ATP.

Photosynthesis

Photosynthesis is the process of converting light energy into chemical energy that is then stored in sugar and other organic molecules. It can be divided into two stages: the light-dependent reactions and the Calvin cycle. In plants, the photosynthetic process takes place in the chloroplast. Inside the chloroplast are membranous sacs, called **thylakoids**. Chlorophyll is a green pigment that lives in the thylakoid membranes and absorbs the light energy, starting the process of photosynthesis. The **Calvin cycle** takes place in the **stroma,** or inner space, of the chloroplasts. The complex series of reactions that take place in photosynthesis can be simplified into the following equation:

$$6\,CO_2 + 12\,H_2O + Light\ Energy \rightarrow C_6H_{12}O_6 + 6\,O_2 + 6\,H_2O$$

Basically, carbon dioxide and water mix with light energy inside the chloroplast to produce organic molecules, oxygen, and water. Note that water is on both sides of the equation. Twelve water molecules are consumed during this process and six water molecules are newly formed as byproducts.

The Light Reactions

During the **light reactions**, chlorophyll molecules absorb light energy, or solar energy. In the thylakoid membrane, chlorophyll molecules, together with other small molecules and proteins, form photosystems, which are made up of a reaction-center complex surrounded by a light-harvesting complex. In the first step of photosynthesis, the light-harvesting complex from photosystem II (PSII) absorbs a photon from light, passes the photon from one pigment molecule to another within itself, and then transfers it to the reaction-center complex.

Inside the reaction-center complex, the energy from the photon enables a special pair of chlorophyll *a* molecules to release two electrons. These two electrons are then accepted by a primary electron acceptor molecule. Simultaneously, a water molecule is split into two hydrogen atoms, two electrons and one oxygen atom. The two

144

electrons are transferred one by one to the chlorophyll *a* molecules, replacing their released electrons. The released electrons are then transported down an electron transport chain by attaching to the electron carrier plastoquinone (Pq), a cytochrome complex, and then a protein called plastocyanin (Pc) before they reach photosystem I (PS I). As the electrons pass through the cytochrome complex, protons are pumped into the thylakoid space, providing the concentration gradient that will eventually travel through ATP synthase to make ATP (like in aerobic respiration).

PS I absorbs photons from light, similar to PS II. However, the electrons that are released from the chlorophyll *a* molecules in PS I are replaced by the electrons coming down the electron transport chain (from PS II). A primary electron acceptor molecule accepts the released electrons in PS I and passes the electrons onto another electron transport chain involving the protein ferredoxin (Fd). In the final steps of the light reactions, electrons are transferred from Fd to Nicotinamide adenine dinucleotide phosphate (NADP+) with the help of the enzyme NADP+ reductase and NADPH is produced. The ATP and nicotinamide adenine dinucleotide phosphate-oxidase (NADPH) produced from the light reactions are used as energy to form organic molecules in the Calvin cycle.

The Calvin Cycle

There are three phases in the Calvin cycle: carbon fixation, reduction, and regeneration of the CO_2 acceptor. **Carbon fixation** is when the first carbon molecule is introduced into the cycle, when CO_2 from the air is absorbed by the chloroplast. Each CO_2 molecule enters the cycle and attaches to ribulose bisphosphate (RuBP), a five-carbon sugar. The enzyme RuBP carboxylase-oxygenase, also known as rubisco, catalyzes this reaction. Next, two three-carbon 3-phosphoglycerate sugar molecules are formed immediately from the splitting of the six-carbon sugar.

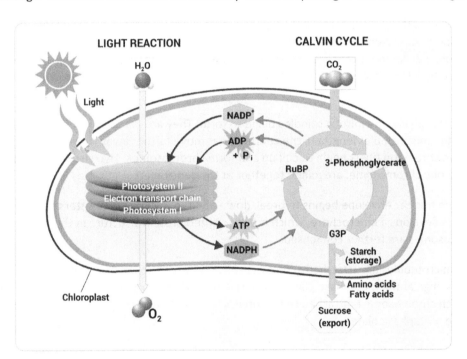

Next, during the **reduction** phase, an ATP molecule is reduced to ADP and the phosphate group attaches to 3-phosphoglycerate, forming 1,3-bisphosphoglycerate. An NADPH molecule then donates two high-energy electrons to the newly formed 1,3-bisphosphate, causing it to lose the phosphate group and become glyceraldehyde 3-phosphate (G3P), which is a high-energy sugar molecule. At this point in the cycle, one G3P molecule exits the cycle and is used by the plant. However, to regenerate RuBP molecules, which are the CO_2 acceptors in the cycle, five G3P molecules continue in the cycle. It takes three turns of the cycle and three CO_2 molecules entering the cycle to form one G3P molecule.

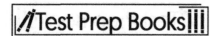

In the final phase of the Calvin cycle, three RuBP molecules are formed from the rearrangement of the carbon skeletons of five G3P molecules. It is a complex process that involves the reduction of three ATP molecules. At the end of the process, RuBP molecules are again ready to enter the first phase and accept CO_2 molecules.

Although the Calvin cycle is not dependent on light energy, both steps of photosynthesis usually occur during daylight, as the Calvin cycle is dependent upon the ATP and NADPH produced by the light reactions, because that energy can be invested into bonds to create high-energy sugars. The Calvin cycle invests nine ATP molecules and six NADPH molecules into every one molecule of G3P that it produces. The G3P that is produced can be used as the starting material to build larger organic compounds, such as glucose.

Cellular Reproduction

Cellular reproduction is the process that cells use to divide into two new cells. The ability of a multi-cellular organism to generate new cells to replace dying and damaged cells is vital for sustaining its life. There are two processes by which a cell can divide: mitosis and meiosis. In **mitosis,** the daughter cells produced from parental cell division are identical to each other and the parent. **Meiosis** produces genetically unique haploid cells due to two stages of cell division. Meiosis produces **haploid** cells, or **gametes** (sperm and egg cells), which only have one set of chromosomes. Humans are **diploid** because we have two sets of chromosomes – one from each parent. **Somatic** (body) cells are all diploid and are produced via mitosis.

Mitosis

Mitosis is the division of the genetic material in the nucleus of a cell, and is immediately followed by **cytokinesis**, which is the division of the cytoplasm of the cell. The two processes make up the mitotic phase of the cell cycle. Mitosis can be broken down into five stages: prophase, prometaphase, metaphase, anaphase, and telophase. Mitosis is preceded by **interphase**, where the cell spends the majority of its life while growing and replicating its DNA.

Prophase: During this phase, the mitotic spindles begin to form. They are made up of centrosomes and microtubules. As the microtubules lengthen, the centrosomes move farther away from each other. The nucleolus disappears and the chromatin fibers begin to coil up and form chromosomes. Two sister **chromatids**, which are two identical copies of one chromosome, are joined together at the centromere.

Prometaphase: The nuclear envelope begins to break down and the microtubules enter the nuclear area. Each pair of chromatin fibers develops a **kinetochore**, which is a specialized protein structure in the middle of the adjoined fibers. The chromosomes are further condensed.

Metaphase: The microtubules are stretched across the cell and the centrosomes are at opposite ends of the cell. The chromosomes align at the metaphase plate, which is a plane that is exactly between the two centrosomes. The centromere of each chromosome is attached to the kinetochore microtubules that are stretching from each centrosome to the metaphase plate.

Anaphase: The sister chromatids break apart, forming individual chromosomes. The two daughter chromosomes move to opposite ends of the cell. The microtubules shorten toward opposite ends of the cell as well. The cell elongates and, by the end of this phase, there is a complete set of chromosomes at each end of the cell.

Telophase: Two nuclei form at each end of the cell and nuclear envelopes begin to form around each nucleus. The nucleoli reappear and the chromosomes become less condensed. The microtubules are broken down by the cell and mitosis is complete.

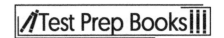

Cytokinesis divides the cytoplasm by pinching off the cytoplasm, forming a cleavage furrow, and the two daughter cells then enter interphase, completing the cycle.

Plant cell mitosis is similar except that it lacks centromeres, and instead has a microtubule organizing center. Cytokinesis occurs with the formation of a cell plate.

Meiosis

Meiosis is a type of cell division in which the parent cell has twice as many sets of chromosomes as the daughter cells into which it divides. Although the first stage of meiosis involves the duplication of chromosomes, similar to that of mitosis, the parent cell in meiosis divides into four cells, as opposed to the two produced in mitosis.

Meiosis has the same phases as mitosis, except that they occur twice: once in meiosis I and again in meiosis II. The diploid parent has two sets of homologous chromosomes, one set from each parent. During meiosis I, each chromosome set goes through a process called **crossing over**, which jumbles up the genes on each chromatid. In anaphase one, the separated chromosomes are no longer identical and, once the chromosomes pull apart, each daughter cell is haploid (one set of chromosomes with two non-identical sister chromatids). Next, during meiosis II, the two intermediate daughter cells divide again, separating the chromatids, producing a total of four total haploid cells that each contains one set of chromosomes.

Genetics

Genetics is the study of heredity, which is the transmission of traits from one generation to the next, and hereditary variation. The chromosomes passed from parent to child contain hereditary information in the form of genes. Each gene has specific sequences of DNA that encode proteins, start pathways, and result in inherited traits. In the human life cycle, one haploid sperm cell joins one haploid egg cell to form a diploid cell. The diploid cell is the zygote, the first cell of the new organism, and from then on mitosis takes over and nine months later, there is a fully developed human that has billions of identical cells.

The monk Gregor Mendel is referred to as the father of genetics. In the 1860s, Mendel came up with one of the first models of inheritance, using peapods with different traits in the garden at his abbey to test his theory and develop his model. His model included three laws to determine which traits are inherited; his theories still apply today, after genetics has been studied more in depth.

> 1. The **Law of Dominance:** Each characteristic has two versions that can be inherited. The gene that encodes for the characteristic has two variations, or alleles, and one is dominant over the other.

> 2. The **Law of Segregation:** When two parent cells form daughter cells, the alleles segregate and each daughter cell only inherits one of the alleles from each parent.

> 3. The **Law of Independent Assortment:** Different traits are inherited independent of one another because in metaphase, the set of chromosomes line up in random fashion – mom's set of chromosomes do not line up all on the left or right, there is a random mix.

Dominant and Recessive Traits

Each gene has two **alleles**, one inherited from each parent. **Dominant alleles** are noted in capital letters (A) and **recessive alleles** are noted in lower case letters (a). There are three possible combinations of alleles among dominant and recessive alleles: AA, Aa (known as a heterozygote), and aa. Dominant alleles, when mixed with recessive alleles, will mask the recessive trait. The recessive trait would only appear as the phenotype when the allele combination is aa because a dominant allele is not present to mask it.

Although most genes follow the standard dominant/recessive rules, there are some genes that defy them. Examples include cases of co-dominance, multiple alleles, incomplete dominance, sex-linked traits, and polygenic inheritance.

In cases of **co-dominance**, both alleles are expressed equally. For example, blood type has three alleles: I^A, I^B, and i. I^A and I^B are both dominant to i, but co-dominant with each other. An $I^A I^B$ has AB blood. With incomplete dominance, the allele combination Aa actually makes a third phenotype. An example: certain flowers can be red (AA), white (aa), or pink (Aa).

Punnett Square

For simple genetic combinations, a **Punnett square** can be used to assess the phenotypes of subsequent generations. In a 2×2 cell square, one parent's alleles are set up in columns and the other parent's alleles are in rows. The resulting allele combinations are shown in the four internal cells.

Mutations

Genetic **mutations** occur when there is a permanent alteration in the DNA sequence that codes for a specific gene. They can be small, affecting only one base pair, or large, affecting many genes on a chromosome. Mutations are classified as either hereditary, which means they were also present in the parent gene, or acquired, meaning they occurred after the genes were passed down from the parents. Although mutations are not common, they are an important aspect of genetics and variation in the general population.

DNA

DNA is made of nucleotide and contains the genetic information of a living organism. It consists of two polynucleotide strands that are twisted and linked together in a double-helix structure. The polynucleotide strands are made up of four nitrogenous bases: adenine (A), thymine (T), guanine (G), and cytosine (C). Adenine and guanine are purines while thymine and cytosine are pyrimidines. These bases have specific pairings of A with T, and G with C. The bases are ordered so that these specific pairings will occur when the two polynucleotide strands coil together to form a DNA molecule. The two strands of DNA are described as antiparallel because one strand runs 5' → 3' while the other strand of the helix runs 3' → 5'.

Before chromosome replication and cell division can occur, DNA replication must happen in interphase. There are specific base pair sequences on DNA, called origins of replication, where DNA replication begins. The proteins that begin the replication process attach to this site and begin separating the two strands and creating a replication bubble. Each end of the bubble has a replication fork, which is a Y-shaped area of the DNA that is being unwound. Several types of proteins are important to the beginning of DNA replication. **Helicases** are enzymes responsible for untwisting the two strands at the replication fork. Single-strand binding proteins bind to the separated strands so that they do not join back together during the replication process. While part of the DNA is unwound, the remainder of the molecule becomes even more twisted in response. Topoisomerase enzymes help relieve this strain by breaking, untwisting, and rejoining the DNA strands.

Once the DNA strand is unwound, an initial primer chain of RNA from the enzyme primase is made to start replication. Replication of DNA can only occur in the 5' → 3' direction. Therefore, during replication, one strand of the DNA template creates the leading strand in the 5' → 3' direction and the other strand creates the lagging strand. While the leading strand is created efficiently and in one piece, the lagging strand is generated in fragments, called **Okazaki fragments**, then are pieced together to form a complete strand by DNA ligase. Following the primer chain of RNA, DNA polymerases are the enzymes responsible for extending the DNA chains by adding on base pairs.

148

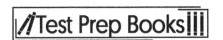

Scientific Method

Human beings are, by nature, very curious. Since long before the scientific method was established, people have been making observations and predicting outcomes, manipulating the physical world to create extraordinary things—from the first man-made fire in 6000 B.C.E. to the satellite that orbited Pluto in 2016. Although the history of the scientific method is sporadic and attributed to many different people, it remains the most reliable way to obtain and utilize knowledge about the observable universe. The scientific method consists of the following steps:

- Make an observation: An observation is the analysis of information using basic human senses: sight, sound, touch, taste, and smell. Observations can be two different types—qualitative or quantitative. A qualitative observation describes what is being observed, such as the color of a house or the smell of a flower. Quantitative observations measure what is being observed, such as the number of windows on a house or the intensity of a flower's smell on a scale of 1-5.
- Create a question: Observations lead to the identification of a problem, also called an inference. Inferences are logical predictions based on experience or education that lead to the formation of a hypothesis.
- Form a hypothesis: A hypothesis is a testable explanation of an observed scenario and is presented in the form of a statement. It's an attempt to answer a question based on an observation, and it allows a scientist to predict an outcome. A hypothesis makes assumptions on the relationship between two different variables, and answers the question: "If I do this, what happens to that?"
- Conduct an experiment: Once a hypothesis has been formed, it must be tested to determine whether it's true or false. To test a hypothesis, one must conduct a carefully designed experiment.
- Collect and analyze data: Once the experiment begins, a disciplined scientist must always record the observations in meticulous detail, usually in a journal. Upon reading this journal, a different scientist should be able to clearly understand the experiment and recreate it exactly. The journal includes all collected data, or any observed changes.
- Form a conclusion: The final step of the scientific method is to make inferences from observed data, which is also known as forming a conclusion.

Science Investigations

Designing a Science Investigation

Human beings are, by nature, very curious. Since long before the scientific method was established, people have been making and predicting outcomes, manipulating the physical world to create extraordinary things—from the first man-made fire in 6000 B.C.E. to the satellite that orbited Pluto in 2016. Although the history of the scientific method is sporadic and attributed to many different people, it remains the most reliable way to obtain and utilize knowledge about the observable universe. Designing a science investigation is based on the scientific method, which consists of the following steps:

- Make an observation
- Create a question
- Form a hypothesis
- Conduct an experiment
- Collect and analyze data
- Form a conclusion

The first step is to identify a problem based on an observation—the who, what, when, where, why, and how. An **observation** is the analysis of information using basic human senses: sight, sound, touch, taste, and smell. Observations can be two different types—qualitative or quantitative. A **qualitative observation** describes what is being observed, such as the color of a house or the smell of a flower. **Quantitative observations** measure what is being observed, such as the number of windows on a house or the intensity of a flower's smell on a scale of 1–5.

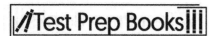
Observations lead to the identification of a problem, also called an **inference**. For example, if a fire truck is barreling down a busy street, the inferences could be:

- There's a fire.
- Someone is hurt.
- Some kid pulled the fire alarm at a local school.

Inferences are logical predictions based on experience or education that lead to the formation of a hypothesis.

Forming and Testing a Hypothesis

A hypothesis is a testable explanation of an observed scenario and is presented in the form of a statement. It's an attempt to answer a question based on an observation, and it allows a scientist to predict an outcome. A hypothesis makes assumptions on the relationship between two different variables, and answers the question: "If I do this, what happens to that?"

In order to form a hypothesis, there must be an independent variable and a dependent variable that can be measured. The **independent variable** is the variable that is manipulated, and the **dependent variable** is the result of the change.

For example, suppose a student wants to know how light affects plant growth. Based upon what he or she already knows, the student proposes (hypothesizes) that the more light to which a plant is exposed, the faster it will grow.

- Observation: Plants exposed to lots of light seem to grow taller.
- Question: Will plants grow faster if there's more light available?
- Hypothesis: The more light the plant has, the faster it will grow.
- Independent variable: The amount of time exposed to light (able to be manipulated)
- Dependent variable: Plant growth (the result of the manipulation)

Once a hypothesis has been formed, it must be tested to determine whether it's true or false. (How to test a hypothesis is described in a subsequent section.) After it has been tested and validated as true over and over, then a hypothesis can develop into a theory, model, or law.

Experimental Design

To test a hypothesis, one must conduct a carefully designed experiment. There are four basic requirements that must be present for an experiment to be valid:

- A control
- Variables
- A constant
- Repeated and collected data

The control is a standard to which the resultant findings are compared. It's the baseline measurement that allows for scientists to determine whether the results are positive or negative. For the example of light affecting plant growth, the control may be a plant that receives no light at all.

The independent variable is manipulated (a good way to remember this is I manipulate the Independent variable), and the dependent variable is the result of changes to the independent variable. In the plant example, the independent variable is the amount of time exposed to light, and the dependent variable is the resulting growth (or lack thereof) of the plant. For this experiment, there may be three plants—one that receives a minimal amount of light, the control, and one that receives a lot of light.

150

Finally, there must be constants in an experiment. A constant is an element of the experiment that remains unchanged. Constants are extremely important in minimizing inconsistencies within the experiment that may lead to results outside the parameters of the hypothesis. For example, some constants in the above case are that all plants receive the same amount of water, all plants are potted in the same kind of soil, the species of the plant used in each condition is the same, and the plants are stored at the same temperature. If, for instance, the plants received different amounts of water as well as light, it would be impossible to tell whether the plants responded to changes in water or light.

Once the experiment begins, a disciplined scientist must always record the observations in meticulous detail, usually in a journal. A good journal includes dates, times, and exact values of both variables and constants. Upon reading this journal, a different scientist should be able to clearly understand the experiment and recreate it exactly. The journal includes all collected data, or any observed changes. In this case, the data is rates of plant growth, as well as any other phenomena that occurred as a result of the experiment. A well-designed experiment also includes repetition in order to get the most accurate possible readings and to account for any errors, so several trials may be conducted.

Even in the presence of diligent constants, there are an infinite number of reasons that an experiment can (and will) go wrong, known as sources of error. All experimental results are inherently accepted as imperfect, if ever so slightly, because experiments are conducted by human beings, and no instrument can measure anything perfectly. The goal of scientists is to minimize those errors to the best of their ability.

Identifying and Explaining Independent and Dependent Variables

In an experiment, variables are the key to analyzing data, especially when data is in a graph or table. Variables can represent anything, including objects, conditions, events, and amounts of time.

Covariance is a general term referring to how two variables move in relation to each other. Take for example an employee that gets paid by the hour. For them, hours worked and total pay have a positive covariance. As hours worked increases, so does pay.

Constant variables remain unchanged by the scientist across all trials. Because they are held constant for all groups in an experiment, they aren't being measured in the experiment, and they are usually ignored. Constants can either be controlled by the scientist directly like the nutrition, water, and sunlight given to plants, or they can be selected by the scientist specifically for an experiment like using a certain animal species or choosing to investigate only people of a certain age group.

Independent variables are also controlled by the scientist, but they are the same only for each group or trial in the experiment. Each group might be composed of students that all have the same color of car or each trial may be run on different soda brands. The independent variable of an experiment is what is being indirectly tested because it causes change in the dependent variables.

Dependent variables experience change caused by the independent variable and are what is being measured or observed. For example, college acceptance rates could be a dependent variable of an experiment that sorted a large sample of high school students by an independent variable such as test scores. In this experiment, the scientist groups the high school students by the independent variable (test scores) to see how it affects the dependent variable (their college acceptance rates).

Note that most variables can be held constant in one experiment, but also serve as the independent variable or a dependent variable in another. For example, when testing how well a fertilizer aids plant growth, its amount of sunlight should be held constant for each group of plants, but if the experiment is being done to determine the

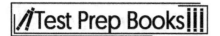

proper amount of sunlight a plant should have, the amount of sunlight is an independent variable because it is necessarily changed for each group of plants.

Identifying and Improving Hypotheses for Science Investigations

When presented with fundamental, scientific concepts, it is important to read for understanding. The most basic skill in achieving this literacy is to understand the concept of hypothesis and, moreover, to be able to identify it in a particular passage. A **hypothesis** is a proposed idea that needs further investigation in order to be proven true or false. While it can be considered an educated guess, a hypothesis goes more in depth in its attempt to explain something that is not currently accepted within scientific theory. It requires further experimentation and data gathering to test its validity and is subject to change, based on scientifically conducted test results. Being able to read a science passage and understand its main purpose, including any hypotheses, helps the test taker understand data-driven evidence. It helps the test taker to be able to correctly answer questions about the science excerpt they are asked to read.

When reading to identify a hypothesis, a test taker should ask, "What is the passage trying to establish? What is the passage's main idea? What evidence does the passage contain that either supports or refutes this idea?" Asking oneself these questions will help identify a hypothesis. Additionally, hypotheses are logical statements that are testable and use very precise language.

Review the following hypothesis example:

Consuming excess sugar in the form of beverages has a greater impact on childhood obesity and subsequent weight gain than excessive sugar from food.

While this is likely a true statement, it is still only a conceptual idea in a text passage regarding how sugar consumption affects childhood obesity, unless the passage also contains tested data that either proves or disproves the statement. A test taker could expect the rest of the passage to cite data proving that children who drink empty calories and don't exercise will, in fact, be obese.

A hypothesis goes further in that, given its ability to be proven or disproven, it may result in further hypotheses that require extended research. For example, the hypothesis regarding sugar consumption in drinks, after undergoing rigorous testing, may lead scientists to state another hypothesis such as the following:

Consuming excess sugar in the form of beverages as opposed to food items is a habit found in mostly sedentary children.

This new, working hypothesis further focuses not just on the source of an excess of calories, but tries an "educated guess" that empty caloric intake has a direct, subsequent impact on physical behavior.

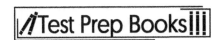

The data-driven chart below is similar to an illustration a test taker might see in relation to the hypothesis on sugar consumption in children:

Behaviors of Healthy and Unhealthy Kids

Healthful

Unhealthful

Exercise daily | Video games daily | Fruits daily | Vegetables daily | Chips daily | Sugar daily

While this guide will address other data-driven passages a test taker could expect to see within a given science excerpt, note that the hypothesis regarding childhood sugar intake and rate of exercise has undergone scientific examination and yielded results that support its truth.

When reading a science passage to determine its hypothesis, a test taker should look for a concept that attempts to explain a phenomenon, is testable, is logical, is precisely worded, and yields data-driven results. The test taker should scan the presented passage for any word or data-driven clues that will help identify the hypothesis, and then be able to correctly answer test questions regarding the hypothesis by using their critical thinking skills.

Identifying Possible Errors in a Science Investigation and Changing the Design to Correct Them

For a hypothesis to be proven true or false, all experiments are subject to multiple trials in order to verify accuracy and precision. A measurement is **accurate** if the observed value is close to the "true value." For example, if someone measured the pH of water at 6.9, this measurement would be considered accurate (the pH of water is 7). On the other hand, a measurement is **precise** if the measurements are consistent—that is, if they are reproducible. If someone had a series of values for a pH of water that were 6.9, 7.0, 7.2, and 7.3, their measurements would not be precise. However, if all measured values were 6.9, or the average of these values was 6.9 with a small range, then their measurements would be precise. Measurements can fall into the following categories:

- Both accurate and precise
- Accurate but not precise
- Precise but not accurate
- Neither accurate nor precise

The accuracy and precision of observed values most frequently correspond to the amount of error present in the experiment. Aside from general carelessness, there are two primary types of error: random and systematic. **Random errors** are unpredictable variations in the experiment that occur by chance. They can be difficult to detect, but they can often be nullified using a statistical analysis and minimized by taking repeated measurements and taking an average. **Systematic errors** occur when there are imperfections in the design of the experiment itself—usually errors that affect the accuracy of the measurements. These errors can be minimized by using the most accurate equipment available and by taking proper care of instruments and measuring techniques. Common examples of errors are listed below.

Random	Systematic
Environmental factors (random changes in vibration, temperature, humidity, etc.)	Poorly maintained instruments
	Old or out-of-date instruments
Differences in instrument use among scientists	Faulty calibration of instruments
Errors in judgment—can be affected by state of mind	Reading the instruments at an angle (parallax error) or other faulty reading errors
Incorrectly recorded observations	Not accounting for lag time

The most basic method to account for the possibility of errors is to take an average (also called a **mean**) of all observed values. To do so, one must divide the number of measurements taken from the sum of all measurements.

$$\frac{Sum\ of\ Measurements}{Total\ \#\ of\ Measurements}$$

For the above example of the pH values, the average is calculated by finding the sum of the pH values ascertained and dividing by the number of values recorded.

$$\frac{6.9 + 7.0 + 7.2 + 7.3}{4} = 7.1$$

The more observations recorded, the greater the precision. It's important to first assess the accuracy of measurements before proceeding to collect multiple trials of data. If a particular trial results in measurements that are vastly different from the average, it may indicate that a random or systematic error occurred during the trial. When this happens, a scientist might decide to "throw out" the trial and run the experiment again.

Identifying the Strengths and Weaknesses of Different Types of Science Investigations

In order to address the strengths and weaknesses of different types of scientific investigations, GED test takers must first strengthen their capacity for scientific literacy and numeracy. It is important to familiarize oneself with methods for decoding highly specialized scientific terms, formulas, and symbols. Additionally, test takers can take the following suggestions to help identify unique weaknesses and strengths in different types of scientific investigations:

- Using critical analysis, test takers begin asking questions about the accuracy of the methods used to collect, analyze, and display data. They should carefully look at text and graphics that show scientific findings.

- Test takers should determine whether or not the words, data, and symbols provided by the author actually offer information that is relevant for testing a hypothesis or making an inference.

- When two or more passages on the same topic are offered, test takers should cross-analyze the findings to determine what data is accurate or relevant and which findings are most objective.

- Although scientific research strives for objectivity, test takers should highlight any subjective biases that may be embedded in a text. In particular, they should be aware of certain historical or ethical biases that might appear.

- Test takers should double check for any computational inaccuracies.

- Test takers should make suggestions for better ways to present the findings in both texts and visual images.

Human Anatomy and Physiology

General Anatomy and Physiology of a Human

Anatomy may be defined as the structural makeup of an organism. The study of anatomy may be divided into microscopic/fine anatomy and macroscopic/gross anatomy. Fine anatomy concerns itself with viewing the features of the body with the aid of a microscope, while gross anatomy concerns itself with viewing the features of the body with the naked eye. Physiology refers to the functions of an organism, and it examines the chemical or physical functions that help the body function appropriately.

Levels of Organization of the Human Body

All the parts of the human body are built of individual units called *cells*. Groups of similar cells are arranged into **tissues**, different tissues are arranged into **organs**, and organs working together form entire **organ systems**. The human body has twelve organ systems that govern circulation, digestion, immunity, hormones, movement, support, coordination, urination & excretion, reproduction (male and female), respiration, and general protection. Here are some of the systems of the body:

HUMAN BODY SYSTEMS

Circulatory System   Central nervous System   Respiratory System   Digestive System   Skeletal System   Muscular System

Body Cavities

The body is partitioned into different hollow spaces that house organs. The human body contains the following cavities:

- Cranial cavity: The cranial cavity is surrounded by the skull and contains organs such as the brain and pituitary gland.

- Thoracic cavity: The thoracic cavity is encircled by the sternum (breastbone) and ribs. It contains organs such as the lungs, heart, trachea (windpipe), esophagus, and bronchial tubes.

155

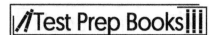

- Abdominal cavity: The abdominal cavity is separated from the thoracic cavity by the diaphragm. It contains organs such as the stomach, gallbladder, liver, small intestines, and large intestines. The abdominal organs are held in place by a membrane called the peritoneum.

- Pelvic cavity: The pelvic cavity is enclosed by the pelvis, or bones of the hip. It contains organs such as the urinary bladder, urethra, ureters, anus, and rectum. It contains the reproductive organs as well. In females, the pelvic cavity also contains the uterus.

- Spinal cavity: The spinal cavity is surrounded by the vertebral column. The vertebral column has five regions: cervical, thoracic, lumbar, sacral, and coccygeal. The spinal cord runs through the middle of the spinal cavity.

Human Tissues

Human tissues can be grouped into four categories:

Muscle: Muscle tissue supports the body and allows it to move, and muscles are special as their cells have the ability to contract. There are three distinct types of muscle tissue: skeletal, smooth, and cardiac. Skeletal muscle is voluntary, or under conscious control, and is usually attached to bones. Most body movement is directly caused by the contraction of skeletal muscle. Smooth muscle is typically involuntary, or not under conscious control, and may be found in blood vessels, the walls of hollow organs, and the urinary bladder. Cardiac muscle is involuntary and found in the heart, which helps propel blood throughout the body.

Nervous: Nervous tissue is unique in that it is able to coordinate information from sensory organs as well as communicate the proper behavioral responses. Neurons, or nerve cells, are the workhorses of the nervous system. They communicate via action potentials (electrical signals) and neurotransmitters (chemical signals).

Epithelial: Epithelial tissue covers the external surfaces of organs and lines many of the body's cavities. Epithelial tissue helps to protect the body from invasion by microbes (bacteria, viruses, parasites), fluid loss, and injury.

Epithelial cell shapes can be:

- Squamous: cells with a flat shape
- Cuboidal: cells with a cubed shape
- Columnar: cells shaped like a column

Epithelial cells can be arranged in four patterns:

- Simple: a type of epithelium composed solely from a single layer of cells
- Stratified: a type of epithelium composed of multiple layers of cells
- Pseudostratified: a type of epithelium that appears to be stratified but actually consists of only one layer of cells
- Transitional: a type of epithelium noted for its ability to expand and contract

Connective: Connective tissue supports and connects the tissues and organs of the body. Connective tissue is composed of cells dispersed throughout a matrix which can be gel, liquid, protein fibers, or salts. The primary protein fibers in the matrix are collagen (for strength), elastin (for flexibility), and reticulum (for support). Connective tissue can be categorized as either *loose* or *dense*. Examples of connective tissue include bones, cartilage, ligaments, tendons, blood, and adipose (fat) tissue.

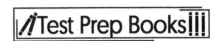

Three Primary Body Planes

A plane is an imaginary flat surface. The three primary planes of the human body are frontal, sagittal, and transverse. The frontal, or coronal, plane is a vertical plane that divides the body or organ into front (anterior) and back (posterior) portions. The **sagittal plane**, or lateral plane, is a vertical plane that divides the body or organ into right and left sides. The transverse plane is a horizontal plane that divides the body or organ into upper and lower portions. In medical imaging, **computed tomography (CT)** scans are oriented only in the transverse plane; while **magnetic resonance imaging (MRI)** scans may be oriented in any of the three planes.

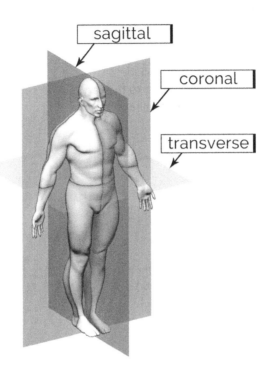

Terms of Direction

Medial refers to a structure being closer to the midline of the body. For example, the nose is medial to the eyes.

Lateral refers to a structure being farther from the midline of the body, and it is the opposite of *medial*. For example, the eyes are lateral to the nose.

Proximal refers to a structure or body part located near an attachment point. For example, the elbow is proximal to the wrist.

Distal refers to a structure or body part located far from an attachment point, and it is the opposite of *proximal*. For example, the wrist is distal to the elbow.

Anterior means toward the front in humans. For example, the lips are anterior to the teeth. The term *ventral* can be used in place of *anterior* and refers to the abdominal region, or underside, of an organism.

Posterior means toward the back in humans, and it is the opposite of *anterior*. For example, the teeth are posterior to the lips. The term *dorsal* can be used in place of *posterior* and refers to the back or upper side of an organism.

Superior means above and refers to a structure closer to the head. For example, the head is superior to the neck. The terms *cephalic* or *cranial* may be used in place of *superior*.

157

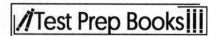

Inferior means below and refers to a structure farther from the head, and it is the opposite of *superior*. For example, the neck is inferior to the head. The term *caudal* may be used in place of *inferior* and refers to a structure near the tail or posterior of the body.

Superficial refers to a structure closer to the surface. For example, the muscles are superficial because they are just beneath the surface of the skin.

Deep refers to a structure farther from the surface, and it is the opposite of *superficial*. For example, the femur is a deep structure lying beneath the muscles.

Body Regions

- Terms for general locations on the body include:
- Cervical: relating to the neck (can also refer to the cervix, as in cervical cancer)
- Clavicular: relating to the clavicle, or collarbone
- Ocular: relating to the eyes
- Acromial: relating to the shoulder
- Cubital: relating to the elbow
- Brachial: relating to the arm
- Carpal: relating to the wrist
- Thoracic : relating to the chest
- Abdominal: relating to the abdomen
- Pubic: relating to the groin
- Pelvic: relating to the pelvis, or bones of the hip
- Femoral: relating to the femur, or thigh bone
- Geniculate: relating to the knee
- Pedal: relating to the foot
- Palmar: relating to the palm of the hand
- Plantar: relating to the sole of the foot

Abdominopelvic Regions and Quadrants

The abdominopelvic region may be defined as the combination of the abdominal and the pelvic cavities. The region's upper border is the breasts and its lower border is the groin region. The region is divided into the following nine sections:

- Right hypochondriac: region below the cartilage of the ribs
- Epigastric: region above the stomach between the hypochondriac regions
- Left hypochondriac: region below the cartilage of the ribs
- Right lumbar: region of the waist
- Umbilical: region between the lumbar regions where the umbilicus, or belly button (navel), is located
- Left lumbar: region of the waist
- Right inguinal: region of the groin
- Hypogastric: region below the stomach between the inguinal regions
- Left inguinal: region of the groin

A simpler way to describe the abdominopelvic area is to divide it into the following quadrants:

- Right upper quadrant (RUQ): Encompasses the right hypochondriac, right lumbar, epigastric, and umbilical regions.

158

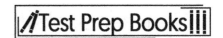

- Right lower quadrant (RLQ): Encompasses the right lumbar, right inguinal, hypogastric, and umbilical regions.

- Left upper quadrant (LUQ): Encompasses the left hypochondriac, left lumbar, epigastric, and umbilical regions.

- Left lower quadrant (LLQ): Encompasses the left lumbar, left inguinal, hypogastric, and umbilical regions.

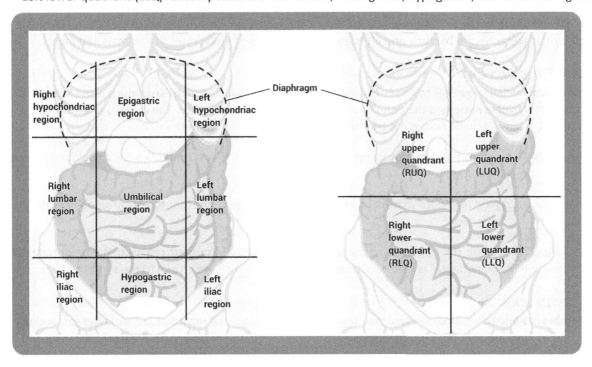

Cell Structure and Function

The cell is the main functional and structural component of all living organisms. Robert Hooke, an English scientist, coined the term "cell" in 1665. Hooke's discovery laid the groundwork for the cell theory, which is composed of three principals:

1. All organisms are composed of cells.

2. All existing cells are created from other living cells.

3. The cell is the most fundamental unit of life.

Organisms can be unicellular (composed of one cell) or multicellular (composed of many cells). All cells must be bounded by a cell membrane, be filled with cytoplasm of some sort, and be coded by a genetic sequence.

The cell membrane separates a cell's internal and external environments. It is a selectively permeable membrane, which usually only allows the passage of certain molecules by diffusion. Phospholipids and proteins are crucial components of all cell membranes. The cytoplasm is the cell's internal environment and is aqueous, or water-based. The genome represents the genetic material inside the cell that is passed on from generation to generation.

Prokaryotes and Eukaryotes

Prokaryotic cells are much smaller than eukaryotic cells. The majority of prokaryotes are unicellular, while the majority of eukaryotes are multicellular. Prokaryotic cells have no nucleus, and their genome is found in an area

159

known as the nucleoid. They also do not have membrane-bound organelles, which are "little organs" that perform specific functions within a cell.

Eukaryotic cells have a proper nucleus containing the genome. They also have numerous membrane-bound organelles such as lysosomes, endoplasmic reticula (rough and smooth), Golgi complexes, and mitochondria. The majority of prokaryotic cells have cell walls, while most eukaryotic cells do not have cell walls. The DNA of prokaryotic cells is contained in a single circular chromosome, while the DNA of eukaryotic cells is contained in multiple linear chromosomes. Prokaryotic cells divide using binary fission, while eukaryotic cells divide using mitosis. Examples of prokaryotes are bacteria and archaea while examples of eukaryotes are animals and plants.

Nuclear Parts of a Cell

Nucleus (plural nuclei): Houses a cell's genetic material, deoxyribonucleic acid (DNA), which is used to form chromosomes. A single nucleus is the defining characteristic of eukaryotic cells. The nucleus of a cell controls gene expression. It ensures genetic material is transmitted from one generation to the next.

Chromosomes: Complex thread-like arrangements composed of DNA that is found in a cell's nucleus. Humans have 23 pairs of chromosomes for a total of 46.

Chromatin: An aggregate of genetic material consisting of DNA and proteins that forms chromosomes during cell division.

Nucleolus (plural nucleoli): The largest component of the nucleus of a eukaryotic cell. With no membrane, the primary function of the nucleolus is the production of ribosomes, which are crucial to the synthesis of proteins.

Cell Membranes

Cell membranes encircle the cell's cytoplasm, separating the intracellular environment from the extracellular environment. They are selectively permeable, which enables them to control molecular traffic entering and exiting cells. Cell membranes are made of a double layer of phospholipids studded with proteins. Cholesterol is also dispersed in the phospholipid bilayer of cell membranes to provide stability. The proteins in the phospholipid bilayer aid the transport of molecules across cell membranes.

Scientists use the term "fluid mosaic model" to refer to the arrangement of phospholipids and proteins in cell membranes. In that model, phospholipids have a head region and a tail region. The head region of the phospholipids is attracted to water (hydrophilic), while the tail region is repelled by it (hydrophobic). Because they are hydrophilic, the heads of the phospholipids are facing the water, pointing inside and outside of the cell. Because they are hydrophobic, the tails of the phospholipids are oriented inward between both head regions. This orientation constructs the phospholipid bilayer.

Cell membranes have the distinct trait of selective permeability. The fact that cell membranes are amphiphilic (having hydrophilic and hydrophobic zones) contributes to this trait. As a result, cell membranes are able to regulate the flow of molecules in and out of the cell.

Factors relating to molecules such as size, polarity, and solubility determine their likelihood of passage across cell membranes. Small molecules are able to diffuse easily across cell membranes compared to large molecules. Polarity refers to the charge present in a molecule. Polar molecules have regions, or poles, of positive and negative charge and are water soluble, while nonpolar molecules have no charge and are fat-soluble. Solubility refers to the ability of a substance, called a solute, to dissolve in a solvent. A soluble substance can be dissolved in a solvent, while an insoluble substance cannot be dissolved in a solvent. Nonpolar, fat-soluble substances have a much easier time passing through cell membranes compared to polar, water-soluble substances.

160

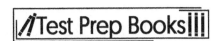

Passive Transport Mechanisms

Passive transport refers to the migration of molecules across a cell membrane that does not require energy. The three types of passive transport include simple diffusion, facilitated diffusion, and osmosis.

Simple diffusion relies on a concentration gradient, or differing quantities of molecules inside or outside of a cell. During simple diffusion, molecules move from an area of high concentration to an area of low concentration. Facilitated diffusion utilizes carrier proteins to transport molecules across a cell membrane. Osmosis refers to the transport of water across a selectively permeable membrane. During osmosis, water moves from a region of low solute concentration to a region of high solute concentration.

Active Transport Mechanisms

Active transport refers to the energy-requiring migration of molecules across a cell membrane. It's a useful way to move molecules from an area of low concentration to an area of high concentration. Adenosine triphosphate (ATP), the currency of cellular energy, is needed to work against the concentration gradient.

Active transport can involve carrier proteins that cross the cell membrane to pump molecules and ions across the membrane, like in facilitated diffusion. The difference is that active transport uses the energy from ATP to drive this transport, as typically the ions or molecules are going against their concentration gradient. For example, glucose pumps in the kidney pump all of the glucose into the cells from the lumen of the nephron even though there is a higher concentration of glucose in the cell than in the lumen. This is because glucose is a precious fuel source, and the body wants to conserve as much as possible. Pumps can either send a molecule in one direction, multiple molecules in the same direction (symports), or multiple molecules in different directions (antiports).

Active transport can also involve the movement of membrane-bound particles, either into a cell (endocytosis) or out of a cell (exocytosis). The three major forms of endocytosis are: pinocytosis, where the cell is *drinking* and intakes only small molecules; phagocytosis, where the cell is *eating* and intakes large particles or small organisms; and receptor-mediated endocytosis, where the cell's membrane splits off to form an internal vesicle as a response to molecules activating receptors on its surface. Exocytosis is the inverse of endocytosis, and the membranes of the vesicle join to that of the cell's surface while the molecules inside the vesicle are released outside. This is common in nervous and muscle tissue for the release of neurotransmitters and in endocrine cells for the release of hormones. The two major categories of exocytosis are excretion and secretion. Excretion is defined as the removal of waste from a cell. Secretion is defined as the transport of molecules, such as hormones or enzymes, from a cell.

Structure and Function of Cellular Organelles

Organelles are specialized structures that perform specific tasks in a cell. The term literally means "little organ." Most organelles are membrane bound and serve as sites for the production or degradation of chemicals. The following are organelles found in eukaryotic cells:

Nucleus: A cell's nucleus contains genetic information in the form of DNA. The nucleus is surrounded by the nuclear envelope. A single nucleus is the defining characteristic of eukaryotic cells. The nucleus is also the most important organelle of the cell. It contains the nucleolus, which manufactures ribosomes (another organelle) that are crucial in protein synthesis (also called gene expression).

Mitochondria: Mitochondria are oval-shaped and have a double membrane. The inner membrane has multiple folds called cristae. Mitochondria are responsible for the production of a cell's energy in the form of adenosine triphosphate (ATP). ATP is the principal energy transfer molecule in eukaryotic cells. Mitochondria also participate in cellular respiration.

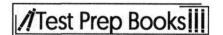
Rough Endoplasmic Reticulum: The rough endoplasmic reticulum (RER) is composed of linked membranous sacs called cisternae with ribosomes attached to their external surfaces. The RER is responsible for the production of proteins that will eventually get shipped out of the cell.

Smooth Endoplasmic Reticulum: The smooth endoplasmic reticulum (SER) is composed of linked membranous sacs called cisternae without ribosomes, which distinguishes it from the RER. The SER's main function is the production of carbohydrates and lipids, which can be created expressly for the cell, or to modify the proteins from the RER that will eventually get shipped out of the cell.

Golgi Apparatus: The Golgi apparatus is located next to the SER. Its main function is the final modification, storage, and shipping of products (proteins, carbohydrates, and lipids) from the endoplasmic reticulum.

Lysosomes: Lysosomes are specialized vesicles that contain enzymes capable of digesting food, surplus organelles, and foreign invaders such as bacteria and viruses. They often destroy dead cells in order to recycle cellular components. Lysosomes are found only in animal cells.

Secretory Vesicles: Secretory vesicles transport and deliver molecules into or out of the cell via the cell membrane. Endocytosis refers to the movement of molecules into a cell via secretory vesicles. Exocytosis refers to the movement of molecules out of a cell via secretory vesicles.

Ribosomes: Ribosomes are not membrane bound. They are responsible for the production of proteins as specified from DNA instructions. Ribosomes can be free or bound.

Cilia and Flagella: Cilia are specialized hair-like projections on some eukaryotic cells that aid in movement, while flagella are long, whip-like projections that are used in the same capacity.

Here is an illustration of the cell:

162

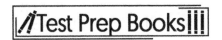

The following organelles are not found in animal cells:

- Cell Walls: Cell walls can be found in plants, bacteria, and fungi, and are made of cellulose, peptidoglycan, and lignin, depending on the organism it surrounds. Each of these materials is a type of sugar recognized as a structural carbohydrate. The carbohydrates are rigid structures located outside of the cell membrane. Cell walls protect the cell, help maintain a cell's shape, and provide structural support.

- Vacuoles: Plant cells have central vacuoles, which are essentially a membrane surrounding a body of water. They may store nutrients or waste products. Since vacuoles are large, they also help to support the structure of plant cells.

- Chloroplasts: Chloroplasts are membrane-bound organelles that perform photosynthesis. They contain structural units called thylakoids. Chlorophyll, a green pigment that circulates within the thylakoids, harnesses light energy (sunlight) and helps convert it into chemical energy (glucose).

Anatomy and Physiology of the Respiratory System

The respiratory system enables breathing and supports the energy-making process in cells. The respiratory system transports an essential reactant, oxygen, to cells so that they can produce energy in their mitochondria via cellular respiration. The respiratory system also removes carbon dioxide, a waste product of cellular respiration.

This system is divided into the upper respiratory system and the lower respiratory system. The upper system comprises the nose, the nasal cavity and sinuses, and the pharynx. The lower respiratory system comprises the larynx (voice box), the trachea (windpipe), the small passageways leading to the lungs, and the lungs.

The pathway of oxygen to the bloodstream begins with the nose and the mouth. Upon inhalation, air enters the nose and mouth and passes into the sinuses where it gets warmed, filtered, and humidified. The throat, or the pharynx, allows the entry of both food and air; however, only air moves into the trachea, or windpipe, since the epiglottis covers the trachea during swallowing and prevents food from entering. The trachea contains mucus and cilia. The mucus traps many airborne pathogens while the cilia act as bristles that sweep the pathogens away toward the top of the trachea where they are either swallowed or coughed out.

The top of the trachea itself has two vocal cords, which make up the larynx. At its bottom, the trachea forks into two major bronchi—one for each lung. These bronchi continue to branch into smaller and smaller bronchioles before terminating in grape-like air sacs called alveoli; these alveoli are surrounded by capillaries and provide the body with an enormous amount of surface area to exchange oxygen and carbon dioxide gases, in a process called external respiration.

Bronchial branching

163

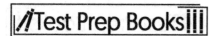
In total, the lungs contain about 1500 miles of airway passages. The right lung is divided into three lobes (superior, middle, and inferior), and the left lung is divided into two lobes (superior and inferior).

The left lung is smaller than the right lung, likely because it shares its space in the chest cavity with the heart.

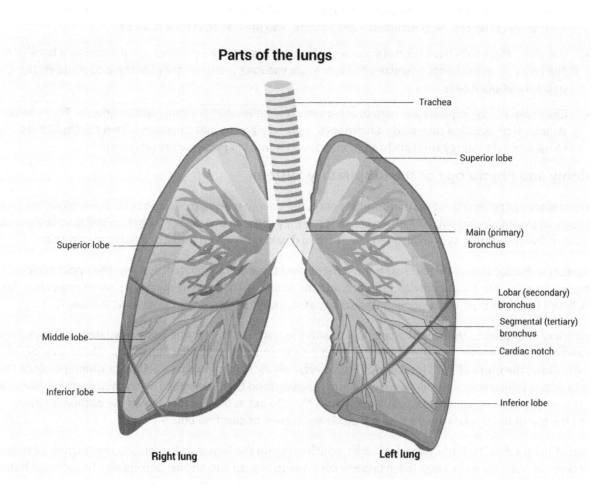

A flat muscle underneath the lungs called the diaphragm controls breathing. When the diaphragm contracts, the volume of the chest cavity increases and indirectly decreases its air pressure. This decrease in air pressure creates a vacuum, and the lungs pull in air to fill the space. This difference in air pressure pulls the air from outside of the body into the lungs in a process called negative pressure breathing.

Upon inhalation or inspiration, oxygen in the alveoli diffuses into the capillaries to be carried by blood to cells throughout the body, in a process called internal respiration. A protein called hemoglobin in red blood cells easily bonds with oxygen, removing it from the blood and allowing more oxygen to diffuse in. This protein allows the blood to take in 60 times more oxygen than the body could without it, and this explains how oxygen can become so concentrated in blood even though it is only 21% of the atmosphere. While oxygen diffuses from the alveoli into the capillaries, carbon dioxide diffuses from the capillaries into the alveoli. When the diaphragm relaxes, the elastic lungs snap back to their original shape; this decreases the volume of the chest cavity and increases the air pressure until it is back to normal. This increased air pressure pushes the carbon dioxide waste from the alveoli through exhalation or *expiration*.

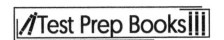

The autonomic nervous system controls breathing. The medulla oblongata gets feedback regarding the carbon dioxide levels in the blood and will send a message to the diaphragm that it is time for a contraction. While breathing can be voluntary, it is mostly under autonomic control.

Functions of the Respiratory System

The respiratory system has many functions. Most importantly, it provides a large area for gas exchange between the air and the circulating blood. It protects the delicate respiratory surfaces from environmental variations and defends them against pathogens. It is responsible for producing the sounds that the body makes for speaking and singing, as well as for non-verbal communication. It also helps regulate blood volume and blood pressure by releasing vasopressin, and it is a regulator of blood pH due to its control over carbon dioxide release, as the aqueous form of carbon dioxide is the chief buffering agent in blood.

Anatomy and Physiology of the Cardiovascular System

The cardiovascular system (also called the circulatory system) is a network of organs and tubes that transport blood, hormones, nutrients, oxygen, and other gases to cells and tissues throughout the body. It is also known as the cardiovascular system. The major components of the circulatory system are the blood vessels, blood, and heart.

Blood Vessels

In the circulatory system, blood vessels are responsible for transporting blood throughout the body. The three major types of blood vessels in the circulatory system are arteries, veins, and capillaries. Arteries carry blood from the heart to the rest of the body. Veins carry blood from the body back to the heart. Capillaries connect arteries to veins and form networks that exchange materials between the blood and the cells.

In general, arteries are stronger and thicker than veins, as they withstand high pressures exerted by the blood as the heart pumps it through the body. Arteries control blood flow through either vasoconstriction (narrowing of the blood vessel's diameter) or vasodilation (widening of the blood vessel's diameter). The blood in veins is under much lower pressures, so veins have valves to prevent the backflow of blood.

Most of the exchange between the blood and tissues takes place through the capillaries. There are three types of capillaries: continuous, fenestrated, and sinusoidal.

Continuous capillaries are made up of epithelial cells tightly connected together. As a result, they limit the types of materials that pass into and out of the blood. Continuous capillaries are the most common type of capillary. Fenestrated capillaries have openings that allow materials to be freely exchanged between the blood and tissues. They are commonly found in the digestive, endocrine, and urinary systems. Sinusoidal capillaries have larger openings and allow proteins and blood cells through. They are found primarily in the liver, bone marrow, and spleen.

Blood

Blood is vital to the human body. It is a liquid connective tissue that serves as a transport system for supplying cells with nutrients and carrying away their wastes. The average adult human has five to six quarts of blood circulating through their body. Approximately 55% of blood is plasma (the fluid portion), and the remaining 45% is composed of solid cells and cell parts. There are three major types of blood cells:

- **Red blood cells**, or erythrocytes, transport oxygen throughout the body. They contain a protein called hemoglobin that allows them to carry oxygen. The iron in the hemoglobin gives the cells and the blood their red colors.

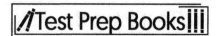

- **White blood cells**, or leukocytes, are responsible for fighting infectious diseases and maintaining the immune system. There are five types of white blood cells: neutrophils, lymphocytes, eosinophils, monocytes, and basophils.

- **Platelets** are cell fragments that play a central role in the blood clotting process.

All blood cells in adults are produced in the bone marrow—red blood cells and most white blood cells are produced in the red marrow, and some white blood cells are produced in the yellow bone marrow.

Heart

The heart is a two-part, muscular pump that forcefully pushes blood throughout the human body. The human heart has four chambers—two upper atria and two lower ventricles separated by a partition called the septum. There is a pair on the left and a pair on the right. Anatomically, *left* and *right* correspond to the sides of the body that the patient themselves would refer to as left and right.

Four valves help to section off the chambers from one another. Between the right atrium and ventricle, the three flaps of the tricuspid valve keep blood from backflowing from the ventricle to the atrium, similar to how the two flaps of the mitral valve work between the left atrium and ventricle. As these two valves lie between an atrium and a ventricle, they are referred to as atrioventricular (AV) valves. The other two valves are semilunar (SL) and control blood flow into the two great arteries leaving the ventricles. The pulmonary valve connects the right ventricle to the pulmonary artery, while the aortic valve connects the left ventricle to the aorta.

166

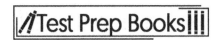

Use this image to better understand the components of the heart:

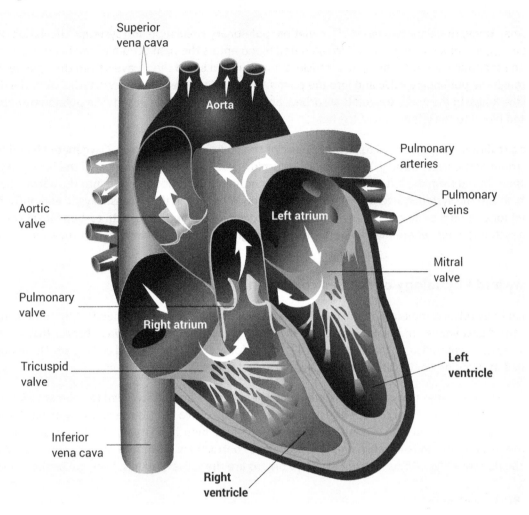

Cardiac Cycle

A **cardiac cycle** is one complete sequence of cardiac activity. The cardiac cycle represents the relaxation and contraction of the heart and can be divided into two phases: diastole and systole.

Diastole is the phase during which the heart relaxes and fills with blood. It gives rise to the **diastolic blood pressure (DBP)**, which is the bottom number of a blood pressure reading. Systole is the phase during which the heart contracts and discharges blood. It gives rise to the **systolic blood pressure (SBP)**, which is the top number of a blood pressure reading. The heart's electrical conduction system coordinates the cardiac cycle.

Types of Circulation

Five major blood vessels manage blood flow to and from the heart: the superior vena cava and inferior vena cava, the aorta, the pulmonary artery, and the pulmonary vein.

The superior vena cava is a large vein that drains blood from the head and the upper body. The inferior vena cava is a large vein that drains blood from the lower body. The aorta is the largest artery in the human body and carries

167

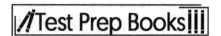

blood from the heart to body tissues. The pulmonary arteries carry blood from the heart to the lungs. The pulmonary veins transport blood from the lungs to the heart.

In the human body, there are two types of circulation: pulmonary circulation and systemic circulation. Pulmonary circulation supplies blood to the lungs. Deoxygenated blood enters the right atrium of the heart and is routed through the tricuspid valve into the right ventricle. Deoxygenated blood then travels from the right ventricle of the heart through the pulmonary valve and into the pulmonary arteries. The pulmonary arteries carry the deoxygenated blood to the lungs. In the lungs, oxygen is absorbed, and carbon dioxide is released. The pulmonary veins carry oxygenated blood to the left atrium of the heart.

Systemic circulation supplies blood to all other parts of the body, except the lungs. Oxygenated blood flows from the left atrium of the heart through the mitral, or bicuspid, valve into the left ventricle of the heart. Oxygenated blood is then routed from the left ventricle of the heart through the aortic valve and into the aorta. The aorta delivers blood to the systemic arteries, which supply the body tissues. In the tissues, oxygen and nutrients are exchanged for carbon dioxide and other wastes. The deoxygenated blood along with carbon dioxide and wastes enter the systemic veins, where they are returned to the right atrium of the heart via the superior and inferior vena cava.

Anatomy and Physiology of the Gastrointestinal System

The human body relies completely on the digestive system to meet its nutritional needs. After food and drink are ingested, the digestive system breaks them down into their component nutrients and absorbs them so that the circulatory system can transport them to other cells to use for growth, energy, and cell repair. These nutrients may be classified as proteins, lipids, carbohydrates, vitamins, and minerals.

The digestive system is thought of chiefly in two parts: the digestive tract (also called the alimentary tract or gastrointestinal tract) and the accessory digestive organs. The digestive tract is the pathway in which food is ingested, digested, absorbed, and excreted. It is composed of the mouth, pharynx, esophagus, stomach, small and large intestines, rectum, and anus. *Peristalsis*, or wave-like contractions of smooth muscle, moves food and wastes through the digestive tract. The accessory digestive organs are the salivary glands, liver, gallbladder, and pancreas.

Mouth and Stomach

The mouth is the entrance to the digestive system. Here, the mechanical and chemical digestion of the food begins. The food is chewed mechanically by the teeth and shaped into a *bolus* by the tongue so that it can be more easily swallowed by the esophagus. The food also becomes more watery and pliable with the addition of saliva secreted from the salivary glands, the largest of which are the parotid glands. The glands also secrete amylase in the saliva, an enzyme which begins chemical digestion and breakdown of the carbohydrates and sugars in the food.

The food then moves through the pharynx and down the muscular esophagus to the stomach.

The stomach is a large, muscular sac-like organ at the distal end of the esophagus. Here, the bolus is subjected to more mechanical and chemical digestion. As it passes through the stomach, it is physically squeezed and crushed while additional secretions turn it into a watery nutrient-filled liquid that exits into the small intestine as **chyme**.

The stomach secretes a great many substances into the **lumen** of the digestive tract. Some cells produce gastrin, a hormone that prompts other cells in the stomach to secrete a gastric acid composed mostly of hydrochloric acid (HCl). The HCl is at such a high concentration and low pH that it denatures most proteins and degrades a lot of organic matter. The stomach also secretes mucous to form a protective film that keeps the corrosive acid from dissolving its own cells. Gaps in this mucous layer can lead to peptic ulcers. Finally, the stomach also uses digestive

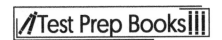

enzymes like proteases and lipases to break down proteins and fats; although there are some gastric lipases here, the stomach is most known for breaking down proteins.

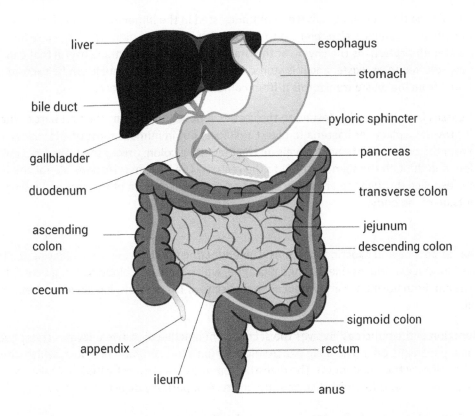

Small Intestine

The chyme from the stomach enters the first part of the small intestine, the **duodenum**, through the **pyloric sphincter**, and its extreme acidity is partly neutralized by sodium bicarbonate secreted along with mucous. The presence of chyme in the duodenum triggers the secretion of the hormones secretin and cholecystokinin (CCK). Secretin acts on the pancreas to dump more sodium bicarbonate into the small intestine so that the pH is kept at a reasonable level, while CCK acts on the gallbladder to release the **bile** that it has been storing. Bile, a substance produced by the liver and stored in the gallbladder, helps to emulsify or dissolve fats and lipids.

Because of the bile (which aids in lipid absorption) and the secreted lipases (which break down fats), the duodenum is the chief site of fat digestion in the body. The duodenum also represents the last major site of chemical digestion in the digestive tract, as the other two sections of the small intestine (the *jejunum* and *ileum*) are instead heavily involved in absorption of nutrients.

The small intestine reaches 40 feet in length, and its cells are arranged in small finger-like projections called villi. This is due to its key role in the absorption of nearly all nutrients from the ingested and digested food, effectively transferring them from the lumen of the GI tract to the bloodstream, where they travel to the cells that need them. These nutrients include simple sugars like glucose from carbohydrates, amino acids from proteins, emulsified fats, electrolytes like sodium and potassium, minerals like iron and zinc, and vitamins like D and B12. Vitamin B12's

169

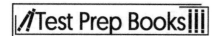

absorption, though it takes place in the intestines, is actually aided by **intrinsic factor** that was released into the chyme back in the stomach.

Large Intestine

The leftover parts of food that remain unabsorbed or undigested in the lumen of the small intestine next travel through the large intestine, which is also referred to as the large bowel or colon. The large intestine is mainly responsible for water absorption. As the chyme at this stage no longer has anything useful that can be absorbed by the body, it is now referred to as *waste*, and it is stored in the large intestine until it can be excreted from the body. Removing the liquid from the waste transforms it from liquid to solid stool, or feces.

This waste first passes from the small intestine to the cecum, a pouch that forms the first part of the large intestine. In herbivores, it provides a place for bacteria to digest cellulose, but in humans most of it is vestigial and is known as the appendix. From the cecum, waste next travels up the ascending colon, across the transverse colon, down the descending colon, and through the sigmoid colon to the rectum. The rectum is responsible for the final storage of waste before it is expelled through the anus. The anal canal is a small portion of the rectum leading through to the anus and the outside of the body.

Pancreas

The **pancreas** has endocrine and exocrine functions. The **endocrine function** involves releasing the hormone insulin, which decreases blood sugar (glucose) levels, and glucagon, which increases blood sugar (glucose) levels, directly into the bloodstream. Both hormones are produced in the islets of Langerhans, insulin in the beta cells and glucagon in the alpha cells.

The **exocrine function** of the pancreas involves the secretion of inactive digestive enzymes (zymogens) from acinar cells into the main pancreatic duct. The main pancreatic duct joins the common bile duct, which empties into the small intestine (specifically the duodenum). The digestive enzymes are then activated and take part in the digestion of carbohydrates, proteins, and fats within chyme (the mixture of partially digested food and digestive juices).

Anatomy and Physiology of the Neuromuscular System

Nervous System

The **human nervous system** coordinates the body's response to stimuli from inside and outside the body. There are two major types of nervous system cells: neurons and neuroglia. **Neurons** are the workhorses of the nervous system and form a complex communication network that transmits electrical impulses termed action potentials, while neuroglia connect and support the neurons.

Although some neurons monitor the senses, some control muscles, and some connect the brain to other neurons, all neurons have four common characteristics:

- **Dendrites**: These receive electrical signals from other neurons across small gaps called *synapses*.
- **Nerve cell body**: This is the hub of processing and protein manufacture for the neuron.
- **Axon**: This transmits the signal from the cell body to other neurons.
- **Terminals**: These bridge the neuron to dendrites of other neurons and deliver the signal via chemical messengers called neurotransmitters.

Here is an illustration of this:

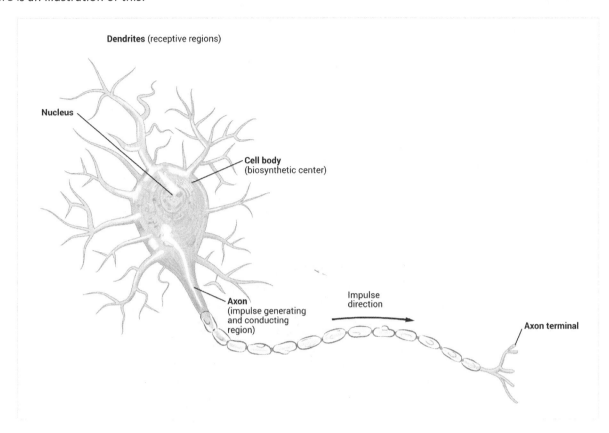

There are two major divisions of the nervous system, central and peripheral:

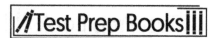
Central Nervous System

The **central nervous system (CNS)** consists of the brain and spinal cord. Three layers of membranes called the meninges cover and separate the CNS from the rest of the body.

The major divisions of the brain are the forebrain, the midbrain, and the hindbrain.

The forebrain consists of the cerebrum, the thalamus and hypothalamus, and the rest of the limbic system. The **cerebrum** is the largest part of the brain, and its most well-documented part is the outer cerebral cortex. The cerebrum is divided into right and left hemispheres, and each cerebral cortex hemisphere has four discrete areas, or lobes: frontal, temporal, parietal, and occipital. The frontal lobe governs duties such as voluntary movement, judgment, problem solving, and planning, while the other lobes are more sensory. The temporal lobe integrates hearing and language comprehension, the parietal lobe processes sensory input from the skin, and the occipital lobe processes visual input from the eyes. For completeness, the other two senses, smell and taste, are processed via the olfactory bulbs. The thalamus helps organize and coordinate all of this sensory input in a meaningful way for the brain to interpret.

172

The **hypothalamus** controls the endocrine system and all of the hormones that govern long-term effects on the body. Each hemisphere of the limbic system includes a hippocampus (which plays a vital role in memory), an amygdala (which is involved with emotional responses like fear and anger), and other small bodies and nuclei associated with memory and pleasure.

The **midbrain** is in charge of alertness, sleep/wake cycles, and temperature regulation, and it includes the substantia nigra which produces melatonin to regulate sleep patterns. The notable components of the hindbrain include the medulla oblongata and cerebellum. The **medulla oblongata** is located just above the spinal cord and is responsible for crucial involuntary functions such as breathing, swallowing, and regulating heart rate and blood pressure. Together with other parts of the hindbrain, the midbrain and medulla oblongata form the brain stem. The brain stem connects the spinal cord to the rest of the brain. To the rear of the brain stem sits the cerebellum, which plays key roles in posture, balance, and muscular coordination. The spinal cord itself, which is encapsulated by the protective bony spinal column, carries sensory information to the brain and motor information to the body.

Peripheral Nervous System

The **peripheral nervous system (PNS)** includes all nervous tissue besides the brain and spinal cord. The PNS consists of the sets of cranial and spinal nerves and relays information between the CNS and the rest of the body. The PNS has two divisions: the autonomic nervous system and the somatic nervous system.

Autonomic Nervous System

The **autonomic nervous system (ANS)** governs involuntary, or reflexive, body functions. Ultimately, the autonomic nervous system controls functions such as breathing, heart rate, digestion, body temperature, and blood pressure.

The ANS is split between parasympathetic nerves and sympathetic nerves. These two nerve types are antagonistic and have opposite effects on the body. Parasympathetic nerves predominate resting conditions, and decrease heart rate, decrease breathing rate, prepare digestion, and allow urination and excretion. Sympathetic nerves, on the other hand, become active when a person is under stress or excited, and they increase heart rate, increase breathing rates, and inhibit digestion, urination, and excretion.

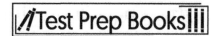
Somatic Nervous System and the Reflex Arc

The **somatic nervous system (SNS)** governs the conscious, or voluntary, control of skeletal muscles and their corresponding body movements. The SNS contains afferent and efferent neurons. Afferent neurons carry sensory messages from the skeletal muscles, skin, or sensory organs to the CNS. Efferent neurons relay motor messages from the CNS to skeletal muscles, skin, or sensory organs.

The SNS also has a role in involuntary movements called reflexes. A reflex is defined as an involuntary response to a stimulus. They are transmitted via what is termed a **reflex arc**, where a stimulus is sensed by an effector and its afferent neuron, interpreted and rerouted by an interneuron, and delivered to effector muscles by an efferent neuron where they respond to the initial stimulus. A reflex is able to bypass the brain by being rerouted through the spinal cord; the interneuron decides the proper course of action rather than the brain. The reflex arc results in an instantaneous, involuntary response. For example, a physician tapping on the knee produces an involuntary knee jerk referred to as the patellar tendon reflex.

Muscular System

The **muscular system** is responsible for involuntary and voluntary movement of the body. There are three types of muscle: skeletal, cardiac, and smooth.

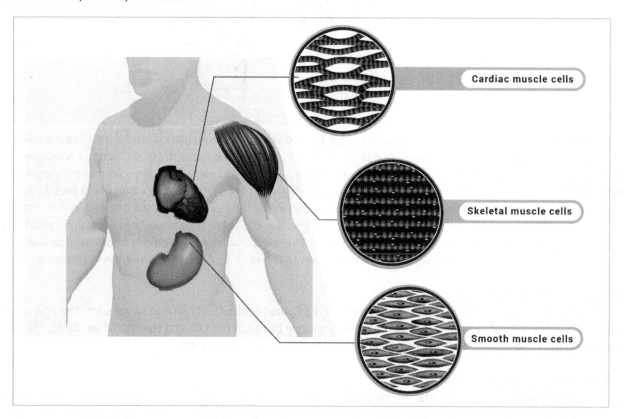

Skeletal Muscles

Skeletal muscles, or **voluntary muscles**, are attached to bones by tendons and are responsible for voluntary movement. The connecting tendons are made up of dense bands of connective tissue and have collagen fibers that firmly attach the muscle to the bone. Their fibers are actually woven into the coverings of the bone and muscle so that they can withstand pressure and tension. They usually work in opposing pairs like the biceps and triceps, for example.

174

Skeletal muscles are made of bundles of long fibers that are composed of cells with many nuclei due to their length. These fibers contain myofibrils, and myofibrils are made of alternating filaments. The thicker myosin filaments are in between the smaller actin filaments in a unit called a **sarcomere**, and the overlapping regions of these filaments give the muscle its characteristic striated, or striped, appearance. Actin filaments are attached to exterior Z lines, myosin filaments are attached to a central M line, and when a muscle is at rest, there is a gap between the Z line and the myosin filaments. Only when the muscle contracts and the actin filaments slide over the myosin filaments does the myosin reach the Z line, as illustrated in the picture below. This sliding-filament model of muscle contraction is dependent on myosin molecules forming and breaking cross-bridges with actin in order to pull the actin filaments closer to the M line.

Skeletal muscles are controlled by the nervous system. Motor neurons connect to muscle fibers via neuromuscular junctions. Motor neurons must release the neurotransmitter acetylcholine which releases calcium ions to stimulate myosin cross-bridging and contraction. As the acetylcholine stops being released, the contraction ends.

Smooth Muscles

Smooth muscles are responsible for involuntary movement, such as moving food through the digestive tract and moving blood through vessels. Their cells have only one nucleus and do not have striations because actin and myosin filaments do not have an organized arrangement like they do in skeletal muscles. Unlike skeletal muscle, smooth muscle doesn't rely on neuromuscular junctions for intercellular communication. Instead, they operate via gap junctions, which send impulses directly from cell to cell.

Trapezius
Shrugs
Upright Rows
Lateral and Front Raises

Triceps
Triceps Dips
Triceps Extensions
Triceps Pulldowns

Latissimus Dorsi
Lat Pulldowns
Rows
Pull-ups

Forearms
Pull-ups
Reverse Curls
Biceps Curls

Gluteals
Lunges
Squats
Deadlifts

Hamstrings
Lunges
Leg Curls
Squats

Biceps
Biceps Curls
Pull-ups
Reverse Curls

Upper Abdominals
Crunches
V-sits
Plank

Lower Abdominals
Bent and Straight Legs Raises
Barbell Rollouts
Plank

Adductors
Lateral Lunges
Machine Adductions
Squats

Calves
Calf Raises
Squats
Deadlifts

Deltoid
Shoulder Press
Lateral and Front Raises
Upright Rows and Shrugs

Pectorals
Bench Press
Dumbbell Flys
Press-ups

Obliques
Lower Body Twists
Wood Chopper
Oblique Crunches

Quadriceps
Lunges
Squats
Deadlifts

176

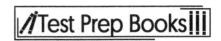

Cardiac Muscles

Cardiac muscle cells are found only in the heart where they control the heart's rhythm and blood pressure. Like skeletal muscle, cardiac muscle has striations, but cardiac muscle cells are smaller than skeletal muscle cells, so they typically have only one nucleus. Like smooth muscle, cardiac muscles do not require neurotransmitter release by motor neurons to function, and they instead operate via gap junctions.

Anatomy and Physiology of the Reproductive System

The **reproductive system** is responsible for producing, storing, nourishing, and transporting functional reproductive cells, or gametes, in the human body. It includes the reproductive organs, also known as gonads, the reproductive tract, the accessory glands and organs that secrete fluids into the reproductive tract, and the perineal structures, which are the external genitalia.

Reproduction involves the passing of genes from one generation to the next, and that is accomplished through haploid gametes. Gametes have gone through meiosis and have 23 chromosomes, half the normal number. The male gamete is sperm, and the female gamete is an egg or ovum. When a sperm fertilizes an egg, they create a zygote, which is the first cell of a new organism. The zygote has a full set of 46 chromosomes because it received 23 from each parent. Because of gene shuffling during sperm and egg development, sperm and egg chromosome sets are all different, which results in the variety seen in humans.

Male Reproductive System

The entire male reproductive system is designed to generate sperm and produce semen that facilitate fertilization of eggs, the female gametes. The testes are the endocrine glands that secrete testosterone, a hormone that is important for secondary sex characteristics and sperm development, or spermatogenesis. Testosterone is in the androgen steroid-hormone family. The testes also produce and store 500 million spermatocytes, which are the male gametes, each day. Testes are housed in the scrotum, which is a sac that hangs outside the body so that spermatogenesis occurs at cooler and optimal conditions.

The seminiferous tubules within the testes produce spermatocytes, which then travel to the epididymis where they are stored as they mature. Then, the sperm move to the ejaculatory duct via the vas deferens. The ejaculatory duct contains more than just sperm. The seminal vesicles secrete an alkaline substance that will help sperm survive in the acidic vagina. The prostate gland secretes enzymes bathed in a milky white fluid that is important for thinning semen after ejaculation to increase its likelihood of reaching the egg. The bulbourethral gland, or Cowper's gland, secretes an alkaline fluid that lubricates the urethra prior to ejaculation to neutralize any acidic urine residue.

The sperm along with all the exocrine secretions are collectively called semen. Their destination is the vagina, and they can only get there if the penis is erect due to arousal and increased circulation. During sexual intercourse, ejaculation will forcefully expel the contents of the semen and effectively deliver the sperm to the egg. The muscular prostate gland is important for ejaculation. Each ejaculation releases 2 to 6 million sperm. Sperm has a whip-like flagellum tail that facilitates movement.

Female Reproductive System

The vagina is the passageway that sperm must travel through to reach an egg, the female gamete. Surrounding the vagina are the labia minor and labia major, both of which are folds that protect the urethra, which is used for urination and is part of the urinary system, and the vaginal opening. The clitoris is rich in nerve-endings, making it sensitive and highly stimulated during sexual intercourse. It is above the vagina and urethra. An exocrine gland called the Bartholin's glands secretes a fluid during arousal that is important for lubrication.

The female gonads are the ovaries. Ovaries generally alternate producing one gamete, an egg or oocyte, per month. They are also responsible for secreting the hormones estrogen and progesterone. Fertilization cannot happen unless

177

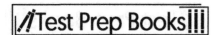

the ejaculated sperm finds the egg, which is only available at certain times of the month. Eggs, or ova, develop in the ovaries in clusters surrounded by follicles, and after puberty, they are delivered to the uterus once a month via the fallopian tubes. The 28-day average journey of the egg to the uterus is called the menstrual cycle, and it is highly regulated by the endocrine system. The regulatory hormones Gonadotropin releasing hormone (GnRH), luteinizing hormone (LH), and follicle-stimulating hormone (FSH) orchestrate the menstrual cycle. Ovarian hormones estrogen and progesterone are also important in timing as well as for vascularization of the uterus in preparation for pregnancy. Fertilization usually happens around ovulation, which is when the egg is inside the fallopian tube. The resulting zygote travels down the tube and implants into the uterine wall. The uterus protects and nourishes the developing embryo for nine months until it is ready for the outside environment.

If the egg released is unfertilized, the uterine lining will slough off during menstruation. Should a fertilized egg, called a zygote, reach the uterus, it will embed itself into the uterine wall due to uterine vascularization that will deliver blood, nutrients, and antibodies to the developing embryo. The uterus is where the embryo will develop for the next nine months. Mammary glands are important female reproductive structures because they produce the milk provided for babies during lactation. Milk contains nutrients and antibodies that benefit the baby.

Anatomy and Physiology of the Integumentary System

The **integumentary system** includes skin, hair, nails, oil glands, and sweat glands. The largest organ of the integumentary system (and of the body), the skin, acts as a barrier and protects the body from mechanical impact, variations in temperature, microorganisms, chemicals, and UV radiation from the sun. It regulates body temperature, peripheral circulation, and excretes waste through sweat. It also contains a large network of nerve cells that relay changes in the external environment to the brain.

Layers of Skin

Skin consists of three layers, the surface epidermis, the inner dermis, and the subcutaneous hypodermis, located below the dermis and containing a layer of fat and connective tissue, which are both important for insulation.

The whole epidermis is composed of epithelial cells that lack blood vessels. The outer epidermis is composed of dead cells which surround the living cells underneath. The most inner epidermal tissue is a single layer of cells called the stratum basale which is composed of rapidly dividing cells that push old cells to the skin's surface. When being pushed out, the cells' organelles disappear, and they start producing a protein called keratin that eventually forms a tough waterproof layer. This outer layer sloughs off every four to five weeks. The melanocytes in the stratum basale produce the pigment melanin that absorbs UV rays and protects the skin. Skin also produces vitamin D if exposed to sunlight.

The dermis underneath the epidermis contains supporting collagen fibers peppered with nerves, blood vessels, hair follicles, sweat glands, oil glands, and smooth muscles.

Skin's Involvement in Temperature Homeostasis

The skin has a thermoregulatory role in the human body that is controlled by a negative feedback loop. The control center of temperature regulation is the hypothalamus in the brain. When the hypothalamus is alerted by receptors from the dermis, it secretes hormones that activate effectors to keep internal temperature at a set point of 98.6°F (37°C). If the environment is too cold, the hypothalamus will initiate a pathway that induces muscle shivering to release heat energy as well as constrict blood vessels to limit heat loss. In hot conditions, the hypothalamus will initiate a pathway that vasodilates blood vessels to increase heat loss and stimulate sweating for evaporative cooling. Evaporative cooling occurs when the hottest water particles evaporate and leave behind the coolest ones. This cools down the body.

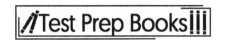

Sebaceous Glands vs. Sweat Glands

The skin also contains oil glands, or sebaceous glands, and sweat glands that are exocrine because their substances are secreted through ducts. Endocrine glands secrete substances into the blood stream instead. Oil glands are attached to hair follicles. They secrete sebum, an oily substance that moisturizes the skin, protecting it from water loss. Sebum also keeps the skin elastic. Also, sebum's slight acidity provides a chemical defense against bacterial and fungal infections.

Sweat glands not attached to hair follicles are called eccrine glands. They are all over the body, and are the sweat glands responsible for thermoregulation. They also remove bodily waste by secreting water and electrolytes. Sweat glands attached to hair follicles are apocrine glands, and there are far fewer apocrine sweat glands than eccrine sweat glands in the body. Apocrine glands are only active post-puberty. They secrete a thicker, viscous substance that is attractive to bacteria, leading to the unpleasant smell in armpits, feet, and the groin. They are stimulated during stress and arousal.

Anatomy and Physiology of the Endocrine System

The **endocrine system** is made up of the ductless tissues and glands that secrete hormones directly into the bloodstream. It is similar to the nervous system in that it controls various functions of the body, but it does so via secretion of hormones in the bloodstream as opposed to nerve impulses. The endocrine system is also different because its effects last longer than that of the nervous system. Nerve impulses are immediate while hormone responses can last for minutes or even days.

The endocrine system works closely with the nervous system to regulate the physiological activities of the other systems of the body in order to maintain homeostasis. Hormone secretions are controlled by tight feedback loops that are generally regulated by the hypothalamus, the bridge between the nervous and endocrine systems. The hypothalamus receives sensory input via the nervous system and responds by stimulating or inhibiting the pituitary gland, which, in turn, stimulates or inhibits several other glands. The tight control is due to hormone secretions.

Hormones are chemicals that bind to specific target cells. Each hormone will only bind to a target cell that has a specific receptor that has the correct shape. For example, testosterone will not attach to skin cells because skin cells have no receptor that recognizes testosterone.

There are two types of hormones: steroid and protein. Steroid hormones are lipid, nonpolar substances, and most are able to diffuse across cell membranes. Once they do, they bind to a receptor that initiates a signal transduction cascade that affects gene expression. Non-steroid hormones bind to receptors on cell membranes that also initiate a signal transduction cascade that affects enzyme activity and chemical reactions.

Major Endocrine Glands

Hypothalamus: This gland is a part of the brain. It connects the nervous system to the endocrine system because it receives sensory information through nerves, and it sends instructions via hormones delivered to the pituitary.

Pituitary Gland: This gland is pea-sized and is found at the bottom of the hypothalamus. It has two lobes called the anterior and posterior lobes. It plays an important role in regulating other endocrine glands. For example, it secretes growth hormone, which regulates growth. Other hormones that are released by this gland control the reproductive system, childbirth, nursing, blood osmolarity, and metabolism.

The hormones and glands respond to each other via feedback loops, and a typical feedback loop is illustrated in the following picture. The hypothalamus and pituitary gland are master controllers of most of the other glands.

Observe this flow chart:

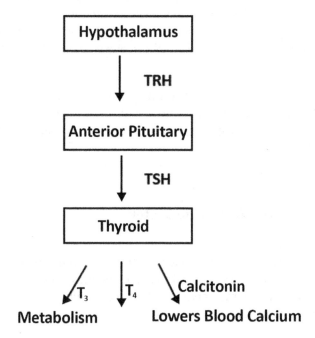

Thymus Gland*:* This gland is located in the chest cavity, embedded in connective tissue. It produces several hormones that are important for development and maintenance of T lymphocytes, which are important cells for immunity.

Adrenal Gland*:* One adrenal gland is attached to the top of each kidney. It produces epinephrine and norepinephrine which cause the "fight or flight" response in the face of danger or stress. These hormones raise heart rate, blood pressure, dilate bronchioles, and deliver blood to the muscles. All of these actions increase circulation and release glucose so that the body has an energy burst.

Pineal Gland*:* The pineal gland secretes melatonin, which is a hormone that regulates the body's circadian rhythm, which governs the natural wake-sleep cycle.

Testes and **Ovaries**: They secrete testosterone and both estrogen and progesterone, respectively. They are responsible for secondary sex characteristics, gamete development, and female hormones are important for embryonic development.

Thyroid Gland*:* This gland releases hormones like thyroxine and calcitonin. Thyroxine stimulates metabolism, and calcitonin monitors the amount of circulating calcium. Calcitonin signals the body to regulating calcium from bone reserves as well as kidney reabsorption of calcium.

Parathyroid Glands*:* These are four pea-sized glands located on the posterior surface of the thyroid. The main hormone that is secreted is called parathyroid hormone (PTH), which influences calcium levels like calcitonin, except it is antagonistic. PTH increases extracellular levels of calcium while calcitonin decreases it.

Pancreas*:* The pancreas is an organ that has both endocrine and exocrine functions. It functions outside of a typical feedback loop in that blood sugar seems to signal the pancreas itself. The endocrine functions are controlled by the pancreatic islets of Langerhans, which are groups of beta cells scattered throughout the gland that secrete insulin to

180

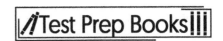

lower blood sugar levels in the body. Neighboring alpha cells secrete glucagon to raise blood sugar. These complementary hormones keep blood sugar in check.

Anatomy and Physiology of the Genitourinary System

The **urinary system** is made up of the kidneys, ureters, urinary bladder, and the urethra. It is the system responsible for removing waste products and balancing water and electrolyte concentrations in the blood. The urinary system has many important functions related to waste excretion. It regulates the concentrations of sodium, potassium, chloride, calcium, and other ions in the filtrate by controlling the amount of each that is reabsorbed during filtration. The reabsorption or secretion of hydrogen ions and bicarbonate contributes to the maintenance of blood pH. Certain kidney cells can detect any reductions in blood volume and pressure. If that happens, they secrete renin, which activates a hormone that causes increased reabsorption of sodium ions and water, raising volume and pressure. Under hypoxic conditions, kidney cells will secrete erythropoietin in order to stimulate red blood cell production. Kidney cells also synthesize calcitriol, which is a hormone derivative of vitamin D3 that aids in calcium ion absorption by the intestinal epithelium.

Under normal circumstances, humans have two functioning kidneys in the lower back and on either side of the spinal cord. They are the main organs that are responsible for filtering waste products out of the blood and regulating blood water and electrolyte levels. Blood enters the kidney through the renal artery, and urea and wastes are removed, while water and the acidity/alkalinity of the blood is adjusted. Toxic substances and drugs are also filtered. Blood exits through the renal vein, and the urine waste travels through the ureter to the bladder, where it is stored until it is eliminated through the urethra.

The kidneys have an outer renal cortex and an inner renal medulla that contain millions of tiny filtering units called nephrons. Nephrons have two parts: a glomerulus, which is the filter, and a tubule. The glomerulus is a network of capillaries covered by the Bowman's capsule, which is the entrance to the tubule. As blood enters the kidneys via the renal artery, the glomerulus allows for fluid and waste products to pass through it and enter the tubule. Blood cells and large molecules, such as proteins, do not pass through and remain in the blood.

The filtrate passes through the tubule, which has several parts. The proximal tubule comes first, and then the descending and ascending limbs of the loop of Henle dip into the medulla, followed by the distal tubule and collecting duct. The journey through the tubule involves a balancing act that regulates blood osmolarity, pH, and electrolytes exchange of materials between the tubule and the bloodstream. The final product at the collecting tubule is called urine, and it is delivered to the bladder by the ureter. The most central part of the kidney is the **renal pelvis**, and it acts as a funnel by delivering the urine from the millions of collecting tubules to the **ureters**. The filtered blood exits through the renal vein and is returned to circulation.

Here's a look at the genitourinary system:

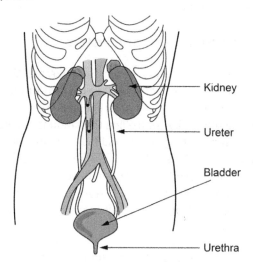

Here's a close up look at the kidney:

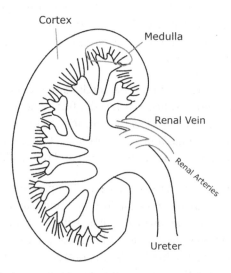

Waste Excretion

Once urine accumulates, it leaves the kidneys. The urine travels through the ureters into the urinary bladder, a muscular organ that is hollow and elastic. As more urine enters the urinary bladder, its walls stretch and become thinner so there is no significant difference in internal pressure. The urinary bladder stores the urine until the body is ready for urination, at which time the muscles contract and force the urine through the urethra and out of the body.

Anatomy and Physiology of the Immune System

The **immune system** is the body's defense against invading microorganisms (bacteria, viruses, fungi, and parasites) and other harmful, foreign substances. It is capable of limiting or preventing infection.

There are two general types of immunity: innate immunity and acquired immunity. Innate immunity uses physical and chemical barriers to block microorganism entry into the body. The biggest barrier is the skin; it forms a physical barrier that blocks microorganisms from entering underlying tissues. Mucous membranes in the digestive,

182

respiratory, and urinary systems secrete mucus to block and remove invading microorganisms. Other natural defenses include saliva, tears, and stomach acids, which are all chemical barriers intended to block infection with microorganisms. Acid is inhospitable to pathogens, as are tears, mucus, and saliva, which all contain a natural antibiotic called lysozyme. The respiratory passages contain microscopic cilia, which are like bristles that sweep out pathogens. In addition, macrophages and other white blood cells can recognize and eliminate foreign objects through phagocytosis or toxic secretions.

Acquired immunity refers to a specific set of events used by the body to fight a particular infection. Essentially, the body accumulates and stores information about the nature of an invading microorganism. As a result, the body can mount a specific attack that is much more effective than innate immunity. It also provides a way for the body to prevent future infections by the same microorganism.

Acquired immunity is divided into a primary response and a secondary response. The **primary immune response** occurs the first time a particular microorganism enters the body, where macrophages engulf the microorganism and travel to the lymph nodes. In the lymph nodes, macrophages present the invader to helper T lymphocytes, which then activate humoral and cellular immunity. Humoral immunity refers to immunity resulting from antibody production by B lymphocytes. After being activated by helper T lymphocytes, B lymphocytes multiply and divide into plasma cells and memory cells. Plasma cells are B lymphocytes that produce immune proteins called antibodies, or immunoglobulins. Antibodies then bind the microorganism to flag it for destruction by other white blood cells. Cellular immunity refers to the immune response coordinated by T lymphocytes. After being activated by helper T lymphocytes, other T lymphocytes attack and kill cells that cause infection or disease.

The **secondary immune response** takes place during subsequent encounters with a known microorganism. Memory cells respond to the previously encountered microorganism by immediately producing antibodies. Memory cells are B lymphocytes that store information to produce antibodies. The secondary immune response is swift and powerful because it eliminates the need for the time-consuming macrophage activation of the primary immune response. Suppressor T lymphocytes also take part to inhibit the immune response as an overactive immune response could cause damage to healthy cells.

Inflammation occurs if a pathogen evades the barriers and chemical defenses. It stimulates pain receptors, alerting the individual that something is wrong. It also elevates body temperature to speed up chemical reactions, although if a fever goes unchecked it can be dangerous due to the fact that extreme heat unfolds proteins. Histamine is secreted which dilates blood vessels and recruits white blood cells that destroy invaders non-specifically. The immune system is tied to the lymphatic system. The thymus, one of the lymphatic system organs, is the site of maturation of T-cells, a type of white blood cell. The lymphatic system is important in the inflammatory response because lymph vessels deliver leukocytes and collect debris that will be filtered in the lymph nodes and the spleen.

Antigen and Typical Immune Response

Should a pathogen evade barriers and survive through inflammation, an antigen-specific adaptive immune response will begin. Immune cells recognize these foreign particles by their antigens, which are their unique and identifying surface proteins. Drugs, toxins, and transplanted cells can also act as antigens. The body even recognizes its own cells as potential threats in autoimmune diseases.

When a macrophage engulfs a pathogen and presents its antigens, helper T cells recognize the signal and secrete cytokines to signal T lymphocytes and B lymphocytes so that they launch the cell-mediated and humoral response, respectively. The cell-mediated response occurs when the T lymphocytes kill infected cells by secreting cytotoxins. The humoral response occurs when B lymphocytes proliferate into plasma and memory cells. The plasma cells secrete antigen-specific antibodies, which bind to the pathogens so that they cannot bind to host cells. Macrophages and other phagocytic cells called neutrophils engulf and degrade the antibody/pathogen complex. The

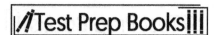

memory cells remain in circulation and initiate a secondary immune response should the pathogen dare enter the host again.

Types of Leukocytes

There are many **leukocytes**, or **white blood cells**, involved in both innate and adaptive immunity. All are developed in bone marrow. Many have been mentioned in the text above, but a comprehensive list is included here for reference.

- **Monocytes** are large phagocytic cells.
  - Macrophages engulf pathogens and present their antigen. Some circulate, but others reside in lymphatic organs like the spleen and lymph nodes.
  - Dendritic cells are also phagocytic and antigen-presenting.
- **Granulocytes** are cells that contain secretory granules.
  - Neutrophils are the most abundant white blood cell. They are circulating and aggressive phagocytic cells that are part of innate immunity. They also secrete substances that are toxic to pathogens.
  - Basophils and mast cells secrete histamine, which stimulates the inflammatory response.
  - Eosinophils are found underneath mucous membranes and defend against multi-cellular parasites like worms. They have low phagocytic activity and primarily secrete destructive enzymes.
- **T lymphocytes** mature in the thymus.
  - Helper T cells recognize antigens presented by macrophages and dendritic cells and secrete cytokines, which mount the humoral and cell-mediated immune response.
  - Killer T cells are cytotoxic cells involved in the cell-mediated response by recognizing and poisoning infected cells.
  - Suppressor T cells suppress the adaptive immune response when there is no threat to conserve resources and energy.
  - Memory T cells remain in circulation to aid in the secondary immune response.
- **B lymphocytes** mature in bone marrow.
  - Plasma B cells secrete antigen-specific antibodies when signaled by Helper T cells and are degraded after the immune response.
  - Memory B cells store antigen-specific antibody making instructions and remain circulating after the immune response is over.
- **Natural killer cells** are part of innate immunity and patrol and identify suspect-material. They respond by secreting cytotoxic substances.

Anatomy and Physiology of the Skeletal System

Axial Skeleton and Appendicular Skeleton

The skeletal system is composed of 206 bones interconnected by tough connective tissue called ligaments. The axial skeleton can be considered the north-south axis of the skeleton. It includes the spinal column, sternum, ribs, and skull. There are 80 bones in the axial skeleton, and 33 of them are vertebrae. The ribs make up 12 of the bones in the axial skeleton.

The remaining 126 bones are in the appendicular skeleton, which contains bones of the appendages like the collarbone (clavicle), shoulders (scapula), arms, hands, hips, legs, and feet. The arm bones consist of the upper humerus with the radius and ulna that attach to the hands. The wrists, hands, and fingers are composed of the carpals, metacarpals, and phalanges, respectively. The femur attaches to the hips. The patella or kneecap connects the femur to the fibula and tibia. The ankles, feet, and toes are composed of the tarsals, metatarsals, and phalanges, respectively.

185

ience

Functions of the Skeletal System

One of the skeletal system's most important functions is to protect vital internal organs. The skull protects the brain, the ribs protect the lungs and heart, the vertebrae protect the spinal column, and the pelvis protects the uterus and other reproductive organs. Red bone marrow produces red and white blood cells as well as platelets in a process known as **hemopoiesis**. The bones themselves store the essential minerals calcium and phosphorus. The organization of the skeleton allows us to stand upright and acts as a foundation for organs and tissues to attach and maintain their location. This is similar to how the wooden frame of a house has room partitions to designate the type of room and floors that furniture can attach to.

The skeletal system and the muscular system are literally interconnected and allow for voluntary movement. Strong connective tissues called tendons attach bones to muscles. Most muscles work in opposing pairs and act as levers. For example, flexing the biceps brings the arm bones together and flexing the triceps pushes them apart. Synovial joints are movable joints, and they are rich with cartilage, connective tissue, and synovial fluid which acts as a lubricant. The majority of joints are synovial joints, and they include hinge joints, like the one at the elbow, which allows for opening and closing.

The vertebrae are cartilaginous joints which have spaces between them filled with cushion-like discs that act as shock absorbers and glue that holds the vertebrae together. The reason for the tight packing of the vertebrae is to protect the spinal cord inside. This limits their movement, but because there are so many of them it allows the backbone to be flexible.

Fibrous joints like those in the skull have fibrous tissue between the bones and no cavity between them. These are fixed joints that are immobile.

Compact and Spongy Bone

Osteoclasts, osteoblasts, and osteocytes are the three types of bone cells. **Osteoclasts** break down old bone, **osteoblasts** make new bone, and **osteocytes** are the mature functional bone cells. Bone is constantly regenerating due to the osteoblasts/osteoclasts that line all types of bones and the blood vessels inside them. The cells exist within a matrix of collagen fibers and minerals. The collagen fibers provide resistance to tension and the minerals provide resistance to compression. Because of the collagen and mineral matrix, bones have ample reinforcement to collectively support the entire human body.

Bones can be classified as any of the following:

- **Long bones** include tube-like rods like the arm and leg bones.
- **Short bones** are tube-like rods that are smaller than long bones like the fingers and toes.
- **Flat bones** are thin and flat like the ribs and breastbone.
- **Irregular bones**, like the vertebrae, are compact and don't fit into the other categories.

The outer tissue of the bone is surrounded by connective tissue known as periosteum. It appears shiny, smooth, and white. It protects the bone, anchors the bone to the connective tissue that surrounds muscles, and links the bone to the circulatory and nervous system. Compact bone is underneath the periosteum and is made of a dense blend of tightly packed osteocytes. It serves as a mineral reservoir of calcium and phosphorus. Compact bones have a Haversian system that is composed of embedded blood vessels, lymph vessels, and nerve bundles that span the interior of the bone from one end to the other. Branching from the central canal to the surface of the bone are the canals of Volkmann which deliver materials to peripheral osteocytes. Concentric circles surround the central Haversian canal, and these lamallae have gaps between them called lacunae where osteocytes are embedded.

This material is provided for exam preparation purposes only and does not indicate an endorsement of any specific scientific, political, or religious point of view. © TPB Publishing. You have been licensed one copy of this document for personal use only. Any other reproduction or redistribution is strictly prohibited. All rights reserved.

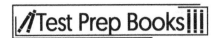

In contrast, spongy bone is very porous and more flexible than compact bone. It is at the ends of long bones and the central part of flat bones. It looks like a honeycomb, and the open spaces are connected by trabeculae which are beams of tissue that add support. They add strength without adding mass.

Cartilage is a very flexible connective tissue made of collagen and flexible elastin. It has no blood vessels and obtains materials via diffusion. It is replaced by bone starting in infancy in a process called ossification.

Chemistry

Scientific Notation and Temperature Scales

Scientific Notation

Scientific notation is the conversion of extremely small or large numbers into a format that is easier to comprehend and manipulate. It changes the number into a product of two separate numbers: a digit term and an exponential term.

Scientific notation = digit term x exponential term

To put a number into scientific notation, one should use the following steps:

- Move the decimal point to after the first non-zero number to find the digit number.
- Count how many places the decimal point was moved in step 1.
- Determine if the exponent is positive or negative.
- Create an exponential term using the information from steps 2 and 3.
- Combine the digit term and exponential term to get scientific notation.

For example, to put 0.0000098 into scientific notation, the decimal should be moved so that it lies between the last two numbers: 000009.8. This creates the digit number: *9.8*

Next, the number of places that the decimal point moved is determined; to get between the 9 and the 8, the decimal was moved six places to the right. It may be helpful to remember that a decimal moved to the right creates a negative exponent, and a decimal moved to the left creates a positive exponent. Because the decimal was moved six places to the right, the exponent is negative.

Now, the exponential term can be created by using the base 10 (this is *always* the base in scientific notation) and the number of places moved as the exponent, in this case: 10^{-6}

Finally, the digit term and the exponential term can be combined as a product. Therefore, the scientific notation for the number 0.0000098 is:

$$9.8 \times 10^{-6}$$

Temperature Scales

There are three main temperature scales used in science. The scale most often used in the United States is the **Fahrenheit** scale. This scale is based on the measurement of water freezing at 32°F and water boiling at 212°F. The **Celsius** scale uses 0°C as the temperature for water freezing and 100°C for water boiling. The Celsius scale is the most widely used in the scientific community. The accepted measurement by the **International System of Units** (from the French Système international d'unités), or SI, for temperature is the Kelvin scale. This is the scale employed in thermodynamics, since its zero is the basis for absolute zero, or the unattainable temperature, when matter no longer exhibits degradation.

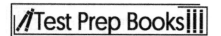

The conversions between the temperature scales are as follows:

$$°\text{Fahrenheit to }°\text{Celsius: } °C = \frac{5}{9}(°F - 32)$$

$$°\text{Celsius to }°\text{Fahrenheit: } °F = \left(\frac{9}{5}°C\right) + 32$$

$$°\text{Celsius to Kelvin: } K = °C + 273.15$$

Atomic Structure and the Periodic Table

Atomic Structure

The structure of an atom has two major components: the atomic nucleus and the atomic shells (also known as orbitals). The **nucleus** is found in the center of an atom. The three major subatomic particles are protons, neutrons, and electrons and are found in the atomic nucleus and shells.

Protons are found in the atomic nucleus and are positively charged particles. The addition or removal of protons from an atom's nucleus creates an entirely different element. **Neutrons** are also found in the atomic nucleus and are neutral particles, meaning they have no net electrical charge. The addition or removal of neutrons from an atom's nucleus does not create a different element but instead creates a lighter or heavier form of that element called an isotope. **Electrons** are found orbiting in the atomic shells around the nucleus and are negatively charged particles. A proton or a neutron has nearly 2,000 times the mass of an electron.

Electrons orbit the nucleus in atomic shells, or electron clouds, each of which can accommodate a certain number of electrons. For example, the first atomic shell can accommodate two electrons, the second atomic shell can hold a maximum of eight electrons, and the third atomic shell can house a maximum of eight electrons. The negatively charged electrons orbiting the nucleus are attracted to the positively charged protons in the nucleus via electromagnetic force. The attraction of opposite electrical charges gives rise to chemical bonds, which refers to the ways atoms are attached to each other.

The **atomic number** of an atom is determined by the number of protons within the nucleus. When a substance is composed of atoms that all have the same atomic number, it is called an **element**. Elements are arranged by atomic number and grouped by properties in the **Periodic table.**

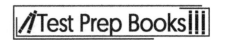

An atom's **mass number** is determined by the sum of the total number of protons and neutrons in the atom. Most nuclei have a net neutral charge, and all atoms of one type have the same atomic number. However, there are some atoms of the same type that have a different mass number, due to an imbalance of neutrons. These are called **isotopes**. In isotopes, the atomic number, which is determined by the number of protons, is the same, but the mass number, which is determined by adding the protons and neutrons, is different due to the irregular number of neutrons.

Chemical Bonding

Chemical bonding typically results in the formation of a new substance, called a compound. Only the electrons in the outermost atomic shell are able to form chemical bonds. These electrons are known as **valence electrons**, and they are what determines the chemical properties of an atom.

Chemical bonding occurs between two or more atoms that are joined together. There are three types of chemical bonds: ionic, covalent, and metallic. The characteristics of the different bonds are determined by how electrons behave in a compound. **Lewis structures** were developed to help visualize the electrons in molecules; they are a method of writing a compound structure formula and including its electron composition. A Lewis symbol for an element consists of the element symbol and a dot for each valence electron. The dots are located on all four sides of the symbol, with a maximum of two dots per side, and eight dots, or electrons, total. The octet rule states that atoms tend to gain, lose, or share electrons until they have a total of eight valence electrons.

Ionic bonds are formed from the electrostatic attractions between oppositely charged atoms. They result from the transfer of electrons from a metal on the left side of the periodic table to a nonmetal on the right side. The metallic substance often has low ionization energy and will transfer an electron easily to the nonmetal, which has a high electron affinity. An example of this is the compound NaCl, which is sodium chloride or table salt, where the Na atom transfers an electron to the Cl atom. Due to strong bonding, ionic compounds have several distinct characteristics. They have high melting and boiling points and are brittle and crystalline. They are arranged in rigid, well-defined structures, which allow them to break apart along smooth, flat surfaces. The formation of ionic bonds is a reaction that is exothermic. In the opposite scenario, the energy it takes to break up a one mole quantity of an ionic compound is referred to as lattice energy, which is generally endothermic. The Lewis structure for NaCl is written as follows:

Covalent bonds are formed when two atoms share electrons, instead of transferring them as in ionic compounds. The atoms in covalent compounds have a balance of attraction and repulsion between their protons and electrons, which keeps them bonded together. Two atoms can be joined by single, double, or even triple covalent bonds. As the number of electrons that are shared increases, the length of the bond decreases. Covalent substances have low melting and boiling points and are poor conductors of heat and electricity.

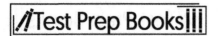

The Lewis structure for Cl_2 is written as follows:

Lewis structure Cl_2

$$:\overset{\cdot\cdot}{\underset{\cdot\cdot}{Cl}}{\cdot} \; + \; {\cdot}\overset{\cdot\cdot}{\underset{\cdot\cdot}{Cl}}: \; \longrightarrow \; :\overset{\cdot\cdot}{\underset{\cdot\cdot}{Cl}}:\overset{\cdot\cdot}{\underset{\cdot\cdot}{Cl}}:$$

Metallic bonds are formed by electrons that move freely through metal. They are the product of the force of attraction between electrons and metal ions. The electrons are shared by many metal cations and act like glue that holds the metallic substance together, similar to the attraction between oppositely-charged atoms in ionic substances, except the electrons are more fluid and float around the bonded metals and form a sea of electrons. Metallic compounds have characteristic properties that include strength, conduction of heat and electricity, and malleability. They can conduct electricity by passing energy through the freely moving electrons, creating a **current**. These compounds also have high melting and boiling points. Lewis structures are not common for metallic structures because of the free-roaming ability of the electrons.

Periodic Table

The periodic table catalogues all of the elements known to man, currently 118. It is one of the most important references in the science of chemistry. Information that can be gathered from the periodic table includes the element's atomic number, atomic mass, and chemical symbol. The first periodic table was rendered by Mendeleev in the mid-1800s and was ordered according to increasing atomic mass. The modern periodic table is arranged in order of increasing atomic number. It is also arranged in horizontal rows known as **periods,** and vertical columns known as **families,** or **groups**. The periodic table contains seven periods and eighteen families. Elements in the periodic table can also be classified into three major groups: metals, metalloids, and nonmetals. **Metals** are concentrated on the left side of the periodic table, while **nonmetals** are found on the right side. **Metalloids** occupy the area between the metals and nonmetals.

Due to the fact the periodic table is ordered by increasing atomic number, the electron configurations of the elements show periodicity. As the atomic number increases, electrons gradually fill the shells of an atom. In general, the start of a new period corresponds to the first time an electron inhabits a new shell.

Periodic Table of the Elements

1A																	8A
1 H hydrogen 1.008	2A											3A	4A	5A	6A	7A	2 He helium 4.003
3 Li lithium 6.94	4 Be beryllium 9.012											5 B boron 10.81	6 C carbon 12.01	7 N nitrogen 14.01	8 O oxygen 16.00	9 F fluorine 19.00	10 Ne neon 20.18
11 Na sodium 22.99	12 Mg magnesium 24.31	3B	4B	5B	6B	7B	8B	8B	8B	11B	12B	13 Al aluminum 26.98	14 Si silicon 28.09	15 P phosphorus 30.97	16 S sulfur 32.06	17 Cl chlorine 35.45	18 Ar argon 39.95
19 K potassium 39.10	20 Ca calcium 40.08	21 Sc scandium 44.96	22 Ti titanium 47.88	23 V vanadium 50.94	24 Cr chromium 52.00	25 Mn manganese 54.94	26 Fe iron 55.85	27 Co cobalt 58.93	28 Ni nickel 58.69	29 Cu copper 63.55	30 Zn zinc 65.39	31 Ga gallium 69.72	32 Ge germanium 72.64	33 As arsenic 74.92	34 Se selenium 78.96	35 Br bromine 79.90	36 Kr krypton 83.79
37 Rb rubidium 85.47	38 Sr strontium 87.62	39 Y yttrium 88.91	40 Zr zirconium 91.22	41 Nb niobium 92.91	42 Mo molybdenum 95.96	43 Tc technetium (98)	44 Ru ruthenium 101.1	45 Rh rhodium 102.9	46 Pd palladium 106.4	47 Ag silver 107.9	48 Cd cadmium 112.4	49 In indium 114.8	50 Sn tin 118.7	51 Sb antimony 121.8	52 Te tellurium 127.6	53 I iodine 126.9	54 Xe xenon 131.3
55 Cs cesium 132.9	56 Ba barium 137.3	57-71	72 Hf hafnium 178.5	73 Ta tantalum 180.9	74 W tungsten 183.9	75 Re rhenium 186.2	76 Os osmium 190.2	77 Ir iridium 192.2	78 Pt platinum 195.1	79 Au gold 197.0	80 Hg mercury 200.5	81 Tl thallium 204.4	82 Pb lead 207.2	83 Bi bismuth 209.0	84 Po polonium (209)	85 At astatine (210)	86 Rn radon (222)
87 Fr francium (223)	88 Ra radium (226)	89-103	104 Rf rutherfordium (265)	105 Db dubnium (268)	106 Sg seaborgium (271)	107 Bh bohrium (270)	108 Hs hassium (277)	109 Mt meitnerium (276)	110 Ds darmstadtium (281)	111 Rg roentgenium (280)	112 Cn copernicum (285)	113 Uut ununtrium (284)	114 Fl flerovium (289)	115 Uup ununpentium (288)	116 Lv livermorium (293)	117 Uus ununseptium (294)	118 Uuo ununoctium (294)

Lanthanide Series	57 La lanthanum 138.9	58 Ce cerium 140.1	59 Pr praseodymium 140.9	60 Nd neodymium 144.2	61 Pm promethium (145)	62 Sm samarium 150.4	63 Eu europium 152.0	64 Gd gadolinium 157.2	65 Tb terbium 158.9	66 Dy dysprosium 162.5	67 Ho holmium 164.9	68 Er erbium 167.3	69 Tm thulium 168.9	70 Yb ytterbium 173.0	71 Lu lutetium 175.0
Actinide Series	89 Ac actinium (227)	90 Th thorium 232	91 Pa protactinium 231	92 U uranium 238	93 Np neptunium (237)	94 Pu plutonium (244)	95 Am americium (243)	96 Cm curium (247)	97 Bk berkelium (247)	98 Cf californium (251)	99 Es einsteinium (252)	100 Fm fermium (257)	101 Md mendelevium (258)	102 No nobelium (259)	103 Lr lawrencium (262)

Legend:
- Alkaline Metal
- Alkaline Earth
- Transition Metal
- Basic Metal
- Semimetal
- Nonmetal
- Halogen
- Noble Gas
- Lanthanide
- Actinide

191

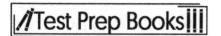

Science

Other trends in the properties of elements in the periodic table are:

Atomic radius: One-half the distance between the nuclei of atoms of the same element

Electronegativity: A measurement of the tendency of an atom to form a chemical bond

Ionization energy: The amount of energy needed to remove an electron from a gas or ion

Electron affinity: The ability of an atom to accept an electron

Trends in the Periodic Table

Chemical Equations

Chemical reactions are represented by **chemical equations**. The equations help to explain how the molecules change during the reaction. For example, when hydrogen gas (H_2) combines with oxygen gas (O_2), two molecules of

192

water are formed. The equation is written as follows, where the "+" sign means *reacts with* and the "→" means *produces*:

$$2\,H_2 + O_2 \rightarrow 2\,H_2O$$

Two hydrogen molecules react with an oxygen molecule to produce two water molecules. In all chemical equations, the quantity of each element on the reactant side of the equation should equal the quantity of the same element on the product side of the equation due to the law of conservation of matter. If this is true, the equation is described as balanced. To figure out how many of each element there is on each side of the equation, the coefficient of the element should be multiplied by the subscript next to the element. Coefficients and subscripts are noted for quantities larger than one. The **coefficient** is the number located directly to the left of the element.

The **subscript** is the small-sized number directly to the right of the element. In the equation above, on the left side, the coefficient of the hydrogen is two and the subscript is also two, which makes a total of four hydrogen atoms. Using the same method, there are two oxygen atoms. On the right side, the coefficient two is multiplied by the subscript in each element of the water molecule, making four hydrogen atoms and two oxygen atoms. This equation is balanced because there are four hydrogen atoms and two oxygen atoms on each side. The states of the reactants and products can also be written in the equation: gas (g), liquid (l), solid (s), and dissolved in water (aq). If they are included, they are noted in parentheses on the right side of each molecule in the equation.

States of Matter and Factors that Affect Phase Changes

Matter is most commonly found in three distinct states or phases: solid, liquid, and gas. A solid has a distinct shape and a defined volume. A liquid has a more loosely defined shape and a definite volume, while a gas has no definite shape or volume. The *Kinetic Theory of Matter* states that matter is composed of a large number of small particles (specifically, atoms and molecules) that are in constant motion. The distance between the separations in these particles determines the state of the matter: solid, liquid, or gas. In gases, the particles have a large separation and no attractive forces. In liquids, there is moderate separation between particles and some attractive forces to form a loose shape. Solids have almost no separation between their particles, causing a defined and set shape. The constant movement of particles causes them to bump into each other, thus allowing the particles to transfer energy between each other. This bumping and transferring of energy helps explain the transfer of heat and the relationship between pressure, volume, and temperature.

The *Ideal Gas Law* states that pressure, volume, and temperature are all related through the equation: $PV=nRT$, where P is pressure, V is volume, n is the amount of the substance in moles, R is the gas constant, and T is temperature.

Through this relationship, volume and pressure are both proportional to temperature, but pressure is inversely proportional to volume. Therefore, if the equation is balanced, and the volume decreases in the system, pressure needs to proportionately increase to keep both sides of the equation balanced. In contrast, if the equation is unbalanced and the pressure increases, then the temperature would also increase, since pressure and temperature are directly proportional.

When pressure, temperature, or volume change in matter, a change in state can occur. Changes in state include solid to liquid (melting), liquid to gas (evaporation), solid to gas (sublimation), gas to solid (deposition), gas to liquid (condensation), and liquid to solid (freezing). There is one other state of matter called *plasma*, which is seen in lightning, television screens, and neon lights. Plasma is most commonly converted from the gas state at extremely high temperatures.

The amount of energy needed to change matter from one state to another is labeled by the terms for phase changes. For example, the temperature needed to supply enough energy for matter to change from a liquid to a gas is called the *heat of vaporization*. When heat is added to matter in order to cause a change in state, there will be an increase in temperature until the matter is about to change its state. During its transition, all of the added heat is used by the matter to change its state, so there is no increase in temperature. Once the transition is complete, then the added heat will again yield an increase in temperature.

Reaction Rates, Equilibrium, and Reversibility

Chemical reactions are conveyed using chemical equations. Chemical equations must be balanced with equivalent numbers of atoms for each type of element on each side of the equation. Antoine Lavoisier, a French chemist, was the first to propose the **Law of Conservation of Mass** for the purpose of balancing a chemical equation. The law states, "Matter is neither created nor destroyed during a chemical reaction."

The **reactants** are located on the left side of the arrow, while the **products** are located on the right side of the arrow. Coefficients are the numbers in front of the chemical formulas. Subscripts are the numbers to the lower right of chemical symbols in a formula. To tally atoms, one should multiply the formula's coefficient by the subscript of each chemical symbol. For example, the chemical equation $2 H_2 + O_2 \rightarrow 2 H_2O$ is balanced. For H, the coefficient of 2 multiplied by the subscript 2 equals 4 hydrogen atoms. For O, the coefficient of 1 multiplied by the subscript 2 equals 2 oxygen atoms. Coefficients and subscripts of 1 are understood and never written.

Reaction Rates

The rate of a reaction is the measure of the change in concentration of the reactants or products over a certain period of time. Many factors affect how fast or slow a reaction occurs, such as concentration, pressure, or temperature. As the concentration of a reactant increases, the rate of the reaction also increases, because the frequency of collisions between elements increases. High-pressure situations for reactants that are gases cause the gas to compress and increase the frequency of gas molecule collisions, similar to solutions with higher concentrations. Reactions rates are then increased with the higher frequency of gas molecule collisions. Higher temperatures usually increase the rate of the reaction, adding more energy to the system with heat and increasing the frequency of molecular collisions.

Equilibrium

Equilibrium is described as the state of a system when no net changes occur. Chemical equilibrium occurs when opposing reactions occur at equal rates. In other words, the rate of reactants forming products is equal to the rate of the products breaking down into the reactants—the concentration of reactants and products in the system doesn't change. This happens in **reversible chemical reactions** as opposed to irreversible chemical reactions. In **irreversible chemical reactions**, the products cannot be changed back to reactants. Although the concentrations are not changing in equilibrium, the forward and reverse reactions are likely still occurring. This type of equilibrium is called a **dynamic equilibrium**. In situations where all reactions have ceased, a **static equilibrium** is reached. Chemical equilibriums are also described as homogeneous or heterogeneous. **Homogeneous equilibrium** involves substances that are all in the same phase, while **heterogeneous equilibrium** means the substances are in different phases when equilibrium is reached. For example, when a reaction is in heterogeneous equilibrium, the general form may be written as:

$$aA \text{ (s)} + bB \text{ (aq)} \leftrightarrow cC \text{ (s)} + dD \text{ (aq)}$$

Catalysts are substances that accelerate the speed of a chemical reaction. A catalyst remains unchanged throughout the course of a chemical reaction. In most cases, only small amounts of a catalyst are needed. Catalysts increase the rate of a chemical reaction by providing an alternate path requiring less activation energy. Activation energy refers to the amount of energy required for the initiation of a chemical reaction.

Catalysts can be homogeneous or heterogeneous. Catalysts in the same phase of matter as its reactants are homogeneous, while catalysts in a different phase than reactants are heterogeneous. It is important to remember catalysts are selective. They don't accelerate the speed of all chemical reactions, but catalysts do accelerate specific chemical reactions.

Mixtures

Solutions and Solution Concentrations

A homogeneous mixture, also called a **solution,** has uniform properties throughout a given sample. An example of a homogeneous solution is salt fully dissolved in warm water. In this case, any number of samples taken from the parent solution would be identical. A **tincture** is a solution in which the solvent is an alcohol.

One **mole** is the amount of matter contained in 6.02×10^{23} of any object, such as atoms, ions, or molecules. It is a useful unit of measure for items in large quantities. This number is also known as **Avogadro's number**. One mole of $^{12}_{6}C$ atoms is equivalent to 6.02×10^{23} $^{12}_{6}C$ atoms. Avogadro's number is often written as an inverse mole, or as $6.02 \times 10^{23}/mol$.

Molarity is the concentration of a solution. It is based on the number of moles of solute in one liter of solution and is written as the capital letter M. A 1.0 molar solution, or 1.0 M solution, has one mole of solute per liter of solution. The molarity of a solution can be determined by calculating the number of moles of the solute and dividing it by the volume of the solution in liters. The resulting number is the mol/L or M for molarity of the solution.

Emulsions

Non-sterile emulsions are thermodynamically unstable mixtures composed of at least two liquids that are immiscible, which are liquids that are insoluble in one another and do not mix easily. The procedure for compounding these types of nonsterile formulations depends on the type of emulsion being prepared. Simple emulsions can either be oil in water or water in oil, while more complicated emulsions include water in oil in water and oil in water in oil. An emulsion consists of two phases; the dispersed liquid makes up the **internal phase**, while the medium which it is dispersed in composes the **external phase**. **Emulsifying agents**, which have chemical properties that make them both water and oil soluble, or amphiphilic, are used to stabilize the emulsion. The emulsifying agent acts by creating a barrier between the two phases. The Dry Gum Method and the Wet Gum Method of emulsion preparation involve the same ratio of 4:2:1, or four parts oil, two parts water, and one part emulsifying agent, but the order of application differs.

The nonsterile preparation of compounded solutions involves dissolving the active pharmaceutical ingredients in purified water, titrating to the necessary pH, and packaging the solution in individual bottles for dispensing. Referring to a master formulation, the procedure to compound would be to first weigh out the active pharmaceutical ingredient (API). The weighed API or solute is added to a solvent. When adding the API to a solvent, it is important to consider the displacement of the solvent by the API. It is generally best to add the API to a percentage of the final volume, which is typically specified in the master formula. A magnetic stirring rod should be used to thoroughly dissolve the API to achieve a homogenous mixture. The pH of the solution should be verified to make sure it is within the specified range for the specific enema being made. Then the solution should be brought to its final volume, and its pH checked again. If necessary, the pH can be adjusted to meet the specific range required in the quality assurance portion of the formula. The solution can then be poured into individual enema bottles and labeled appropriately.

Chemical Reactions

Chemical reactions are characterized by a chemical change in which the starting substances, or reactants, differ from the substances formed, or products. Chemical reactions may involve a change in color, the production of gas, the formation of a precipitate, or changes in heat content. The following are the basic types of chemical reactions:

- **Decomposition Reactions:** A compound is broken down into smaller elements. For example, $2\,H_2O \rightarrow 2\,H_2 + O_2$. This is read as, "2 molecules of water decompose into 2 molecules of hydrogen and 1 molecule of oxygen."

- **Combination/Synthesis Reactions:** Two or more elements or compounds are joined together. For example, $2\,H_2 + O_2 \rightarrow 2\,H_2O$. This is read as, "2 molecules of hydrogen react with 1 molecule of oxygen to produce 2 molecules of water."

- **Single Displacement Reactions:** A single element or ion takes the place of another element in a compound. It is also known as a substitution reaction. For example, $Zn + 2\,HCl \rightarrow ZnCl_2 + H_2$. This is read as, "zinc reacts with 2 molecules of hydrochloric acid to produce one molecule of zinc chloride and one molecule of hydrogen." In other words, zinc replaces the hydrogen in hydrochloric acid.

- **Double Displacement Reactions:** Two elements or ions exchange a single element to form two different compounds, resulting in different combinations of cations and anions in the final compounds. It is also known as a metathesis reaction. For example, $H_2SO_4 + 2\,NaOH \rightarrow Na_2SO_4 + 2\,H_2O$

  - Special types of double displacement reactions include:

    - **Oxidation-Reduction (or Redox) Reactions:** Elements undergo a change in oxidation number. For example, $2\,S_2O_3{}^{2-}\,(aq) + I_2\,(aq) \rightarrow S_4O_6{}^{2-}\,(aq) + 2\,I^-\,(aq)$.

    - **Acid-Base (or Neutralization) Reactions:** Involves a reaction between an acid and a base, which produces a salt and water. For example, $HBr + NaOH \rightarrow NaBr + H_2O$.

    - **Combustion Reactions:** A hydrocarbon (a compound composed of only hydrogen and carbon) reacts with oxygen (O_2) to form carbon dioxide (CO_2) and water (H_2O). For example, $CH_4 + 2\,O_2 \rightarrow CO_2 + 2\,H_2O$.

Stoichiometry

Stoichiometry investigates the quantities of chemicals that are consumed and produced in chemical reactions. Chemical equations are made up of reactants and products; stoichiometry helps elucidate how the changes from reactants to products occur, as well as how to ensure the equation is balanced.

Chemical reactions are limited by the amount of starting material, or reactants, available to drive the process forward. The reactant that has the smallest amount of substance is called the limiting reactant. The **limiting reactant** is completely consumed by the end of the reaction. The other reactants are called **excess reactants**. For example, gasoline is used in a combustion reaction to make a car move and is the limiting reactant of the reaction. If the gasoline runs out, the combustion reaction can no longer take place, and the car stops.

The quantity of product that should be produced after using up all of the limiting reactant can be calculated and is called the **theoretical yield of the reaction**. Since the reactants do not always act as they should, the actual amount of resulting product is called the **actual yield**. The actual yield is divided by the theoretical yield and then multiplied by 100 to find the **percent yield** for the reaction.

Solution stoichiometry deals with quantities of solutes in chemical reactions that occur in solutions. The quantity of a solute in a solution can be calculated by multiplying the molarity of the solution by the volume. Similar to chemical

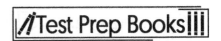

equations involving simple elements, the number of moles of the elements that make up the solute should be equivalent on both sides of the equation.

When the concentration of a particular solute in a solution is unknown, a **titration** is used to determine that concentration. In a titration, the solution with the unknown solute is combined with a standard solution, which is a solution with a known solute concentration. The point at which the unknown solute has completely reacted with the known solute is called the **equivalence point**. Using the known information about the standard solution, including the concentration and volume, and the volume of the unknown solution, the concentration of the unknown solute is determined in a balanced equation. For example, in the case of combining acids and bases, the equivalence point is reached when the resulting solution is neutral. HCl, an acid, combines with NaOH, a base, to form water, which is neutral, and a solution of Cl^- ions and Na^+ ions. Before the equivalence point, there are an unequal number of cations and anions and the solution is not neutral.

Oxidation and Reduction

Oxidation and reduction reactions, also known as **redox reactions**, are those in which electrons are transferred from one element to another. Batteries and fuel cells are two energy-related technologies that utilize these reactions. When an atom, ion, or molecule loses its electrons and becomes more positively charged, it is described as being oxidized. When a substance gains electrons and becomes more negatively charged, it is reduced. In chemical reactions, if one element or molecule is oxidized, another must be reduced for the equation to be balanced. Although the transfer of electrons is obvious in some reactions where ions are formed, redox reactions also include those in which electrons are transferred but the products remain neutral.

Keep track of oxidation states or oxidation numbers to ensure the chemical equation is balanced. **Oxidation numbers** are assigned to each atom in a neutral substance or ion. For ions made up of a single atom, the oxidation number is equal to the charge of the ion. For atoms in their original elemental form, the oxidation number is always zero. Each hydrogen atom in an H_2 molecule, for example, has an oxidation number of zero. The sum of the oxidation numbers in a molecule should be equal to the overall charge of the molecule. If the molecule is a positively charged ion, the sum of the oxidation number should be equal to overall positive charge of the molecule. In ionic compounds that have a cation and anion joined, the sum of the oxidation numbers should equal zero.

All chemical equations must have the same number of elements on each side of the equation to be balanced. Redox reactions have an extra step of counting the electrons on both sides of the equation to be balanced. Separating redox reactions into oxidation reactions and reduction reactions is a simple way to account for all of the electrons involved. The individual equations are known as **half-reactions**. The number of electrons lost in the oxidation reaction must be equal to the number of electrons gained in the reduction reaction for the redox reaction to be balanced.

The oxidation of tin (Sn) by iron (Fe) can be balanced by the following half-reactions:

Oxidation: $Sn^{2+} \rightarrow Sn^{4+} + 2\,e^-$

Reduction: $2\,Fe^{3+} + 2\,e^- \rightarrow 2\,Fe^{2+}$

Complete redox reaction: $Sn^{2+} + 2\,Fe^{3+} \rightarrow Sn^{4+} + 2\,Fe^{2+}$

Acids and Bases

Acids and bases are defined in many different ways. An **acid** can be described as a substance that increases the concentration of H^+ ions when it is dissolved in water, as a proton donor in a chemical equation, or as an electron-pair acceptor. A **base** can be a substance that increases the concentration of OH^- ions when it is dissolved in water, accepts a proton in a chemical reaction, or is an electron-pair donor.

pH refers to the power or potential of hydrogen atoms and is used as a scale for a substance's acidity. In chemistry, pH represents the hydrogen ion concentration (written as $[H^+]$) in an aqueous, or watery, solution. The hydrogen ion concentration, $[H^+]$, is measured in moles of H^+ per liter of solution.

The pH scale is a logarithmic scale used to quantify how acidic or basic a substance is. pH is the negative logarithm of the hydrogen ion concentration: $pH = -\log[H^+]$. A one-unit change in pH correlates with a ten-fold change in hydrogen ion concentration. The pH scale typically ranges from zero to 14, although it is possible to have pHs outside of this range. Pure water has a pH of 7, which is considered **neutral**. pH values less than 7 are considered **acidic**, while pH values greater than 7 are considered **basic**, or **alkaline**.

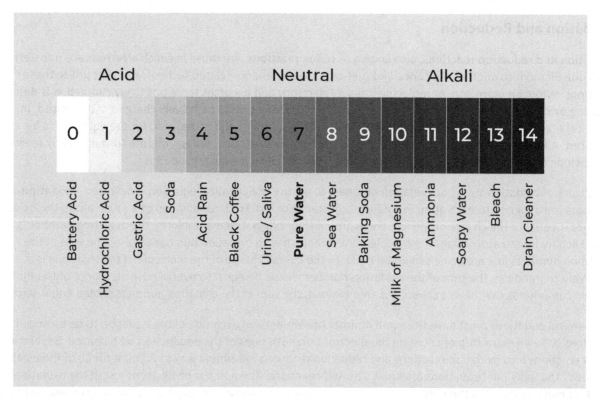

Generally speaking, an acid is a substance capable of donating hydrogen ions, while a base is a substance capable of accepting hydrogen ions. A **buffer** is a molecule that can act as either a hydrogen ion donor or acceptor. Buffers are crucial in the blood and body fluids and prevent the body's pH from fluctuating into dangerous territory. pH can be measured using a pH meter, test paper, or indicator sticks.

Water can act as either an acid or a base. When mixed with an acid, water can accept a proton and become an H_3O^+ ion. When mixed with a base, water can donate a proton and become an OH^- ion. Sometimes water molecules donate and accept protons from each other; this process is called **autoionization**. The chemical equation is written as follows: $H_2O + H_2O \rightarrow OH^- + H_3O^+$.

Acids and bases are characterized as strong, weak, or somewhere in between. Strong acids and bases completely or almost completely ionize in aqueous solution. The chemical reaction is driven completely forward, to the right side of the equation, where the acidic or basic ions are formed. Weak acids and bases do not completely dissociate in aqueous solution. They only partially ionize and the solution becomes a mixture of the acid or base, water, and the

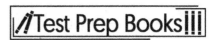

acidic or basic ions. Strong acids are complemented by weak bases, and vice versa. A **conjugate acid** is an ion that forms when its base pair gains a proton. For example, the conjugate acid NH_4^+ is formed from the base NH_3. The **conjugate base** that pairs with an acid is the ion that is formed when an acid loses a proton. NO_2^- is the conjugate base of the acid HNO_2.

Health

Health Dimensions

For all patient populations, one of the most important topics to discuss is their diet. Especially for older adults, proper **nutrition** is critical. Income fluctuations due to retirement or lost income from a deceased or divorced spouse may affect the grocery budget. Vitamin deficiencies can quickly become problematic, resulting in a brief or prolonged hospitalization. Neurological concerns may also affect memory, and patients may simply forget to eat. Simple questions regarding favorite meals, restaurants, or eating preferences can yield answers. It is important to note that missing meals can also become commonplace if a depression diagnosis exists. Inserting a brief depression inventory early in the visit may reveal the major reason for the patient's current health status and uncover areas of concern regarding daily nutrition.

Exercise is also a crucial piece of the assessment puzzle when discussing healthy lifestyle choices. Chronological age is not synonymous with physical decline, and patients should be encouraged to continue with exercise as tolerated. Simply walking daily for 30 minutes, broken into segments if necessary, is a great starting point. Weight-bearing exercise, isometrics, swimming, yoga, Pilates, or Tai-Chi all provide patients with the opportunity for gentle movement if some mobility issues exist. If needed, physical or occupational therapies can aid in the restoration of mobility and should be suggested after injury or with sedentary patients. Older patients must be reminded that retirement is not a signal to simply age, but the opportunity to age well.

Apart from the maintenance of diet and exercise is the importance of **socialization** and hobbies. Aging can be an isolating experience, especially as adult children move away and manage separate families. Less time may be spent with extended family and, once retired, the older adult may see less need for meeting new people in general. It is important for the nurse to assess the patient's perceived need for companionship. What do they do for fun? How do they unwind? Do they have a bucket list and what's on it? These types of open-ended questions not only create dialogue but can quickly become a goal-setting session.

When discussing high-risk behaviors with members of the aged population, it is imperative that the nurse include sexual activity. Although thought to be less sexually active than younger patients, this age group has seen a dramatic increase in sexually transmitted disease (STD) in recent years. Many have lost a spouse or life partner to death or divorce, and experience bouts of profound loneliness and sexual frustration. Although some may be seeking to remarry, most are interested in companionship and may not consider STDs to be a major concern. It is not as necessary to discuss birth control with a postmenopausal woman or elderly man as it is to discuss chlamydia, gonorrhea, herpes, and HIV. A simple question regarding intimate partners or social life will likely yield more information that the nurse can use to gently introduce the subject.

Nurses must carefully assess the likelihood of the progression of both medical and mental health concerns. Historically, the longer an individual manages chronic disease, the more complicated the illness becomes. More biological systems are impacted, leading to further physiological compromise. For example, diabetes mellitus, if managed well over a number of years, may still result in renal, visual, and cardiovascular complications in later years. The nurse must discuss basic diabetic care with the patient at every encounter. Annual eye exams, podiatric care, consultation with a diabetic nutritionist or dietician, and adhering closely to the diet plan, are all essential.

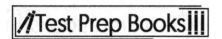

Mental Health

The mental status of a patient has the potential to impact every area of their life, resulting in an inability to respond to any nursing intervention. Compromised mental health has been known to affect a patient's coping mechanisms, lifestyle choices, and ability to manage stress effectively. Nurses who work with patients impacted by mental illness need to maintain awareness of numerous concepts. Chief among them is the nurse's effectiveness in conducting the initial interview. It is essential to assess the patient's mood, affect, body language, and tone. Asking open-ended questions about daily living, employment and relationship status, hobbies, and habits can help the nurse determine if any socialization deficits are present. Once the patient begins to respond, this will create an atmosphere of trust, which is necessary when conducting an assessment for depression.

One of the most frequently diagnosed mental illnesses is clinical depression. Once the nurse has completed the depression inventory and determines that some risk for clinical depression does exist, the next step will be to discuss how the patient's symptoms affect daily life. Within the last two weeks, has the patient felt increasingly depressed, hopeless, or helpless? Has the patient struggled to fall asleep, woken up early, or slept longer than expected? Are meal times less or more frequent? Has anyone that knows the patient remarked about a change in their mood? Have there been sudden bouts of tearfulness, sadness, or feelings of worthlessness? Is the patient engaging in self-harm or high-risk behaviors? Has the patient considered hurting themselves? If so, is there a plan? Does the patient have access to weapons or medications, and have there been suicide attempts in the past? This line of questioning will help the nurse to determine if the patient needs to be referred to a psychologist or other mental health professional. It will also help the nurse determine what is safe or not safe to have around the patient and how to best respond to them.

Once it is determined that the patient is not in imminent danger or planning to commit suicide, the nurse can begin discussing nursing interventions to alleviate the patient's symptoms. If suicidal ideation does exist, safety planning and hospitalization may be necessary. Utilizing motivational interviewing to reveal the patient's readiness for change, the nurse can open the discussion from where the patient sits on the continuum. This type of nursing style is often necessary to confirm the feasibility of proposed nursing interventions.

Mood Disorders, Depression, Anxiety

A **mood disorder** is a mental health classification for all of the disorders that alter or change a person's mood that are inconsistent with the situation they are experiencing (i.e., depression and bipolar). The following are the most common types of mood disorders:

1. **Major depression:** having a lack of interest in day-to-day activities, feelings of hopelessness, anxiety, anger, or having suicidal thoughts that last for two or more weeks

2. **Dysthymia:** a low-grade feeling of depression that lasts for a minimum of two years

3. **Bipolar disorder:** a disorder characterized by periods of depression followed by periods of mania

4. **Mood disorder related to another health condition:** having an acute or chronic medical illnesses can trigger symptoms of depression.

5. **Substance-induced mood disorder:** when depression is related to or caused by the use of drugs, alcohol, or other harmful substances

Mood disorders may be caused by an imbalance of brain chemicals. Life events, abrupt changes in routine, and stress may also contribute to a depressed mood. Mood disorders also tend to run in families and are more intense and harder to manage than normal feelings of sadness. Children, teens, or adults who have a parent with a mood disorder have a greater chance of also having a mood disorder. Rates of depression are nearly twice as high as in

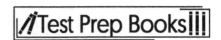

women as they are in men. Once a person in the family has this diagnosis, their brothers, sisters, or children have a higher chance of the same diagnosis. Depending on age and the type of mood disorder, a person may have different symptoms of depression. The following are the most common symptoms of a mood disorder:

- Ongoing sad, anxious, or empty affect
- Feeling hopeless or helpless
- Having low self-esteem
- Feeling inadequate or worthless
- Excessive guilt
- Repeating thoughts of death or suicide
- Loss of interest in usual activities or activities that were once enjoyed, including sex
- Relationship problems
- Trouble sleeping or sleeping too much
- Changes in appetite and/or weight
- Decreased energy
- Trouble concentrating
- A decrease in the ability to make decisions
- Frequent physical complaints that don't get better with treatment
- Very sensitive to failure or rejection
- Irritability, hostility, or aggression

With a mood disorders, these feelings are more intense than what a person may feel occasionally. If these feelings continue over time, interfere with interest in family, friends, community, or work, or if there are thoughts of suicide, medical intervention is needed.

Antidepressant and mood stabilizing medicines, especially when combined with psychotherapy, have been shown to work very well in the treatment of depression. Treatment of bipolar disorder may include mood stabilizers such as lithium and carbamazepine, along with second-generation antipsychotics such as aripiprazole and risperidone. Psychotherapy is focused on changing the person's distorted views of self and the environment. It also helps to improve interpersonal relationship skills, identify stressors in the environment, and assist with avoiding them. Family therapy, electroconvulsive therapy, and transcranial stimulation may also be therapeutic.

Support Systems
Another contributing factor for overall patient well-being is a well-functioning support system. Even if there is no disease process present, a support system, as defined by the patient, is vital to healthy stress and disease management. During the assessment, the nurse must ask open-ended questions about patients' support systems: What hobbies do they enjoy? How do they spend the holidays, and with whom? Are they married or single? Do they have children? Answers to these few questions will help quickly decide if there are any gaps in socialization and open the discussion on how to fill them.

Whether it's family members, friends, or coworkers, some sort of support network usually exists for most patients. The nurse must make sure to encourage discussion about who the patient confides in and trusts. Those individuals can either add to or subtract from the patient's progression through and whole-hearted commitment to treatment. For those patients who report having no supportive network, the nurse can guide the patient toward viable options. One of the most effective and influential options would be to match the patient to a support group according to any comorbidities that they currently manage. Thousands of independent groups exist to provide a much-needed communal experience. Often run by health professionals or counselors, members of these groups can gain knowledge about their condition, daily symptom management, and possibly gain new supportive friends. Overall, the presence of a network of trusted friends and advisors is an invaluable facet of the therapeutic environment.

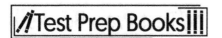

Religious and Spiritual Influences on Health

Religious and spiritual beliefs can heavily influence a patient's decision to receive care. It is important for the nurse to determine if any specific religious or spiritual beliefs exist for the patient, and how those beliefs inform their decisions. Many people value certain dietary customs in accordance with their religion and strictly adhere to them. For example, for those who identify as Jewish, adherence to a strict Kosher diet is non-negotiable. Any attempts by the nurse to suggest any changes to this diet would be viewed as insensitive. It is for this same reason that religious and spiritual beliefs of any kind must be respected.

Congregants of the Church of Scientology have received significant media attention for what some perceive to be controversial beliefs. Some who self-identify as a part of this group have also expressed particular mistrust of mental health practitioners in general. Although they do not forego all medical treatments, a nurse attending to patients following this religion must consider those beliefs when developing interventions and treatment plans. It may be more advantageous to encourage the patient to consult a church advisor and incorporate the tenants of Scientology into direct practice, if permitted.

Another religious group well known for their healthcare choices is Jehovah's Witnesses. Founded by Charles Taze Russell in the late 1800s, this group does not believe in accepting blood transfusions under any circumstances. A nurse caring for a patient who holds this belief must be prepared to discuss any viable options with the patient and church elders. Not all instances of receiving blood products are prohibited, so it will be important to confirm if the patient would consider using plasma, volume expanders, or artificial blood.

Additionally, ethical considerations regarding how to provide sensitive and compassionate care are important to highlight. It is the nurse's responsibility to seek a consultation with the unit chaplain, social worker, or facility ethics board to discuss any areas where there is a potential conflict of interest.

Influencing Factors

Personal Hygiene

Personal hygiene is most important upon a patient's initial admission assessment because how well they are groomed walking into the facility speaks to how well they take care of themselves on a day-to-day basis at home. The nurse will very quickly be able to make a judgment about how hygienic the patient is when doing the standard head-to-toe assessment.

Components of personal hygiene include evidence of washing themselves, how they care for their feet and nails, how they dress, the cleanliness of their clothes, whether or not they have shaved, if their hair is clean and maintained, and their level of oral hygiene.

Different people uphold themselves, their families, and their households to different standards of cleanliness. There are certain "accepted" standards of cleanliness, but not everyone maintains every single one at all times. The nurse keeps the client's personal hygiene in the context of their physical abilities, state of illness, and cultural context. Some cultures may be used to a lower or higher level of cleanliness, and the nurse keeps this in mind when performing the assessment.

Examples of cultural differences include how often it is acceptable to bathe or shower in a week. Some cultures may stick to a daily routine, while others may think weekly is acceptable. The presence or absence of hair on certain parts of the body on males and females may be different from culture to culture. The tolerance of bodily odor may also vary as to how strong of an odor is present and acceptable. The practice of bathing or showering may be an exclusively private act in some cultures, while in other cultures it is a public, communal activity. The nurse endeavors to understand the cultural context from which their client hails.

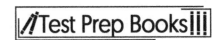

Rest and Sleep

Sleep and rest are essential to optimal health and healing. Patients can have difficulty sleeping. Whenever possible, plan the patient's care routine to correspond with periods when the patient is awake. Care activities should be grouped together when appropriate to avoid disturbing the patient more than necessary. Although patients need adequate rest periods, they should be encouraged to get out of bed and participate in activities when they're able, which aids in better rest. For a patient who's unable to leave their bed, encourage them to perform active range of motion exercises.

Patients in unfamiliar surroundings, or in facilities with constant lighting and noise, can become disoriented to day and night. Provide these patients with as many environmental cues as possible, such as dimming the lights and keeping the noise level low at night, turning the lights on and opening curtains and blinds in the morning, etc. Performing activities of daily living on a set schedule can also help the patient to stay oriented.

Stress Management

Stress management is a crucial piece of overall patient well-being. Poorly managed stress has the potential to cause significant health decline. When conducting an assessment, the nurse must carefully approach the topic of stress management. Since many of life's stressors cannot be completely changed, the nurse will be best served to listen actively, remarking about how certain activities or situations can worsen health conditions. Odd work hours, late night shifts, or working multiple jobs can negatively impact sleep patterns. Without restorative sleep, the patient will have difficulties focusing on treatment-plan adherence. As the lack of sleep continues, the patient can begin to lose focus on a previous goal of maintaining healthy lifestyle choices and return to easier high-risk behaviors.

Once the topic of known sources of stress has been initiated, the nurses can go one step further to inquire what steps have been taken to ameliorate those stressors. Next, the patient can be encouraged to state how they have worked to manage the stressors and what has been least effective. It is during this exchange that the patient is more likely to accept recommendations and institute them in daily life. Notably, it is also necessary to uncover sources of stress that are not readily apparent. Ask probing questions about preferred forms of stress relief and relaxation techniques. Encourage patients to seek out trusted members of their support network to communicate their needs and ask for help. Overall, a patient's ability to institute the checks and balances required to alleviate stress is crucial.

Health Threats

High Risk Behaviors

High-risk behaviors can be defined as actions that have a high probability of yielding a negative consequence. Nurses must develop a rapport with patients in an effort to create open communication so the patient will be more likely to reveal conduct that could have detrimental health outcomes. This technique can also encourage patients to ask questions about their risky behaviors. The nurse can then use the established rapport to discern if the patient's level of comfort and commitment to the behaviors is amenable to change.

One of the most effective methods of encouraging open communication with patients is motivational interviewing. Nurses use motivational interviewing to assess, collaborate, plan, and implement treatment with patients. There are five major components of motivational interviewing: express empathy, illustrate incongruity, manage resistance, encourage self-validation, and promote independence. The nurse can employ these steps when combatting ambivalence to change. For example, when working with a patient who is considering smoking cessation, begin with simple statements regarding the difficulties involved with quitting.

This often results in the patient remarking about the number of attempts to quit, along with reasons why their prior attempts did not end in success. Next, draw from earlier statements concerning lifestyle choices, the patient's own reasons for quitting, and the potential for negative outcomes. In the next step, the nurse can tie the elements together, choosing carefully which area of resistance to target. What might the patient gain from quitting? What are the potential barriers to success from the patient's viewpoint? Asking these open-ended questions will help patients draw their own conclusions, validating the ability to self-navigate through possible obstacles. Once able to verbalize how the desired outcome could be achieved, the patient has managed to break through their own resistance, and the groundwork has been set for more internal dialogue.

Lifestyle Choices

Traditionally, nursing interventions are designed to target the lifestyle choices that affect disease processes. During every patient encounter, the nurse must ask open-ended questions in order to determine which interventions should be implemented. The acronym **SMART (specific, measurable, attainable, relevant, and timely)** is a concise reference for patients. When it is clearly what the main objective is, the likelihood of achieving that goal is increased.

When addressing multiple issues, chose one area with the highest likelihood of success to build momentum and patient confidence in the process. For example, when discussing diet, it is important for the nurse to first establish what the patient's current diet and exercise plan includes. This dialogue will open the door to likes, dislikes, preferred cooking methods, and diet history. As the discussion expands, inquire about budgetary constraints and actual access to healthy food options. Once eating habits are known, define daily scheduling conflicts that may become barriers to success. Create a contingency plan, with multiple options. Another major area of importance for lifestyle choices is exercise. Upon reviewing current diagnoses, medications, and any mobility or chronic pain concerns, the nurse can partner with the patient to formulate a reasonable plan. Set a specific goal on the type and duration of exercise; measure steps or activity as accurately as possible with a pedometer. Can they commit to exercise daily? What is an appropriate form of exercise? Maintain the stance of advocate and collaborator to preserve patients' autonomy and validate their experiences whenever possible.

Substance Use and Other Disorders and Dependencies

Substance abuse is defined, most simply, as extreme use of a drug. Abuse occurs for many reasons, such as mental health instability, inability to cope with everyday life stressors, the loss of a loved one, or enjoyment of the euphoric state that the overindulgence in a substance causes. Abused substances create some type of intoxication that alters decision-making, awareness, attentiveness, or physical impulses.

Substance abuse results in tolerance, withdrawal, and compulsive drug-taking behavior. **Tolerance** occurs when increased amounts of the substance are needed to achieve the desired effects. **Withdrawal** manifests as physiological and substance-specific cognitive symptoms (e.g., cold sweats, shivering, nausea, vomiting, paranoia, hallucinations). Withdrawal not only happens when an individual stops abusing the substance, but also occurs when he or she attempts to reduce the amount taken in an effort to stop using altogether.

Some of the most commonly abused substances include the following:

Tobacco

People abuse tobacco either in cigarette, cigar, pipe, or snuff form. People report many reasons for tobacco use, including a calming effect, suppression of appetite, and relief of depression. The primary addictive component in tobacco is nicotine, but tobacco smoke also contains about seven hundred carcinogens (cancer-causing agents) that may result in lung and throat cancers as well as heart disease, emphysema, peptic ulcer disease, and stroke. Withdrawal indicators include insomnia, irritability, overwhelming nicotine craving, anxiety, and depression.

Alcohol

Some individuals feel the need to have a drink, as it is a central nervous system (CNS) depressant, which tends to calm and soothe individuals and lower inhibitions. However, it also slurs speech and impairs muscle control,

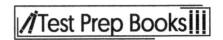

coordination, and reflex time. Alcohol abuse can cause cirrhosis of the liver; liver, esophagus, and stomach cancers; heart enlargement; chronic inflammation of the pancreas; vitamin deficiencies; certain anemias; and brain damage. Physical dependence is a biological need for alcohol in order to avoid physical withdrawal symptoms, which include anxiety, erratic pulse rate, tremors, seizures, and hallucinations. In its most serious form, withdrawal combined with malnourishment can lead to a potentially fatal condition known as **delirium tremens (DTs),** which is a psychotic disorder that involves tremors, disorientation, and hallucinations.

Other Prescriptions

Prescription medications, such as anti-anxiety, sleep, and pain medications, are commonly abused.

Marijuana

Marijuana is considered the most frequently abused illicit drug in the United States. General effects of marijuana use include pleasure, relaxation, and weakened dexterity and memory. The active addictive ingredient in marijuana is tetrahydrocannabinol (THC). It is normally smoked (but can be eaten), and its smoke has more carcinogens than that of tobacco. The individual withdrawing from marijuana will experience increased irritability and anxiety.

Cocaine

Cocaine is a stimulant that is also known as **coke, snow**, or **rock**. It can be smoked, injected, snorted, or swallowed. Reported effects include pleasure, enhanced alertness, and increased energy. Both temporary and prolonged use have been known to contribute to damage to the brain, heart, lungs, and kidneys. Withdrawal symptoms include severe depression and reduced energy.

Heroin

Heroin is also known as **smack** and **horse**, its use continues to increase. Effects of heroin abuse include pleasure, slower respirations, and drowsiness. Overdose and/or overuse of heroin can cause respiratory depression, resulting in death. Use of heroin as an injectable substance can lead to other complications such as heart valve damage, tetanus, botulism, hepatitis B, or human immunodeficiency virus (HIV)/AIDS infection from sharing dirty needles. Withdrawal is usually intense and includes vomiting, abdominal cramps, diarrhea, confusion, body aches, and diaphoresis.

Methamphetamines

Methamphetamine is also known as **meth, crank**, and **crystal,** and its use also continues to increase, especially in the West and Midwest regions of the United States. Methamphetamine is categorized as a stimulant that produces such effects as pleasure, increased alertness, and decreased appetite. Similar to cocaine, it can be snorted, smoked, or injected, and it can be eaten as well. Like cocaine, it shares many of the same detrimental effects, such as myocardial infarction, hypertension, and stroke. Other prolonged usage effects include paranoia, hallucinations, damage to and loss of dentition, and heart damage. Withdrawal symptoms involve depression, abdominal cramps, and increased appetite.

Nursing interventions for the individual addicted to tobacco, alcohol, and other drugs centers around the prevention of relapse, and treatment depends on the individual and the substance that is abused. Behavioral treatment assists with recognition of abuse triggers, habits, and drug cravings, as well as providing the tactics to help one cope with these issues. A physician may prescribe nicotine patches for the tobacco abuser and methadone or Suboxone to manage withdrawal symptoms and certain drug yearnings.

Non-Substance-Related Dependencies

Even some behaviors—such as exercise and work—are recognized as positive behaviors, but when taken to extremes, unpleasant consequences develop. For example, exercise addiction, in its least damaging form, may create anxiety when physical or weather conditions prevent participation. In more extreme cases, certain athletes

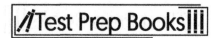

Science

will continue to train in spite of illness or injury, exacerbating the physical problem and sometimes causing permanent disabilities.

Overworking—sometimes referred to as "**workaholism**"—may also be viewed as positive by some standards. In the end, however, those working many hours of overtime may result in a life out of balance. They may also be using work as a means to avoid other responsibilities, such as family life. It can create stress and low energy, and it can lead to physical and emotional problems.

Sexual addiction, also known as **hypersexuality**, involves a preoccupation with sexual pleasures that can manifest itself in a multitude of ways. These behaviors prove harmful to themselves and potentially other people. One example is pornography. Those addicted to pornography find that having close and intimate contact with their long-term partner is less exciting than viewing stimulating films or pictures. This creates intimacy problems and difficulty in one's primary relationship. The Internet has made it easier for people to access these materials, sometimes at no cost, creating a greater number of persons who view it addictively.

Gambling addiction may involve a desire for the adrenaline rush of making bets or a cycle of losing money via gambling and then gambling more to try to make up for previously lost money.

Overeating, based upon the number of obese and overweight persons in our culture, is on the rise. Some people use food much in the same way that others use alcohol or drugs—to feel a sense of pleasure or to numb feelings of depression or anxiety. The consequences of obesity are numerous from a social and physical standpoint, with the most severe of these being the high risk for heart disease or stroke.

Some individuals are addicted to **self-harm** in the form of cutting, scratching, or mutilating themselves. This is often described as a means to bring relief from emotional pain as one focuses on the physical sensation of pain to distract from the emotional sensation. It may also be a type of self-punishment. Some people have horrendous scars from this compulsion. Others may contract infections. It is theorized that persons who self-mutilate are at higher risk of suicide than those who do not, making it a possible precursor to suicidal ideations.

Health Promotion/Disease Prevention

Two of the most important aspects of providing exceptional nursing care are health promotion and disease prevention. Both are integral to ensuring the physical and psychological well-being of individuals, groups, and the community at large.

Health promotion can be loosely defined as the direct or indirect presentation of information, specifically designed to influence behaviors that are expected to result in positive health outcomes. When presented directly, the instruction may be in written form such as brochures, books, or articles in magazines or newspapers. Historically, these publications were typically available in physician's offices, clinics, and hospitals. For nurses, health promotion is no longer relegated to easily discarded brochures or pamphlets. With the introduction of the Internet, information targeting healthy activities can be found instantly after several keystrokes. Nursing interventions can be provided via webinars, face-to-face coaching sessions, telephonic care, and social media sites. These mediums allow the nurse to contact thousands of individuals at once and increase exposure.

Indirect presentation of healthy lifestyle choices often occurs through billboards, signage, or posters in physicians' offices, as well as strategic mention or product placement in movies and television shows. Increasing numbers of "reality TV" stars can be seen holding bottles of a specific brand of vitamins or diet pills, or leaving a restaurant noted for healthy dishes. Albeit not as successful as the direct-to-consumer approach, this allows for health promotion to sneak in the back doors of viewers' minds, slowly affecting their daily habits. Traditionally, nurses are not involved in this type of health promotion, but nurses can use this type of behavior when interacting with

This material is provided for exam preparation purposes only and does not indicate an endorsement of any specific scientific, political, or religious point of view. © TPB Publishing. You have been licensed one copy of this document for personal use only. Any other reproduction or redistribution is strictly prohibited. All rights reserved.

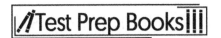

patients. Ensuring that hand washing posters are present in restrooms, display cases of vitamins and supplements in the office waiting area, and sponsorship or participation in local health fairs all support higher awareness.

In an effort to actively guide the prevention of disease, community health nurses employ numerous tactics. Each strategy is specific to a particular population to intervene at several stages of the disease process.

Primary prevention consists of the nursing strategies implemented to prevent the onset of a particular disease process. One well-known example of primary disease prevention is the "say no to drugs" movement. Nurses in this campaign can specifically target young children and teens to prevent their initial use of drugs with the use of buttons, posters, commercials, and rallies. **Secondary prevention** focuses on the early detection of disease and prevention of considerable damage from the disease process. Finally, **tertiary prevention** efforts with this same patient population would be nursing interventions implemented in drug treatment centers, clinics, and detox units in the hospital. These nurses work with the patients actively addicted to substances and collaborate to manage their disease.

Home Safety

The nurse works to promote patient safety by ensuring their home environment is safe. The nurse will begin this process by first assessing the client's home for safety opportunities. This can be done by walking through the client's home taking mental and written notes as well as interviewing the patient and their caregiver.

The patient themselves must be assessed for their ability to live safely in their own home. Patients with dementia, Alzheimer's, and other cognitive dysfunctions present more of a risk to themselves than a patient whose cognitive faculties are well intact. The nurse may assess whether the patient is able to live independently, need constant supervision, or need assistance with only a few daily activities. An important consideration is how well the patient can follow their own medication regime. The nurse should consider whether the use of divided days-of-the-week pill boxes would be appropriate, for example. Once the client's cognitive function is assessed and addressed, the nurse can then move on to ensuring the external environment is safe.

The external environment of the patient's home poses many potential safety hazards. The patient may live in a multiple-story house, in which case the stairs present a fall risk for elderly and deconditioned patients. A hand rail may be helpful if it is not already present, as well as safety treads on the staircase. Some patients with chronic conditions that restrict them from climbing up and down stairs may require a chair elevator. The nurse can connect the patient and their family to community resources for such items.

The lighting in the home is as important as the lighting in a hospital room. One of the classic fall prevention tips in the hospital is to ensure the patient's room is adequately lit both in the daytime and at night. The same goes for the client's home. The nurse needs to ensure nightlights are available in rooms that the client may need to ambulate across during the night, such as the bedroom. Visits to the bathroom should be unencumbered and easily navigated, without fall risks in the way. Due to medication and chronic illnesses such as heart failure, visits to the bathroom often increase in the elderly patient, thus increasing fall risk.

The nurse should discourage the use of throw rugs in the homes of patients at risk for a fall. This type of rug can easily catch the client's foot, throwing them off balance and potentially causing a fall.

The house should be well kept, clean, and sanitary. If the client is not able to keep up with their normal housekeeping duties, assistance should be sought. The nurse can, again, connect the client to community resources in this case. Perhaps a church friend, community volunteer, or local housekeeping service if affordable for the client may be used. A cluttered home may present a fall risk, and it also negatively affects the mental health of the client, causing anxiety and depressive symptoms.

Some clients, such as those with diabetes, may have syringes to administer insulin that will need proper disposal. The nurse may provide the client with a sharps container for syringe disposal as well as educating the patient on proper syringe hygiene and disposal. The nurse should ensure that the client understands these concepts to prevent at-home injuries.

Food hygiene is an important topic to address with the client if they are still preparing their own food. Hand hygiene before, after, and during food preparation is vital to preventing the spread of food-borne illnesses. The client should be educated on the proper handling of meats, ensuring that they not only perform frequent hand hygiene, but that they properly sanitize surfaces that raw meat touches, such as cutting boards.

The nurse needs to assess household alarms such as fire, smoke, and carbon monoxide alarms and ensure that they have fresh batteries and are in working order. The client should be educated to monitor these alarms as needed so they are ready to go in the case of a fire or carbon monoxide leak.

Patients receiving oxygen therapy should be educated on proper oxygen use and maintenance of their oxygen tank. They will be taught not to smoke while receiving oxygen, because this is a fire hazard. They will also need to monitor the tank's gauges to make sure they know when they are running low on oxygen and need a replacement tank.

Emergency First Aid

In the event of a medical emergency, there are specific steps to take depending on the situation. There will be written policies for these types of emergencies in the workplace that are used for patients, staff, and/or visitors.

Below are some examples of medical emergencies:

- Choking
- Unresponsive or unconscious person or patient
- Excessive bleeding
- Head injury
- Broken bones
- Severe burns
- Seizures
- Chest pain
- Difficulty breathing
- Allergic reactions that cause swelling and/or breathing difficulties
- Inhalation or swallowing of a toxic substance
- Accidental poisoning

Choking

If someone is choking, the victim will most likely grab at their throat, or they may have a cough that eventually stops, indicating blockage of the airway. If the airway is blocked, they will need the Heimlich maneuver to be performed immediately. Oftentimes people cough and may leave the room to get a drink or to avoid disrupting others. It is best to follow that person to ensure they are not choking.

When someone is choking and conscious, the responder, or person at the scene who witnesses and intervenes, should:

- Ask the victim if they are choking and tell them help is here.
- Assist the victim to a standing position.
- Stand behind the victim and wrap the arms around the victim's waist.
- Make a fist with one hand and place the thumb against the victim's stomach just above their belly button.

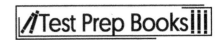

- Place the other hand on top of the fisted hand.
- Thrust quick, hard, and upward on the victim's stomach.
- Continue this until the food or object comes out of the victim's mouth.
- Do *not* swipe the victim's mouth with one finger, as this could push the blockage further down the airway.

If the victim is still choking and goes unconscious:

- Lower the victim to the floor, shout for help, and have someone call 911.
- Begin cardiopulmonary resuscitation (CPR) by following the basic life support steps until emergency medical services (EMS) arrives.

Unconsciousness or Unresponsiveness

First, try to arouse the person by shaking or tapping them. If they are indeed unresponsive, call for help, have someone call 911, and proceed to:

- Make sure the patient is lying flat and place a backboard under them for CPR.
- Follow basic life support (BLS) protocol.
- Look and listen for breathing (chest rise).
- Check for a pulse in radial artery (wrist).
- If patient is breathing, stay with them until EMS arrives. If there is a pulse but no breathing, begin rescue breaths. Give one breath every five or six seconds. Check pulse every two minutes.
- If no pulse, begin CPR and continue until EMS arrives.
- Direct someone else to get the **automated external defibrillator (AED)** as CPR is continued.
- CPR: Thirty chest compressions then two breaths, repeat for two-minute cycles.
- Chest compressions should be firm and deep, to the rhythm of the disco song "Stayin' Alive," about one hundred beats per minute. This ensures adequate perfusion of organs with blood since the heart is not pumping on its own.
- When the AED arrives, turn it on and follow the prompts for use.

If the patient recovers, turn them onto their left side and continue to monitor them until EMS arrive. Healthcare workers will be trained and certified on BLS, CPR, and AED use.

Excessive Bleeding

Call for help and call 911. Then:

- Have the patient sit down or lie down.
- Use a towel or shirt to hold continuous pressure on the bleeding area.
- Elevate the area above their heart. For example, if the leg is bleeding, have the patient lie down and put their leg on a chair.
- Talk to the patient and monitor their responsiveness. Stay with them until EMS arrives.

Head Injury

Concussions, contusions, and skull fractures are all common types of traumatic brain injuries. **Concussions** occur when the brain is jarred against the skull, usually during sports, hard contact with another person, or hitting the head on the ground. Concussions can cause mental confusion and lead to disruptions in normal brain functioning. The effects of a concussion can show up immediately, or they may not show up for hours or days. Normally, concussions do not cause a loss of consciousness, so it is important to pay attention to other possible symptoms. Another type of traumatic brain injury is a contusion, which is a bruise on the brain. This bruise can swell in the

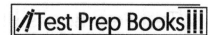

brain and cause a hematoma, or bleeding in the brain. A skull fracture is a break in the skull bone and can occur with or without brain damage. The following list includes symptoms of traumatic brain injuries:

- Confusion
- Depression
- Dizziness or balance problems
- Foggy feeling
- Double vision or changes in vision
- Tiredness
- Headache
- Memory loss
- Nausea
- Sensitivity to light
- Trouble remembering and concentrating

If a patient has a known head injury, or they stated that they hit their head, stay with the patient and call for a supervisor. Monitor the patient for mild symptoms from the list above. If the symptoms are not serious, the patient may require a visit from the physician. If the patient is elderly or has other serious health issues, hospitalization may be required to rule out more serious consequences from the head injury. The pie chart below depicts the leading causes of traumatic brain injury, with falls being the largest percentage.

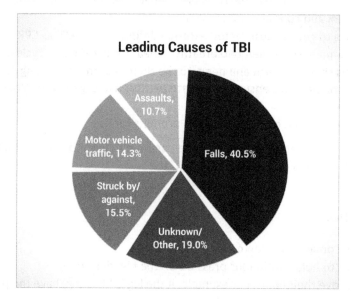

Symptoms of a head injury that are more serious and require immediate emergency treatment include:

- Unequal pupils
- Convulsions
- Fracture of the skull or face
- Inability to move legs or arms
- Clear or bloody fluid coming from the ears, nose, or mouth
- Loss of consciousness
- Persistent vomiting
- Severe headache

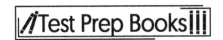
- Slurred speech and distorted vision
- Restlessness and irritability

If any of the above symptoms appear after a head injury, call for help and call 911.

Broken Bones (Compound Fractures)

A **compound fracture** is a fracture in which the bone is protruding through the skin. Other symptoms include pain, swelling, deformity in the fractured area, and bruising. This is the most serious type of fracture and requires immediate attention. The following comprises first aid for fractures:

- Call for help and call 911, especially if a fracture in the head, back or neck is suspected.
- Don't move the patient unless they are in danger of further injury.
- Keep the injured area still and stay with the patient.
- Treat any bleeding by holding pressure with a towel or gauze.
- Look for signs of shock in the patient (shallow, fast breathing, or feeling faint) and lay them down with their feet elevated.
- Wrap ice packs in a towel and ice the injured area.
- Wait for EMS to arrive.

Burns

Burn injuries can range from mild to severe, but the initial treatment for all burns is the same. **First-degree burns** affect the top layer of the skin, **second-degree burns** affect two layers, and **third-degree burns** affect all three layers. Call for an emergency response if:

- The burn is through all the skin layers.
- The person is a baby or elderly and the burn is severe.
- The hands, feet, face, or genitals are burned.
- The burn is larger than two inches or is oozing.
- The burn is charred and leathery, or has white, brown, or black patches.

Initial treatment for all burns includes:

- Remove the source of the burn, put out the fire, smother the burning area, or have the person stop, drop, and roll.
- Remove any hot or burned clothing.
- Remove clothing that is tight and remove jewelry (burns can swell very quickly).
- Hold the burned area under cool, running water for twenty minutes.
- Use two cold cloths if running water is not available. Alternate holding them on the area every two minutes.
- Do not put ice on the burn.
- Keep the patient warm by covering the rest of the body.
- Wrap or cover the burn loosely with gauze, or a use a sheet for large areas.
- If EMS has been called, stay with the patient and keep them warm until help arrives.

Seizures

Seizures have many symptoms depending on the type of seizure. Some symptoms include jerking motions, shaking, unconsciousness, stiffness, and blank staring. If someone is having a violent seizure, the steps to follow include:

- Protect the victim's head by moving hard objects out of the way and placing a blanket under their head.
- Loosen clothing around their neck.
- Do not try to hold them down and do not try to put something in their mouth.

- Get help to control bystanders so that the victim has some space.
- When the seizure is over, have the victim lie on their side and make sure their airway is open.
- Call 911 if the seizure lasts more than five minutes, if the victim has other medical conditions, or if the person has never had a seizure before.
- People with known epilepsy may have seizures that are short and frequent, so calling 911 may not be necessary.

Chest Pain

Chest pain can be a symptom of a heart attack or other serious heart or lung condition. Prompt attention is necessary so that the person can be treated before serious heart damage or death occurs. Chest pain can also be a result of a lung infection, excessive coughing, broken ribs from an injury, anxiety, indigestion, or muscular injury. If the patient has not fallen or does not have any outward physical signs of injury to the chest area, assume that the chest pain is cardiac related. When someone complains of chest pain, do the following:

- Have the person sit down and ask where the pain is located.
- Call for the supervisor immediately.
- Assess if they have any injuries on or near their chest.
- Call 911 (if not in a medical facility) if the pain lasts more than a few minutes, or they have the following symptoms:
- Pain in the arms, shoulders, back and chest
- Difficulty breathing
- Fatigue
- Nausea
- Sweating
- Dizziness
- If there is oxygen available, a respiratory therapist or nurse will place a nasal cannula in their nose and give between two and four liters of oxygen.
- If available and the person is not allergic or taking any blood-thinner medication, the nurse will have the person chew a regular-strength aspirin. Aspirin helps the blood flow to the heart.
- Stay with the person until EMS arrives.
- If the person becomes unconscious, follow BLS guidelines and initiate CPR.

Difficulty Breathing

Breathing difficulties or shortness of breath can be caused by many factors, such as asthma, bronchitis, pneumonia, heart conditions, pulmonary embolism, anxiety, or exercise. People may occasionally have shortness of breath because of an underlying condition that is being monitored by a physician. They may take medication for this symptom and be able to continue to live relatively normal lives. However, if a person has sudden difficulty catching their breath, and it is not relieved with rest, change of position, or their inhaler medication, immediate attention is required. Do the following if a person begins to struggle with breathing:

- Call for help and have the person sit up in their chair or in their bed.

- Instruct the person to try to take slow breaths, inhaling though their nose and exhaling out of their mouth.

- Continue to talk to them reassuringly and soothingly. Anxiety can actually make breathing even more difficult.

- If their breathing becomes easier and they seem to calm down, have a physician see them as soon as possible, especially if this is something new for this person.

- If breathing continues to be difficult, call 911 (if not in medical facility).

- Place oxygen on the patient with a mask or nasal cannula, if available.

- Stay with the patient until help arrives and monitor their level of consciousness and breathing rate.

Allergic Reactions

Allergies can cause many symptoms from mild to severe. Some examples of mild symptoms might include itching, redness on the skin, hives, sneezing, runny nose, and itchy eyes. Wheezing may occur and may be treated with a prescribed inhaler. Life-threatening allergic reactions include swelling of the tongue or throat, difficulty breathing, and **anaphylaxis**, which is a systemic reaction. Anaphylaxis is rare but can lead to death if it is not recognized and treated quickly. Allergies to foods, medications, latex, and insect bites can cause anaphylaxis. Normally a person who has serious allergic reactions will have an **epinephrine pen**, or "**epi-pen**," with them at all times, to be administered in case of a reaction. If the following symptoms associated with anaphylaxis are observed outside of a medical facility, call 911. Otherwise, report any of the following symptoms to the nurse:

- Difficulty breathing
- Swollen tongue or throat tightness
- Wheezing
- Nausea and vomiting
- Fainting or dizziness
- Low blood pressure
- Rapid heart beat
- Feeling strange or sense of impending doom
- Chest pain

Call 911 even if an epi-pen has been administered for the allergic reaction. Reaction symptoms can continue to occur or can reoccur later.

Poisoning

Poison can be something eaten, inhaled, or absorbed in excess, or exposure to toxic substances. This type of emergency can happen to patients and employees. If there is an accidental poisoning and the person is awake and alert, call the poison-control hotline at 1-800-222-1222. Stay on the phone with poison control and stay with the victim. Try to have the following information available for the responders:

- Weight and age of the victim
- The label or bottle of the substance taken
- The time of exposure to the substance (how long it has been)
- The address of where the victim is located

If the person goes unconscious or is not breathing, call 911.

Many chemical labels, such as cleaning supplies, have warning labels and instructions for dealing with toxic exposure. The eyes may need to be flushed with water, for example. Read labels but also call for help. In healthcare facilities, protocols for chemical spills or exposure exist so that clean up and injury can be dealt with quickly. Always follow the policy provided by the facility or workplace.

Self-Care

The job of a nurse is physically, mentally, and emotionally stressful. The strain of moving and lifting patients, along with going from room to room constantly answering the needs of the patients for a long shift, can be physically exhausting. One must organize one's time, prioritize tasks, answer questions, and have countless conversations with the health care team and patients and their families, all of which can take a mental toll. Dealing with patients who are sick, in pain, suffering, and, in some cases, facing death, can drain a nurse's emotional reserves, which can quickly lead to burnout if left unaddressed. Being aware of this potential for overall fatigue is the first step to managing stress and maintaining one's own health.

It is important that a nurse knows how to cope with the effects of stress positively. **Negative coping mechanisms** include unhealthy eating habits and binging behavior, abusing substances such as alcohol and drugs, acting recklessly with one's own safety, and becoming abusive in personal relationships.

Positive coping mechanisms include finding an activity to engage in to unwind and relieve stress in a healthy way. Activities such as daily exercise, spending quality time with friends and family, cooking, yoga, biking, and hiking are all ways to deal with the stress of a demanding job in a healthy way.

The nurse should be careful not to work too many hours as well. It can be tempting to take on extra shifts continually to earn extra money for gifts, vacations, or simply to pay the bills and support a family. These extra shifts and long hours can put a nurse in a danger zone if they are using up too much mental, physical, and/or emotional energy. It is better to be well rested and have adequate mental and physical energy for a shift than to put the patient and oneself at risk for harm.

Being properly nourished, getting adequate exercise, and maintaining healthy sleep habits will all positively contribute to a nurse's health. The nurse's health is vital to helping their patients regain or maintain their own health and, thus, should be made a high priority. If one needs help learning healthy eating habits, meal planning, how to get involved in an exercise program or routine, or other methods of managing stress, many facilities have programs to help guide employees toward better health. There are a plethora of available online resources aimed at improving one's health as well.

Health Screening

Historically, nurses have been primarily responsible for conducting health screenings. Every biological system within the human body should be screened periodically to ensure that it is operating at optimal levels. At the start of every developmental stage, it is recommended that patients be screened and, if found deficient, treated and monitored for progress. Health screenings are suggested based on chronological age to guide both individual treatment and trends for developing community outreach. Armed with the data, nurses collaborate with patients, providers, and caregivers to formulate an effective treatment plan.

Nurses working within the community health sector also utilize health screenings to guide disease-prevention efforts on a larger scale. Nurse researchers can use the data to aid in the creation of medications and advertisement campaigns to target those individuals on the borderlines of a particular disease process. Further, community-health nurses can conduct health screenings to identify gaps in access to healthcare, barriers to care, and disease maintenance. Once the information is disseminated to surrounding healthcare providers, clinics, and local government officials, the community-health nurse can begin the dialogue to effect policy changes. More engagement with health fairs, educational seminars, and print and social media campaigns may also result from health screenings.

Overall, health screenings are an integral piece of the healthcare puzzle. As nurses, it is often necessary to discuss the importance of annual health-screening recommendations upon each patient encounter. If patients reject or accept the recommended testing, they become aware of any present risk factors. Nurses can probe for information as to their ambivalence. For example, while completing a depression screening, a nurse can determine if an individual is at risk for depression. A patient who scores higher on the questionnaire can reveal if the answers are an accurate representation of daily high-risk behavior, or situational in nature.

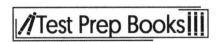

Techniques of Physical Assessment

One of the most important skills that a nurse can possess is that of the physical assessment. Practically every area of nursing practice requires that a nurse have an accurate recall of normal physical functioning and be capable of observing areas of compromise. The nurse's awareness of baseline functioning for a patient within the specific age group and associated health concerns is essential. Physicians, nurse practitioners, and other healthcare providers routinely depend on the nurse's initial assessment of patients to guide their overall treatment of patients.

The initial assessment of a patient does not begin in the face-to-face interaction. As an expert, the nurse must start with any available historical data. Review prior history and physical records, diagnoses, medications, and treatment plans. Certain medications and disease processes can impact daily functioning and the nurse must consider this prior to patient interaction. Immediately upon introduction, the nurse must observe: gait, posture, and balance, skin tone, voice intonation, responsiveness, eye contact, hand grip with handshake, and general stature. While taking vital signs, assess mood, **level of consciousness (LOC)**, orientation, short-term and long-term memory, bowel and urinary habits, and medication list. The aforementioned portions of the assessment can aid in the formulation of the rest of the clinical picture. It is also necessary to discuss daily habits, work schedule, social interactions, and physical activity. Those factors can influence adherence to suggested treatment plans. Once a full clinical picture falls into place, the nurse can utilize the findings to discuss interventions that would be helpful to the patient.

Cancer Screening

Cancer screening tests relevant to several organ systems have effectively decreased the incidence and mortality of cancer in those systems. Common screening tests include the Papanicolaou (PAP) test for cervical cancer, colonoscopy for colon cancer, and mammography for breast cancer. Recently, screening for lung cancer with advanced computed tomography (CT) technology in patients with a history of smoking has been proposed, in an effort to identify lung cancers at an earlier stage that may be treated more successfully. Conversely, the research indicates that there is insufficient evidence to support any relationship between decreased disease incidence and morbidity and the prostate-specific antigen test (PSA) measurements for prostate cancer, or the annual full-body skin assessments by a dermatologist. In addition, there are no screening tests available for ovarian cancer.

Osteoporosis Screening/Bone-Density Scan

Osteoporosis is the "thinning" of the bone, which most commonly affects postmenopausal women. The degree and progression of the changes associated with osteoporosis can be measured by the bone-density exam, which compares a patient's test results with the results of younger patients who are disease free.

Domestic Violence Screening and Detection

The efficiency of domestic violence screening and detection is often hampered by the reluctance of the abused individual to report the abuse. Institutions and insurance companies have included routine assessment questions related to a patient's perceptions of personal safety; however, the widespread acceptance and effectiveness of these measures are not known.

Depression Screening

Depression is prevalent in adolescents and more commonly observed in females. In the elderly, symptoms of depression differ from other age groups and often go unnoticed because they commonly occur in combination with other medical illnesses and disabilities. Symptoms of depression in the older adult include confusion, changes in weight or appetite, physical aches and pains, irritability, trouble sleeping, and suicidal thoughts. A caregiver may attribute confusion to a cognitive disorder such as dementia and not address it as possible depression. Nurses can use various screening tools to assess for depression.

The **Beck Depression Inventory (BDI)** is used to measure the behavioral manifestations of depression and assess its severity. The BDI is a twenty-one-item self-report inventory that can be used in clients between the ages of 13 and

80. The **Hamilton Depression Rating Scale (HAM-D)** is a useful tool that measures depression before, during, and after treatments. This twenty-one-item test is measured on a three-point or five-point scale. **The Children's Depression Inventory (CDI)** is a modified BDI used in children. The CDI can be used in adolescents up until the age of 17 and assesses the severity of depression.

Vaccinations

Active and Passive Immunity

Acquired immunity occurs after the first antigen encounter. The first time the body mounts this immune response is called the primary immune response. Because the memory B cells store information about the antigen's structure, any subsequent immune response causes a secondary immune response, which is much faster and produces substantially more antibodies due to the presence of memory B cells. If the secondary immune response is strong and fast enough, it will fight off the pathogen before an individual becomes symptomatic. This is a natural means of acquiring immunity.

Vaccination is the process of inducing immunity. **Active immunization** refers to immunity gained by exposure to infectious microorganisms or viruses and can be *natural* or *artificial*. Natural immunization refers to an individual being exposed to an infectious organism as a part of daily life. For example, it was once common for parents to expose their children to childhood diseases such as measles or chicken pox. Artificial immunization refers to therapeutic exposure to an infectious organism as a way of protecting an individual from disease. Today, the medical community relies on artificial immunization as a way to induce immunity.

Vaccines are used for the development of active immunity. A vaccine contains a killed, weakened, or inactivated microorganism or virus that is administered through injection, by mouth, or by aerosol. Vaccinations are administered to prevent an infectious disease but do not always guarantee immunity. Due to circulating memory B cells after administration, the secondary response will fight off the pathogen should it be encountered again in many cases. Both illnesses and vaccinations cause active immunity.

Passive immunity refers to immunity gained by the introduction of antibodies. This introduction can also be natural or artificial. The process occurs when antibodies from the mother's bloodstream are passed on to the bloodstream of the developing fetus. Breast milk can also transmit antibodies to a baby. Babies are born with passive immunity, which provides protection against general infection for approximately the first six months of its life.

Practice Quiz

1. Nociceptors detect which of the following?
    a. Deep pressure
    b. Vibration
    c. Pain
    d. Temperature

2. A cluster of capillaries that functions as the main filter of the blood entering the kidney is known as which of the following?
    a. The Bowman's capsule
    b. The loop of Henle
    c. The glomerulus
    d. The nephron

3. What is an alteration in the normal gene sequence called?
    a. DNA mutation
    b. Gene migration
    c. Polygenetic inheritance
    d. Incomplete dominance

4. Blood type is a trait determined by multiple alleles, and two of them are co-dominant: I^A codes for A blood and I^B codes for B blood. The i allele codes for O blood and is recessive to both. If an A heterozygous individual and an O individual have a child, what is the probability that the child will have A blood?
    a. 25%
    b. 50%
    c. 75%
    d. 100%

5. Which of the choices below are the reproductive cells produced by meiosis?
    a. Zygotes
    b. Germ cells
    c. Blastocyst
    d. Gametes

See answers on the next page.

217

Answer Explanations

1. C: Nociceptors are a type of touch receptor that detect pain. They relay this information to the CNS via afferent nerves. Efferent nerves then carry motor signals back, which may cause muscle contractions that move the body part away from the source of the pain. For example, if a person places their hand on a hot stove, nociceptors detect the painful burning sensation. Then they relay this information up to the brain, where a response signal travels down the efferent nerves that control the muscles of the shoulder, arm, forearm, and hand to retract the hand from the hot stove. Choice *A* is incorrect because that is mainly the function of Ruffini endings. Choice *B* describes the function of several mechanoreceptors such as Meissner's corpuscles, Pacinian corpuscles, and Merkel's discs. Lastly, thermoreceptors detect changes in temperature, so Choice *D* is incorrect.

2. C: A cluster of capillaries that functions as the main filter of the blood entering the kidney is known as the glomerulus, so Choice *C* is correct. The Bowman's capsule surrounds the glomerulus and receives fluid and solutes from it; therefore, Choice *A* is incorrect. The loop of Henle is a part of the kidney tubule where water and nutrients are reabsorbed, so *B* is false. The nephron is the unit containing all of these anatomical features, making Choice *D* incorrect as well.

3. A: An alteration in the normal gene sequence is called a DNA point mutation. Mutations can be harmful, neutral, or even beneficial. Sometimes, as seen in natural selection, a genetic mutation can improve fitness, providing an adaptation that will aid in survival. DNA mutations can happen as a result of environmental damage, for example, from radiation or chemicals. Mutations can also happen during cell replication as a result of incorrect pairing of complementary nucleotides by DNA polymerase. There are also chromosomal mutations as well, where entire segments of chromosomes can be deleted, inverted, duplicated, or sent or received from a different chromosome.

4. B: According to the Punnett square, the child has a 2 out of 4 chance of having A-type blood, since the dominant allele I^A is present in two of the four possible offspring. The type O blood allele is masked by the type A blood allele since it is recessive.

$I^A i$	ii
$I^A i$	ii

5. D: Reproductive cells are referred to as gametes: egg (female) and sperm (male). These cells have only one set of 23 chromosomes and are haploid so that when they combine during fertilization, the zygote has the correct diploid number, 46. Reproductive cell division is called meiosis, which is different from mitosis, the type of division process for body (somatic) cells.

Verbal

Word Knowledge

Select the word that most correctly completes the sentence.

1. After Kira wrote her first book, she pledged to her fans the sequel would be just as exciting as the first. Pledged to means:
    a. denied
    b. promised
    c. invigorated
    d. germinated

2. When I heard the wolf howl from my tent, my hands started trembling and my heart stopped... hopefully I would make it through this night alive! Trembling means:
    a. dancing
    b. glowing
    c. shaking
    d. throbbing

3. Unlike Leo, who always played basketball in the park after school, Gabriel would consistently go to the library and study after school. Consistently means:
    a. infrequently
    b. occasionally
    c. hardly
    d. usually

4. As soon as the shot rang out, the runners dashed toward the finish line. Dashed means:
    a. sprinted
    b. skipped
    c. rejoiced
    d. herded

5. Resolved to get an *A* on her paper, LaShonda began writing it two weeks before it was due. Resolved means:
    a. resumed
    b. content
    c. enthusiastic
    d. determined

6. After Colby's mom picked him up from school, they went to the bank to install a check. Install means:
    a. celebrate
    b. neutralize
    c. eliminate
    d. deposit

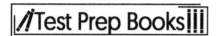

7. The sale at the grocery store motivated my dad to buy four avocados instead of two. Motivated means:
   a. intimidated
   b. inspired
   c. dismayed
   d. berated

8. My mom recently started drinking fruit and vegetable smoothies in order to enhance the quality of her health. Enhance means:
   a. increase
   b. decrease
   c. curtail
   d. request

9. In the middle of our vacation, we had a sojourn in a remote cabin in the woods. Believe it or not, we got snowed in and had to stay for two weeks! Sojourn means:
   a. soiree
   b. presentation
   c. layover
   d. cohort

10. Cooking dinner was her favorite activity until she triggered the fire alarm by burning the casserole in the oven. Triggered means:
   a. activated
   b. offended
   c. unplugged
   d. disbanded

11. Much to her consternation, she had to go to the dentist's office to get a tooth pulled, so she did some breathing exercises before she walked in. Consternation means:
   a. refresh
   b. creative
   c. rapture
   d. dread

12. The yellow feathers and purple markings told us that this bird was native to the southeast part of the United States. Native means:
   a. entertaining
   b. indigenous
   c. impudent
   d. monotonous

13. When we caught the eels, their bodies wriggled out of our hands and back into the water. Wriggled means:
   a. exploded
   b. deteriorated
   c. thundered
   d. slithered

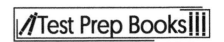

14. Even though at the restaurant my mom requested the eggplant with no cheese, she received a huge serving of parmesan on top. Serving means:
    a. portion
    b. directed
    c. mourning
    d. endorsement

15. I promise, I did not instigate the fight. Instigate means:
    a. Begin
    b. Ponder
    c. Swim
    d. Overwhelm

16. The nurse measured her sublingual temperature against her axillary temperature. Sublingual means:
    a. In the ear
    b. In the rectum
    c. Under the armpit
    d. Under the tongue

17. Given his rude comments, her reaction seemed plausible. Plausible means:
    a. Conceivable
    b. Skeptical
    c. Diurnal
    d. Erudite

18. The young boy seemed to be capable of nothing, other than his uncanny ability to exasperate his babysitter. Exasperate means:
    a. Annoy
    b. Breathe
    c. Disappoint
    d. Stifle

19. The student wanted to become a phlebotomist. Phlebotomist means:
    a. A professional who takes x-rays
    b. A professional who makes artificial limbs
    c. A professional who draws blood
    d. A professional who counsels patients

20. The patient's eyes appeared glassy. Glassy means:
    a. Sad
    b. Expressionless
    c. Emotional
    d. Blind

21. The patient had aphasia after his stroke. Aphasia means:
    a. Memory loss
    b. Droopy face
    c. Impairment in facial recognition
    d. Language impairment

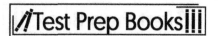

22. The professor was notorious for his jejune lectures. Jejune means:
    a. Dull
    b. Stimulating
    c. Interactive
    d. Expert

23. The patient had a difficulty with proprioception. Proprioception means:
    a. Spatial awareness of the body
    b. Balance and agility
    c. Pain detection
    d. Sensory integration

24. The patient's cheeks appeared ruddy. Ruddy means:
    a. Swollen or puffy
    b. Edematous
    c. Flushed
    d. Discolored or blotchy

25. The nurse informed the toddler's mother that the boy should start to sleep better once the cause of his pruritis was identified and treated. Pruritis means:
    a. Vomiting
    b. Ringing in the ears
    c. Insomnia
    d. Itchiness

26. The medication side effects that the patient experienced were diaphoresis and dizziness. Diaphoresis means:
    a. Excessive sweating
    b. Dyspnea
    c. Wheezing
    d. Frequent urination

27. The nurse explained the risk factors for contracting a venereal disease. Venereal means:
    a. Vector-borne
    b. Sexually-transmitted
    c. Relating to the gums
    d. Parasitic

28. The doctor studied the newborn's face for nuances in expression. Nuances means:
    a. Apparent disparities
    b. Subtle differences
    c. Drastic changes
    d. Visual cues
    e. Ancillary

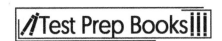

Reading Comprehension

Questions 29–33 are based upon the following passage:

My gentleness and good behaviour had gained so far on the emperor and his court, and indeed upon the army and people in general, that I began to conceive hopes of getting my liberty in a short time. I took all possible methods to cultivate this favourable disposition. The natives came, by degrees, to be less apprehensive of any danger from me. I would sometimes lie down, and let five or six of them dance on my hand; and at last the boys and girls would venture to come and play at hide-and-seek in my hair. I had now made a good progress in understanding and speaking the language. The emperor had a mind one day to entertain me with several of the country shows, wherein they exceed all nations I have known, both for dexterity and magnificence. I was diverted with none so much as that of the rope-dancers, performed upon a slender white thread, extended about two feet, and twelve inches from the ground. Upon which I shall desire liberty, with the reader's patience, to enlarge a little.

This diversion is only practised by those persons who are candidates for great employments, and high favour at court. They are trained in this art from their youth, and are not always of noble birth, or liberal education. When a great office is vacant, either by death or disgrace (which often happens), five or six of those candidates petition the emperor to entertain his majesty and the court with a dance on the rope; and whoever jumps the highest, without falling, succeeds in the office. Very often the chief ministers themselves are commanded to show their skill, and to convince the emperor that they have not lost their faculty. Flimnap, the treasurer, is allowed to cut a caper on the straight rope, at least an inch higher than any other lord in the whole empire. I have seen him do the summerset several times together, upon a trencher fixed on a rope which is no thicker than a common packthread in England. My friend Reldresal, principal secretary for private affairs, is, in my opinion, if I am not partial, the second after the treasurer; the rest of the great officers are much upon a par.

from Jonathan Swift's Gulliver's Travels into Several Remote Nations of the World

29. Which of the following statements best summarizes the central purpose of this text?
    a. Gulliver details his fondness for the archaic, yet interesting, practices of his captors.
    b. Gulliver conjectures about the intentions of the aristocratic sector of society.
    c. Gulliver becomes acquainted with the people and practices of his new surroundings.
    d. Gulliver's differences cause him to become penitent around new acquaintances.

30. What is the word *principal* referring to in the following text?
    My friend Reldresal, principal secretary for private affairs, is, in my opinion, if I am not partial, the second after the treasurer; the rest of the great officers are much upon a par.

    a. Primary or chief
    b. An acolyte
    c. An individual who provides nurturing
    d. One in a subordinate position

31. What can the reader infer from the following text?
   I would sometimes lie down, and let five or six of them dance on my hand; and at last the boys and girls would venture to come and play at hide-and-seek in my hair.

   a. The children tortured Gulliver.
   b. Gulliver traveled because he wanted to meet new people.
   c. Gulliver is considerably larger than the children who are playing around him.
   d. Gulliver has a genuine love and enthusiasm for people of all sizes.

32. What is the significance of the word *mind* in the following passage?
   The emperor had a mind one day to entertain me with several of the country shows, wherein they exceed all nations I have known, both for dexterity and magnificence.

   a. The ability to think
   b. A collective vote
   c. A definitive decision
   d. A mythological question

33. How do Flimnap and Reldresal demonstrate the community's emphasis on physical strength and leadership abilities?
   a. Only children used Gulliver's hands as a playground.
   b. The two men who exhibited superior abilities held prominent positions in the community.
   c. Only common townspeople, not leaders, walk the straight rope.
   d. No one could jump higher than Gulliver.

Questions 34–38 are based upon the following passage:

Three years ago, I think there were not many bird-lovers in the United States who believed it possible to prevent the total extinction of both egrets from our fauna. All the known rookeries accessible to plume-hunters had been totally destroyed. Two years ago, the secret discovery of several small, hidden colonies prompted William Dutcher, President of the National Association of Audubon Societies, and Mr. T. Gilbert Pearson, Secretary, to attempt the protection of those colonies. With a fund contributed for the purpose, wardens were hired and duly commissioned. As previously stated, one of those wardens was shot dead in cold blood by a plume hunter. The task of guarding swamp rookeries from the attacks of money-hungry desperadoes, to whom the accursed plumes were worth their weight in gold, is a very chancy proceeding. There is now one warden in Florida who says that "before they get my rookery they will first have to get me."

Thus far, the protective work of the Audubon Association has been successful. Now there are 20 colonies, which contain, all told, about 5,000 egrets and about 120,000 herons and ibises which are guarded by the Audubon wardens. One of the most important is on Bird Island, a mile out in Orange Lake, Central Florida, and it is ably defended by Oscar E. Baynard. To-day, the plume hunters who do not dare to raid the guarded rookeries are trying to study out the lines of flight of the birds, to and from their feeding-grounds, and shoot them in transit. Their motto is "Anything to beat the law, and get the plumes." It is there that the state of Florida should take part in the war.

The success of this campaign is attested by the fact that last year a number of egrets were seen in eastern Massachusetts—for the first time in many years. And so to-day the question is, can the wardens continue to hold the plume-hunters at bay?

From *Our Vanishing Wildlife*, by William T. Hornaday

224

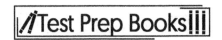

34. What purpose does the quote serve at the end of the first paragraph?
    a. The quote shows proof of a hunter threatening one of the wardens.
    b. The quote lightens the mood by illustrating the colloquial language of the region.
    c. The quote provides an example of a warden protecting one of the colonies.
    d. The quote provides much needed comic relief in the form of a joke.

35. What is the meaning of the word *rookeries* in the following text?

    To-day, the plume hunters who do not dare to raid the guarded rookeries are trying to study out the lines of flight of the birds, to and from their feeding-grounds, and shoot them in transit.

    a. Houses in a slum area
    b. A place where hunters gather to trade tools
    c. A place where wardens go to trade stories
    d. A colony of breeding birds

36. What is on Bird Island?
    a. Hunters selling plumes
    b. An important bird colony
    c. Bird Island Battle between the hunters and the wardens
    d. An important egret with unique plumes

37. What is the main purpose of the passage?
    a. To persuade the audience to act in preservation of the bird colonies
    b. To show the effect hunting egrets has had on the environment
    c. To argue that the preservation of bird colonies has had a negative impact on the environment
    d. To demonstrate the success of the protective work of the Audubon Association

38. Why are hunters trying to study the lines of flight of the birds?
    a. To further their studies of ornithology
    b. To help wardens preserve the lives of the birds
    c. To have a better opportunity to hunt the birds
    d. To build their homes under the lines of flight because they believe it brings good luck

Questions 39–43 are based upon the following passage:

Insects as a whole are preeminently creatures of the land and the air. This is shown not only by the possession of wings by a vast majority of the class, but by the mode of breathing to which reference has already been made, a system of branching air-tubes carrying atmospheric air with its combustion-supporting oxygen to all the insect's tissues. The air gains access to these tubes through a number of paired air-holes or spiracles, arranged segmentally in series.

It is of great interest to find that, nevertheless, a number of insects spend much of their time under water. This is true of not a few in the perfect winged state, as for example aquatic beetles and water-bugs ('boatmen' and 'scorpions') which have some way of protecting their spiracles when submerged, and, possessing usually the power of flight, can pass on occasion from pond or stream to upper air. But it is advisable in connection with our present subject to dwell especially on some insects that remain continually under water till they are ready to undergo their final moult and attain the winged state, which they pass entirely in the air. The preparatory instars of such insects are aquatic; the adult instar is aerial. All may-flies, dragon-flies, and caddis-flies, many beetles and two-winged flies, and a few moths thus divide their life-story between the water and the air. For

225

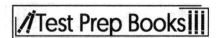

the present we confine attention to the Stone-flies, the May-flies, and the Dragon-flies, three well-known orders of insects respectively called by systematists the Plecoptera, the Ephemeroptera, and the Odonata.

In the case of many insects that have aquatic larvae, the latter are provided with some arrangement for enabling them to reach atmospheric air through the surface-film of the water. But the larva of a stone-fly, a dragon-fly, or a may-fly is adapted more completely than these for aquatic life; it can, by means of gills of some kind, breathe the air dissolved in water.

Excerpt from *The Life-Story of Insects*, by Geo H. Carpenter

39. Which statement best details the central idea in this passage?
    a. It introduces certain insects that transition from water to air.
    b. It delves into entomology, especially where gills are concerned.
    c. It defines what constitutes insects' breathing.
    d. It invites readers to have a hand in the preservation of insects.

40. Which definition most closely relates to the usage of the word *moult* in the passage?
    a. An adventure of sorts, especially underwater
    b. Mating act between two insects
    c. The act of shedding part or all of the outer shell
    d. Death of an organism that ends in a revival of life

41. What is the purpose of the first paragraph in relation to the second paragraph?
    a. The first paragraph serves as a cause, and the second paragraph serves as an effect.
    b. The first paragraph serves as a contrast to the second.
    c. The first paragraph is a description for the argument in the second paragraph.
    d. The first and second paragraphs are merely presented in a sequence.

42. Which of the statements reflect information that one could reasonably infer based on the author's tone?
    a. The author's tone is persuasive and attempts to call the audience to action.
    b. The author's tone is passionate due to excitement over the subject and personal narrative.
    c. The author's tone is informative and exhibits interest in the subject of the study.
    d. The author's tone is somber, depicting some anger at the state of insect larvae.

43. Which statement best describes stoneflies, mayflies, and dragonflies?
    a. They are creatures of the land and the air.
    b. They have a way of protecting their spiracles when submerged.
    c. Their larvae can breathe the air dissolved in water through gills of some kind.
    d. The preparatory instars of these insects are aerial.

Questions 44–48 are based on the following passage.

In the quest to understand existence, modern philosophers must question if humans can fully comprehend the world. Classical Western approaches to philosophy tend to hold that one can understand something, be it an event or object, by standing outside of the phenomenon and observing it. It is then by unbiased observation that one can grasp the details of the world. This seems to hold true for many things. Scientists conduct experiments and record their findings, and thus many natural phenomena become

226

comprehensible. However, many of these observations were possible because humans used tools in order to make these discoveries.

This may seem like an extraneous matter. After all, people invented things like microscopes and telescopes in order to enhance their capacity to view cells or the movement of stars. While humans are still capable of seeing things, the question remains if human beings have the capacity to fully observe and see the world in order to understand it. It would not be an impossible stretch to argue that what humans see through a microscope is not the exact thing itself but rather a human interpretation of it.

This would seem to be the case in the "Business of the Holes" experiment conducted by Richard Feynman. To study the way electrons behave, Feynman set up a barrier with two holes and a plate. The plate was there to indicate how many times the electrons would pass through the hole(s). Rather than casually observing the electrons acting under normal circumstances, Feynman discovered that electrons behave in two totally different ways depending on whether or not they are observed. The electrons that were observed had passed through either one of the holes or were caught on the plate as particles. However, electrons that weren't observed acted as waves instead of particles and passed through both holes. This indicated that electrons have a dual nature. Electrons seen by the human eye act like particles, while unseen electrons act like waves of energy.

This dual nature of the electrons presents a conundrum. While humans now have a better understanding of electrons, the fact remains that people cannot entirely perceive how electrons behave without the use of instruments. We can only observe one of the mentioned behaviors, which only provides a partial understanding of the entire function of electrons. Therefore, we're forced to ask ourselves whether the world we observe is objective or if it is subjectively perceived by humans. Or, an alternative question: can humans understand the world only through machines that will allow them to observe natural phenomena?

Both questions humble humanity's capacity to grasp the world. However, those ideas don't take into account that many phenomena have been proven by human beings without the use of machines, such as the discovery of gravity. Like all philosophical questions, whether humanity's reason and observation alone can understand the universe can be approached from many angles.

44. Which of the following best describes how paragraph four is structured?
    a. It offers one solution, questions the solution, and then ends with an alternative solution.
    b. It presents an inquiry, explains the detail of that inquiry, and then offers a solution.
    c. It presents a problem, explains the details of that problem, and then ends with more inquiries.
    d. It gives a definition, offers an explanation, and then ends with an inquiry.

45. For the classical approach of understanding to hold true, which of the following is required?
    a. The person observing must use a telescope.
    b. The person observing must prove their theory beyond a doubt.
    c. Multiple witnesses must be present.
    d. The person observing must be unbiased.

46. Which best describes how the electrons in the experiment behaved like waves?
    a. The electrons moved up and down like ocean waves.
    b. The electrons passed through both holes and then onto the plate.
    c. The electrons converted to photons upon touching the plate.
    d. Electrons were seen passing through one hole or the other.

227

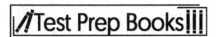

47. Which situation best parallels the revelation of the dual nature of electrons discovered in Feynman's experiment?
    a. A man is born color-blind and grows up observing everything in lighter or darker shades. With the invention of special goggles he puts on, he discovers that there are other colors in addition to different shades.
    b. The coelacanth was thought to be extinct, but a live specimen was just recently discovered. There are now two living species of coelacanth known, and both are believed to be endangered.
    c. In the Middle Ages, blacksmiths added carbon to iron, thus inventing steel. This important discovery would have its biggest effects during the industrial revolution.
    d. The x-ray machine was invented to help doctors better examine and treat broken bones. It was put to use in hospitals and medical centers.

48. Which statement about technology would the author likely disagree with?
    a. Technology can help expand the field of human vision.
    b. Technology renders human observation irrelevant.
    c. Developing tools used in observation and research indicates growing understanding of our world in itself.
    d. Studying certain phenomena necessitates the use of tools and machines.

Questions 49–53 are based on the following passage:

The Middle Ages were a time of great superstition and theological debate. Many beliefs were developed and practiced, while some died out or were listed as heresy. Boethianism is a Medieval theological philosophy that attributes sin to gratification and righteousness with virtue and God's providence. Boethianism holds that sin, greed, and corruption are means to attain temporary pleasure, but that they inherently harm the person's soul as well as other human beings.

In *The Canterbury Tales,* we observe more instances of bad actions punished than goodness being rewarded. This would appear to be some reflection of Boethianism. In the "Pardoner's Tale," all three thieves wind up dead, which is a result of their desire for wealth. Each wrongdoer pays with their life, and they are unable to enjoy the wealth they worked to steal. Within his tales, Chaucer gives reprieve to people undergoing struggle, but also interweaves stories of contemptible individuals being cosmically punished for their wickedness.

The thieves idolize physical wealth, which leads to their downfall. This same theme and ideological principle of Boethianism is repeated in the "Friar's Tale," in which the summoner character attempts to gain further wealth by partnering with a demon. The summoner's refusal to repent for his avarice and corruption leads to the demon dragging his soul to Hell. Again, we see the theme of the individual who puts faith and morality aside in favor for a physical prize. The result, of course, is that the summoner loses everything.

The examples of the righteous being rewarded tend to appear in a spiritual context within the *Canterbury Tales*. However, there are a few instances where we see goodness resulting in physical reward. In the "Prioress' Tale," we see corporal punishment for barbarism *and* a reward for goodness. The Jews are punished for their murder of the child, giving a sense of law and order (though racist) to the plot. While the boy does die, he is granted a lasting reward by being able to sing even after his death, a miracle that marks that the murdered youth led a pure life. Here, the miracle represents eternal favor with God.

Again, we see the theological philosophy of Boethianism in Chaucer's *The Canterbury Tales* through acts of sin and righteousness and the consequences that follow. When pleasures of the world are sought instead of God's favor, we see characters being punished in tragic ways. However, the

228

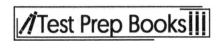

absence of worldly lust has its own set of consequences for the characters seeking to obtain God's favor.

49. What would be a potential reward for living a good life, as described in Boethianism?
    a. A long life sustained by the good deeds one has done over a lifetime
    b. Wealth and fertility for oneself and the extension of one's family line
    c. Vengeance for those who have been persecuted by others who have a capacity for committing wrongdoing
    d. God's divine favor for one's righteousness

50. What might be the main reason why the author chose to discuss Boethianism through examining *The Canterbury Tales*?
    a. *The Canterbury Tales* is a well-known text.
    b. *The Canterbury Tales* is the only known fictional text that contains use of Boethianism.
    c. *The Canterbury Tales* presents a manuscript written in the medieval period that can help illustrate Boethianism through stories and show how people of the time might have responded to the idea.
    d. Within each individual tale in *The Canterbury Tales*, the reader can read about different levels of Boethianism and how each level leads to greater enlightenment.

51. What "ideological principle" is the author referring to in the middle of the second paragraph when talking about the "Friar's Tale"?
    a. The principle that the act of ravaging another's possessions is the same as ravaging one's soul
    b. The principle that thieves who idolize physical wealth will be punished in an earthly sense as well as eternally
    c. The principle that fraternization with a demon will result in one losing everything, including their life
    d. The principle that a desire for material goods leads to moral malfeasance punishable by a higher being

52. Which of the following words, if substituted for the word avarice in paragraph two, would least change the meaning of the sentence?
    a. Perniciousness
    b. Pithiness
    c. Covetousness
    d. Precariousness

53. Based on the passage, what view does Boethianism take on desire?
    a. Desire does not exist in the context of Boethianism.
    b. Desire is a virtue and should be welcomed.
    c. Having desire is evidence of demonic possession.
    d. Desire for pleasure can lead toward sin.

Questions 54–58 are based on the following passage:

It was a heavy disappointment to Maggie that she was not allowed to go with her father in the gig when he went to fetch Tom home from the academy; but the morning was too wet, Mrs. Tulliver said, for a little girl to go out in her best bonnet. Maggie took the opposite view very strongly, and it was a direct consequence of this difference of opinion that when her mother was in the act of brushing out the reluctant black crop Maggie suddenly rushed from under her hands and dipped her head in a basin of water standing near, in the vindictive determination that there should be no more chance of curls that day.

"Maggie, Maggie!" exclaimed Mrs. Tulliver, sitting stout and helpless with the brushes on her lap, "what is to become of you if you're so naughty? I'll tell your aunt Glegg and your aunt Pullet when

229

they come next week, and they'll never love you any more. Oh dear, oh dear! look at your clean pinafore, wet from top to bottom. Folks 'ull think it's a judgment on me as I've got such a child,— they'll think I've done summat wicked."

Before this remonstrance was finished, Maggie was already out of hearing, making her way toward the great attic that ran under the old high-pitched roof, shaking the water from her black locks as she ran, like a Skye terrier escaped from his bath. This attic was Maggie's favourite retreat on a wet day, when the weather was not too cold; here she fretted out all her ill humours, and talked aloud to the worm-eaten floors and the worm-eaten shelves, and the dark rafters festooned with cobwebs; and here she kept a Fetish which she punished for all her misfortunes. This was the trunk of a large wooden doll, which once stared with the roundest of eyes above the reddest of cheeks; but was now entirely defaced by a long career of vicarious suffering.

An excerpt from The Mill on the Floss *by George Eliot*

54. Why was Maggie disappointed?
   a. She does not enjoy having her hair brushed.
   b. She wants Mrs. Tulliver to be fired from her job.
   c. She wants her aunt Glegg and aunt Pullet to visit sooner than next week.
   d. She could not join her father when he left to go to the academy.

55. It can be inferred from the passage that:
   a. Maggie's father does not enjoy her company.
   b. It is societally expected that young girls are presentable.
   c. Maggie's aunts share Maggie's carefree spirit.
   d. Mrs. Tulliver is a stay-at-home mother.

56. What does Maggie do with her doll?
   a. She takes her emotions out by damaging the doll.
   b. She brings her doll to the attic because toys are not allowed in her home.
   c. She plays pretend with her doll in a dollhouse.
   d. She steals the doll since it belongs to her sibling.

57. What does the text mean when it uses the term *ill humours* in Paragraph 3?
   a. Sickly health
   b. Poor mood
   c. Dark sense of humor
   d. Anxious habits

58. What does the word *vicarious* in Paragraph 3 most nearly mean?
   a. Savage
   b. Untimely
   c. Secondhand
   d. Continuous

Math

1. Which of the following numbers has the greatest value?
   a. 1.43785
   b. 1.07548
   c. 1.43592
   d. 0.89409

2. The value of 6×12 is the same as:
   a. $2 \times 4 \times 4 \times 2$
   b. $7 \times 4 \times 3$
   c. $6 \times 6 \times 3$
   d. $3 \times 3 \times 4 \times 2$

3. This chart indicates how many sales of CDs, vinyl records, and MP3 downloads occurred over the last year. Approximately what percentage of the total sales was from CDs?

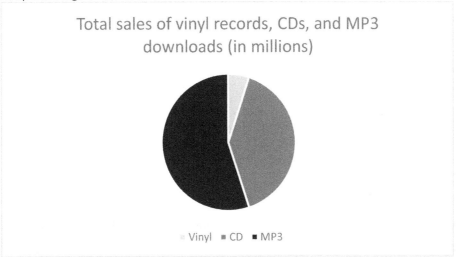

Total sales of vinyl records, CDs, and MP3 downloads (in millions)

Vinyl   CD   MP3

   a. 55%
   b. 25%
   c. 40%
   d. 5%

4. After a 20% sale discount, Frank purchased a new refrigerator for $850. How much money did he save off of the original price?
   a. $170
   b. $212.50
   c. $105.75
   d. $200

5. Which of the following values is the largest?
   a. 0.45
   b. 0.096
   c. 0.3
   d. 0.313

231

6. What is the value of b in this equation?

$$5b - 4 = 2b + 17$$

    a. 13
    b. 24
    c. 7
    d. 21

7. A school's faculty consists of 15 teachers and 20 teaching assistants. They have 200 students. What is the ratio of faculty to students?
    a. $3 : 20$
    b. $4 : 17$
    c. $3 : 2$
    d. $7 : 40$

8. Evaluate the expression. Give the result in decimal form.

$$\frac{3}{5} \times \frac{7}{10} \div \frac{1}{2}$$

    a. 0.042
    b. 84%
    c. 0.84
    d. 0.42

9. A student gets an 85% on a test with 20 questions. How many questions did the student solve correctly?
    a. 15
    b. 16
    c. 17
    d. 18

10. If Sarah reads at an average rate of 21 pages in 4 nights, how long will it take her to read 140 pages?
    a. 6 nights
    b. 26 nights
    c. 8 nights
    d. 27 nights

11. Alan currently weighs 200 pounds, but he wants to lose weight to get down to 175 pounds. What is this difference in kilograms? (1 pound is approximately equal to 0.45 kilograms.)
    a. 9 kg
    b. 11.25 kg
    c. 78.75 kg
    d. 90 kg

12. Johnny earns $2,334.50 from his job each month. He pays $1,437 for monthly expenses and saves the rest. Johnny is planning a vacation in 3 months that he estimates will cost $1,750 total. How much will Johnny have left over from 3 months of saving once he pays for his vacation?
    a. $948.50
    b. $584.50
    c. $852.50
    d. $942.50

13. What is $\frac{420}{98}$ rounded to the nearest integer?
   a. 3
   b. 4
   c. 5
   d. 6

14. A small reptile travels 340 millimeters in 4 seconds. What is the average speed in centimeters per second?
   a. 10.2
   b. 3.4
   c. 8.5
   d. 85

15. The total perimeter of a rectangle is 36 cm. If the length is 12 cm, what is the width?
   a. 3 cm
   b. 12 cm
   c. 6 cm
   d. 8 cm

16. Dwayne has received the following scores on his math tests: 78, 92, 83, 97. What score must Dwayne get on his next math test to have an overall average of 90?
   a. 89
   b. 98
   c. 95
   d. 100

17. What is the overall median of Dwayne's current scores: 78, 92, 83, 97?
   a. 19
   b. 85
   c. 83
   d. 87.5

18. Evaluate:

$$\left(\sqrt{36} \times \sqrt{16}\right) - 3^2$$

   a. 30
   b. 21
   c. 15
   d. 13

19. In Jim's school, there are a total of 650 students. There are three girls for every two boys. How many students are girls?
   a. 260 girls
   b. 130 girls
   c. 65 girls
   d. 390 girls

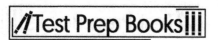

20. What is the value of the expression: $7^2 - 3 \times (4 + 2) + 15 \div 5$?
    a. 12.2
    b. 40.2
    c. 34
    d. 58.2

21. Kimberley earns $10 an hour babysitting, and after 10 p.m., she earns $12 an hour. The time she works is rounded to the nearest hour for pay purposes. On her last job, she worked from 5:30 p.m. to 11:00 p.m. In total, how much did Kimberley earn on her last job?
    a. $45
    b. $57
    c. $62
    d. $42

22. What value of x would solve the following equation?
$$9x + x - 7 = 16 + 2x$$

    a. $x = -4$
    b. $x = 3$
    c. $x = \frac{9}{8}$
    d. $x = \frac{23}{8}$

23. Stephanie has a piece of wrapping paper left over that is 60 inches by 20 inches. Does she have enough paper to cover a cubic box that has a side of length 14 inches?
    a. No. She is 20 square inches short.
    b. No. She is 12 square inches short.
    c. Yes. She has 24 square inches extra.
    d. There is not enough information to answer this question.

24. Keith's bakery had 252 customers go through its doors last week. This week, that number increased to 378. Express this increase as a percentage.
    a. 26%
    b. 50%
    c. 35%
    d. 12%

25. What is the perimeter of the following triangle? Round your answer to the nearest tenth of a unit.

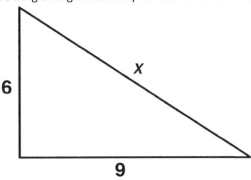

a. 117.0
b. 25.8
c. 15.0
d. 12.9

26. The formula that allows us to convert degrees Celsius to degrees Fahrenheit is $F = \frac{9}{5}C + 32$. Convert 54° Celsius to Fahrenheit.

a. 97.2 °F
b. −2 °F
c. 129.2 °F
d. 12.2 °F

27. The following graph compares the various test scores of the top three students in each of these teachers' classes. Based on the graph, which teacher's students had the lowest range of test scores?

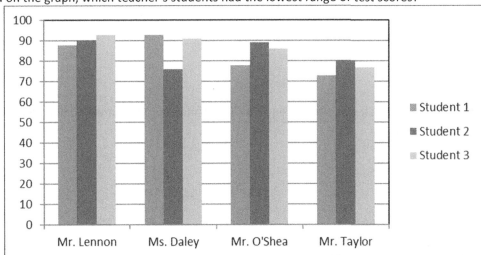

a. Mr. Lennon
b. Mr. O'Shea
c. Mr. Taylor
d. Ms. Daley

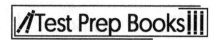

28. Bernard can make $80 per day. If he needs to make $300 and only works full days, how many days will this take?
    a. 2
    b. 3
    c. 4
    d. 5

29. Using the following diagram, calculate the total circumference, rounding to the nearest tenth.

    a. 25.0 cm
    b. 15.7 cm
    c. 78.5 cm
    d. 31.4 cm

30. Which measure for the center of a small sample set would be most affected by outliers?
    a. Mean
    b. Median
    c. Mode
    d. None of the above

31. A line that travels from the lower left of a graph to the upper right of the graph indicates what kind of relationship between an independent and a dependent variable?
    a. Positive
    b. Negative
    c. Exponential
    d. Logarithmic

32. How many kilometers is 4,382 feet if 1 foot is equal to 0.3048 meters? There are 0.3048 meters in 1 foot.
    a. 1.336 kilometers
    b. 14,376 kilometers
    c. 1.437 kilometers
    d. 13,336 kilometers

33. Which of the following is the best description of the relationship between x and y?

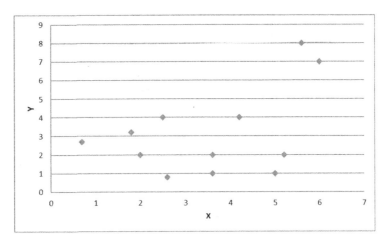

a. The data has normal distribution
b. x and y have a negative relationship
c. x and y have no apparent relation.
d. x and y have a positive relationship

34. What is the slope of this line?

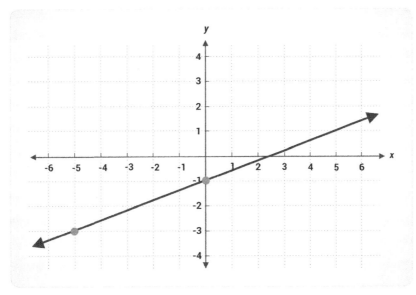

a. 2

b. $\frac{5}{2}$

c. $\frac{1}{2}$

d. $\frac{2}{5}$

237

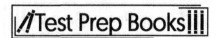
35. What is the perimeter of the figure below? Note that the solid outer line is the perimeter.

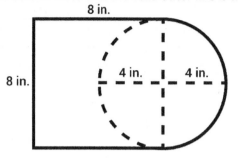

8 in.

8 in.

4 in.   4 in.

a.   48.565 in
b.   36.565 in
c.   39.78 in
d.   39.565 in

36. Which of the following equations best represents the problem below?

The width of a rectangle is 2 centimeters less than the length. If the perimeter of the rectangle is 44 centimeters, then what are the dimensions of the rectangle?

a. $2l + 2(l - 2) = 44$
b. $(l + 2) + (l + 2) + l = 48$
c. $l \times (l - 2) = 44$
d. $(l + 2) + (l + 2) + l = 44$

37. Simplify:

$$\frac{4a^{-1}b^3}{a^4b^{-2}} \times \frac{3a}{b}$$

a. $12a^3b^5$

b. $12\frac{b^4}{a^4}$

c. $\frac{12}{a^4}$

d. $7\frac{b^4}{a}$

38. A shoebox has a volume of 358,150 cubic centimeters. If its height is 47.5 cm and its width is 72.5 cm, what is the length of the box?
a.   51.5 cm
b.   208 cm
c.   47.5 cm
d.   104 cm

238

39. The graph shows the position of a car over a 10-second time interval. Which of the following is the correct interpretation of the graph for the interval 1 to 3 seconds?

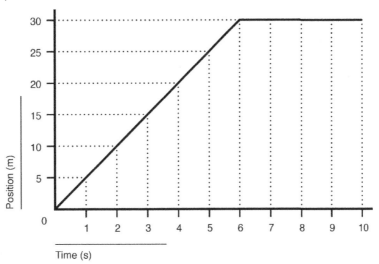

a. The car remains in the same position.
b. The car is traveling at a speed of 5 m/s.
c. The car is traveling up a hill.
d. The car is traveling at 5 mph.

40. Determine the missing value: $70 \text{ cm} + \rule{1cm}{0.15mm} = 2 \text{ m}$.
a. 30 cm
b. 130 cm
c. −68 cm
d. 140 cm

41. List the following numbers in increasing order: $\frac{1}{5}, -\frac{1}{2}, .5, \frac{3}{4}, -1$.
a. $-1, -\frac{1}{2}, \frac{1}{5}, .5, \frac{3}{4}$
b. $-\frac{1}{2}, \frac{1}{5}, .5, \frac{3}{4}, -1$
c. $-1, -\frac{1}{2}, .5, \frac{1}{5}, \frac{3}{4}$
d. $\frac{1}{5}, .5, \frac{3}{4}, -\frac{1}{2}, -1$

42. Which fraction is 0.45 equivalent to?
a. $\frac{4}{5}$
b. $\frac{9}{10}$
c. $\frac{9}{20}$
d. $\frac{5}{4}$

43. A runner went out for a 2.5 mile run this morning. How many kilometers was their run?
a. 1.5 km

239

b. 4 km

    c. 1 km

    d. 6 km

44. Solve the following equation for x: $21x - 8 = -13x + 40$

    a. 48

    b. $\dfrac{24}{17}$

    c. $\dfrac{17}{24}$

    d. 6

45. Compute the mean of the following salaries: $40,000, $36,000, $41,000, $35,000, $39,000.

    a. $36,000

    b. $38,200

    c. $39,000

    d. $47,750

Science

1. Which statement about white blood cells is true?

    a. B cells are responsible for antibody production.

    b. White blood cells are made in the white/yellow cartilage before they enter the bloodstream.

    c. Platelets, a special class of white blood cell, function to clot blood and stop bleeding.

    d. The majority of white blood cells only activate during the age of puberty, which explains why children and the elderly are particularly susceptible to disease.

2. Which locations in the digestive system are sites of chemical digestion?

    I. Mouth

    II. Stomach

    III. Small Intestine

    a. II only

    b. III only

    c. II and III only

    d. I, II, and III

3. Which of the following are functions of the urinary system?

    I. Synthesizing calcitriol and secreting erythropoietin

    II. Regulating the concentrations of sodium, potassium, chloride, calcium, and other ions

    III. Reabsorbing or secreting hydrogen ions and bicarbonate

    IV. Detecting reductions in blood volume and pressure

    a. I, II, and III

    b. II and III

    c. II, III, and IV

    d. All of the above are functions of synergists.

4. Which of the following structures is unique to eukaryotic cells?
   a. Cell walls
   b. Nuclei
   c. Cell membranes
   d. Organelles

5. Which cellular organelle is used for digestion to recycle materials?
   a. The Golgi apparatus
   b. The lysosome
   c. The centrioles
   d. The mitochondria

6. A rock has a mass of 14.3 grams (g) and a volume of 5.4 cm3, what is its density?
   a. 8.90 g/cm^3
   b. 0.38 g/cm^3
   c. 77.22 g/cm^3
   d. 2.65 g/cm^3

7. Why do arteries have valves?
   a. They have valves to maintain high blood pressure so that capillaries diffuse nutrients properly.
   b. Their valves are designed to prevent backflow due to their low blood pressure.
   c. They have valves due to a leftover trait from evolution that, like the appendix, are useless.
   d. Arteries do not have valves, but veins do.

8. If the pressure in the pulmonary artery is increased above normal, which chamber of the heart will be affected first?
   a. The right atrium
   b. The left atrium
   c. The right ventricle
   d. The left ventricle

9. What is the purpose of sodium bicarbonate when released into the lumen of the small intestine?
   a. It works to chemically digest fats in the chyme.
   b. It decreases the pH of the chyme so as to prevent harm to the intestine.
   c. It works to chemically digest proteins in the chyme.
   d. It increases the pH of the chyme so as to prevent harm to the intestine.

10. Nurses can use knowledge of family functions and their structures to empower families through evidence-based practices or interventions. A family function that discusses disease prevention and illness management is called:
    a. Economic function
    b. Affective function
    c. Health care function
    d. Socialization function

11. Nursing interventions or approaches to family nursing are based on many factors. A nursing intervention that focuses on interactions among family members is an approach known as:
    a. Family as a system
    b. Family as a client
    c. Family as a component of society
    d. Family as a context

12. Using anatomical terms, what is the relationship of the sternum relative to the deltoid?
    a. Medial
    b. Lateral
    c. Superficial
    d. Posterior

13. Ligaments connect what?
    a. Muscle to muscle
    b. Bone to bone
    c. Bone to muscle
    d. Muscle to tendon

Use the following image to answer question 14:

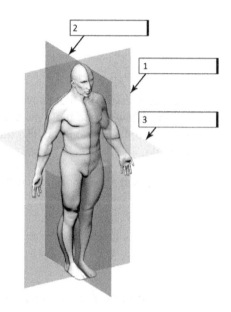

14. Identify the correct sequence of the 3 primary body planes as numbered 1, 2, and 3 in the above image.
    a. Plane 1 is coronal, plane 2 is sagittal, and plane 3 is transverse.
    b. Plane 1 is sagittal, plane 2 is coronal, and plane 3 is medial.
    c. Plane 1 is coronal, plane 2 is sagittal, and plane 3 is medial.
    d. Plane 1 is sagittal, plane 2 is coronal, and plane 3 is transverse.

15. Which of the following is NOT a major function of the respiratory system in humans?
    a. It provides a large surface area for gas exchange of oxygen and carbon dioxide.
    b. It helps regulate the blood's pH.
    c. It helps cushion the heart against jarring motions.
    d. It is responsible for vocalization.

16. Which of the following is NOT a function of the forebrain?
    a. To regulate blood pressure and heart rate
    b. To perceive and interpret emotional responses like fear and anger
    c. To perceive and interpret visual input from the eyes
    d. To integrate voluntary movement

17. What is the major difference between somatic and germline mutations?
   a. Somatic mutations usually benefit the individual, while germline mutations usually harm them.
   b. Since germline mutations only affect one cell, they are less noticeable than the rapidly dividing somatic cells.
   c. Somatic mutations are not expressed for several generations, but germline mutations are expressed immediately.
   d. Germline mutations are usually inherited, while somatic mutations will affect only the individual.

18. A child complains of heavy breathing even when relaxing. They are an otherwise healthy child with no history of respiratory problems. What might be the issue?
   a. Asthma
   b. A blood clot
   c. Hyperventilation
   d. Exercising too hard

19. Which statement is NOT true about DNA?
   a. It has guanine.
   b. DNA enables living organisms to pass on their genetic information.
   c. It contains uracil.
   d. DNA replication happens in interphase.

20. What is the process of cell division in somatic (most body) cells called?
   a. Mitosis
   b. Meiosis
   c. Respiration
   d. Cytogenesis

21. Which of the following is NOT a function of lipids?
   a. They provide cellular instructions.
   b. They can be chemical messages.
   c. They provide energy.
   d. They compose cell membranes.

22. Which is true regarding DNA?
   a. It is the genetic code.
   b. It provides energy.
   c. It is single-stranded.
   d. All of the above

23. Which is the cellular organelle used to tag, package, and ship out proteins destined for other cells or locations?
   a. The Golgi apparatus
   b. The lysosome
   c. The centrioles
   d. The mitochondria

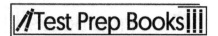

24. How do cellulose and starch differ?
    a. Cellulose and starch are proteins with different R groups.
    b. Cellulose is a polysaccharide made up of glucose molecules, and starch is a polysaccharide made up of galactose molecules.
    c. Cellulose and starch are both polysaccharides made up of glucose molecules, but they are connected with different types of bonds.
    d. Cellulose and starch are the same molecule, but cellulose is made by plants and starch is made by animals.

25. Esther is left-handed. Hand dominance is a genetic factor. If being right-handed is a dominant trait over being left-handed, which of the following must NOT be true about Esther's parents?
    a. Her parents are both right-handed.
    b. Her parents are both left-handed.
    c. Only one parent is right-handed.
    d. All of the above can be true.

26. What is the order of filtration in the nephron?
    a. Collecting duct → Proximal tubule → Loop of Henle
    b. Proximal tubule → Loop of Henle → Collecting duct
    c. Loop of Henle → Collecting duct → Proximal tubule
    d. Loop of Henle → Proximal tubule → Collecting duct

27. A patient's body is not properly filtering blood. Which of the following body parts is most likely malfunctioning?
    a. Medulla
    B. Heart
    C. Nephrons
    D. Renal cortex

28. A pediatrician notes that an infant's cartilage is disappearing and being replaced by bone. What process has the doctor observed?
    a. Mineralization
    b. Ossification
    c. Osteoporosis
    d. Calcification

29. The epidermis is composed of what type of cells?
    a. Osteoclasts
    b. Connective
    c. Dendritic
    d. Epithelial

30. Which of the following is directly transcribed from DNA and represents the first step in protein building?
    a. siRNA
    b. rRNA
    c. mRNA
    d. tRNA

31. What information does a genotype give that a phenotype does not?
    a. The genotype necessarily includes the proteins coded for by its alleles.
    b. The genotype will always show an organism's recessive alleles.
    c. The genotype must include the organism's physical characteristics.
    d. The genotype shows what an organism's parents looked like.

Use the following Punnett square to answer question 32:

32. Which statement is supported by the Punnett square above, if "T" = Tall and "t" = short?
    a. Both parents are homozygous tall.
    b. 100% of the offspring will be tall because both parents are tall.
    c. There is a 25% chance that an offspring will be short.
    d. The short allele will soon die out.

33. Which of the following is a chief difference between evaporation and boiling?
    a. Liquids boil only at the surface, while they evaporate equally throughout the liquid.
    b. Evaporating substances change from gas to liquid, while boiling substances change from liquid to gas.
    c. Evaporation happens in nature, while boiling is a man-made phenomenon.
    d. Evaporation can happen below a liquid's boiling point.

34. Which of the following cannot be found in a human cell's genes?
    a. Sequences of amino acids to be transcribed into mRNA
    b. Lethal recessive traits like sickle cell anemia
    c. Mutated DNA
    d. DNA that codes for proteins the cell doesn't use

35. Which of the following is a special property of water?
    a. Water easily flows through phospholipid bilayers.
    b. A water molecule's oxygen atom allows fish to breathe.
    c. Water is highly cohesive which explains its high boiling point.
    d. Water can self-hydrolyze and decompose into hydrogen and oxygen.

36. For any given element, an isotope is an atom with which of the following?
    a. A different atomic number
    b. A different number of protons
    c. A different number of electrons
    d. A different mass number

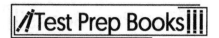

37. What is the electrical charge of the nucleus?
    a. A nucleus always has a positive charge.
    b. A stable nucleus has a positive charge, but a radioactive nucleus may be neutral with no charge.
    c. A nucleus is always neutral with no charge.
    d. A stable nucleus is neutral with no charge, but a radioactive nucleus may have a charge.

38. What is the probability of *AaBbCcDd* × *AAbbccDD* having a child with genotype *AAbbccDD*?
    a. $\frac{1}{2}$

    b. $\frac{1}{4}$

    c. $\frac{1}{8}$

    d. $\frac{1}{16}$

39. Which of the following creates sperm?
    a. Prostate gland
    b. Seminal vesicles
    c. Scrotum
    d. Seminiferous tubules

40. Which statement regarding meiosis is correct?
    a. Meiosis produces four diploid cells.
    b. Meiosis contains two cellular divisions separated by interphase II.
    c. Meiosis produces cells with two sets of chromosomes.
    d. Crossing over occurs in the prophase of meiosis I.

41. Which of the following lists of joint types is in the correct order for increasing amounts of permitted motion (least mobile to most mobile)?
    a. Hinge, condyloid, saddle
    b. Saddle, hinge, condyloid
    c. Saddle, condyloid, hinge
    d. Hinge, saddle, condyloid

42. The function of synergists can best be described as which of the following?
    I. They assist primary movers in completing the specific movement.
    II. They stabilize the point of origin and provide extra pull near the insertion.
    III. They help prevent unwanted movement at a joint.

    a. I, II
    b. I, III
    c. II, III
    d. All of the above

43. Which of the following correctly lists the four properties that all types of muscle tissue share?
    a. Contractile, excitable, elastic, extensible
    b. Contractile, voluntary, elastic, extensible
    c. Contractile, excitable, voluntary, extensible
    d. Contractile, excitable, elastic, voluntary

44. Which of the following statements about the autonomic nervous system (ANS) is true?
    a. It controls the reflex arc.
    b. It contains motor (efferent) neurons.
    c. It contains sensory (afferent) neurons.
    d. It contains both parasympathetic nerves and sympathetic nerves.

45. What is the function of the sinuses?
    a. To trap the many airborne pathogens
    b. To direct air down the trachea rather than the esophagus
    c. To warm, humidify, and filter air
    d. To sweep away pathogens and direct them toward the top of the trachea

46. Farmworkers and their families have a higher risk of exposure to pesticides when living near chemically treated fields. A public health nurse creating a program that focuses on chemical toxin screenings for exposed farmworkers, in addition to treatment referrals for those who have high levels of toxin contamination, is an example of:
    a. Primary prevention
    b. Secondary prevention
    c. Tertiary prevention
    d. Quaternary prevention

47. Health risks are generally controlled by health promotion and disease prevention. Which of the following is NOT an example of a general family health risk?
    a. Behavioral risks
    b. Environmental risks
    c. Biological risks
    d. Single risks

48. Nurses can use several educational principles or domains of learning to present health information to individuals, families, and the community. The domain that discusses attitude changes and value development is known as the:
    a. Cognitive domain
    b. Affective domain
    c. Effective domain
    d. Psychomotor domain

49. Salts like sodium iodide (NaI) and potassium chloride (KCl) use what type of bond?
    a. Ionic bonds
    b. Disulfide bridges
    c. Covalent bonds
    d. London dispersion forces

50. What type of chemical reaction produces a salt?
    a. An oxidation reaction
    b. A neutralization reaction
    c. A synthesis reaction
    d. A decomposition reaction

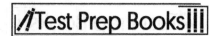

51. What types of molecules can move through a cell membrane by passive transport?
    a. Complex sugars
    b. Non-lipid-soluble molecules
    c. Oxygen
    d. Molecules moving from areas of low concentration to areas of high concentration

52. What is one feature that prokaryotes and eukaryotes have in common?
    a. A plasma membrane
    b. A nucleus enclosed by a membrane
    c. Organelles
    d. A nucleoid

53. What is the last phase of mitosis?
    a. Prophase
    b. Telophase
    c. Anaphase
    d. Metaphase

54. How many daughter cells are formed from one parent cell during meiosis?
    a. One
    b. Two
    c. Three
    d. Four

55. Which level of protein structure is defined by the folds and coils of the protein's polypeptide backbone?
    a. Primary
    b. Secondary
    c. Tertiary
    d. Quaternary

56. What is the sensory threshold?
    a. The smallest amount of stimulus required for an individual to feel a sensation
    b. The amount of stimulus required for an individual to feel pain
    c. The amount of stimulus required to cause an individual to move away from the stimulus
    d. The place where the stimulus is coming from

57. How many neurons generally make up a sensory pathway?
    a. 1
    b. 2
    c. 3
    d. 4

58. In which part of the eye does visual processing begin?
    a. Cornea
    b. Optic nerve
    c. Retina
    d. Eyelid

59. What type of vessel carries oxygen-rich blood from the heart to other tissues of the body?
    a. Veins
    b. Intestines
    c. Bronchioles
    d. Arteries

60. The somatic nervous system is responsible for which of the following?
    a. Breathing
    b. Thought
    c. Movement
    d. Fear

Answer Explanations #1

Verbal

Word Knowledge

1. B: She pledged to, or *promised* her fans the sequel would be just as exciting as the first. Choice *A*, denied, is the opposite of the word *promised* and does not fit with the word *excited*. Choice *C*, invigorated, means energized, and might fit the tone of the sentence with the word *excited.* However, *promised* is the better word to use here. Choice *D*, germinated, means to grow.

2. C: My hands started shaking and my heart stopped. *Shaking* is most closely related to the word *trembling*. Choice *A*, dancing, is not a synonym of shaking. Choice *B*, glowing, is incorrect; hands usually do not glow when one is afraid of something. Choice *D*, throbbing, is closer than *A* or *B*, but Choice *C,* shaking, is closer to the answer than *throbbing*.

3. D: Gabriel would consistently, or *usually* go to the library and study after school. Consistently and usually mean similar things. *Infrequently*, *occasionally*, and *hardly* are the opposite of *consistently* so they do not fit here.

4. A: The runners sprinted, or *dashed* toward the finish line. Choice *B* is incorrect; runners who begin a race usually don't skip toward the finish line. Choice *C* is incorrect, as *rejoice* means to celebrate, not dash or run. Choice *D*, herded, means to gather around something; usually *herded* is used for animals and not for runners.

5. D: *Resolved* means driven or determined, Choice *D*. Choice *A*, resumed, means to start again. Choice *B*, content, means to be satisfied with something. Choice *C*, enthusiastic, means hopeful.

6. D: They went to the bank to install, or *deposit* a check. When people go to the bank with a check, they usually don't celebrate it, Choice *A*, but do something more practical with it, like deposit it. Choice *B*, neutralize, means to counteract something, and is incorrect in this sentence. Choice *C,* eliminate, means to get rid of something, and is also incorrect here.

7. B: The sale at the grocery store inspired, or *motivated* my dad to buy four avocados instead of two. The rest of the words (intimidated, dismayed, and berated) have negative connotations and therefore do not fit within the context of the sentence.

8. A: In order to increase, or *enhance* the quality of her health. Enhance or increase means to make better. Becoming healthier is a direct effect of consuming fruits and vegetables, so Choice *A* is the best answer choice here. Becoming healthier might lead to Choices *B, C,* and *D*, but these are not synonyms of *enhance.*

9. C: Sojourn means a brief stop, *layover*, or break. Choice *A*, soiree, means party. Choice *B*, presentation, means something displayed or proposed. Choice *D*, cohort, means partner in activity.

10. A: Until she activated, or *triggered* the fire alarm by burning the casserole in the oven. Triggered means to activate something or initiate something. Choice *B*, offended, is the wrong choice here. You can offend a person because they have emotions, but you cannot offend a fire alarm. Choice *C*, unplugged, is also incorrect. Choice *D*, disbanded, is the opposite of *activated* and is incorrect in this context.

11. D: Consternation means dread or dismay. Choice *A*, refresh, is not an adjective used to describe a dentist's office, especially when the patient is about to take care of a cavity. Choices *B*, creative, is not a synonym of consternation. Choice *C*, rapture, means ecstatic or happy, and is the opposite sentiment of what we are looking for.

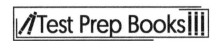

12. B: Told us that the bird was indigenous, or *native* to the southeast part of the United States. Indigenous means native or belonging to a certain area, so Choice *B* is the best answer here. Choice *A*, entertaining, means amusing. Choice *C*, impudent, means bold or shameless. Choice *D*, monotonous, means remaining the same or dull.

13. D: Their bodies wriggled, or *slithered* out of our hands and back into the water. Choices *A* and *C*, exploded and thundered, are too extreme for the context. Deteriorated, Choice *B*, means to crumble or disintegrate, which is not a synonym of wriggled. Choice *D* is the best answer for this sentence.

14. A: Serving means *portion*, Choice *A*. Directed, Choice *B*, means to supervise or conduct, and does not make sense in the context of the sentence. Choice *C*, mourning, means to grieve over, and is also incorrect. Choice *D*, endorsement, means to approve or support something.

15. A: *Instigate* refers to initiating or bringing about an action. While instigating something can be overwhelming, one does not overwhelm a fight. Ponder means to think carefully about something, and swim refers to moving through water.

16. D: The correct answer Choice is *D*, under the tongue. The root word of *sublingual* is *lingual*, which means tongue. The prefix is *sub*, which means under. Therefore, if we pay attention the prefix and how it relates to the root word, we get "under the tongue." Choice *A*, in the ear, would be the word *tympanic*. Choice *B*, in the rectum, would be the word *rectal*. Choice *C*, under the armpit, would be the word *axillary*.

17. A: *Plausible* means likely to be possible or accepted, the opposite of *skeptical*. *Diurnal* relates to daytime, so it is unrelated. *Erudite* means clever or intelligent, but not necessarily possible or correct. *Conceivable* means that something is able to be thought of or able to be done. Conceivable is the best match for plausible.

18. A: The Latin root, *asper*, means rough. *Exasperate*, then, means to make relations with someone rough or to rub them the wrong way. *Disappointment* can be the result of an exasperating situation, but it is not the same as exasperation itself. *Annoy* is a synonym, meaning to irritate and make someone slightly angry.

19. C: A professional who draws blood. An x-ray technician takes x-rays, a prosthetist makes artificial limbs, and a psychologist, social worker, or therapist counsels patients.

20. B: Expressionless. Glassy eyes, like a doll's, are shiny and empty; they are expressionless. Someone with glassy eyes may have a fixed stare. Different conditions, such as severe dehydration and cholera, can cause glassy eyes.

21. D: Language impairment. *Aphasia* is a loss in the ability to express or understand speech, so it is language impairment. It is often caused by brain damage, whether due to a stroke, TBI, or other cause. An inability to recognize things is *agnosia*.

22. A: Dull. Something that is *jejune* is simplistic, naïve, or unoriginal.

23. A: Spatial awareness of the body. The body has sensory receptors, called proprioceptors, which help the body sense and respond to position and movement.

24. C: Flushed. *Ruddy* means red and flushed.

25. D: Itchiness. The intense itchiness of pruritis may be caused by dry skin, allergies, pregnancy, or other causes.

26. A: Excessive sweating. Causes of diaphoresis are varied and can include anxiety, medication side effects, malaria, and diabetes.

27. B: Sexually-transmitted. Syphilis and chlamydia are examples of venereal diseases.

251

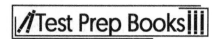

28. B: Subtle differences. *Nuances* are shades or subtle differences, particularly in tone, expression, or sound.

Reading Comprehension

29. C: Choice *C* is the correct answer because it most extensively summarizes the entire passage. While Choices *A* and *B* are reasonable possibilities, they reference portions of Gulliver's experiences, not the whole. Choice *D* is incorrect because Gulliver doesn't express repentance or sorrow in this particular passage.

30. A: Principal refers to *chief* or *primary* within the context of this text. Choice *A* is the answer that most closely aligns with this definition. Choices *B* and *D* make reference to a helper or followers while Choice *C* doesn't meet the description of Reldresal from the passage.

31. C: One can reasonably infer that Gulliver is considerably larger than the children who were playing around him because multiple children could fit into his hand. Choice *A* is incorrect because there is no indication of stress in Gulliver's tone. Choices *B* and *D* aren't the best answer because though Gulliver seems fond of his new acquaintances, he didn't travel there with the intentions of meeting new people, nor does he express a definite love for them in this particular portion of the text.

32. C: The emperor made a definitive decision to expose Gulliver to their native customs. In this instance, the word *mind* was not related to a vote, question, or cognitive ability.

33. B: Choice *B* is the only option that mentions the correlation between physical ability and leadership positions. Choices *A* and *D* are unrelated to physical strength and leadership abilities. Choice *C* does not make a deduction that would lead to the correct answer—it only comments upon the abilities of common townspeople.

34. C: The quote gives the warden's direct statement regarding his dedication to the rookery. Choice *A* is incorrect because the speaker of the quote is a warden, not a hunter. Choice *B* is incorrect because the quote does not lighten the mood but shows the danger of the situation between the wardens and the hunters. Choice *D* is incorrect because there is no humor found in the quote.

35. D: Although *rookeries* could mean Choice *A*, houses in a slum area, it does not make sense in this context. Choices *B* and *C* are both incorrect, as this is not a place for hunters to trade tools or for wardens to trade stories.

36. B: The previous sentence is describing "20 colonies" of birds, so what follows should be a bird colony. Choice *A* may be true, but we have no evidence of this in the text. Choice *C* does touch on the tension between the hunters and wardens, but there is no official "Bird Island Battle" mentioned in the text. Choice *D* does not exist in the text.

37. D: The text mentions several different times how and why the association has been successful and gives examples to back this fact. Choice *A* is incorrect because the passage doesn't mention the need for people to take action. Likewise, Choices *B* and *C* are not mentioned in the text.

38. C: Choice *A* might be true in a general sense, but it is not relevant to the text. Choice *B* is incorrect because the hunters are not studying lines of flight to help wardens, but to hunt birds. Choice *D* is incorrect because nothing in the text mentions that hunters are trying to build homes underneath lines of flight of birds for good luck.

39. A: Choice *B* is incorrect because although the passage talks about gills, it is not the central idea of the passage. Choices *C* and *D* are incorrect because the passage does not "define" or "invite," but only serves as an introduction to stoneflies, dragonflies, and mayflies and their transition from water to air.

40. C: To moult is to shed part or all of the outer shell, as noted in Choice *C*. Choices *A*, *B*, and *D* are incorrect.

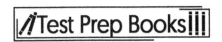

41. B: Notice how the first paragraph goes into detail describing how insects are able to breathe air. The second paragraph acts as a contrast to the first by stating "[i]t is of great interest to find that, nevertheless, a number of insects spend much of their time under water." Watch for transition words such as *nevertheless* to help find what type of passage you're dealing with.

42. C: Overall, the author presents us with information on the subject. One moment where personal interest is depicted is when the author states, "It is of great interest to find that, nevertheless, a number of insects spend much of their time under water."

43. C: Their larvae can breathe the air dissolved in water through gills of some kind. This is stated in the last paragraph. Choice *A* is incorrect because the text mentions this in a general way at the beginning of the passage concerning "insects as a whole." Choice *B* is incorrect because this is stated of beetles and water-bugs, and not the insects in question. Choice *D* is incorrect because this is the opposite of what the text says of instars.

44. C: The beginning of this paragraph literally "presents a conundrum," explains the problem of partial understanding, and then ends with more questions, or inquiries. There is no solution offered in this paragraph, making Choices *A* and *B* incorrect. Choice *D* is incorrect because the paragraph does not begin with a definition.

45. D: Looking back in the text, the author describes that classical philosophy holds that understanding can be reached by careful observation. This will not work if they are overly invested or biased in their pursuit. Choices *A* and *C* are in no way related and are completely unnecessary. A specific theory is not necessary to understanding, according to classical philosophy mentioned by the author. Again, the key to understanding is observing the phenomena outside of it, without bias or predisposition. Thus, Choice *B* is wrong.

46. B: Choices *A* and *C* are incorrect because such behavior is not mentioned at all in the text. In the passage, the author says that electrons that were physically observed appeared to pass through one hole or another. Remember, the electrons that were observed doing this were described as acting like particles. Therefore, Choice *D* is incorrect. Recall that the plate actually recorded electrons passing through both holes simultaneously and hitting the plate. This behavior, the electron activity that wasn't seen by humans, was characteristic of waves. Thus, Choice *B* is the correct answer.

47. A: The important thing to keep in mind is that we must choose a scenario that best parallels, or is most similar to, the discovery of the experiment mentioned in the passage. The important aspects of the experiment can be summed up like so: humans directly observed one behavior of electrons, and then, through analyzing a tool (the plate that recorded electron hits), discovered that there was another electron behavior that could not be physically seen by human eyes. This best parallels the scenario in Choice *A*. Like Feynman, the color-blind person is able to observe one aspect of the world, but through the special goggles (a tool), he is able to see a natural phenomenon that he could not physically see on his own. While Choice *D* is compelling, the x-ray does not necessarily reveal that a bone is broken. Usually, the x-ray helps to see a bone that is already known to be broken. The other choices do not parallel the scenario in question. Therefore, Choice *A* is the best choice.

48. B: Choice *A* is incorrect because much of the passage discusses how technology helps humans observe what cannot be seen with the naked eye, therefore the author would agree with this statement. This line of reasoning is also why the author would agree with Choice *D*, making it incorrect as well. As indicated in the second paragraph, the author seems to think that humans create inventions and tools with the goal of studying phenomena more precisely. This indicates increased understanding as people recognize limitations and develop items to help bypass the limitations and learn. Therefore, Choice *C* is incorrect as well.

49. D: The author explains that Boethianism is a Medieval theological philosophy that attributes sin to temporary pleasure and righteousness with virtue and God's providence. Other than Choice *D*, the choices listed are all physical things. While these could still be divine rewards, Boethianism holds that the true reward for being virtuous is in

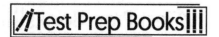

God's favor. It is also stressed in the article that physical pleasures cannot be taken into the afterlife. Therefore, the best choice is *D, God's favor*.

50. C: Choices *A* and *B* are generalized statements, and we have no evidence to support Choice *B*. Choice *D* is very compelling, but it looks at Boethianism in a way that the author does not. The author does not mention "different levels of Boethianism" when discussing the tales, only that the concept appears differently in different tales. Boethianism also doesn't focus on enlightenment.

51. D: Choice *A* is incorrect; while the text does mention thieves ravaging others' possessions, it is only meant as an example and not as the principle itself. Choice *B* is incorrect for the same reason as Choice *A*. Choice *C* is mentioned in the text and is part of the example that proves the principle, but it is not the principle itself. Choice *B* is incorrect for the same reason as *A*. Choice *C* is mentioned in the text and is part of the example that proves the principle, and also not the principle itself.

52. C: The word *avarice* most nearly means *covetousness*, an extreme desire for money or wealth. Choice A means evil or mischief and does not relate to the context of the sentence. Choice *B* is also incorrect, because pithiness means shortness or conciseness. Choice *D* is close because *precariousness* means danger or instability, which goes well with the context. However, we are told of the summoner's specific characteristic of greed, which makes Choice *C* the best answer.

53. D: Boethianism acknowledges desire as something that leads out of holiness, so Choice *A* is incorrect. Choice *B* is incorrect because in the passage, Boethianism is depicted as being wary of desire and anything that binds people to the physical world. Choice *C* can be eliminated because the author never says that desire indicates demonic possession.

54. D: Choice *D* best describes why Maggie is disappointed. It is stated in Paragraph 1 that she was disappointed that she could not go with her father to the academy to pick up Tom. She then gets in a squabble about her hair. Choice *A* is incorrect because although Maggie does not want her hair to be styled, that is not why she is disappointed. Choice *B* is incorrect because Mrs. Tulliver is her mother, not a caretaker to be fired. Choice *C* is incorrect because there is nothing to suggest that she wants her aunts to visit sooner.

55. B: Choice *B* identifies a reasonable inference that can be made from the text. Mrs. Tulliver is distressed with Maggie's resistance to having her hair done. She stresses about what other people will think. Therefore, it is a reasonable assumption that it would be societally unacceptable for Maggie to go about with unkempt hair. Choice *A* is incorrect because Maggie is forbidden to go due to wet weather, not due to her father's wishes. Choice *C* is incorrect because it is implied that Maggie's aunts would take her mother's side regarding her poor behavior. Choice *D* is incorrect because although Mrs. Tulliver is at home taking care of Maggie, it is unclear if that is her full-time occupation.

56. A: Choice *A* explains what Maggie does with her doll. As the text explains, Maggie goes into the attic and defaces the doll for the misfortunes she has gone through. Choice *B* is incorrect because there is nothing stating that Maggie cannot play in other parts of the home. Choice *C* is incorrect because Maggie's destruction of the doll cannot be considered normal playtime. Choice *D* is incorrect because Maggie's siblings are not discussed.

57. B: Choice *B* identifies what *ill humours* means in this text. Maggie defaces the doll due to her misfortunes. Therefore, readers can assume that *ill humours* refers to Maggie's poor moods. Choice *A* is incorrect because Maggie does not appear to be in poor health. Choice *C* is incorrect because the term is not referring to Maggie's actual sense of comedic humor. Choice *D* is incorrect because Maggie appears to be angry rather than anxious, based on the text.

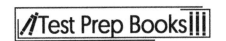

58. C: Choice *C* accurately describes the meaning of the word *vicarious* in this text. The suffering that the doll goes through is due to the suffering that Maggie feels she is going through. In this sense, *vicarious* means secondhand. Choice *A* is incorrect because although the defacement is vicious, that is not the meaning of the word. Choice *B* is incorrect because the timing of the suffering is irrelevant. Choice *D* is incorrect because although the suffering appears to be ongoing, that is also not the meaning of the word.

Math

1. A: Compare each number after the decimal point to figure out which overall number is greatest. In Choices *A* (1.43785) and *C* (1.43592), both have the same tenths place (4) and hundredths place (3). However, the thousandths place is greater in Choice *A* (7), so *A* has the greatest value overall.

2. D: By rearranging and grouping the factors in Choice *D*, we can notice that $3 \times 3 \times 4 \times 2 = (3 \times 2) \times (4 \times 3) = 6 \times 12$, which is what we were looking for.

3. C: The total percentage of a pie chart equals 100%. We can see that CD sales make up less than half of the chart (50%) but more than a quarter (25%), and the only answer choice that meets these criteria is Choice *C*, 40%.

4. B: Since $850 is the price after a 20% discount, $850 represents 80% (or 0.8) of the original price. In other words, $850 = 0.8x$ (where x is the original price). Solving this, we find $x = \frac{850}{0.8} = 1,062.5$. Now, to find the savings, calculate the original price minus the sale price: $1,062.50 - 850 = 212.50$.

5. A: To figure out which value is the largest, look at the first nonzero digits. Choice *B*'s first nonzero digit is in the hundredths place. The other three all have nonzero digits in the tenths place, so it must be Choice *A*, *C*, or *D*. Of these, Choice *A*'s first nonzero digit is the largest.

6. C: To solve for the value of b, isolate the variable b on one side of the equation.

Start by moving the lower value of −4 to the other side by adding 4 to both sides:

$$5b - 4 = 2b + 17$$

$$5b - 4 + 4 = 2b + 17 + 4$$

$$5b = 2b + 21$$

Then, subtract $2b$ from both sides:

$$5b - 2b = 2b + 21 - 2b$$

$$3b = 21$$

Then, divide both sides by 3 to get the value of b:

$$\frac{3b}{3} = \frac{21}{3}$$

$$b = 7$$

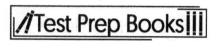

7. D: The total faculty is:

$$15 + 20 = 35$$

So, the ratio is 35 : 200. Then, divide both of these numbers by 5, since 5 is a common factor to both, with a result of 7 : 40.

8. C: The first step in solving this problem is expressing the result in fraction form. Multiplication and division are typically performed in order from left to right, but they can be performed in any order. For this problem, let's start with the division operation between the last two fractions. When dividing one fraction by another, invert or flip the second fraction and then multiply the numerators and denominators.

$$\frac{7}{10} \times \frac{2}{1} = \frac{14}{10}$$

Next, multiply the first fraction by this value:

$$\frac{3}{5} \times \frac{14}{10} = \frac{42}{50}$$

In this instance, to find the decimal form, we can multiply the numerator and denominator by 2 to get 100 in the denominator.

$$\frac{42}{50} \times \frac{2}{2} = \frac{84}{100}$$

In decimal form, this would be expressed as 0.84.

9. C: To find what 85% of 20 questions is, multiply 20 by

$$.85: 20 \times .85 = 17 \text{ questions}$$

10. D: This problem can be solved by setting up a proportion involving the given information and the unknown value. The proportion is:

$$\frac{21 \text{ pages}}{4 \text{ nights}} = \frac{140 \text{ pages}}{x \text{ nights}}$$

We can cross-multiply to get $21x = 4 \times 140$. Solving this, we find $x \approx 26.67$. Since this is not an integer, we round up to 27 nights because 26 nights would not give Sarah enough time to finish.

11. B: Using the conversion rate, multiply the projected weight loss of 25 lb by $0.45\frac{\text{kg}}{\text{lb}}$ to get the amount in kilograms (11.25 kg).

12. D: First, subtract $1,437 from $2,334.50 to find Johnny's monthly savings; this equals $897.50. Then, multiply this amount by 3 to find out how much he will have (in 3 months) before he pays for his vacation; this equals $2,692.50. Finally, subtract the cost of the vacation ($1,750) from this amount to find how much Johnny will have left: $942.50.

13. B: Dividing by 98 can be approximated by dividing by 100, which would mean shifting the decimal point of the numerator to the left by 2. The result is 4.2, which rounds to 4.

14. C: First, we find the speed in mm/s. Divide 340 by 4 to obtain 85 mm/s. Then, to convert mm to cm, divide by 10. The correct answer is 8.5 cm/s.

15. C: The formula for the perimeter of a rectangle is $P = 2L + 2W$, where P is the perimeter, L is the length, and W is the width. The first step is to substitute all of the data into the formula:

$$36 = 2(12) + 2W$$

Simplify by multiplying 2×12:

$$36 = 24 + 2W$$

Simplifying this further by subtracting 24 on each side gives:

$$36 - 24 = 24 - 24 + 2W$$

$$12 = 2W$$

Divide by 2:

$$6 = W$$

The width is 6 cm. Remember to test this answer by substituting this value into the original formula:

$$36 = 2(12) + 2(6)$$

16. D: To find the average of a set of values, add the values together and then divide by the total number of values. In this case, include the unknown value, x, of what Dwayne needs to score on his next test. The average must equal 90. Set up the equation and solve:

First, combine like terms:

$$\frac{78 + 92 + 83 + 97 + x}{5} = 90$$

Next, divide both sides by 5:

$$\frac{350 + x}{5} = 90$$

Lastly, subtract 350 from both sides:

$$350 + x = 450$$

$$x = 100$$

Dwayne would need to get a perfect score of 100 in order to get an average of at least 90.

Test this answer by substituting 100 back into the original formula.

$$\frac{78 + 92 + 83 + 97 + 100}{5} = 90$$

257

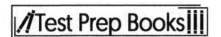

17. D: For an even number of total values, the median is calculated by finding the mean, or average, of the two middle values once all values have been arranged in ascending order from least to greatest. In this case, $(83 + 92) \div 2$ would equal the median 87.5, Choice *D*.

18. C: Follow the order of operations in order to solve this problem. Evaluate inside the parentheses first, being sure to follow the order of operations inside the parentheses as well. First, simplify the square roots:

$$(6 \times 4) - 3^2$$

Then, multiply inside the parentheses:

$$24 - 3^2$$

Next, simplify the exponent:

$$24 - 9$$

Finally, subtract to get 15, Choice *C*.

19. D: Three girls for every two boys can be expressed as a ratio: 3 : 2. This can be visualized as splitting the school into five groups: three girl groups and two boy groups. The number of students that are in each group can be found by dividing the total number of students by five:

$$\frac{650 \text{ students}}{5 \text{ groups}} = \frac{130 \text{ students}}{\text{group}}$$

To find the total number of girls, multiply the number of students per group (130) by the number of girl groups in the school (3). This equals 390, Choice *D*.

20. C: 34 When performing calculations consisting of more than one operation, the order of operations should be followed: parentheses, exponents, multiplication & division, addition & subtraction.

Parentheses:

$$7^2 - 3 \times (4 + 2) + 15 \div 5$$
$$7^2 - 3 \times (6) + 15 \div 5$$

Exponents:

$$49 - 3 \times 6 + 15 \div 5$$

Multiplication & division (from left to right):

$$49 - 18 + 3$$

Addition & subtraction (from left to right):

$$49 - 18 + 3 = 34$$

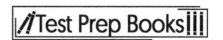

21. C: Kimberley worked 4.5 hours at the rate of $10 / h and 1 hour at the rate of $12 / h. The problem states that her time is rounded to the nearest hour, so the 4.5 hours would round up to 5 hours at the rate of $10 / h.

$$(5 \text{ h}) \times \left(\frac{\$10}{\text{h}}\right) + (1 \text{ h}) \times \left(\frac{\$12}{\text{h}}\right) = \$50 + \$12 = \$62$$

22. D:

$9x + x - 7 = 16 + 2x$	Combine $9x$ and x.
$10x - 7 = 16 + 2x$	
$10x - 7 + 7 = 16 + 2x + 7$	Add 7 to both sides to remove the -7.
$10x = 23 + 2x$	
$10x - 2x = 23 + 2x - 2x$	Subtract $2x$ from both sides to move it to the other side of the equation.
$8x = 23$	
$\dfrac{8x}{8} = \dfrac{23}{8}$	Divide by 8 to get x by itself.
$x = \dfrac{23}{8}$	

23. C: The cube box has a surface area of 1,176 square inches. We know this because it has 6 faces that are each 14 by 14 inches: $6 \times 14 \times 14 = 1,176$. She has 1,200 square inches of wrapping paper because the dimensions are 60 by 20, and the area of the wrapping paper is $60 \times 20 = 1,200$. Therefore, she has $1,200 - 1,176 = 24$ square inches extra.

24. B: First, calculate the difference between the larger value and the smaller value.

$$378 - 252 = 126$$

To calculate this difference as a percentage of the original value, and thus calculate the percentage *increase*, divide 126 by 252 to get 0.5, then multiply by 100 to reach the percentage 50%, Choice *B*.

25. B: First, we need to use the Pythagorean theorem to find the missing length: $x^2 = 6^2 + 9^2$, so $x^2 = 117$. Therefore, $x = \sqrt{117} \approx 10.8$, rounded to one decimal place. The perimeter is the sum of the three sides: $6 + 9 + 10.8 = 25.8$.

26. A: C: Plug 54 in for C in the given equation: $F = \frac{9}{5}(54) + 32 = 97.2 + 32 = 129.2$.

27. A: To calculate the range in a set of data, subtract the lowest value from the highest value. In this graph, the range of Mr. Lennon's students is 4, which can be be seen physically in the graph as having the smallest difference compared with the other teachers between the highest value and the lowest value.

28. C: The number of days can be found by taking the total amount Bernard needs to make and dividing it by the amount he earns per day:

$$\frac{300}{80} = \frac{30}{8} = \frac{15}{4} = 3.75$$

259

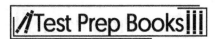

Bernard will need to work four days since he is only working full days and three days is not enough time.

29. D: To calculate the circumference of a circle, use the formula $2\pi r$, where r equals the radius (half of the diameter) of the circle and $\pi \approx 3.14$. Substitute the given information to get:

$$2 \times 3.14 \times 5 = 31.4$$

30. A: Mean. An outlier is a data value that's either far above or below the majority of values in a sample set. The mean is the average of all values in the set. In a small sample, a very high or low number could greatly change the average. The median is the middle value when arranged from lowest to highest. Outliers would have no more of an effect on the median than any other value. Mode is the value that repeats most often in a set. Assuming that the same outlier doesn't repeat, outliers would have no effect on the mode of a sample set.

31. A: This kind of line indicates a positive relationship. A negative relationship would match a line traveling from the upper left of the graph to the lower right. Exponential and logarithmic functions aren't linear—their graphs do not make a straight line.

32. A: The conversion can be obtained by setting up and evaluating the following expression:

$$4{,}382 \text{ ft } \times \frac{0.3048 \text{ m}}{1 \text{ ft}} \times \frac{1 \text{ km}}{1{,}000 \text{ m}} = 1.336 \text{ km}$$

33. C: The data points do not appear to form any sort of line, even approximately, as we would expect for a positive or negative relation. They also do not form the characteristic bell-shaped curve of a normal distribution. No relation is apparent.

34. D: The slope is given by the change in y divided by the change in x. Specifically, it's:

$$slope = \frac{y_2 - y_1}{x_2 - x_1}$$

The first point is $(-5, -3)$, and the second point is $(0, -1)$. Work from left to right when identifying coordinates. Thus, the point on the left is point 1 $(-5, -3)$ and the point on the right is point 2 $(0, -1)$.

Now we just need to plug those numbers into the equation:

$$slope = \frac{-1 - (-3)}{0 - (-5)}$$

It can be simplified to:

$$slope = \frac{-1 + 3}{0 + 5}$$

$$slope = \frac{2}{5}$$

35. B: The figure is composed of three sides of a square and a semicircle. The sides of the square are simply added:

$$8 \text{ in} + 8 \text{ in} + 8 \text{ in} = 24 \text{ in}$$

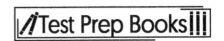

The circumference of a circle is found by the equation $C = 2\pi r$. The radius is 4 in, so the circumference of the circle is approximately 25.13 in. Only half of the circle makes up the outer border of the figure (part of the perimeter), and half of 25.13 in is 12.565 in. Therefore, the total perimeter is:

$$24 \text{ in} + 12.565 \text{ in} = 36.565 \text{ in}$$

The other answer choices use the incorrect formula or fail to include all of the necessary sides.

36. A: The perimeter of a rectangle is $P = 2l + 2w$. We are told $P = 44$, so $2l + 2w = 44$. We are also told that the width is 2 cm less than the length: $w = l - 2$. Substituting this for w in the perimeter equation, we get $2l + 2(l - 2) = 44$, which is Choice A. Although it's not necessary to answer the test question, we could solve the equation to find the length and width. The equation simplifies to $4l - 4 = 44$, or $l = 12$, and since $w = l - 2$, we find $w = 10$.

37. B: The first step is to make all exponents positive by moving the terms with negative exponents to the opposite side of the fraction. This expression becomes:

$$\frac{4b^3 b^2}{a^1 a^4} \times \frac{3a}{b}$$

Then the rules for exponents can be used to simplify. Multiplying the same bases means the exponents can be added. Dividing the same bases means the exponents are subtracted. Thus, after multiplying the exponents in the first fraction, the expression becomes:

$$\frac{4b^5}{a^5} \times \frac{3a}{b}$$

Therefore, we can first multiply to get:

$$\frac{12ab^5}{a^5 b}$$

Then, simplifying yields:

$$12\frac{b^4}{a^4}$$

38. D: The volume of a shoebox is length times width times height. Therefore, we have $358{,}150 = L \times 72.5 \times 47.5$. Divide both sides by $72.5 \times 47.5 = 3{,}443.75$ to obtain $L = 104$ cm.

39. B: The car is traveling at a speed of 5 meters per second. On the interval from 1 to 3 seconds, the position changes by 10 meters. This is 10 meters in 2 seconds, or 5 meters in each second.

40. B: 1 m is equal to 100 cm. Therefore, 2 m is equal to 200 cm. The missing amount is $200 - 70 = 130$ cm.

41. A: To put the numbers in increasing order, first change all fractions to decimals by dividing the numerator by the denominator. This gives us $\frac{1}{5} = 0.2$, $-\frac{1}{2} = -0.5$, and $\frac{3}{4} = 0.75$. The negative values are the smallest, with -1 being the smallest value in the group. The positive numbers are compared by looking at the decimal values from left to right. Therefore, the correct order is $-1, -\frac{1}{2}, \frac{1}{5}, .5, \frac{3}{4}$.

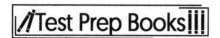

42. C: To change a decimal to a fraction, find the smallest place value in the decimal. The 5 is in the hundredths place. Then, write the decimal values over 100, since it is in the hundredths place. This process results in $\frac{45}{100}$. Reduce to obtain $\frac{9}{20}$.

43. B: 1 mile is approximately equal to 1.6 kilometers. Therefore, multiply 2.5 times 1.6 to obtain 4 km.

44. B: First, add 8 to both sides of the equation to obtain $21x = -13x + 48$. Then, add $13x$ to both sides to obtain $34x = 48$. Finally, divide both sides by 34 to obtain $x = \frac{48}{34} = \frac{24}{17}$.

45. B: First, find the sum of the 5 salaries. The total of the salaries is $191,000. Then, divide by 5 to obtain a mean of $38,200.

Science

1. A: When activated, B cells create antibodies against specific antigens. White blood cells are generated in red and yellow bone marrow, not cartilage. Platelets are not a type of white blood cell and are typically cell fragments produced by megakaryocytes. White blood cells are active throughout nearly all of one's life and have not been shown to specially activate or deactivate because of life events like puberty or menopause.

2. D: Mechanical digestion is physical digestion of food and tearing it into smaller pieces using force. This occurs in the stomach and mouth. Chemical digestion involves chemically changing the food and breaking it down into small organic compounds that can be utilized by the cell to build molecules. The salivary glands in the mouth secrete amylase that breaks down starch, which begins chemical digestion. The stomach contains enzymes such as pepsinogen/pepsin and gastric lipase which chemically digest protein and fats, respectively. The small intestine continues to digest protein using the enzymes trypsin and chymotrypsin. It also digests fats with the help of bile from the liver and lipase from the pancreas. These organs act as exocrine glands because they secrete substances through a duct. Carbohydrates are digested in the small intestine with the help of pancreatic amylase, gut bacterial flora and fauna, and brush border enzymes like lactose. Brush border enzymes are contained in the towel-like microvilli in the small intestine that soak up nutrients.

3. D: The urinary system has many functions, the primary of which is removing waste products and balancing water and electrolyte concentrations in the blood. It also plays a key role in regulating ion concentrations, such as sodium, potassium, chloride, and calcium, in the filtrate. The urinary system helps maintain blood pH by reabsorbing or secreting hydrogen ions and bicarbonate as necessary. Certain kidney cells can detect reductions in blood volume and pressure and then can secrete renin to activate a hormone that causes increased reabsorption of sodium ions and water. This serves to raise blood volume and pressure. Kidney cells secrete erythropoietin under hypoxic conditions to stimulate red blood cell production. They also synthesize calcitriol, a hormone derivative of vitamin D3, which aids in calcium ion absorption by the intestinal epithelium.

4. B: The structure exclusively found in eukaryotic cells is the nucleus. Animal, plant, fungi, and protist cells are all eukaryotic. DNA is contained within the nucleus of eukaryotic cells, and they also have membrane-bound organelles that perform complex intracellular metabolic activities. Prokaryotic cells (archaea and bacteria) do not have a nucleus or other membrane-bound organelles and are less complex than eukaryotic cells.

5. B: The cell structure responsible for cellular storage, digestion, and waste removal is the lysosome. Lysosomes are like recycle bins. They are filled with digestive enzymes that facilitate catabolic reactions to regenerate monomers. The Golgi apparatus is designed to tag, package, and ship out proteins destined for other cells or locations. The centrioles typically play a large role only in cell division when they ratchet the chromosomes from the mitotic plate to the poles of the cell. The mitochondria are involved in energy production and are the powerhouses of the cell.

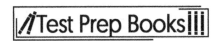
6. D: Density is found by dividing mass by volume:

$$density = \frac{mass}{volume}$$

The unit for mass (in this case grams) and the units for volume (in this case cm^3) need to be combined together. They're combined as grams over volume since that's how they were set up in the equation:

$$d = \frac{14.3 \text{ g}}{5.4 \text{ cm}^3} = 2.65 \text{ g/cm}^3$$

7. D: Veins have valves, but arteries do not. Valves in veins are designed to prevent backflow since they are the furthest blood vessels from the pumping action of the heart and steadily increase in volume (which decreases the available pressure). Capillaries diffuse nutrients properly because of their thin walls and high surface area and are not particularly dependent on positive pressure.

8. C: The blood leaves the right ventricle through a semi-lunar valve and goes through the pulmonary artery to the lungs. Any increase in pressure in the artery will eventually affect the contractibility of the right ventricle. Blood enters the right atrium from the superior vena cava and inferior vena cava, and blood leaves the right atrium through the tricuspid valve to the right ventricle. Blood enters the left atrium from the pulmonary veins carrying oxygenated blood from the lungs. Blood flows from the left atrium to the left ventricle through the mitral valve and leaves the left ventricle through a semi-lunar valve to enter the aorta.

9. D: Sodium bicarbonate, a very effective base, functions chiefly to increase the pH of the chyme. Chyme leaving the stomach has a very low pH due to the high amounts of acid that are used to digest and break down food. If this is not neutralized, the walls of the small intestine will be damaged and may form ulcers. Sodium bicarbonate is produced by the pancreas and released in response to pyloric stimulation so that it can neutralize the acid. It has little to no digestive effect.

10. C: Health care functions are a way for the family to learn about health concepts, health promotion/maintenance, illness management, and disease prevention. For example, a family member can provide care to ill family members and serve as the main source of support and information. The other four family functions are economic function, reproductive function, socialization function, and affective function.

11. A: Family as a system is a nursing approach that focuses on one individual family member and other parts of the family simultaneously. An example of a question a nurse might ask is, "What has changed between you and your significant other since your child's leg injury?" Choice *B* is incorrect because family as a client is an approach that focuses on how the family reacts to an event as a whole. Choice *C* is incorrect because family as a component of society is an approach that incorporates interactions between the family and other institutions. Choice *D* is incorrect because family as a context is an approach where the nurse focuses on the individual and how the family influences the individual's health.

12. A: The sternum is medial to the deltoid because it is much closer to (typically right on) the midline of the body, while the deltoid is lateral at the shoulder cap. Superficial means that a structure is closer to the body surface and posterior means that it falls behind something else. For example, skin is superficial to bone and the kidneys are posterior to the rectus abdominis.

13. B: Ligaments connect bone to bone. Tendons connect muscle to bone. Both are made of dense, fibrous connective tissue (primary Type 1 collagen) to give strength. However, tendons are more organized, especially in the long axis direction like muscle fibers themselves, and they have more collagen. This arrangement makes more sense because muscles have specific orientations of their fibers, so they contract in somewhat predictable directions. Ligaments are less organized and have more of a woven pattern because bone connections are not as organized as bundles of muscle fibers, so ligaments must have strength in multiple directions to protect against injury.

14. A: The three primary body planes are coronal, sagittal, and transverse. The coronal or frontal plane, named for the plane in which a corona or halo might appear in old paintings, divides the body vertically into front and back sections. The sagittal plane, named for the path an arrow might take when shot at the body, divides the body vertically into right and left sections. The transverse plane divides the body horizontally into upper or superior and lower or inferior sections. There is no medial plane, per se. The anatomical direction medial simply references a location close or closer to the center of the body than another location.

15. C: Although the lungs may provide some cushioning for the heart when the body is violently struck, this is not a major function of the respiratory system. Its most notable function is that of gas exchange for oxygen and carbon dioxide, but it also plays a vital role in the regulation of blood pH. The aqueous form of carbon dioxide, carbonic acid, is a major pH buffer of the blood, and the respiratory system directly controls how much carbon dioxide stays and is released from the blood through respiration. The respiratory system also enables vocalization and forms the basis for the mode of speech and language used by most humans.

16. A: The forebrain contains the cerebrum, the thalamus, the hypothalamus, and the limbic system. The limbic system is chiefly responsible for the perception of emotions through the amygdala, while the cerebrum interprets sensory input and generates movement. Specifically, the occipital lobe receives visual input, and the primary motor cortex in the frontal lobe is the controller of voluntary movement. The hindbrain, specifically the medulla oblongata and brain stem, control and regulate blood pressure and heart rate.

17. D: Germline mutations in eggs and sperm are permanent, can be on the chromosomal level, and will be inherited by offspring. Somatic mutations cannot affect eggs and sperm, and therefore are not inherited by offspring. Mutations of either kind are rarely beneficial to the individual but do not necessarily harm them. Germline cells divide much more rapidly than do somatic cells, and a mutation in a sex cell would promulgate and affect many thousands of its daughter cells.

18. A: It is most likely asthma. Any of the answer choices listed can cause heavy breathing. A blood clot in the lung (*B*) could cause this, but this would be very uncommon for a child. Choices *C* and *D* can both be ruled out because the question mentions that it occurs even when the patient is relaxing. Hyperventilation is usually caused by a panic attack or some sort of physical activity. Asthma often develops during childhood. It would stand to reason then that the child may have not yet been diagnosed. While asthma attacks can be caused by exercise, they can also occur when a person is not exerting themselves.

19. C: DNA contains chemical bases that form chemical bonds with each other. The four bases in DNA are adenine, cytosine, thymine, and guanine. Uracil is a chemical base found in RNA, not DNA, so Choice *C* is the correct answer.

20. A: The process of cell division in somatic cells is called mitosis. In interphase, which precedes mitosis, cells prepare for division by copying their DNA. Once mitotic machinery has been assembled in interphase, mitosis occurs, which has five distinct phases: prophase, prometaphase, metaphase, anaphase, and telophase, followed by cytokinesis, which is the final splitting of the cytoplasm. The two diploid daughter cells are genetically identical to the parent cell.

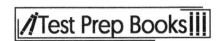

21. A: Choice *B* is true because steroid hormones are lipid based. Long-term energy is one of the most important functions of lipids, so *C* is true. *D* is also true because the cell membrane is not only composed of a lipid bilayer, but it also has cholesterol (another lipid) embedded within it to regulate membrane fluidity.

22. A: Choice *B* is incorrect because DNA does not provide energy—that's the job of carbohydrates and glucose. Choice *C* is incorrect because DNA is double-stranded. Because Choices *B* and *C* are incorrect, Choice *D*, all of the above, is incorrect.

23. A: The Golgi apparatus is designed to tag, package, and ship out proteins destined for other cells or locations. The centrioles typically play a large role only in cell division when they ratchet the chromosomes from the mitotic plate to the poles of the cell. The mitochondria are involved in energy production and are the powerhouses of the cell. The cell structure responsible for cellular storage, digestion, and waste removal is the lysosome. Lysosomes are like recycle bins. They are filled with digestive enzymes that facilitate catabolic reactions to regenerate monomers.

24. C: Cellulose and starch are both polysaccharides, which are long chains of glucose molecules. However, they are connected by different types of bonds, which gives them different structures and different functions.

25. D: Let's label *R* as the right-handed allele and *r* as the left-handed allele. Esther has to have the combination rr since she's left-handed. She had to get at least one recessive allele from each parent. So, mom could either be Rr or rr (right-handed or left-handed), and dad can also be Rr or rr. As long as each parent carries one recessive allele, it is possible that Esther is left-handed. Therefore, all answer choices are possible.

26. B: Kidneys filter blood using nephrons that span the outer renal cortex and inner renal medulla. The inner kidneys are composed of the renal pelvis, which collects urine and sends it to the bladder via the ureters. Filtrate first enters the filtering tube of the nephron via the glomerulus, a bundle of capillaries where blood fluid (but not cells) diffuses into the Bowman's capsule, the entryway into the kidney filtration canal. Bowman's capsule collects fluid, but the nephron actually starts filtering blood in the proximal tubule, where necessary ions, nutrients, wastes, and (depending on blood osmolarity) water are absorbed or released. Also, blood pH is regulated here, as the proximal tubule fine-tunes pH by utilizing the blood buffering system, adjusting amounts of hydrogen ions, bicarbonate, and ammonia in the filtrate. Down the loop of Henle in the renal medulla, the filtrate becomes more concentrated as water exits, while on the way back up the loop of Henle, ion concentration is regulated with ion channels. The distal tubule continues to regulate ion and water concentrations, and the collecting duct delivers the filtrate to the renal pelvis.

27. C: Nephrons are responsible for filtering blood. When functioning properly they allow blood cells and nutrients to go back into the bloodstream while sending waste to the bladder. However, nephrons can fail at doing this, particularly when blood flood to the kidneys is limited. The medulla (also called the renal medulla) (*A*) and the renal cortex (*D*) are both parts of the kidney but are not specifically responsible for filtering blood. The medulla is in the inner part of the kidney and contains the nephrons. The renal cortex is the outer part of the kidney. The heart (*B*) is responsible for pumping blood throughout the body rather than filtering it.

28. B: Ossification is the process by which cartilage, a soft, flexible substance is replaced by bone throughout the body. All humans regardless of age have cartilage, but cartilage in some areas is replaced by bones as a person grows.

29. D: The outermost layer of the skin, the epidermis, consists of epithelial cells. This layer of skin is dead, as it has no blood vessels. Osteoclasts are cells that make up bones. Notice the prefix "osteo-," which means bone. Connective tissue macrophage cells can be found in a variety of places, and dendritic cells are part of the lymphatic system.

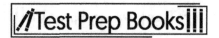

30. C: mRNA is directly transcribed from DNA before being taken to the cytoplasm and translated by rRNA into a protein. tRNA transfers amino acids from the cytoplasm to the rRNA for use in building these proteins. siRNA is a special type of RNA which interferes with other strands of mRNA, typically by causing them to get degraded by the cell rather than translated into protein.

31. B: Since the genotype is a depiction of the specific alleles that an organism's genes code for, it includes recessive genes that may or may not be otherwise expressed. The genotype does not have to name the proteins that its alleles code for; indeed, some of them may be unknown. The phenotype is the physical, visual manifestations of a gene, not the genotype. The genotype does not necessarily include any information about the organism's physical characteristics. Although some information about an organism's parents can be obtained from its genotype, its genotype does not actually show the parents' phenotypes.

32. C: One in four offspring (or 25%) will be short, so all four offspring cannot be tall. Although both of the parents are tall, they are hybrid or heterozygous tall, not homozygous. Although it may seem intuitive that the short allele will be expressed by lower numbers of the population than the tall allele, it still appears in 75% of the offspring (although its effects are masked in 2/3 of those). Besides, conditions could favor the recessive allele and kill off the tall offspring.

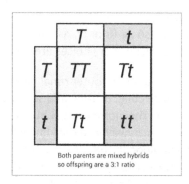

Both parents are mixed hybrids
so offspring are a 3:1 ratio

33. D: Evaporation takes place at the surface of a fluid, while boiling takes place throughout the fluid. The liquid will boil when it reaches its boiling or vaporization temperature, but evaporation can happen due to a liquid's volatility. Volatile substances often coexist as a liquid and as a gas, depending on the pressure forced on them. The phase change from gas to liquid is condensation, and both evaporation and boiling take place in nature.

34. A: Human genes are strictly DNA and do not include proteins or amino acids. A human's genome and collection of genes will include even their recessive traits, mutations, and unused DNA.

35. C: Water's polarity lends it to be extremely cohesive and adhesive; this cohesion keeps its atoms very close together. Because of this, it takes a large amount of energy to boil its liquid form. Phospholipid bilayers are made of nonpolar lipids; water, a polar liquid, cannot easily flow through it. Cell membranes use proteins called aquaporins to solve this issue and let water flow in and out. Fish breathe by capturing dissolved oxygen through their gills. Water can self-ionize, wherein it decomposes into a hydrogen ion (H^+) and a hydroxide ion (OH^-), but it cannot self-hydrolyze.

36. D: An isotope of an element has an atomic number equal to its number of protons, but a different mass number because of the additional neutrons. Even though there are differences in the nucleus, the behavior and properties of isotopes of a given element are identical. Atoms with different atomic numbers also have different numbers of protons and are different elements, so they cannot be isotopes.

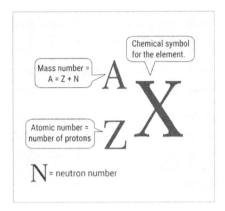

37. A: The neutrons and protons make up the nucleus of the atom. The nucleus is positively charged due to the presence of the protons. The negatively charged electrons are attracted to the positively charged nucleus by the electrostatic or Coulomb force; however, the electrons are not contained in the nucleus. The positively charged protons create the positive charge in the nucleus, and the neutrons are electrically neutral, so they have no effect. Radioactivity does not directly have a bearing on the charge of the nucleus.

38. D: The probability of each specified genotype can be determined by individual Punnett squares. Each probability should then be then multiplied (law of multiplication) to find the value, which in this case is $\frac{1}{2} \times \frac{1}{2} \times \frac{1}{2} \times \frac{1}{2} = \frac{1}{16}$.

	A	a
A	AA	Aa
A	AA	Aa

	B	b
b	Bb	bb
b	Bb	bb

	C	C
c	Cc	cc
c	Cc	cc

	D	d
D	DD	Dd
D	DD	Dd

Probabilities: $AA = \frac{1}{2}$ $\qquad$ $bb = \frac{1}{2}$ $\qquad$ $cc = \frac{1}{2}$ $\qquad$ $DD = \frac{1}{2}$

39. D: The seminiferous tubules are responsible for sperm production. Had *testicles* been an answer choice, it would also have been correct since it houses the seminiferous tubules. The prostate gland (*A*) secretes enzymes that help nourish sperm after creation. The seminal vesicles (*B*) secrete some of the components of semen. The scrotum (*C*) is the pouch holding the testicles.

40. D: Choice *A* is incorrect because meiosis produces haploid cells. Choice *B* is incorrect because there is no interphase II. Otherwise, gametes would be diploid instead of haploid. Choice *C* is incorrect because the resulting cells only have one set of chromosomes. Choice *D* is the only correct answer because each chromosome set goes through a process called crossing over, which jumbles up the genes on each chromatid during meiosis I.

41. A: All three joint types given are synovial joints, allowing for a fair amount of movement (compared with fibrous and cartilaginous joints). Of the three given, hinge joints, such as the elbow, permit the least motion because they are uniaxial and permit movement in only one plane. Saddle joints and condyloid joints both have reciprocating surfaces that mate with one another and allow a variety of motions in numerous planes, but saddle joints, such as

267

the thumb carpal-metacarpal joint, allow more motion than condyloid joints. In saddle joints, two concave surfaces articulate, and in a condyloid joint, such as the wrist, a concave surface articulates with a convex surface, allowing motion in mainly two planes.

42. D: All of the above are functions of synergists. Synergists are responsible for helping the primary movers or agonists carry out their specific movements. Synergists can help stabilize the point of origin of a muscle or provide extra pull near the insertion; in this sense, they can be considered "fixators." Some synergists can help prevent undesired movement at a joint. For example, for elbow flexion, the brachialis is a synergist to the biceps.

43. A: All three types of muscle tissue (skeletal, cardiac, and smooth) share four important properties: they are contractile, meaning they can shorten and pull on connective tissue; excitable, meaning they respond to stimuli; elastic, meaning they rebound to their original length after a contraction; and extensible, meaning they can be stretched repeatedly but maintain the ability to contract. While skeletal muscle is under voluntary control, both cardiac and smooth muscle are involuntary.

44. D: The autonomic nervous system (ANS), a division of the PNS, controls involuntary functions such as breathing, heart rate, blood pressure, digestion, and body temperature via the antagonistic parasympathetic and sympathetic nerves. Choices *A, B,* and *C* are incorrect because they describe characteristics of the somatic nervous system, which is the other division of the PNS. It controls skeletal muscles via afferent and efferent neurons. Afferent neurons carry sensory messages from skeletal muscles, skin, or sensory organs to the central nervous system (CNS), while efferent neurons relay motor messages from the CNS to skeletal muscles, skin, or sensory organs. While skeletal muscle movement is under voluntary control, the somatic nervous system also plays a role in the involuntary reflex arc.

45. C: The sinuses function to warm, filter, and humidify air that is inhaled. Choice *A* is incorrect because mucus traps airborne pathogens. Choice *B* is incorrect because the epiglottis is the structure in the pharynx that covers the trachea during swallowing to prevent food from entering it. Lastly, Choice *D,* sweeping away pathogens and directing them toward the top of the trachea, is the function of cilia. Respiratory structures, such as the nasal passages and trachea, are lined with mucus and cilia.

46. B: Secondary prevention requires that public health nurses stop disease progression through early detection/treatment, which will minimize the chronicity or prevalence of the exposure. Choice *A* is incorrect because primary preventions use general measures in a community to promote health, e.g., developing a health education program for students that teaches the effects of pesticide exposure. Choice *C* is incorrect because, in tertiary prevention, the public health nurse attempts to stop deterioration in the patient through nursing and medical care. For example, the nurse might create a clinic, unit, or center in which self-care is provided for a specific community. Choice *D* is incorrect because there are only three levels of prevention.

47. D: Single risk factors can be a subset of the general health risks mentioned in Choices *A–C.* For instance, a family history of cardiovascular disease can be considered a single biological risk that is worsened by smoking or unhealthy eating; a behavioral risk has a higher probability of occurring if other family members have the same practice. Biological risks can include age-related risks, and environmental risks are attributed to physical, social, and economic factors.

48. B: The affective domain discusses changes in attitudes and the development of specific values in regard to health. This domain requires that nurses listen to patients, who may have deeply rooted beliefs, to help them follow a series of steps that involve knowledge, comprehension, and evaluation of information. Choice *A* is incorrect; the cognitive domain involves memory, reasoning, and problem-solving. Choice *C* is incorrect, as it is not a domain of learning. Choice *D* is incorrect; the psychomotor domain emphasizes the performance of skills or motor skills such as giving injections and performing health promotion exercises.

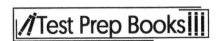

49. A: Salts are formed from compounds that use ionic bonds. Disulfide bridges are special bonds in protein synthesis which hold the protein in their secondary and tertiary structures. Covalent bonds are strong bonds formed through the sharing of electrons between atoms and are typically found in organic molecules like carbohydrates and lipids. London dispersion forces are fleeting, momentary bonds which occur between atoms that have instantaneous dipoles but quickly disintegrate.

50. B: A solid produced during a reaction in solution is called a precipitate. In a neutralization reaction, the products (an acid and a base) react to form a salt and water. Choice *A*, an oxidation reaction, involves the transfer of an electron. Choice *C*, a synthesis reaction, involves the joining of two molecules to form a single molecule. Choice *D*, a decomposition reaction, involves the separation of a molecule into two other molecules.

51. C: Molecules that are soluble in lipids, like fats, sterols, and vitamins (A, D, E, and K), for example, are able to move in and out of a cell using passive transport. Water and oxygen are also able to move in and out of the cell without the use of cellular energy. Complex sugars and non-lipid-soluble molecules are too large to move through the cell membrane without relying on active transport mechanisms. Molecules naturally move from areas of high concentration to those of lower concentration. It requires active transport to move molecules in the opposite direction, as suggested by Choice *D*.

52. A: Both types of cells are enclosed by a cell membrane, which is selectively permeable. Selective permeability essentially means that the membrane is a gatekeeper, allowing certain molecules and ions in and out, and keeping unwanted ones at bay, at least until they are ready for use. Prokaryotes contain a nucleoid and do not have organelles; eukaryotes contain a nucleus enclosed by a membrane, as well as organelles.

53. B: During telophase, two nuclei form at each end of the cell and nuclear envelopes begin to form around each nucleus. The nucleoli reappear, and the chromosomes become less compact. The microtubules are broken down by the cell, and mitosis is complete. The process begins with prophase as the mitotic spindles begin to form from centrosomes. Prometaphase follows, with the breakdown of the nuclear envelope and the further condensing of the chromosomes. Next, metaphase occurs when the microtubules are stretched across the cell and the chromosomes align at the metaphase plate. Finally, in the last step before telophase, anaphase occurs as the sister chromatids break apart and form chromosomes.

54. D: Meiosis has the same phases as mitosis, except that they occur twice—once in meiosis I and once in meiosis II. During meiosis I, the cell splits into two. Each cell contains two sets of chromosomes. Next, during meiosis II, the two intermediate daughter cells divide again, producing four total haploid cells that each contain one set of chromosomes.

55. B: The secondary structure of a protein refers to the folds and coils that are formed by hydrogen bonding between the slightly charged atoms of the polypeptide backbone. The primary structure is the sequence of amino acids, similar to the letters in a long word. The tertiary structure is the overall shape of the molecule that results from the interactions between the side chains that are linked to the polypeptide backbone. The quaternary structure is the complete protein structure that occurs when a protein is made up of two or more polypeptide chains.

56. A: The sensory threshold is the smallest amount of stimulus that is required for an individual to experience one of the senses. For example, during a hearing test, the sensory threshold would be the quietest sound that a person could detect. This threshold is an important indicator of whether a person's senses are working within a normal range.

57. C: Generally, all sensory pathways that extend from the sensory receptor to the brain are composed of three long neurons called the primary, secondary, and tertiary neurons. The primary one stretches from the sensory receptor to the dorsal root ganglion of the spinal nerve, and the secondary one stretches from the cell body of the

269

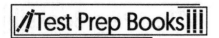

primary neuron to the spinal cord or the brain stem. The tertiary one stretches from the cell body of the secondary one into the thalamus. Each type of sense, such as touch, hearing, and vision, has a different pathway designed specifically for that sensation.

58. C: Visual processing begins in the retina. When an individual sees an image, it is taken in through the cornea and lens and then transmitted upside down onto the retina. The cells in the retina process what is being seen and then send signals to the ganglion cells, whose axons make up the optic nerve. The optic nerve cells connect the retina to the brain, which is where the processing of the visual information is completed and the images are returned to their proper orientation.

59. D: Veins carry oxygen-poor blood back to the heart. Intestines carry digested food through the body. Bronchioles are passageways that carry air from the nose and mouth to the lungs.

60. C: The somatic nervous system is the voluntary nervous system, which is responsible for voluntary movement. It includes nerves that transmit signals from the brain to the muscles of the body. Breathing is controlled by the autonomic nervous system. Thought and fear are complex processes that occur in the brain, which is part of the central nervous system.

Verbal

Word Knowledge

Select the word that most correctly completes the sentence.

1. The charge nurse was a good leader because she had gravitas and commanded respect. Gravitas means:
   a. Intelligence
   b. Dignity
   c. Gratitude
   d. Somberness

2. An ultrasound was ordered to image the patient's hepatic portal system. Hepatic means:
   a. Relating to the pancreas
   b. Relating to the liver
   c. Relating to the kidney
   d. Relating to the gallbladder

3. The vehement speeches from former patients motivated many donors to increase their pledges. Vehement means:
   a. Ardent
   b. Motivational
   c. Novel
   d. Virulent

4. The medication had an intrathecal route of administration. Intrathecal means:
   a. Under tongue
   b. Around the spinal cord
   c. In the ear
   d. Inside the cheek

5. The graduate student's thesis was focused on gerontology. Gerontology means:
   a. The study of diseases
   b. The study of growth
   c. The study of genes
   d. The study of aging

6. The hospital room looked pristine. Pristine means:
   a. Unorganized and dingy
   b. Unfriendly
   c. Sterile
   d. Clean and new

7. The patient's stomach appeared distended. Distended means:
   a. Enlarged or expanded
   b. Sunken or concave
   c. Soft and flaccid
   d. Discolored or blotchy

8. After the trauma, new symptoms of the woman's latent infection emerged. Latent means:
   a. Chronic and debilitating
   b. Acute but not necessarily severe
   c. Present but not active or visible
   d. Uncontrollable or volatile

9. The nurse reported that the patient experienced dyspnea and dizziness. Dyspnea means:
   a. Difficulty breathing
   b. Difficulty sleeping
   c. Rapid pulse
   d. Nasal discharge

10. The nurse explained the symptoms of the patient's acute illness and recommended increasing fluid intake. Acute means:
   a. Serious with a poor prognosis
   b. Sudden or rapid onset
   c. Debilitating and contagious
   d. Chronic and slow to resolve

11. The graduate student noted that the common symptoms of the condition were malaise, weight loss, and anuria. Anuria means:
   a. Lack of urine output
   b. Excessive urine production
   c. Memory loss
   d. Lack of usual reflexes

12. The viscosity of the patient's synovial fluid was abnormal. Viscosity means:
   a. A fluid's cellular and nutrient profile
   b. A fluid's thickness or resistance to flow
   c. A fluid's color and transparency
   d. A fluid's sedimentation rate

13. The prognosis was undetermined because of the aberrant nature of his illness. Aberrant means:
   a. Overt
   b. Grave
   c. Radical
   d. Abnormal

14. The patient's father had a history of chronic renal disease. Renal means:
   a. Relating to the pancreas
   b. Relating to the liver
   c. Relating to the kidney
   d. Relating to hormones

15. During her internship at the hospital, Cassandra got to triage a lot of patients. Triage means:
    a. Diagnose or identify a problem
    b. Develop an effective treatment plan
    c. Evaluate and gather relevant medical history
    d. Sort based on problem severity

16. The nurse noted that the baby appeared indolent. Indolent means:
    a. Underweight
    b. Agitated
    c. Lethargic
    d. Alert

17. The medication had a buccal route of administration. Buccal means:
    a. Under the tongue
    b. In the rectum
    c. Through the nasal cavity
    d. Inside the cheek

18. Immediately after the holiday, staff interest grew rampant. Rampant means:
    a. Stagnant
    b. Mildly
    c. Unrestrained
    d. Wearily

19. An increased pupil size is considered an ominous sign. Ominous means:
    a. Unequivocal
    b. Promising
    c. Auspicious
    d. Threatening

20. The patient had a history of anxiety, emphysema, and a peptic ulcer. Peptic means:
    a. Relating to ingestion
    b. Relating to defecation
    c. Relating to digestion
    d. Relating to the pancreas

21. What is the best definition of the word *retort*?
    a. Conversation
    b. Jest
    c. Counter
    d. Flexible

22. What is the best definition of the word *subliminal*?
    a. Subconscious
    b. Transportation
    c. Underground
    d. Substitute

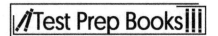

23. What is the best definition of the word *incite*?
    a. Understanding
    b. Illumination
    c. Rally
    d. Judgment

24. What is the best definition of the word *sustain*?
    a. strength
    b. invigorate
    c. embolden
    d. expedite

25. What is the best definition of the word *mitigate*?
    a. alleviate
    b. focus
    c. fiery
    d. conspire

26. What does *abstain* mean?
    a. To regurgitate
    b. To imbibe
    c. To refrain from something
    d. To prolong

27. What is the best definition of the word *venerate*?
    a. Respect
    b. Reject
    c. Expect
    d. Deserve

28. What word meaning "a fungal infection or disease" best fits in the following sentence:
    Ringworm is considered a type of _____.
    a. Lichen
    b. Mycosis
    c. Virus
    d. Pustule

Reading Comprehension

Questions 29–33 are based on the following passage:

Dana Gioia argues in his article that poetry is dying, now little more than a limited art form confined to academic and college settings. Of course, poetry remains healthy in the academic setting, but the idea of poetry being limited to this academic subculture is a stretch. New technology and social networking alone have contributed to poets and other writers' work being shared across the world. YouTube has emerged to be a major asset to poets, allowing live performances to be streamed to billions of users. Even now, poetry continues to grow and voice topics that are relevant to the culture of our time. Poetry is not in the spotlight as it may have been in earlier times, but it's still a relevant art form that continues to expand in scope and appeal.

274

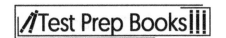

Furthermore, Gioia's argument does not account for live performances of poetry. Not everyone has taken a poetry class or enrolled in university—but most everyone is online. The Internet is a perfect launching point to get all creative work out there. An example of this was Buddy Wakefield's performance of his poem "Hurling Crowbirds at Mockingbars." Wakefield is a well-known poet who has published several collections of contemporary poetry. "Crowbirds" is one of my favorite works by Wakefield, especially because of his performance of it at New York University in 2009. Although his reading was a campus event, views of his performance online number in the thousands. His poetry attracted people outside of the university setting.

Naturally, the poem's popularity can be attributed to both Wakefield's performance and the quality of his writing. "Crowbirds" touches on themes of core human concepts such as faith, personal loss, and growth. These are not ideas that only poets or students of literature understand, but all human beings: "You acted like I was hurling crowbirds at mockingbars / and abandoned me for not making sense. / Evidently, I don't experience things as rationally as you do." Wakefield weaves together a complex description of the perplexed and hurt emotions of the speaker who is undergoing a separation from a romantic interest. The line "You acted like I was hurling crowbirds at mockingbars" conjures up an image of someone confused, seemingly out of their mind... or in the case of the speaker, passionately trying to grasp at a relationship that is fading. The speaker is looking back and finding the words that described how he wasn't making sense. This poem is particularly human and gripping in its message, but the entire effect of the poem is enhanced through the physical performance.

At its core, poetry is about addressing issues and ideas in the world. Part of this is also addressing the perspectives that are exiguously considered. Although the platform may look different, poetry continues to have a steady audience due to the emotional connection the poet shares with the audience.

29. Which of the following best explains how the passage is organized?
   a. The author begins with a long definition of the main topic and then proceeds to prove how that definition has changed over the course of modernity.
   b. The author presents a puzzling phenomenon and uses the rest of the passage to showcase personal experiences in order to explain it.
   c. The author contrasts two different viewpoints and then builds a case showing preference for one over the other.
   d. The passage is an analysis of a theory that the author has no stake in.

30. The author of the passage would likely agree most with which of the following?
   a. Buddy Wakefield is a genius and is considered at the forefront of modern poetry.
   b. Poetry is not irrelevant; it is an art form that adapts to the changing times while retaining its core elements.
   c. Spoken word is the zenith of poetic forms and the premier style of poetry in this decade.
   d. Poetry is on the verge of vanishing from our cultural consciousness.

31. Which of the following words, if substituted for the word exiguously in the last paragraph, would least change the meaning of the sentence?
   a. Indolently
   b. Inaudibly
   c. Interminably
   d. Infrequently

275

32. Which of the following is most closely analogous to the author's opinion of Buddy Wakefield's performance in relation to modern poetry?
    a. Someone's refusal to accept that the Higgs boson particle will validate the Standard Model of physics
    b. An individual's belief that soccer will lose popularity within the next 50 years
    c. A professor's opinion that poetry contains the language of the heart, while fiction contains the language of the mind
    d. A student's insistence that psychoanalysis is a subset of modern psychology

33. What is the primary purpose of the passage?
    a. To educate readers on the development of poetry and describe the historical implications of poetry in media
    b. To disprove Dana Gioia's stance that poetry is becoming irrelevant and is only appreciated in academia
    c. To inform readers of the brilliance of Buddy Wakefield and to introduce them to other poets that have influenced contemporary poetry
    d. To prove that Gioia's article does have some truth to it and to shed light on its relevance to modern poetry

Questions 33–38 are based upon the following passage:

My Good Friends,—When I first imparted to the committee of the projected Institute my particular wish that on one of the evenings of my readings here the main body of my audience should be composed of working men and their families, I was animated by two desires; first, by the wish to have the great pleasure of meeting you face to face at this Christmas time, and accompany you myself through one of my little Christmas books; and second, by the wish to have an opportunity of stating publicly in your presence, and in the presence of the committee, my earnest hope that the Institute will, from the beginning, recognise one great principle—strong in reason and justice—which I believe to be essential to the very life of such an Institution. It is, that the working man shall, from the first unto the last, have a share in the management of an Institution which is designed for his benefit, and which calls itself by his name.

I have no fear here of being misunderstood—of being supposed to mean too much in this. If there ever was a time when any one class could of itself do much for its own good, and for the welfare of society—which I greatly doubt—that time is unquestionably past. It is in the fusion of different classes, without confusion; in the bringing together of employers and employed; in the creating of a better common understanding among those whose interests are identical, who depend upon each other, who are vitally essential to each other, and who never can be in unnatural antagonism without deplorable results, that one of the chief principles of a Mechanics' Institution should consist. In this world, a great deal of the bitterness among us arises from an imperfect understanding of one another. Erect in Birmingham a great Educational Institution, properly educational; educational of the feelings as well as of the reason; to which all orders of Birmingham men contribute; in which all orders of Birmingham men meet; wherein all orders of Birmingham men are faithfully represented—and you will erect a Temple of Concord here which will be a model edifice to the whole of England.

Contemplating as I do the existence of the Artisans' Committee, which not long ago considered the establishment of the Institute so sensibly, and supported it so heartily, I earnestly entreat the gentlemen—earnest I know in the good work, and who are now among us—by all means to avoid the great shortcoming of similar institutions; and in asking the working man for his confidence, to set him the great example and give him theirs in return. You will judge for yourselves if I promise too much for the working man, when I say that he will stand by such an enterprise with the utmost of his patience, his perseverance, sense, and support; that I am sure he will need no charitable aid

276

or condescending patronage; but will readily and cheerfully pay for the advantages which it confers; that he will prepare himself in individual cases where he feels that the adverse circumstances around him have rendered it necessary; in a word, that he will feel his responsibility like an honest man, and will most honestly and manfully discharge it. I now proceed to the pleasant task to which I assure you I have looked forward for a long time.

From Charles Dickens' speech in Birmingham in England on December 30, 1853 on behalf of the Birmingham and Midland Institute

34. Which word is most closely synonymous with the word patronage as it appears in the following statement:
...that I am sure he will need no charitable aid or condescending patronage;

a. Auspices
b. Aberration
c. Acerbic
d. Adulation

35. Which term is most closely aligned with the definition of the term working man as it is defined in the following passage:
You will judge for yourselves if I promise too much for the working man, when I say that he will stand by such an enterprise with the utmost of his patience, his perseverance, sense, and support...

a. Athlete
b. Viscount
c. Entrepreneur
d. Bourgeois

36. Which of the following statements most closely correlates with the definition of the term working man as it is defined in Question 38?
a. A working man is not someone who works for institutions or corporations, but someone who is well-versed in the workings of the soul.
b. A working man is someone who is probably not involved in social activities because the physical demand for work is too high.
c. A working man is someone who works for wages among the middle class.
d. The working man has historically taken to the field, to the factory, and now to the screen.

37. Based upon the contextual evidence provided in the passage above, what is the meaning of the term *enterprise* in the third paragraph?
a. Company
b. Courage
c. Game
d. Cause

38. The speaker addresses his audience as *My Good Friends.* What kind of credibility does this salutation give to the speaker?
a. The speaker is an employer addressing his employees, so the salutation is a way for the boss to bridge the gap between himself and his employees.
b. The speaker's salutation is one from an entertainer to his audience, and he uses this friendly language to connect to his audience before a serious speech.
c. The salutation is used ironically to give a somber tone to the serious speech that follows.
d. The speech is one from a politician to the public, so the salutation is used to grab the audience's attention.

Questions 39–43 are based upon the following passage:

MANKIND being originally equals in the order of creation, the equality could only be destroyed by some subsequent circumstance; the distinctions of rich, and poor, may in a great measure be accounted for, and that without having recourse to the harsh, ill-sounding names of oppression and avarice. Oppression is often the CONSEQUENCE, but seldom or never the MEANS of riches; and though avarice will preserve a man from being necessitously poor, it generally makes him too timorous to be wealthy.

But there is another and greater distinction, for which no truly natural or religious reason can be assigned, and that is, the distinction of men into KINGS and SUBJECTS. Male and female are the distinctions of nature, good and bad the distinctions of heaven; but how a race of men came into the world so exalted above the rest, and distinguished like some new species, is worth enquiring into, and whether they are the means of happiness or of misery to mankind.

In the early ages of the world, according to the scripture chronology, there were no kings; the consequence of which was, there were no wars; it is the pride of kings which throw mankind into confusion. Holland without a king hath enjoyed more peace for this last century than any of the monarchical governments in Europe. Antiquity favors the same remark; for the quiet and rural lives of the first patriarchs hath a happy something in them, which vanishes away when we come to the history of Jewish royalty.

Government by kings was first introduced into the world by the Heathens, from whom the children of Israel copied the custom. It was the most prosperous invention the Devil ever set on foot for the promotion of idolatry. The Heathens paid divine honors to their deceased kings, and the Christian world hath improved on the plan, by doing the same to their living ones. How impious is the title of sacred majesty applied to a worm, who in the midst of his splendor is crumbling into dust!

As the exalting one man so greatly above the rest cannot be justified on the equal rights of nature, so neither can it be defended on the authority of scripture; for the will of the Almighty, as declared by Gideon and the prophet Samuel, expressly disapproves of government by kings. All anti-monarchical parts of scripture have been very smoothly glossed over in monarchical governments, but they undoubtedly merit the attention of countries which have their governments yet to form. "Render unto Caesar the things which are Caesar's" is the scripture doctrine of courts, yet it is no support of monarchical government, for the Jews at that time were without a king, and in a state of vassalage to the Romans.

Now three thousand years passed away from the Mosaic account of the creation, till the Jews under a national delusion requested a king. Till then their form of government (except in extraordinary cases, where the Almighty interposed) was a kind of republic administered by a judge and the elders of the tribes. Kings they had none, and it was held sinful to acknowledge any being under that title but the Lord of Hosts. And when a man seriously reflects on the idolatrous homage which is paid to the persons of kings, he need not wonder that the Almighty, ever jealous of his honor, should disapprove of a form of government which so impiously invades the prerogative of heaven.

Excerpt from *Common Sense* by Thomas Paine

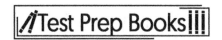

39. According to the passage, what role does avarice, or greed, play in wealth and poverty?
    a. Avarice makes a man poor.
    b. Avarice is the consequence of wealth.
    c. Avarice prevents a man from being poor, but makes him too fearful to be wealthy.
    d. Avarice is what drives a person to be wealthy

40. Of these distinctions, which does the author believe to be beyond natural or religious reason?
    a. Good and bad
    b. Male and female
    c. Human and animal
    d. Kings and subjects

41. According to the passage, what are the Heathens responsible for?
    a. Government by kings
    b. Quiet and rural lives of patriarchs
    c. Paying divine honors to their living kings
    d. Equal rights of nature

42. Which of the following best states Paine's rationale for the denouncement of monarchy?
    a. It is against the laws of nature.
    b. It is against the equal rights of nature and is denounced in scripture.
    c. Despite scripture, a monarchical government is unlawful.
    d. Neither the law nor scripture denounce monarchy.

43. Based on the passage, what is the best definition of the word *idolatrous*?
    a. Worshipping kings
    b. Being deceitful
    c. Sinfulness
    d. Engaging in illegal activities

Questions 44–48 are based on the following passage:

When I got on the coach the driver had not taken his seat, and I saw him talking with the landlady. They were evidently talking of me, for every now and then they looked at me. Some of the people who were sitting on the bench outside the door came and listened, and then looked at me, most of them pityingly. I could hear a lot of words often repeated, queer words, for there were many nationalities in the crowd; so I quietly got my polyglot dictionary from my bag and looked them out. I must say they weren't cheering to me, for amongst them were "Ordog"—Satan, "pokol"—hell, "stregoica"—witch, "vrolok" and "vlkoslak"—both of which mean the same thing, one being Slovak and the other Servian for something that is either were-wolf or vampire.

When we started, the crowd round the inn door, which had by this time swelled to a considerable size, all made the sign of the cross and pointed two fingers towards me. With some difficulty I got a fellow-passenger to tell me what they meant; he wouldn't answer at first, but on learning that I was English, he explained that it was a charm or guard against the evil eye. This was not very pleasant for me, just starting for an unknown place to meet an unknown man; but everyone seemed so kind-hearted, and so sorrowful, and so sympathetic that I couldn't help but be touched. I shall never forget the last glimpse which I had of the inn-yard and its crowd of picturesque figures, all crossing themselves, as they stood round the wide archway, with its background of rich foliage of oleander and orange trees in green tubs clustered in the

279

centre of the yard. Then our driver cracked his big whip over his four small horses, which ran abreast, and we set off on our journey.

I soon lost sight and recollection of ghostly fears in the beauty of the scene as we drove along, although had I known the language, or rather languages, which my fellow-passengers were speaking, I might not have been able to throw them off so easily. Before us lay a green sloping land full of forests and woods, with here and there steep hills, crowned with clumps of trees or with farmhouses, the blank gable end to the road. There was everywhere a bewildering mass of fruit blossoms—apple, plum, pear, cherry; and as we drove by, I could see the green grass under the trees spangled with the fallen petals. In and out amongst these green hills of what they call here the "Mittel Land" ran the road, losing itself as it swept round the grassy curve, or was shut out by the straggling ends of pine woods, which here and there ran down the hillsides like tongues of flame. The road was rugged, but still we seemed to fly over it with a feverish haste. I couldn't understand then what the haste meant, but the driver was evidently bent on losing no time in reaching Borgo Prund.

44. What type of narrator is found in this passage?
    a. First person
    b. Second person
    c. Third-person limited
    d. Third-person omniscient

45. Which of the following is true of the traveler?
    a. He wishes the driver would go faster.
    b. He's returning to the country of his birth.
    c. He has some familiarity with the local customs.
    d. He doesn't understand all of the languages being used.

46. How does the traveler's mood change between the second and third paragraphs?
    a. From relaxed to rushed
    b. From fearful to charmed
    c. From confused to enlightened
    d. From comfortable to exhausted

47. Who is the traveler going to meet?
    a. A kind landlady
    b. A distant relative
    c. A friendly villager
    d. A complete stranger

48. Based on the details in this passage, what can readers probably expect to happen in the story?
    a. The traveler will become a farmer.
    b. The traveler will arrive late at his destination.
    c. The traveler will soon encounter danger or evil.
    d. The traveler will have a pleasant journey and make many new friends.

Questions 49–53 are based on the following passage:

I heartily accept the motto, "That government is best which governs least"; and I should like to see it acted up to more rapidly and systematically. Carried out, it finally amounts to this, which also I believe—"That government is best which governs not at all"; and when men are prepared for it, that will be the kind of government which they will have. Government is at best but an expedient; but most governments are

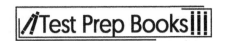

usually, and all governments are sometimes, inexpedient. The objections which have been brought against a standing army, and they are many and weighty, and deserve to prevail, may also at last be brought against a standing government. The standing army is only an arm of the standing government. The government itself, which is only the mode which the people have chosen to execute their will, is equally liable to be abused and perverted before the people can act through it. Witness the present Mexican war, the work of comparatively a few individuals using the standing government as their tool; for, in the outset, the people would not have consented to this measure.

This American government—what is it but a tradition, though a recent one, endeavoring to transmit itself unimpaired to posterity, but each instant losing some of its integrity? It has not the vitality and force of a single living man; for a single man can bend it to his will. It is a sort of wooden gun to the people themselves. But it is not the less necessary for this; for the people must have some complicated machinery or other, and hear its din, to satisfy that idea of government which they have. Governments show thus how successfully men can be imposed on, even impose on themselves, for their own advantage. It is excellent, we must all allow. Yet this government never of itself furthered any enterprise, but by the alacrity with which it got out of its way. It does not keep the country free. It does not settle the West. It does not educate. The character inherent in the American people has done all that has been accomplished; and it would have done somewhat more, if the government had not sometimes got in its way. For government is an expedient by which men would fain succeed in letting one another alone; and, as has been said, when it is most expedient, the governed are most let alone by it. Trade and commerce, if they were not made of india-rubber, would never manage to bounce over the obstacles which legislators are continually putting in their way; and, if one were to judge these men wholly by the effects of their actions and not partly by their intentions, they would deserve to be classed and punished with those mischievous persons who put obstructions on the railroads.

But, to speak practically and as a citizen, unlike those who call themselves no-government men, I ask for, not at once no government, but at once a better government. Let every man make known what kind of government would command his respect, and that will be one step toward obtaining it.

Excerpt from *Civil Disobedience*, by Henry David Thoreau

49. Which phrase best encapsulates Thoreau's use of the term *expedient* in the first paragraph?
    a. A dead end
    b. A state of order
    c. A means to an end
    d. Rushed construction

50. Which best describes Thoreau's view on the Mexican War?
    a. Government is inherently corrupt because it must wage war.
    b. Government can easily be manipulated by a few individuals for their own agenda.
    c. Government is a tool for the people, but it can also act against their interest.
    d. The Mexican War was a necessary action, but not all the people believed this.

51. What is Thoreau's purpose for writing?
    a. His goal is to illustrate how the government can function if ideals are maintained.
    b. He wants to prove that true democracy is the best government, but it can be corrupted easily.
    c. Thoreau reflects on the stages of government abuses.
    d. He is seeking to prove that the government is easily corruptible and inherently restrictive of individual freedoms that can simultaneously affect the whole state.

281

52. Which example best supports Thoreau's argument?
    a. A vote carries in the Senate to create a new road tax.
    b. The president vetoes a new agriculture bill.
    c. Prohibition is passed to outlaw alcohol.
    d. Trade is opened between the United States and Iceland.

53. Which best summarizes this section from the following passage:
    This American government—what is it but a tradition, though a recent one, endeavoring to transmit itself unimpaired to posterity, but each instant losing some of its integrity? It has not the vitality and force of a single living man; for a single man can bend it to his will. It is a sort of wooden gun to the people themselves.
    a. The government may be instituted to ensure the protections of freedoms, but this is weakened by the fact that it is easily manipulated by individuals.
    b. Unlike an individual, the government is uncaring.
    c. Unlike an individual, the government has no will, making it more prone to be used as a weapon against the people.
    d. American government is modeled after other traditions but actually has greater potential to be used to control people.

Questions 54–58 are based on the following passage:

When Jane and Elizabeth were alone, the former, who had been cautious in her praise of Mr. Bingley before, expressed to her sister how very much she admired him.

"He is just what a young man ought to be," said she, "sensible, good-humoured, lively; and I never saw such happy manners! so much ease, with such perfect good breeding!"

"He is also handsome," replied Elizabeth, "which a young man ought likewise to be if he possibly can. His character is thereby complete."

"I was very much flattered by his asking me to dance a second time. I did not expect such a compliment."

"Did not you? I did for you. But that is one great difference between us. Compliments always take you by surprise, and me never. What could be more natural than his asking you again? He could not help seeing that you were about five times as pretty as every other woman in the room. No thanks to his gallantry for that. Well, he certainly is very agreeable, and I give you leave to like him. You have liked many a stupider person."

"Dear Lizzy!"

"Oh, you are a great deal too apt, you know, to like people in general. You never see a fault in anybody. All the world are good and agreeable in your eyes. I never heard you speak ill of a human being in my life."

An excerpt from Pride and Prejudice *by Jane Austen*

54. What is the relationship between Jane and Elizabeth?
    a. They are sisters.
    b. They are cousins.
    c. They are friends.
    d. They are enemies.

55. What does Elizabeth think of Jane?
    a. That Jane is too interested in male attention
    b. That Jane only sees the best in people
    c. That Jane is unworthy of a man like Mr. Bingley
    d. That Jane is too beautiful for her suitor

56. What does Elizabeth believes completes Mr. Bingley's character?
    a. His personality
    b. His money
    c. His looks
    d. His intelligence

57. It can be inferred from the text that:
    a. Elizabeth has taken over a motherly role for Jane.
    b. Both Elizabeth and Jane are uninterested in finding suitors.
    c. Jane is tired of Elizabeth pestering her about relationships.
    d. Elizabeth cares deeply for Jane and how her life turns out.

58. Based on this dialogue, how do Jane and Elizabeth differ?
    a. Elizabeth is more concerned with romance than Jane is.
    b. Elizabeth is more free-spirited than Jane is.
    c. Elizabeth is more judgmental and critical than Jane is.
    d. Elizabeth is less interested in participating in social events than Jane is.

Math

1. $4\frac{1}{3} + 3\frac{3}{4} =$
    a. $6\frac{5}{12}$
    b. $8\frac{1}{12}$
    c. $8\frac{2}{3}$
    d. $7\frac{7}{12}$

2. Five of six numbers have a sum of 25. The average of all six numbers is 6. What is the sixth number?
    a. 8
    b. 10
    c. 11
    d. 12

3. 4.67 miles is equivalent to how many kilometers to three significant digits? Use the conversion 1 mi = 1.609 km.
    a. 7.514 km
    b. 7.51 km
    c. 2.90 km
    d. 2.902 km

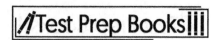

4. If $\frac{5}{2} \div \frac{1}{3} = n$, then n is between:
    a.   5 and 7
    b.   7 and 9
    c.   9 and 11
    d.   3 and 5

5. A closet is filled with red, blue, and green shirts. If $\frac{1}{3}$ of the shirts are green and $\frac{2}{5}$ are red, what fraction of the shirts are blue?
    a. $\frac{4}{15}$
    b. $\frac{1}{5}$
    c. $\frac{7}{15}$
    d. $\frac{1}{2}$

6. What is the sum of $\frac{1}{3}$ and $\frac{2}{5}$?
    a. $\frac{3}{8}$
    b. $\frac{11}{15}$
    c. $\frac{11}{30}$
    d. $\frac{4}{5}$

7. Add and express in reduced form: $\frac{5}{12} + \frac{4}{9}$
    a. $\frac{9}{17}$
    b. $\frac{1}{3}$
    c. $\frac{31}{36}$
    d. $\frac{3}{5}$

8. Divide and reduce: $\frac{4}{13} \div \frac{27}{169}$
    a. $\frac{52}{27}$
    b. $\frac{51}{27}$
    c. $\frac{52}{29}$
    d. $\frac{51}{29}$

9. Express $\frac{54}{15}$ as a mixed number, reduced to lowest terms.

    a. $3\frac{3}{5}$

    b. $3\frac{1}{15}$

    c. $3\frac{3}{54}$

    d. $3\frac{1}{54}$

10. Which of the following is equivalent to the value of the digit 3 in the number 792.134?
    a. 3×10
    b. 3×100
    c. $\frac{3}{10}$
    d. $\frac{3}{100}$

11. Add $101,694 + 623$.
    a. 103,317
    b. 102,317
    c. 102,417
    d. 102,427

12. Add and express in reduced form $\frac{7}{12} + \frac{5}{9}$.

    a. $1\frac{5}{36}$

    b. $\frac{13}{9}$

    c. $\frac{41}{36}$

    d. $1\frac{4}{9}$

13. Subtract $7,236 - 978$.
    a. 6,268
    b. 5,258
    c. 6,358
    d. 6,258

14. A construction company is building a new housing development with the property of each house measuring 30 feet wide. If the length of the street is zoned off at 345 feet, how many houses can be built on the street?
    a. 11 houses
    b. 115 houses
    c. 11.5 houses
    d. 12 houses

15. Subtract $653.4 - 59.38$.
    a. 595.92
    b. 594.11
    c. 594.02
    d. 593.92

16. What is the product of two irrational numbers?
    a. Irrational
    b. Rational
    c. Irrational or rational
    d. Complex and imaginary

17. If $-3(x + 4) = x + 8$, what is the value of x?
    a. $x = 4$
    b. $x = 2$
    c. $x = 5$
    d. $x = -5$

18. If $4x - 3 = 5$, what is the value of x?
    a. 1
    b. 2
    c. 3
    d. 4

19. A grocery store is selling individual bottles of water, and each bottle contains 750 milliliters of water. If a customer purchases 12 bottles, what conversion will correctly determine how many liters the customer will take home?
    a. 100 milliliters equals 1 liter
    b. 1,000 milliliters equals 1 liter
    c. 1,000 liters equals 1 milliliter
    d. 10 liters equals 1 milliliter

20. There are $4x + 1$ treats in each party favor bag. If a total of $60x + 15$ treats are distributed, how many bags are given out?
    a. 15
    b. 16
    c. 20
    d. 22

21. Apples cost $2 each, while bananas cost $3 each. Maria purchased a total of 10 pieces of fruit and spent $22. How many apples did she buy?
    a. 5
    b. 6
    c. 7
    d. 8

22. A circle has a radius of 6 inches. What is the circumference of the circle?
    a. 36π inches
    b. 12π inches
    c. 36 inches
    d. 12 inches

23. What is the value of b in this equation?

$$2b + 11 = 8b - 13$$

   a. 10
   b. 8
   c. 4
   d. -3

24. A cube-shaped box has a side length of 6 inches. It can be filled with peanut butter at a capacity of 75%. How much peanut butter, in cubic inches, can fit inside the box?
   a. 162
   b. 216
   c. 54
   d. 154

25. A truck weighs 3.7 tons. How many pounds does the truck weigh?
   a. 2,100 pounds
   b. 3,700 pounds
   c. 4,700 pounds
   d. 7,400 pounds

26. If a student scored 86, 92, 91, 90, 97, and 100 on six tests, what is their average score? Round your answer to the nearest tenth.
   a. 92.7
   b. 93
   c. 91.5
   d. 90

27. The ratio of dogs to cats to birds at a pet store is 4:5:3. If there are a total of 168 pets (dogs, cats, and birds only), how many of them are birds?
   a. 30
   b. 56
   c. 70
   d. 42

28. Shari wants to paint a border around the walls in the room. Her room is rectangular, with a length of 14 ft and a width of 9.5 ft. How many feet long is the border in total?
   a. 23.5 ft
   b. 47 ft
   c. 5.5 ft
   d. 28 ft

29. The surface area of a cube is 384 cubic inches. What is the length of a single side of the cube?
   a. 4 in
   b. 36 in
   c. 8 in
   d. 16 in

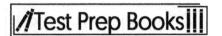

30. Convert 5.625 kg to grams.
    a. 56.25 g
    b. 562.5 g
    c. 0.005625 g
    d. 5,625 g

31. Which of the following is an equivalent measurement for 1.3 cm?
    a. 0.13 m
    b. 0.013 m
    c. 0.13 mm
    d. 0.013 mm

32. Mo needs to buy enough material to cover the walls around the stage for a theater performance. If he needs 79 feet of wall covering, what is the minimum number of yards of material he should purchase if the material is sold only by whole yards?
    a. 23 yards
    b. 25 yards
    c. 26 yards
    d. 27 yards

33. A bag contains 4 red marbles, 8 blue marbles, 7 yellow marbles, and 2 green marbles. If a student selects one marble, what is the probability that it will be either blue or yellow?
    a. $\frac{4}{7}$
    b. $\frac{8}{21}$
    c. $\frac{5}{7}$
    d. $\frac{16}{21}$

34. Convert 1500 hours into a 12-hour clock time.
    a. 3:00 p.m.
    b. 9:00 a.m.
    c. 3:00 a.m.
    d. 9:00 p.m.

35. What is the circumference of a circle with a diameter of 6 cm? Round your answer to the nearest tenth of a centimeter.
    a. 27.7 cm
    b. 18.8 cm
    c. 37.7 cm
    d. 19.1 cm

36. What time is 10:00 a.m. in military (24-hour clock) time?
    a. 0100 hours
    b. 1000 hours
    c. 1200 hours
    d. 0200 hours

37. 1 kilometer is how many centimeters?
    a. 100 cm
    b. 1,000 cm
    c. 10,000 cm
    d. 100,000 cm

38. Find the range of the following data values: 45, 21, 55, 89, 67, 33, 20, 21.
    a. 21
    b. 69
    c. 43.875
    d. 39

39. A piggy bank contains 12 dollars' worth of nickels. A nickel weighs 5 grams, and the empty piggy bank weighs 1,050 grams. What is the total weight of the full piggy bank?
    a. 1,110 grams
    b. 1,200 grams
    c. 2,250 grams
    d. 2,200 grams

40. Last year, the New York City area received approximately $27\frac{3}{4}$ inches of snow. The Denver area received approximately three times as much snow as New York City. How much snow fell in Denver?
    a. 60 inches
    b. $27\frac{1}{4}$ inches
    c. $9\frac{1}{4}$ inches
    d. $83\frac{1}{4}$ inches

41. 85% of a high school graduating class of 1640 students went to college. How many students did not go to college?
    a. 1,394
    b. 246
    c. 1,929
    d. 546

42. Convert 4.5 kL to mL.
    a. 0.00000045
    b. 4,500,000
    c. 4,500
    d. 450,000

43. Solve the equation $(x - 8)^2 = 121$ for x.
    a. -3
    b. -19
    c. 11
    d. -11

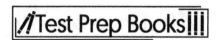

44. Simplify the following expression: $14a^2b^3c \div 21a^{-1}b^2c^3$.
    a. $\frac{2ab}{3c^2}$

    b. $\frac{2a^3}{3bc^2}$

    c. $\frac{2a^3b}{3c^2}$

    d. $\frac{2a^3bc^2}{3}$

45. Compute the median of the following data set: 9, 5, 1, 1, 3, 4, 7, 8, 10, 6.
    a. 5.4
    b. 1
    c. 5.5
    d. 6

Science

1. The process of breaking down large molecules into smaller molecules to provide energy is known as which of the following?
    a. Metabolism
    b. Bioenergetics
    c. Anabolism
    d. Catabolism

2. Which blood component is chiefly responsible for clotting?
    a. Platelets
    b. Red blood cells
    c. Antigens
    d. Plasma cells

3. Which is the first event to happen in a primary immune response?
    a. Macrophages ingest pathogens and present their antigens.
    b. Neutrophils aggregate and act as cytotoxic, nonspecific killers of pathogens.
    c. B lymphocytes make pathogen-specific antibodies.
    d. Helper T cells secrete interleukins to activate pathogen-fighting cells.

4. Where does sperm maturation take place in the male reproductive system?
    a. Seminal vesicles
    b. Prostate gland
    c. Epididymis
    d. Vas deferens

5. What molecule serves as the hereditary material for prokaryotic and eukaryotic cells?
    a. Proteins
    b. Carbohydrates
    c. Lipids
    d. DNA

6. What is the balance of the following chemical equation?

$$\_\,F_2 + \_\,H_2O \rightarrow \_\,HF + \_\,O_2$$

    a. 2:4:2:1
    b. 4:2:8:2
    c. 2:2:4:1
    d. 1:1:2:1

7. What makes bone resistant to shattering?
    a. The calcium salts deposited in the bone
    b. The collagen fibers
    c. The bone marrow and network of blood vessels
    d. The intricate balance of minerals and collagen fibers

8. How do organisms maintain homeostasis?
    a. They increase their body temperature, blood pH, and fluid balance.
    b. They undergo biochemical processes and absorb energy to increase entropy.
    c. They undergo biochemical processes to maintain the order of their external environment.
    d. They use free energy and matter via biochemical processes to work against entropy.

9. What is the purpose of a catalyst?
    a. To increase a reaction's rate by increasing the activation energy
    b. To increase a reaction's rate by increasing the temperature
    c. To increase a reaction's rate by decreasing the activation energy
    d. To increase a reaction's rate by decreasing the temperature

10. Motivational interviewing (MI) is a tool used by nurses to help motivate patients to change their behavior and make better choices that will improve their health. Which of the following steps of motivational interviewing involves person-centered reflective listening?
    a. Evoking the patient's motivation
    b. Guiding or focus
    c. Engaging or empathy
    d. Planning or promotion of independence

11. Which of the following is a core skill in motivational interviewing that is used in the acronym OARS?
    a. Reflections
    b. Outreach
    c. Activation
    d. Response

12. Nurses use contracting, a strategy that involves formally defining the roles of family members and health professionals. Several phases and activities are involved in contracting. The phase that involves the division of responsibilities, setting of time limits, and implementation of a plan is called the:
    a. Beginning or orientation phase
    b. Working phase
    c. Post-visit phase
    d. Termination phase

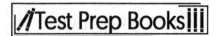
13. Which of the following is the body cavity that contains the urinary bladder, urethra, and ureters?
    a. The thoracic cavity
    b. The pelvic cavity
    c. The abdominal cavity
    d. The spinal cavity

14. Which of the following best defines the term *amphoteric*?
    a. A substance that conducts electricity due to ionization when dissolved in a solvent
    b. A substance that can act as an acid or a base depending on the properties of the solute
    c. A substance that, according to the Brønsted-Lowry Acid-Base Theory, is a proton-donor
    d. A substance that donates its proton and forms its conjugate base in a neutralization reaction

15. Which of the following touch receptors respond to light touch and slower vibrations?
    a. Merkel's discs
    b. Pacinian corpuscles
    c. Meissner's corpuscles
    d. Ruffini endings

16. Which of the following are responsible for the exchange of nutrients, hormones, oxygen, fluids, and electrolytes between blood and the interstitial fluid of body tissues?
    a. Arterioles
    b. Venules
    c. Capillaries
    d. Hemoglobin

17. Which of the following correctly identifies a difference between the primary and secondary immune responses?
    a. In the secondary response, macrophages migrate to the lymph nodes to present the foreign microorganism to helper T lymphocytes.
    b. The humoral immunity that characterizes the primary response is coordinated by T lymphocytes.
    c. The primary response is quicker and more powerful than the secondary response.
    d. Suppressor T cells activate in the secondary response to prevent an overactive immune response.

18. Nurses use several approaches to health risk reduction, which include:
    a. Empowerment and contracting with families
    b. Contracting with families and family policy
    c. Home visits and telehomecare
    d. Care for vulnerable populations and home visits

19. Home visits are an approach that nurses use to minimize health risks in families. Which of the following choices best represents the correct ordering of phases that nurses employ during a home visit process?
    a. Initiation phase, in-home phase, pre-visit phase, termination phase, post-visit phase
    b. Pre-visit phase, initiation phase, in-home phase, termination phase, post-visit phase
    c. Initiation phase, pre-visit phase, in-home phase, termination phase, post-visit phase
    d. Initiation phase, pre-visit phase, in-home phase, post-visit phase, termination phase

20. Routine immunization of adolescents continues to be successful in the prevention of diseases. However, there are several challenges to providing successful immunizations. Since the introduction of the National Childhood Vaccine Injury Act in 1986, providers have counseled patients and parents regarding the risks and benefits of an immunizing agent. The Vaccine Injury Act has most likely reduced which of the following barriers to adolescent immunization?

    a. Vaccine cost
    b. Changes in vaccine schedules
    c. Vaccine shortages
    d. Vaccine refusal

21. What are the functions of the hypothalamus?

       I. Regulate body temperature.
       II. Send stimulatory and inhibitory instructions to the pituitary gland.
       III. Receive sensory information from the brain.

    a. I and II
    b. I and III
    c. II and III
    d. I, II, and III

22. Which of the following statements is accurate regarding the mechanism of food absorption in the stomach?

    a. Polar substances pass through the apical and basolateral membranes passively.
    b. Most nutrients move through the active transport proteins along the apical and basolateral membranes.
    c. Nutrients initially move from the lumen of the intestine through the active transport proteins of the basolateral membrane.
    d. Nonpolar nutrients travel through the basolateral membrane and then through the enterocyte.

23. What is an adaptation?

    a. The original traits found in a common ancestor
    b. Changes that occur in the environment
    c. When one species begins behaving like another species
    d. An inherited characteristic that enhances survival and reproduction

24. If a person with AB blood and a person with O blood have children, what is the probability that their children will have the same phenotype as either parent?

    a. 0%
    b. 25%
    c. 50%
    d. 75%

25. What are the building blocks of DNA called?

    a. Helices
    b. Proteins
    c. Genes
    d. Nucleotides

26. Which element's atoms have the greatest number of electrons?

    a. Hydrogen
    b. Iron
    c. Copper
    d. Iodine

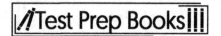

27. Which of the following areas of the body has the highest density of sweat glands?
    a. Upper back
    b. Arms
    c. Palms/soles of the feet
    d. Head

28. With which genotype would the recessive phenotype appear, if the dominant allele is marked with A and the recessive allele is marked with a?
    a. AA
    b. aa
    c. Aa
    d. aA

29. What is the name for the structural and functional units located in the cortex of the kidney that create and transport urine?
    a. Glomerulus
    b. Nephrons
    c. Loops of Henle
    d. Distal tubules

30. The muscular tube that connects the outer surface to the cervix in a woman's birth canal is referred to as which of the following?
    a. The uterus
    b. The cervix
    c. The vagina
    d. The ovaries

31. Which of the following hormones is primarily responsible for regulating metabolism?
    a. Insulin
    b. Testosterone
    c. Adrenaline
    d. Thyroid hormone

32. Which of the following is the gland that helps regulate calcium levels?
    a. Osteoid gland
    b. Pineal gland
    c. Parathyroid glands
    d. Thymus gland

33. What is the name for the sac-shaped structures that facilitate the exchanging of carbon dioxide and oxygen?
    a. Kidneys
    b. Medulla oblongata
    c. Alveoli
    d. Bronchioles

34. Which of the following organs functions as both an endocrine and exocrine gland?
    a. The kidney
    b. The spleen
    c. The pancreas
    d. The stomach

35. Which of the following systems does NOT include a transportation system throughout the body?
    a. Cardiovascular system
    b. Endocrine system
    c. Immune system
    d. Nervous system

36. Which of the following structures receives neurotransmitters that are transmitted across synapses?
    a. Axon
    b. Dendrites
    c. Neuroglia
    d. Node of Ranvier

37. A white blood cell targets and kills parasites attached to tissue via phagocytosis and antihistamine production. Which of the following types of white blood cells is this?
    a. Basophils
    b. Monocytes
    c. Neutrophils
    d. Eosinophils

38. Which of the following describes the correct path of light as it enters a human eye?
    a. Lens, pupil, choroid, retina, optic nerve
    b. Cornea, pupil, lens, vitreous humor, retina
    c. Retina, pupil, lens, aqueous body, optic disk
    d. Lens, cornea, pupil, retina, choroid

39. Which statement about the ear is incorrect?
    a. The organ of Corti converts sound into neural activity.
    b. The middle ear consists of three bones.
    c. The tympanic membrane separates the outer ear from the middle ear.
    d. The cochlea is a component of the middle ear.

40. What structure is referred to as the cubital region?
    a. The foot
    b. The wrist
    c. The elbow
    d. The knee

41. The gallbladder resides in which cavity of the body?
    a. Thoracic
    b. Abdominal
    c. Pelvic
    d. Cranial

42. A tissue sample is observed as a flat, single layer of cells. Which would best describe these cells?
    a. Simple squamous cells
    b. Transitional epithelial cells
    c. Simple columnar cells
    d. Stratified cuboidal cells

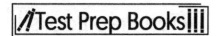

43. A small blood vessel found in the liver has large pores that allow proteins and blood cells to move in and out of the vessel. What type of blood vessel is this?
    a. Continuous capillary
    b. Fenestrated capillary
    c. Sinusoidal capillary
    d. Arteriole

44. Which of the following is the phase when a heart contracts and pushes blood out?
    a. Systole
    b. Cardiac cycle
    c. Diastole
    d. Systemic circulation

45. A person smells a foul odor. What portion of their brain contains the structure that detects the odor?
    a. Cerebrum
    b. Cerebellum
    c. Brain stem
    d. Occipital lobe

46. Which of the following portions of a nephron are permeable to water?
    I. Collecting duct
    II. Ascending limb
    III. Descending limb
    IV. Ureter

    a. I, II, and III
    b. II and III
    c. I and III
    d. I only

47. An enzymatic reaction requires free energy to proceed. Which term best describes this reaction?
    a. Exergonic
    b. Combustion
    c. Endergonic
    d. Redox

48. Which of the following is necessary for swallowing food?
    a. Amylase
    b. Peristalsis
    c. Villi
    d. Trachea

49. Which of the following are functions of a myelin sheath?
    I. Insulates an axon
    II. Structural support for axon
    III. Increases permeability of ions

    a. I only
    b. I and II
    c. III only
    d. I, II, and III

50. Which structure is not a component of the lymphatic system?
    a. Thymus
    b. Spleen
    c. Tonsils
    d. Septal area

51. Where does the process of external respiration occur?
    a. Mitochondria
    b. Within cells
    c. Alveoli
    d. Bronchi

52. Which sensory receptors are located in the skin?
    I. Mechanoreceptors
    II. Photoreceptors
    III. Thermoreceptors
    IV. Chemoreceptors

    a. I only
    b. I and IV
    c. I and III
    d. I, II, III, and IV

53. Which term describes the sensation of balance and spatial orientation?
    a. Kinesthetic sense
    b. Vestibular sense
    c. Somatosensation
    d. Perception

54. Which of the following leukocytes matures in the thymus?
    a. Neutrophils
    b. Suppressor T cells
    c. Memory B cells
    d. Basophils

55. A patient is at a hospital, and they are told that their beta cells are not functioning properly. Which hormone would be affected by malfunctioning beta cells?
    a. Insulin
    b. Glucagon
    c. Antidiuretic hormone
    d. Growth hormone

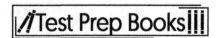

56. Diffusion and osmosis are examples of what type of transport mechanism?
    a.   Active
    b.   Passive
    c.   Extracellular
    d.   Intracellular

57. Which organelle is responsible for generating energy for the cell and is referred to as the powerhouse of the cell?
    a.   Mitochondria
    b.   Nucleus
    c.   Ribosomes
    d.   Cell wall

58. A color-blind male and a carrier female have three children. What is the probability that they are all color blind?
    a. $\frac{1}{4}$

    b. $\frac{1}{8}$

    c. $\frac{1}{16}$

    d. $\frac{1}{32}$

59. What shape does a water molecule form?
    a.   C-shape
    b.   S-shape
    c.   V-shape
    d.   T-shape

60. Which type of biological molecule stores information?
    a.   Carbohydrates
    b.   Nucleic acids
    c.   Proteins
    d.   Lipids

36. What are the building blocks of DNA called?
    a.   Helices
    b.   Proteins
    c.   Genes
    d.   Nucleotides

Answer Explanations #2

Verbal

Word Knowledge

1. B: *Gravitas* is dignity or seriousness of manner.

2. B: *Hepatic* means relating to the liver. The prefix *hepa-* relates to the liver.

3. A: *Vehement*, or *ardent*, means showing passionate feelings or being forceful.

4. B: *Intrathecal* means around the spinal cord. Baclofen, for spastic cerebral palsy, may have an intrathecal route of administration.

5. D: *Gerontology* is the study of aging. The prefix *ger-* or *gero-* means old age as in geriatric.

6. D: *Pristine* means clean and new. Something in pristine condition is unused or appears as it did when it was new.

7. A: *Distended* means enlarged or expanded. A *distended* stomach or other organ is bloated or swollen because of internal pressure.

8. C: A *latent* disease is present but not detectable in a symptomatic way. It may be dormant, but it has the potential to become symptomatic in the future with discernable manifestations for the patient.

9. A: *Dyspnea* means difficulty breathing. The prefix *dys-* means dysfunctional or abnormal. The suffix *-pnea* in a medical context refers to respiration and breathing. Sleep apnea is a breathing disorder that can occur during sleep.

10. B: *Acute* illnesses have a sudden or rapid onset. An *acute* illness is the opposite of a *chronic* one, which is a disease that the patient has had for a long time. A sinus infection is an acute illness, while multiple sclerosis is a chronic one.

11. A: *Anuria* is a lack of urine output. Again, the prefixes *a-* or *an-* mean "without" or "not," and *-uria* refers to urine.

12. B: *Viscosity* refers to a fluid's thickness or resistance to flow. A viscous fluid is in contrast to a runny one. For example, honey is more viscous than water.

13. D: *Aberrant* means abnormal. *Overt* means outwardly demonstrative, *grave* means severe or serious, and *radical* means revolutionary or progressive.

14. C: *Renal* means relating to the kidneys. The renal blood vessels serve the kidneys.

15. D: *Triage* means to sort based on problem severity. Patients entering the ER need to be triaged so that they are treated in order of urgency.

16. C: *Indolent* can mean lethargic, lazy, or aversive to activity.

17. D: *Buccal* means relating to the cheek. An example of a medication with a buccal route of administration is nitroglycerine in the treatment of angina.

18. C: *Rampant* means unrestrained. *Stagnant* means still or unchanging, like a body of water with no active flow.

19. D: Something that is ominous is threatening. Choices *B* and *C*, promising and auspicious, are antonyms of ominous. Unequivocal refers to something that is unambiguous or absolutely certain.

20. C: *Peptic* means relating to digestion. *Peptic* comes from *pepsin,* which is a stomach enzyme that helps degrade proteins.

21. C: *Retort* is a verb that means "to answer back," usually in a sharp manner. This term embodies the idea of a response, emphasized by the "re-" prefix meaning "back, again." While a *retort* can be used in a conversation or as a jest, neither term embodies the idea of addressing someone again. *Counter*, however, means to respond in opposition when used as a verb.

22. A: *Subliminal* and *subconscious* share the Latin prefix "sub-," meaning under or below, or more commonly used when talking about messages the sender doesn't want the receiver to consciously take note of. The word *subliminal* means beneath the consciousness. Thus, *subconscious* is the perfect match.

23. C: Although *incite* usually has negative connotations, leaders can incite their followers to benevolent actions as well. In both cases, people rally to support a cause.

24. B: *Sustain* is to revitalize, or to give strength. *Strength* would be a good choice, but strength alone does not describe the re-strengthening that sustain embodies. The best choice is *invigorate*, which is a verb like sustain, meaning to strengthen. This makes invigorate the better choice. *Expedite* is unrelated. While *embolden* means to give someone courage, which is a form of strength, invigorate and sustain speak more toward physical circumstances.

25. A: *Mitigate* refers to easing tension or making something less severe. *Focus, fiery,* and *conspire* do not relate. *Alleviate* is synonymous, meaning to make less severe. Note the ending -ate, which also indicates function. Both terms reflect the function of easing difficult circumstances.

26. C: *Abstain* means to refrain from something. For example, someone who chooses to abstain from alcohol does not drink alcohol.

27. A: *Venerate* means respect. Someone who is venerated is respected and revered.

28. B: Ringworm is a type of mycosis. The prefix *myco-* means something related to fungus.

Reading Comprehension

29. C: Choice *A* is incorrect because the introduction does not contain an impartial definition, but rather, an opinion. Choice *B* is incorrect. There is no puzzling phenomenon given, as the author doesn't mention any peculiar cause or effect that is in question regarding poetry. Choice *D* does contain another's viewpoint at the beginning of the passage; however, to say that the author has no stake in this argument is incorrect because the author uses personal experiences to build their case.

30. B: Choice *B* accurately describes the author's argument in the text: that poetry is not irrelevant. While the author does praise, and even value, Buddy Wakefield as a poet, the author never heralds him as a genius. Eliminate Choice *A*, as it is an exaggeration. Not only is Choice *C* an exaggerated statement, but the author never mentions spoken word poetry in the text. Choice *D* is incorrect because this statement contradicts the writer's argument.

31. D: *Exiguously* means not occurring often, or occurring rarely, so Choice *D* would least change the meaning of the sentence. Choice *A*, *indolently*, means unhurriedly, or slow, and does not fit the context of the sentence. Choice *B*,

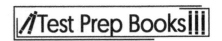

inaudibly, means quietly or silently. Choice *C, interminably*, means endlessly, or all the time, and is the opposite of the word *exiguously*.

32. D: A student's insistence that psychoanalysis is a subset of modern psychology is the most analogous option. The author of the passage tries to insist that performance poetry is a subset of modern poetry, and therefore, tries to prove that modern poetry is not "dying," but thriving on social media for the masses. Choice *A* is incorrect, as the author is not refusing any kind of validation. Choice *B* is incorrect; the author's insistence is that poetry will not lose popularity. Choice *C* mimics the topic but compares two different genres, making it incorrect as the author makes no comparison in this passage.

33. B: The author's purpose is to disprove Gioia's article, which claims that poetry is a dying art form that only survives in academic settings. In order to prove this argument, the author educates the reader about new developments in poetry, Choice *A*, and describes the brilliance of a specific modern poet, Choice *C*, but these serve as examples of a growing poetry trend that counters Gioia's argument. Choice *D* is incorrect because it contradicts the author's argument.

34. A: The word *patronage* most nearly means *auspices* which means protection or support. Choice *B, aberration*, means deformity and does not make sense within the context of the sentence. Choice *C, acerbic*, means bitter and also does not make sense in the sentence. Choice *D, adulation*, is a positive word meaning praise, and thus does not fit with the word *condescending* in the sentence.

35. D: *Working man* is most closely aligned with Choice *D, bourgeois*. In the context of the speech, the word *bourgeois* means working or middle class. Choice *A, athlete*, does suggest someone who works hard, but it does not make sense in this context. Choice *B, viscount*, is a European title used to describe a specific degree of nobility. Choice *C, entrepreneur*, is a person who operates their own business.

36. C: In the context of the speech, the term *working man* most closely correlates with Choice *C*. Choice *A* is not mentioned in the passage and is off-topic. Choice *B* may be true in some cases, but it does not reflect the sentiment described for the term *working man* in the passage. Choice *D* is not a definition, and the topics of the *field, factory,* and *screen* are not mentioned in the passage.

37. D: *Enterprise* most closely means *cause*. Choices *A, B,* and *C* are all related to the term *enterprise*. However, Dickens speaks of a cause here, not a *company, courage,* or a *game*. "He will stand by such an enterprise" is a call to stand by a cause to enable the working man to have a certain autonomy over his own economic standing. The very first paragraph ends with the statement that the working man "shall...have a share in the management of an institution which is designed for his benefit."

38. B: Recall from the first paragraph that the speaker is there to "accompany [the audience]... through one of my little Christmas books," making him an author there to entertain the crowd with his own writing. The speech preceding the reading is the passage itself, and, as the tone indicates, it is a serious speech addressing the "working man." Although the passage speaks of employers and employees, the speaker himself is not an employer of the audience, so Choice *A* is incorrect. Choice *C* is also incorrect, as the salutation is not used ironically, but sincerely, as the speech addresses the well-being of the crowd. Choice *D* is incorrect because the speech is not given by a politician, but by a writer.

39. C: In the final sentence of the first paragraph, it is stated that avarice can prevent a man from being necessitously poor, but it also makes him too timorous, or fearful, to be wealthy. Choice *A* is incorrect because avarice prevents a man from being poor. Choice *B* is incorrect because the passage states that oppression, not avarice, is the consequence of wealth. Choice *D* is incorrect because the passage does not state that avarice drives a person's desire to be wealthy.

301

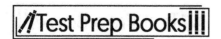

40. D: Paine believes that the distinction that is beyond a natural or religious reason is between king and subjects. Choice *A* is incorrect because he states that the distinction between good and bad is made in heaven. Choice *B* is incorrect because he states that the distinction between male and female is natural. Choice *C* is incorrect because he does not mention anything about the distinction between humans and animals.

41. A: The passage states that the Heathens were the first to introduce government by kings into the world. Choice *B* is incorrect because the quiet lives of patriarchs came before the Heathens introduced this type of government, and Paine puts it in opposition to government by kings. Choice *C* is incorrect because it was Christians, not Heathens, who paid divine honors to living kings. Heathens honored deceased kings. Choice *D* is incorrect because, while equal rights of nature are mentioned in the paragraph, they are not mentioned in relation to the Heathens.

42. B: Paine doesn't say it is against the laws of nature, so Choice *A* is incorrect. He cites parts of scripture that he claims denounce monarchy, so Choices *C* and *D* are incorrect.

43. A: To be *idolatrous* is to worship someone or something other than God, in this case, kings. Choice *B* is incorrect because it is not defined as being deceitful. Choice *C* is incorrect because, while idolatry is considered a sin, it is an example of a sin, not a synonym for it. Choice *D* is incorrect because, while idolatry may have been considered illegal in some cultures, it is not a definition for the term.

44. A: This is a straightforward question that requires readers to know that a first-person narrator speaks from an "I" point of view.

45. D: This can be inferred from the fact that the traveler must refer to his dictionary to understand those around him. Choice *A* isn't a good choice because the traveler seems to wonder why the driver needs to drive so fast. Choice *B* isn't mentioned in the passage and doesn't seem like a good answer choice because he seems wholly unfamiliar with his surroundings. This is why Choice *C* can also be eliminated.

46. B: The answer can be found in the first sentence of the third paragraph, which states, "I soon lost sight and recollection of ghostly fears in the beauty of the scene as we drove along." Also, readers should get a sense of foreboding from the first two paragraphs, where superstitious villagers seem frightened on the traveler's behalf. However, the final paragraph changes to delighted descriptions of the landscape's natural beauty. Choices *A* and *D* can be eliminated because the traveler is anxious, not relaxed or comfortable at the beginning of the passage. Choice *C* can also be eliminated because the traveler doesn't gain any particular insights in the last paragraph, and in fact continues to lament that he cannot understand the speech of those around him.

47. D: The answer to this reading comprehension question can be found in the second paragraph, when the traveler is "just starting for an unknown place to meet an unknown man"—in other words, a complete stranger.

48. C: Answering this prediction question requires readers to understand foreshadowing, or hints that the author gives about what will happen next. There are numerous hints scattered throughout this passage: the villagers' sorrow and sympathy for the traveler, their superstitious actions, the spooky words that the traveler overhears, and the driver's unexplained haste. All of these point to a danger that awaits the protagonist.

49. C: This is a tricky question, but it can be solved through careful context analysis and vocabulary knowledge. One can infer that the use of "expedient," while not necessarily very positive, isn't inherently bad in this context either. Note how in the next line, he says, "but most governments are usually, and all governments are sometimes, inexpedient." This use of "inexpedient" indicates that a government becomes a hindrance rather than a solution; it slows progress rather than helps facilitate progress. Thus, Choice *A* and Choice *D* can be ruled out because they are hindrances or problems and would work better with inexpedient rather than expedient. Choice *B* makes no logical sense. Therefore, Choice *C* is the best description of expedient.

302

50. B: Choice *B* is the most accurate representation of Thoreau's views. Essentially, Thoreau brings to light the fact that the few people in power can twist government and policy for their own needs. Choices *A* and *C* are also correct to a degree, but the answer asks for the best description, which is Choice *B*. While Choice *D* is the only answer that mentions the Mexican War directly, Thoreau clearly thinks the war is unnecessary because the people generally didn't consent to the war.

51. D: Choices *A* and *B* are completely incorrect. Thoreau is not defending the government in any way. His views are set against government. As mentioned in the text, he appreciates little government but favors having no government structure at all. The text is reflective by nature but not reflective on the stages of government abuses as Choice *C* suggests. Choice *D* is the more appropriate answer because of the presence of evidence in the text. Thoreau cites current events and uses them to illustrate the point he's trying to make.

52. C: One of Thoreau's biggest criticisms of government is its capacity to impose on the people's freedoms and liberties, enact rules that the people don't want, and remove power from the individual. None of the scenarios directly impose specific regulations or restrictions on the people, except Prohibition. Prohibition removed the choice to consume alcohol in favor of abstinence, which was favored by the religious conservatives of the time. Thus, Thoreau would point out that this is a clear violation of free choice and an example of government meddling.

53. A: Choice *B* is totally irrelevant. Choice *C* is also incorrect; Thoreau never personifies government. Also, this doesn't coincide with his wooden gun analogy. Choice *D* is compelling because of its language, but it doesn't define the statement. Choice *A* is the most accurate summary of the main point of Thoreau's statement.

54. A: Choice *A* accurately identifies the relationship between Elizabeth and Jane. The first sentence states that Jane is expressing to her sister how she feels about Mr. Bingley. She is talking to Elizabeth; therefore, Elizabeth is her sister. Choices *B*, *C*, and *D* are incorrect due to this analysis.

55. B: Choice *B* captures Elizabeth's thoughts on Jane. In this last paragraph of the passage, Elizabeth states that Jane likes everyone and believes that the world is entirely good. It is a fair conclusion to make that Elizabeth thinks that Jane sees the best in everyone. Choice *A* is incorrect because Elizabeth approves of Jane's male suitor. Choice *C* is incorrect because Elizabeth seems to think that they are a good pairing. Choice *D* is incorrect because, although Elizabeth believes that Jane is more beautiful than other women, Elizabeth also compliments Mr. Bingley on his appearance.

56. C: In the third paragraph of the text, Elizabeth states that he is handsome and that is what completes his character. Choices *A*, *B*, and *D* are incorrect because Elizabeth does not mention these aspects of Mr. Bingley.

57. D: Choice *D* is a strong inference that can reasonably be made. Elizabeth is invested in her sister's choice in a partner. She believes that he needs to be well-rounded in every aspect. She is also complimentary to her sister. This conveys that Elizabeth cares for Jane and what becomes of her romantic prospects. Choice *A* is incorrect because although Elizabeth visibly cares for Jane and judges her partner, there is nothing to suggest that the relationship is similar to that of a mother and daughter. Choice *B* and *C* are incorrect because the conversation is generally positive and there is no conflict between the sisters or with the idea of romantic prospects.

58. C: Choice *C* describes how the sisters differ based on the text. Elizabeth is critical of Jane's romantic partners and has a discerning eye for why Mr. Bingley approached Jane. This is because she is less naïve and positive than Jane. She is more judgmental and critical of people. Choice *A* is incorrect because Jane is the one actively engaging in romance. Choice *B* is incorrect because there is nothing to show that Elizabeth is free-spirited. Choice *D* is incorrect because readers cannot assume that Elizabeth does not enjoy social events based on this dialogue.

303

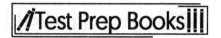

Math

1. B: Separate the whole numbers from the fractions:

$$4 + 3 + \frac{1}{3} + \frac{3}{4} = 7 + \frac{1}{3} + \frac{3}{4}$$

Add the fractions by finding the lowest common denominator:

$$\frac{1}{3} + \frac{3}{4} = \frac{4}{12} + \frac{9}{12} = \frac{13}{12} = 1 + \frac{1}{12}$$

Finally, add the fractions and whole numbers together:

$$7 + \frac{1}{3} + \frac{3}{4} = 7 + 1 + \frac{1}{12} = 8\frac{1}{12}$$

2. C: The average is calculated by adding all six numbers, then dividing by 6. The first five numbers have a sum of 25. This scenario can be expressed by the equation $\frac{(25+n)}{6} = 6$, where n is the unknown number. After multiplying both sides by 6, we get $25 + n = 36$, which means $n = 11$.

3. B: To convert miles to kilometers, we can multiply the number of miles by the miles-per-kilometer conversion factor:

$$4.67 \text{ mi} \times \frac{(1.609 \text{ km})}{(1 \text{ mi})} = 7.51 \text{ km}$$

Because the question asks for an answer with three significant digits, 7.51 kilometers is the correct answer.

4. B: Solve for n:

$$\frac{5}{2} \div \frac{1}{3} = \frac{5}{2} \times \frac{3}{1} = \frac{15}{2} = 7.5$$

Since $n = 7.5$, it falls between 7 and 9. Therefore, Choice *B* is the correct answer.

5. A: The total fraction taken up by green and red shirts will be:

$$\frac{1}{3} + \frac{2}{5} = \frac{5}{15} + \frac{6}{15} = \frac{11}{15}$$

The remaining fraction is:

$$1 - \frac{11}{15} = \frac{15}{15} - \frac{11}{15} = \frac{4}{15}$$

6. B: Fractions must have like denominators to be added. The common denominator is the least common multiple (LCM) of the two original denominators. In this case, the LCM is 15, so both fractions should be changed to equivalent fractions with a denominator of 15. Multiply the bottom of each fraction by whatever number is needed to produce 15, and multiply the top of each fraction by that same number:

$$\frac{1 \times 5}{3 \times 5} = \frac{5}{15} \text{ and } \frac{2 \times 3}{5 \times 3} = \frac{6}{15}$$

Now, add the numerators and keep the denominator the same:

$$\frac{5}{15} + \frac{6}{15} = \frac{11}{15}$$

7. C: To find a common denominator, look for a number that has both denominators (12 and 9) as factors. 36 works. Multiply the top and bottom of each fraction by whatever number will make the denominator 36:

$$\frac{5}{12} \times \frac{3}{3} = \frac{15}{36} \text{ and } \frac{4}{9} \times \frac{4}{4} = \frac{16}{36}$$

Now that we have a common denominator, add the numerators.

$$\frac{15}{36} + \frac{16}{36} = \frac{15+16}{36} = \frac{31}{36}$$

Since 31 and 36 have no common factors except 1, this fraction can't be reduced.

8. A: Flip the second fraction and multiply.

$$\frac{4}{13} \times \frac{169}{27}$$

Simplify the fractions before multiplying to make the numbers simpler to work with.

$$\frac{4}{1} \times \frac{13}{27}$$

Multiply across the top and across the bottom.

$$\frac{4 \times 13}{1 \times 27} = \frac{52}{27}$$

The numerator and denominator do not have any factors in common, so this fraction cannot be reduced.

9. A: Divide 54 by 15:

$$\begin{array}{r} 3 \\ 15{\overline{\smash{\big)}\,54}} \\ \underline{-45} \\ 9 \end{array}$$

The result is 3 with a remainder of 9, which is equivalent to $3\frac{9}{15}$. Reduce the fraction $\frac{9}{15}$ for the final answer, $3\frac{3}{5}$.

10. D: Digits to the left of the decimal point represent the digit value times increasing multiples of 10 (first 1, then 10, 100, 1,000, and so on). Digits to the right of the decimal point represent the digit value divided by increasing multiples of 10 (first $\frac{1}{10}$, then $\frac{1}{100}$, $\frac{1}{1000}$, and so on). So the second digit to the right of the decimal point equals the digit value divided by 100.

11. B: Sup the problem and add each column, starting on the far right (ones). Add, carrying anything over 9 into the next column to the left. Solve from right to left.

305

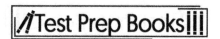

12. A: Find a common denominator. 36 is a multiple of both 12 and 9, so we can use that. Multiply the top and bottom of each fraction by whatever number it takes to make the bottom 36.

$$\frac{7}{12} + \frac{5}{9}$$

Multiply each fraction to convert to a common denominator.

$$\frac{7}{12} \times \frac{3}{3} + \frac{5}{9} \times \frac{4}{4} = \frac{21}{36} + \frac{20}{36}$$

Now add the numerators, keeping the same denominator.

$$\frac{21 + 20}{36} = \frac{41}{36}$$

Convert to a mixed number.

$$\frac{41}{36} = 1\frac{5}{36}$$

The numerator and denominator (5 and 36) do not have any factors in common, so this fraction can't be reduced.

13. D: Set up the problem, with the larger number on top. Begin subtracting with the far-right column (ones). Borrow 10 from the column to the left when necessary.

14. A: To determine the number of houses that can fit on the street, we can divide the length of the street by the width of each house's property:

$$345 \div 30 = 11.5$$

However, the construction company is not going to build half a house, so they will need to build either 11 or 12 houses. Since the width of 12 houses (360 feet) would extend past the length of the street, only 11 houses can be built.

15. C: Set up the problem, with the larger number on top and numbers lined up at the decimal point. Insert 0 in any blank spots to the right of the decimal point as placeholders. Begin subtracting with the far-right column. Borrow 10 from the column to the left when necessary.

16. C: The product of two irrational numbers can be rational or irrational. Sometimes the irrational parts of the two numbers cancel each other out, leaving a rational number. For example, $\sqrt{2} \times \sqrt{2} = 2$ because the roots cancel each other out. Technically, the product of two irrational numbers is a complex number, because real numbers are a type of complex number. However, Choice D is incorrect because the product of two irrational numbers is not an imaginary number.

17. D: First, distribute the -3 on the left side:

$$-3x - 12 = x + 8$$

Subtract x from both sides:

$$-4x - 12 = 8$$

Add 12 to both sides to isolate the variable:

$$-4x = 20$$

Finally, divide both sides by -4 to solve:

$$x = -5$$

18. B: When solving for x, add 3 to both sides to get $4x = 8$. Then divide both sides by 4 to get $x = 2$.

19. B: $12 \times 750 = 9,000$

The amount of water in one bottle is measured in milliliters, but the question asks for an amount in liters. Therefore, the conversion from milliliters to liters is needed. There are 1,000 milliliters in 1 liter.

20. A: The total number of treats distributed will be the number of treats per bag $(4x + 1)$ times the number of bags given out, which can be represented by the variable n. This expression is $n(4x + 1)$. Since this is the amount of treats distributed, set it equal to $60x + 15$.

$$n(4x + 1) = 60x + 15$$

In order to figure out what n is, determine what number times 4 results in 60 $(4n = 60)$ and what number times 1 results in 15 $(1n = 15)$. In both cases, $n = 15$. Therefore, 15 bags are given out.

21. D: Let a be the number of apples and let b represent the number of bananas. The total number of fruits is $a + b = 10$, and the total cost is $2a + 3b = 22$. To solve this pair of equations, we can multiply the first equation by -3:

$$-3(a + b) = -3(10)$$

$$-3a - 3b = -30$$

When we add this to the other equation, the b terms cancel out:

$$(-3a - 3b = -30) + (2a + 3b = 22)$$

$$= (-a = -8)$$

This simplifies to $a = 8$.

22. B: The circumference of a circle with radius r is equal to $2\pi r$. In this case, $r = 6$. Therefore, the circumference is $2(6)\pi = 12\pi$.

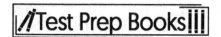

23. C: To solve for the value of b, isolate the variable b on one side of the equation.

Start by adding 13 to both sides of the equation:

$$2b + 11 + 13 = 8b - 13 + 13$$

$$2b + 24 = 8b$$

Then subtract $2b$ from both sides:

$$2b - 2b + 24 = 8b - 2b$$

$$24 = 6b$$

Finally, divide both sides by 6 to get b by itself:

$$24 \div 6 = 6b \div 6$$

$$4 = b$$

The answer is $b = 4$.

24. A: The box has a volume of $6^3 = 216$ cubic inches. Because the capacity is 75%, the total amount of peanut butter that can fit in the box is $0.75 \times 216 = 162$ cubic inches.

25. D: One ton is equal to 2,000 pounds. Multiply 3.7 by 2,000 to obtain 7,400 pounds.

26. A: To find the average, also known as the mean, find the sum of the values and divide by the total number of values. Therefore, the mean is $\frac{86+92+91+90+97+100}{6} = \frac{556}{6} \approx 92.7$, rounded to the nearest tenth.

27. D: Adding the parts of the ratio, we find $4 + 5 + 3 = 12$. Therefore, there are 12 parts of the whole. Because there are 168 total animals, each part is equal to $168 \div 12 = 14$ animals. From the given ratio, we know that 3 parts of the whole are birds. Therefore, there are $3 \times 14 = 42$ birds.

28. B: This question is asking for the perimeter of her room. $P = 2L + 2W = 2(14) + 2(9.5) = 47$ ft.

29. C: The surface area of a cube is equal to $6s^2$, where s is the side length. Therefore, we have $384 = 6s^2$. Divide both sides by 6 and then take the square root to obtain $s = 8$ in.

30. D: 1 kg = 1,000 g. Therefore, we multiply 5.625 by 1,000 to obtain 5,625 g.

31. B: 100 cm is equal to 1 m. 1.3 divided by 100 is 0.013. Therefore, 1.3 cm is equal to 0.013 m. Because 1 cm is equal to 10 mm, 1.3 cm is equal to 13 mm.

32. D: A yard is 3 feet. The equation to calculate the minimum number of yards is $79 \div 3 = 26\frac{1}{3}$.

If the material is sold only by whole yards, then Mo would need to round up to the next whole yard in order to cover the extra $\frac{1}{3}$ yard. Therefore, the answer is 27 yards. None of the other choices meets the minimum whole yard requirement.

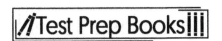

33. C: The probability is equal to the number of desired outcomes divided by the number of possible outcomes. There are $4 + 8 + 7 + 2 = 21$ marbles that could be selected. There are $8 + 7 = 15$ marbles that are blue or yellow. Therefore, the probability of selecting either a blue or a yellow marble is $\frac{15}{21} = \frac{5}{7}$.

34. A: For military (24-hour) times of 1300 and higher, subtract 12 from the hours (the first two digits) and make the time p.m. For 1500, we find $15 - 12 = 3$, so the time is 3:00 p.m.

35. B: The circumference of a circle is equal to $2\pi r$, where r is the radius. The radius is half of the diameter, so the radius of this circle is 3 cm. Therefore, the circumference is $2\pi(3) = 6\pi \approx 18.8$ cm.

36. B: For times from 1:00 a.m. to 12:00 p.m. (noon), we can convert to military time by simply dropping the colon, so 10:00 a.m. becomes 1000 hours.

37. D: There are 1,000 meters per kilometer, and 100 centimeters per meter, so we can calculate:

$$1 \text{ km} \times \frac{1{,}000 \text{ m}}{1 \text{ km}} \times \frac{100 \text{ cm}}{1 \text{ m}} = 100{,}000 \text{ cm}$$

38. B: The range is equal to the largest value minus the smallest value. The largest value is 89, and the smallest value is 20. Therefore, the range is $89 - 20 = 69$.

39. C: A dollar contains 20 nickels. Therefore, if there are 12 dollars' worth of nickels, there are $12 \times 20 = 240$ nickels. Each nickel weighs 5 grams. Therefore, the weight of the nickels is $240 \times 5 = 1{,}200$ grams. To find the total weight of the filled piggy bank, add the weight of the nickels and the weight of the empty bank:

$$1{,}200 + 1{,}050 = 2{,}250 \text{ grams}$$

40. D: To find Denver's total snowfall, multiply $27\frac{3}{4}$ by 3. To do this, convert the mixed number into an improper fraction.

$$27\frac{3}{4} = \frac{27 \times 4 + 3}{4} = \frac{111}{4}$$

Therefore, Denver had approximately $\frac{3 \times 111}{4} = \frac{333}{4}$ inches of snow. The improper fraction can be converted back into a mixed number through division.

$$\frac{333}{4} = 83\frac{1}{4} \text{ inches}$$

41. B: 85% of 1640 is equal to $(0.85)(1640) = 1394$. Therefore, 1394 students went to college and 1640-1394 = 246 students did not.

42. B: 1 kL is equal to 1,000,000 mL. Therefore, multiply 4.5 times 1,000,000 to obtain 4,500,000.

43. A: Take the square root of both sides to obtain $x - 8 = 11$ or $x - 8 = -11$. Add 8 to both sides in each equation, resulting in the two solutions $x = 19$ and $x = -3$.

44. C: We rewrite as a fraction: $\frac{14a^2 b^3 c}{21a^{-1} b^2 c^3}$. The coefficients reduce to $\frac{2}{3}$. We use the exponential rule $\frac{x^m}{x^n} = x^{m-n}$ to simplify the variables. Therefore, we have $\frac{2}{3} a^{2-(-1)} b^{3-2} c^{1-3} = \frac{2a^3 b}{3c^2}$.

45. C: First, place the values in numerical order: 1, 1, 3, 4, 5, 6, 7, 8, 9, 10. Since there are an even number of data values, the median is the mean of the two middle values 5 and 6. The median is 5.5.

Science

1. D: Catabolism is the process of breaking down large molecules into smaller molecules to release energy for work. Carbohydrates and fats are catabolized to provide energy for exercise and daily activities. Anabolism synthesizes larger molecules from smaller constituent building blocks. Bioenergetics and metabolism are more general terms involving overall energy production and usage.

2. A: Platelets are the blood components responsible for clotting. There are between 150,000 and 450,000 platelets in healthy blood. When a clot forms, platelets adhere to the injured area of the vessel and promote a molecular cascade that results in adherence of more platelets. Ultimately, the platelet aggregation results in recruitment of a protein called fibrin, which adds structure to the clot. Too many platelets can cause clotting disorders. Too few platelets leads to bleeding disorders.

3. A: Choice *B* might be an attractive answer choice, but neutrophils are part of the innate immune system and are not considered part of the primary immune response. The first event that happens in a primary immune response is that macrophages ingest pathogens and display their antigens. Then, they secrete interleukin 1 to recruit helper T cells. Once helper T cells are activated, they secrete interleukin 2 to stimulate plasma B and killer T cell production. Only then can plasma B make the pathogen specific antibodies.

4. C: The epididymis stores sperm and is a coiled tube located near the testes. The immature sperm that enters the epididymis from the testes migrates through the 20-foot long epididymis tube in about two weeks, where viable sperm are concentrated at the end. The vas deferens is a tube that transports mature sperm from the epididymis to the urethra. Seminal vesicles are pouches attached that add fructose to the ejaculate to provide energy for sperm. The prostate gland excretes fluid that makes up about a third of semen released during ejaculation. The fluid reduces semen viscosity and contains enzymes that aid in sperm functioning; both effects increase sperm motility and ultimate success.

5. D: DNA serves as the hereditary material for prokaryotic and eukaryotic cells.

6. C: These are the coefficients that follow the law of conservation of matter. The coefficient times the subscript of each element should be the same on both sides of the equation.

7. D: Bone matrix is an intricate lattice of collagen fibers and mineral salts, particularly calcium and phosphorus. The mineral salts are strong but brittle, and the collagen fibers are weak but flexible, so the combination of the two makes bone resistant to shattering and able to withstand the normal forces applied to it.

8. D: The natural tendency in the universe is to increase entropy and disorder, so organisms undergo biochemical processes and use free energy and matter to stabilize their internal environment against this changing external environment in a process called homeostasis. Organisms strive to maintain physiologic factors such as body temperature, blood pH, and fluid balance in equilibrium or around a set point. Choice *A* is incorrect because homeostasis in organisms involves trying to maintain internal conditions around their set point, which doesn't always involve increasing body temperature, blood pH, and fluid balance; the organism may need to work to decrease these values. Choice *B* is incorrect because maintaining homeostasis expends energy; it does not absorb it. Choice *C* is incorrect because homeostasis involves maintaining order in the organism's internal, not external, environment.

310

9. C: A catalyst functions to increase reaction rates by decreasing the activation energy required for a reaction to take place. Inhibitors would increase the activation energy or otherwise stop the reactants from reacting. Although increasing the temperature usually increases a reaction's rate, this is not true in all cases, and most catalysts do not function in this manner.

10. C: Practicing reflective listening expresses empathy and conveys acceptance toward the patient with a nonjudgmental attitude. The nurse will typically rephrase the patient's comments to illustrate active listening and let the patient know that they are being heard. The general steps in motivational interviewing can include engaging, guiding (focus), evoking, and planning. These steps can be organized into the following categories: expressing empathy, highlighting discrepancies (focus), adjusting to resistance, understanding motivations (evoking), and supporting self-efficacy (planning).

11. A: Choice A is the only term included in the acronym OARS, which stands for a set of counseling skills that nurses can use: open-ended questions, affirmations, reflections, and summaries. Reflection or reflective listening is an important skill that expresses empathy.

12. B: During the working phase, nurses actively listen to the client or family to develop a plan of care and an educational plan for the patient based on assessment findings. Nurses set a time to implement interventions that will meet short/long-term goals. They work with the patient to create a list of goals/responsibilities and an individual plan of care. Choice A is incorrect; during the orientation phase, nurses introduce themselves and acquire essential information about their patients/clients. The nurses obtain the family's view of the situation and any problems or concerns. Choice C is incorrect, as it is a phase discussed within in-home visits. Choice D is incorrect; the termination phase is the phase where the patient is discharged from care after a successful working phase. The termination phase is where the family's needs are met successfully through collaboration with nurses or other health care professionals.

13. B: The pelvic cavity is the area formed by the bones of the hip. Housed in that space are the urinary bladder, urethra, ureters, anus, and rectum. This hollow space also contains the uterus in females. The other body cavities listed contain other organs not specified in the question.

14. B: An amphoteric substance can act as an acid or a base depending on the properties of the solute. Water is a common example; because of its amphoteric property, it serves as a universal solvent. Choice A is incorrect because it describes electrolytes. Choices C and D are incorrect because they both describe an acid.

15. C: The body has a variety of touch receptors that detect tactile information, which gets carried via general somatic afferents and general visceral afferents to the CNS. Meissner's corpuscles respond to light touch and slower vibrations. Choice A is incorrect because Merkel's discs respond to sustained pressure. Choice B is incorrect because Pacinian corpuscles detect rapid vibration in the skin and fascia, and Choice D is incorrect because Ruffini endings detect deep touch and tension in the skin and fascia.

16. C: Capillaries are responsible for the exchange of nutrients, hormones, oxygen, fluids, and electrolytes between the blood and interstitial fluid in tissues. Hemoglobin helps carry oxygen and iron in circulating red blood cells. Arterioles and venules are intermediately-sized blood vessels, but their walls are too thick for cellular-level exchange.

17. D: In the secondary immune response, suppressor T lymphocytes are activated to negate the potential risk of damage to healthy cells brought on by an unchecked, overactive immune response. Choice A is incorrect because this activity is characteristic of the primary response, not the secondary response. Choice B is incorrect because humoral immunity is mediated by antibodies produced by B, not T, lymphocytes. Choice C is wrong because the secondary response is faster than the primary response because the primary response entails the time-consuming process of macrophage activation.

18. A: Nurses use home visits, empowerment of families, and contracting with families to reduce health risks in families. Telehomecare, family policy, and care for vulnerable populations are types of community resources that nurses can share with families. Choices *B–D* are not the best answer choices since they are not specific to health risk reduction approaches.

19. C: The correct order of phases during a nurse home visit process is (I) the initiation phase, (II) the pre-visit phase, (III) the in-home phase, (IV) the termination phase, and (V) the post-visit phase.

20. D: Parents' fear of vaccines can prevent adolescents from getting immunized for a specific disease. Due to the rise of internet misinformation, parents are more likely to access incorrect information on vaccines. Therefore, nurses must educate families on the efficacy and safety of vaccines. The Vaccine Injury Act allows providers or nurses to give families up-to-date and correct information by providing vaccine information sheets produced by the CDC, which explain the benefits and risks of taking a vaccine. Choices *A–C* are other barriers to immunizations; however, the legislation indicated above is more likely to reduce fears parents may have regarding adolescent vaccination. A parent who decides not to vaccinate their child can put them and others at risk of spreading disease.

21. D: The hypothalamus is the link between the nervous and the endocrine systems. It receives information from the brain and sends signals to the pituitary gland, instructing it to release or inhibit the release of hormones. Aside from its endocrine function, it controls body temperature, hunger, sleep, and circadian rhythms, and it is part of the limbic system.

22. B: Most nutrients (e.g., large polar molecules) initially move from the lumen of the intestine through a transport protein found on the apical membrane. As the nutrients pass through the enterocyte or epithelial cell, they move to another transport protein on the basolateral membrane and then travel through the interstitial fluid and then to the capillaries. Choice *A* is incorrect since nonpolar substances, not polar substances, pass through the membranes. Choices *C* and *D* are incorrect; nutrients move through the lumen of the intestine and then to the transport proteins of the apical membrane.

23. D: Charles Darwin based the idea of adaptation around his original concept of natural selection. He believed that evolution occurred based on three observations: the unity of life, the diversity of life, and the suitability of organisms to their environments. There was unity in life based on the idea that all organisms descended from a common ancestor. Then, as the descendants of common ancestors faced changes in their environments or moved to new environments, they began adapting new features to help them. This concept explained the diversity of life and how organisms were matched to their environments. Natural selection helps to improve the fit between organisms and their environments by increasing the frequency of features that enhance survival and reproduction.

24. A: There is no chance that an offspring will have O blood or AB blood (see Punnett square).

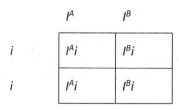

25. D: A nucleotide is a five-carbon sugar with a phosphate group and a nitrogenous base (adenine, guanine, cytosine, and thymine). DNA is a double helix and looks like a spiral ladder. Each side has a sugar/phosphate backbone, and the rungs of the ladder that connect the sides are the nitrogenous bases. Adenine always pairs with thymine via two hydrogen bonds, and cytosine always pairs with guanine via three hydrogen bonds. The weak hydrogen bonds are important because they allow DNA to easily be opened for replication and transcription.

26. D: Iodine has the greatest number of electrons at 53 electrons. The number of electrons increases in elements going from left to right across the periodic table. Hydrogen, Choice *A*, is at the top left corner of the periodic table, so it has the fewest electrons (one electron). Iron has 26 electrons, copper has 29 electrons, Choices *B* and *C*, respectively.

27. C: The relative density of eccrine sweat glands varies in different areas of the body. The palms and soles of the feet have the highest density, reaching values of approximately 400 sweat glands per square centimeter of epidermis. The head also has a high density of sweat glands, though significantly less than on the palms and soles. Areas such as the upper arms and thighs have only around 80 eccrine sweat glands per square inch of skin.

28. B: Dominant alleles are considered to have stronger phenotypes and, when mixed with recessive alleles, will mask the recessive trait. The recessive trait would only appear as the phenotype when the allele combination is aa because a dominant allele is not present to mask it.

29. B: The nephron is the structural and functional unit that creates and transports urine. The glomerulus, loop of Henle, and distal tubule are parts of the nephron involved in creating and transporting urine depending on their respective functions, so Choices *A*, *C*, and *D* are incorrect, as they represent only a part of the unit.

30. C: The uterus and ovaries aren't part of the birth canal, so Choices *A* and *D* are false. The cervix is the uppermost portion of the birth canal, so Choice *B* is incorrect, making Choice *C* the correct answer, as the vagina is the muscular tube on the lowermost portion of the birth canal that connects the exterior environment to the cervix.

31. D: Thyroid hormone is responsible for regulating metabolism, so Choice *D* is the correct answer. Insulin is involved in glucose uptake into tissues, testosterone is for sperm production and secondary male sexual characteristics, and adrenaline is responsible for mechanisms in the fight-or-flight response, making Choices *A*, *B*, and *C* incorrect.

32. C: The parathyroid gland impacts calcium levels by secreting parathyroid hormone (PTH). The osteoid gland is not a real gland. The pineal gland regulates sleep by secreting melatonin, and the thymus gland focuses on immunity. *Thyroid* would also be a correct answer choice as it influences the levels of circulating calcium.

33. C: The alveoli are small sac-shaped structures at the end of the bronchioles where gas exchange takes place. The bronchioles are tubes through which air travels. The kidneys and medulla oblongata do not directly affect oxygen and carbon dioxide exchange.

34. C: The pancreas functions as an exocrine gland because it secretes enzymes that break down food components. It also functions as an endocrine gland because it secretes hormones that regulate blood sugar levels. The kidney isn't a gland; it is an organ located directly below the adrenal glands. The stomach is an exocrine gland because it secretes hydrochloric acid. Like the kidney, the spleen is an organ, not a gland. Therefore, the only correct answer is *C*.

35. B: The endocrine system's organs are glands which are spread throughout the body. The endocrine system itself does not connect the organs or transport the hormones they secrete. Rather, the various glands secrete the hormone into the bloodstream and lets the cardiovascular system pump it throughout the body. The other three body systems each include a network throughout the body:

- Cardiovascular system: veins and arteries
- Immune system: lymphatic vessels (it also uses the circulatory system)
- Nervous system: nerve networks

36. B: An action potential in one nerve triggers the release of neurotransmitters that are stored in synaptic vesicles at the axon terminal. The neurotransmitters then travel across the synaptic cleft where they are received by the

313

dendrites of another neuron. The purpose of an axon is to carry nerve impulses from the cell body of a neuron to the axon terminal where it can trigger the release of neurotransmitters. Neuroglia provide structural, metabolic, and developmental support to neurons. Nodes of Ranvier are gaps between the insulating myelin sheaths that improve the speed of nerve impulses.

37. D: Eosinophils are a type of leukocyte known as a granulocyte. Granulocytes are white blood cells that contain secretory granules. In addition to eosinophils, basophils and neutrophils are also granulocytes. Basophils remedy parasite infections and allergens by producing heparin, histamine, and serotonin, while the function of a neutrophil is to identify and kill microbes. Eosinophils specifically are found beneath mucous membranes, and their primary goal is to destroy multi-cellular parasites through phagocytosis and antihistamine production. Monocytes are another form of white blood cell that detects and eliminate viruses, bacteria, fungi, protozoa, and infected cells.

38. B: When light enters an eye, it first passes through the outside layer, the cornea. From there it passes through the opening of the pupil to the lens which focuses the light through the vitreous humor on to the retina. The retina is where the light is detected by sensory neurons that then send information through the optic nerve to the brain.

39. D: The cochlea is not a component of the middle ear; instead, it resides in the inner ear. Sound travels through the auditory canal of the outer ear to the tympanic membrane, which separates the outer ear from the middle ear. Within the middle ear there are three bones known as ossicles that attach tympanic membrane to the oval window. The remaining choices are true statements.

40. C: The term cubital refers to the body region relating to the elbow. There are many terms that refer to specific portions of the body. *Pedal* describes the foot region, *carpal* describes the wrist, and *geniculate* relates to the knee.

41. B: The gallbladder resides in the abdominal cavity along with other organs such as the stomach, liver, small intestines, and large intestines. The abdominal cavity is separated from the thoracic cavity by the diaphragm. The thoracic cavity contains the heart, trachea, esophagus, and all components of the lungs. Below the abdominal cavity lies the pelvic cavity where the ureters, urinary bladder, urethra, reproductive organs, rectum, and anus reside. Lastly, the cranial cavity is the area within the skull where organs such as the brain and pituitary gland are.

42. A: Simple squamous cells form a single layer of flat cells. Simple refers to a single layer, whereas stratified refers to multiple layers, and transitional refers to multiple layers of different shapes of cells. The squamous shape is a cell that is wider than it is tall. Cuboidal cells are approximately cube shaped, and columnar cells are taller than they are wide.

43. C: There are three variations of capillaries. Sinusoidal capillaries have the largest openings of the three types, which allow proteins and larger cells like erythrocytes to pass through. Continuous capillaries are made of tightly bound cells that do not allow many materials to pass in and out of them. Fenestrated capillaries have openings, smaller than those found in sinusoidal capillaries, that allow materials to pass between the tissues and blood. Arterioles are the smallest form of artery and do not allow materials to pass in and out of them like the capillaries do.

44. A: Systole is a phase during the cardiac cycle when the heart muscle contracts to pump blood out. Diastole is the phase where the heart muscle relaxes to allow it to fill with blood. The process of these two phases repeating is known as the cardiac cycle. Systemic circulation refers to the process of supplying blood to all parts of the body aside from the lungs. The process of blood going to and from the lungs is known as pulmonary circulation.

45. A: The specific structure that is concerned with detecting smells is the olfactory cortex, which is a portion of the cerebrum. The primary objective of the cerebellum is to maintain posture and balance. The brain stem is mostly involved in regulating the autonomic functions of the body. Lastly, the occipital lobe is the rearmost portion of the cerebrum, and it is responsible for all the aspects of vision.

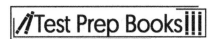

46. C: Within a nephron, waste is removed, and water is needed to remove the waste. Therefore, it is necessary that regions of a nephron are permeable to water. The first portion of a nephron, the proximal convoluted tubule, is permeable to water, salts, amino acids, glucose, and vitamins. Following the proximal convoluted tubule is the descending loop of Henle, where water can be reabsorbed. Next, the base and ascending limb of the loop of Henle is only permeable to salts and urea, while no water is reabsorbed. Lastly, in the distal convoluted tubule and following collecting duct, water is once more reabsorbed.

47. C: Endergonic reactions are nonspontaneous, meaning that they need a positive standard change in free energy to occur. Exergonic reactions are the opposite of endergonic. They are spontaneous reactions that require no energy input to occur and result in energy flowing from the system into the surrounding environment. Combustion reactions are specific chemical reactions where an oxidant and a fuel release heat and result in water and carbon dioxide. Oxidation-reduction reactions, also known as redox reactions, involve the transfer of electrons from one molecule to another. Redox reactions result in one molecule being oxidized while the other is reduced.

48. B: Peristalsis is an involuntary movement in which muscles constrict and relax in a wave-like motion. Peristalsis occurs throughout the digestive tract to move food substances. The process of swallowing a bolus of food is made possible by peristalsis in the esophagus, where food is moved from the oral cavity to the stomach. Amylase is a digestive enzyme that is secreted within the saliva and also found in the pancreas. Amylase is a digestive enzyme that breaks starches down into sugars. Villi are finger-like projections within the small intestines that increase their surface area to aid in nutrient absorption. The trachea is not involved in food consumption and digestion. Its purpose is to provide a firm passage for air to enter and exit the lungs.

49. A: A myelin sheath insulates an axon of a nerve by preventing electrical interference from other nerves or ions. The breaks between myelin sheaths, known as nodes of Ranvier, allow ions to enter. The insulated sections with periodic breaks for ion channels allow the speed of nerve transmission to be increased.

50. D: The septal area is a portion of the brain's limbic system and is not involved in generating certain emotions, such as social bonding. The lymphatic system includes the spleen, thymus gland, tonsils, adenoids, and lymph nodes. Overall, the lymphatic system's function is to remove fluids, maintain immune functions, and maintain fluid levels in a body.

51. C: External respiration occurs in the alveoli within the lungs. Inhaled air passes through the trachea, into the bronchi, bronchioles, then eventually the alveoli. The alveoli are surrounded by capillaries which can replace carbon dioxide with oxygen in the blood. This process of gas exchange is external respiration. The mitochondria are responsible for aerobic respiration within cells but are not involved in external respiration. Internal respiration occurs within the cells of tissues, but external respiration only occurs within the lungs. The bronchi are important for allowing external respiration to occur since they are airways that lead to alveoli. However, external respiration does not occur at the bronchi, as the gasses are exchanged within the alveoli.

52. C: Mechanoreceptors, which detect touches to one's body, are located in the skin, ligaments, and hair follicles. Thermoreceptors, which detect variations in temperature, are located in the skin, liver, hypothalamus, and skeletal muscles. Not within the skin, light detecting photoreceptors reside in the retina, and dissolved substance detecting chemoreceptors are found within blood vessels, the tongue, the nose, and many other locations.

53. B: Vestibular sense is the sensation of balance and orientation in space. The receptors involved in vestibular sensation reside within the inner ear. Vestibular sense is important for coordinated movement. Similar to vestibular sense, kinesthetic sense also comes from receptors in the inner ear to control actions such as talking and moving. Somatosensation is the interpretation of sensory information from certain organs. Somatosensation is the detection of pressure, pain, temperature, and more within specific organs. Perception is different than sensation. It is an interpretation of all sensory information to understand one's environment.

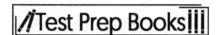

54. B: Suppressor T cells, which mature in the thymus, suppress adaptive immune responses to conserve energy and resources. Neutrophils and basophils are granulocytes that mature within bone marrow. Memory B cells are B lymphocytes, and they mature in bone marrow.

55. A: Insulin is a hormone that lowers one's blood sugar by inducing glucose storage. It is produced by the beta cells in the pancreas. Glucagon is also produced in the pancreas. However, it is made by the alpha cells and has the opposite function of insulin. Antidiuretic hormone and growth hormone are synthesized by the pituitary gland.

56. B: Diffusion and osmosis are examples of passive transport. Unlike active transport, passive transport does not require cellular energy. Diffusion is the movement of particles, such as ions, nutrients, or waste, from high concentration to low. Osmosis is the spontaneous movement of water from an area of high concentration to one of low concentration. Facilitated diffusion is another type of passive transport, in which particles move from high concentration to low concentration via a protein channel.

57. A: Mitochondria is described as the powerhouse of the cell. The nucleus, Choice *B*, contains the cell's DNA. The ribosomes, Choice *C*, build proteins. The cell wall, Choice *D*, maintains the shape of plant cells and protects its contents.

58. B: Color blindness is a recessive, sex-linked trait. The Punnett square below shows the cross between a carrier female and a color-blind male. The two offspring in bold are color blind. The probability of having one child that is color blind is $\frac{1}{2}$. The probability of having three color-blind children is $\frac{1}{2} \times \frac{1}{2} \times \frac{1}{2}$ (law of multiplication) or $\frac{1}{8}$.

	X^C	X^c
X^c	**$X^C X^c$**	**$X^c X^c$**
Y	$X^C Y$	$X^c Y$

59. C: Water molecules form a V-shape because of the uneven sharing of electrons between the atoms. The oxygen atom is slightly negatively charged, and the hydrogen atoms are slightly positively charged, so they pull away from each other and the molecule forms a V-shape.

60. B: Nucleic acids include DNA and RNA, which store an organism's genetic information. Carbohydrates, Choice *A*, are used as an energy source for an organism. Proteins, Choice *C*, are important for the structure and function of organisms. Lipids, Choice *D*, are important for energy storage and insulation.

NEX Practice Tests #3 & #4

To keep the size of this book manageable, save paper, and provide a digital test-taking experience, the 3rd and 4th practice tests can be found online. Scan the QR code or go to this link to access it:

testprepbooks.com/bonus/nex

The first time you access the tests, you will need to register as a "new user" and verify your email address.

If you have any issues, please email support@testprepbooks.com.

Index

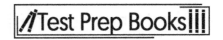

Dear NEX Test Taker,

Thank you for purchasing this study guide for your NEX exam. We hope that we exceeded your expectations.

Our goal in creating this study guide was to cover all of the topics that you will see on the test. We also strove to make our practice questions as similar as possible to what you will encounter on test day. With that being said, if you found something that you feel was not up to your standards, please send us an email and let us know.

We would also like to let you know about other books in our catalog that may interest you.

ATI TEAS 7

This can be found on amazon.com/dp/163775597X

HESI A2

Amazon.com/dp/1637753969

NCLEX RN

Amazon.com/dp/1637759975

We have study guides in a wide variety of fields. If the one you are looking for isn't listed above, then try searching for it on Amazon or send us an email.

Thanks Again and Happy Testing!
Product Development Team
info@studyguideteam.com

FREE Test Taking Tips Video/DVD Offer

To better serve you, we created videos covering test taking tips that we want to give you for FREE. **These videos cover world-class tips that will help you succeed on your test.**

We just ask that you send us feedback about this product. Please let us know what you thought about it—whether good, bad, or indifferent.

To get your **FREE videos**, you can use the QR code below or email freevideos@studyguideteam.com with "Free Videos" in the subject line and the following information in the body of the email:

      a. The title of your product

      b. Your product rating on a scale of 1-5, with 5 being the highest

      c. Your feedback about the product

If you have any questions or concerns, please don't hesitate to contact us at info@studyguideteam.com.

Thank you!

Made in the USA
Las Vegas, NV
12 January 2025

16268132R00184